Developmental Perspectives on Embodiment *and* Consciousness

The Jean Piaget Symposium Series
Series Editor:
Ellin Scholnick
University of Maryland

Available from LEA/Taylor and Francis

Overton, W.F. (Ed.): The Relationship Between Social and Cognitive Development.

Liben, L.S. (Ed): Piaget and the Foundations of Knowledge

Scholnick, E.K. (Ed): New Trends in Conceptual Representations: Challenges to Piaget's Theory?

Niemark, E.D., DeLisi, R. & Newman, J.L. (Eds.): Moderators of Competence.

Bearison, D.J. & Zimiles, H. (Eds.): Thought and Emotion: Developmental Perspectives.

Liben, L.S. (Ed.): Development and Learning: Conflict or Congruence?

Forman, G. & Pufall, P.B. (Eds.): Constructivism in the Computer Age.

Overton, W.F. (Ed.): Reasoning, Necessity, and Logic: Developmental Perspectives.

Keating, D.P. & Rosen, H. (Eds.): Constructivist Perspectives on Developmental Psychopathology and Atypical Development.

Carey, S. & Gelman, R. (Eds.): The Epigenesis of Mind: Essays on Biology and Cognition.

Beilin, H. & Pufall, P. (Eds.): Piaget's Theory: Prospects and Possibilities.

Wozniak, R.H. & Fisher, K.W. (Eds.): Development in Context: Acting and Thinking in Specific Environments.

Overton, W.F. & Palermo, D.S. (Eds.): The Nature and Ontogenesis of Meaning.

Noam, G.G. & Fischer, K.W. (Eds.): Development and Vulnerability in Close Relationships.

Reed, E.S., Turiel, E. & Brown, T. (Eds.): Values and Knowledge.

Amsel, E. & Renninger, K.A. (Eds.): Change and Development: Issues of Theory, Method, and Application.

Langer, J. & Killen, M. (Eds.): Piaget, Evolution, and Development.

Scholnick, E., Nelson, K., Gelman, S.A. & Miller, P.H. (Eds.): Conceptual Development: Piaget's Legacy.

Nucci, L.P., Saxe, G.B. & Turiel, E. (Eds.): Culture, Thought, and Development.

Amsel, E. & Byrnes, J.P. (Eds.): Language, Literacy, and Cognitive Development: The Development and Consequences of Symbolic Communication.

Brown, T. & Smith, L. (Eds.): Reductionism and the Development of Knowledge.

Lightfoot, C., LaLonde, C. & Chandler, M. (Eds.): Changing Conceptions of Psychological Life.

Parker, J., Langer, J., & Milbrath, C. (Eds.): Biology and Knowledge Revisited: From Neurogenesis to Psychogenesis.

Goncu, A., & Gaskins, S. (Eds.): Play and Development: Evolutionary, Sociocultural, and Functional Perspectives.

Overton, W., Müller, U., & Newman., J. (Eds.): Developmental Perspectives on Embodiment and Consciousness.

Wainryb, C., Turiel, E., & Smetana, J. (Eds.): Social Development, Social Inequalities, and Social Justice.

Müller, U., Carpendale, J., Budwig, N., Sokol, B. (Eds.): Social Life and Social Knowledge: Toward a Process Account of Development.

Developmental Perspectives on Embodiment *and* Consciousness

Edited by

Willis F. Overton

Ulrich Müller

Judith L. Newman

Lawrence Erlbaum Associates
Taylor & Francis Group

New York   London

Lawrence Erlbaum Associates
Taylor & Francis Group
270 Madison Avenue
New York, NY 10016

Lawrence Erlbaum Associates
Taylor & Francis Group
2 Park Square
Milton Park, Abingdon
Oxon OX14 4RN

Printed in the United States of America on acid-free paper
10 9 8 7 6 5 4 3 2 1

International Standard Book Number-13: 978-0-8058-5069-7 (Hardcover)

Library of Congress Cataloging-in-Publication Data

Developmental perspectives on embodiment and consciousness / editors, Willis F. Overton, Ulrich Mueller and Judith L. Newman.
    p. cm. -- (The Jean Piaget symposium series)
    Includes bibliographical references and index.
    ISBN-13: 978-0-8058-5069-7 (alk. paper) 1. Mind and body. 2. Consciousness. I. Overton, Willis F. II. Mueller, Ulrich, 1949- III. Newman, Judith L.

BF151.D48 2008
150--dc22   2007032110

Visit the Taylor & Francis Web site at
http://www.taylorandfrancis.com

and the LEA and Routledge Web site at
http://www.routledge.com

DEDICATION

We dedicate this volume to the memory of our friends and colleagues, Professors Harry Beilin and Irving E. Sigel. Both highly esteemed scholars were deeply involved in the founding and growth of the field of cognitive development; both contributed heavily to introducing the work of Jean Piaget to developmental psychology in North America; both strongly and continuously supported the development of the Jean Piaget Society over more than a quarter of a century; and both participated in and encouraged lively debate and discussion at numerous Annual Symposia of the Jean Piaget Society.

CONTENTS

CONTRIBUTORS

Jeremy I. M. Carpendale
Department of Psychology, Simon Fraser University
Burnaby, British Columbia

Nicole Charles
Graduate School of Education, University of Pennsylvania
Philadelphia, Pennsylvania

Giovanna Colombetti
Post-Doctoral Fellow at the Cognitive Science Laboratory
University of Trento, Italy

Thomas J. Csordas
Department of Anthropology, University of California, San Diego
La Jolla, California

Suzanne G. Fegley
Graduate School of Education, University of Pennsylvania
Philadelphia, Pennsylvania

Helena Hong Gao
School of Humanities and Social Sciences, Nanyang Technological
University, Singapore

Tyhesha N. Goss
Graduate School of Education, University of Pennsylvania
Philadelphia, Pennsylvania

Vinay Harpalani
Graduate School of Education, University of Pennsylvania
Philadelphia, Pennsylvania

Mark Johnson
Department of Philosophy, University of Oregon
Eugene, Oregon

Lynn S. Liben
Department of Psychology, Pennsylvania State University
University Park, Pennsylvania

Patricia H. Miller
Department of Psychology, University of Georgia
Athens, Georgia

Ulrich Müller
Department of Psychology, University of Victoria
Victoria, British Columbia

Judith L. Newman
Department of Human Development and Family Studies,
Pennsylvania State University, Abington, Pennsylvania

Willis F. Overton
Department of Psychology, Temple University
Philadelphia, Pennsylvania

Timothy P. Racine
Department of Psychology, Simon Fraser University
Burnaby, British Columbia

Ellin Kofsky Scholnick
University of Maryland
College Park, Maryland

Margaret B. Spencer
Graduate School of Education, University of Pennsylvania
Philadelphia, Pennsylvania

Esther Thelen (Deceased)
Department of Psychology, Formerly of Indiana University
Bloomington, Indiana

Evan Thompson
University College, University of Toronto
Toronto, Ontario

Jacques Vonèche
University of Geneva, Archives Jean Piaget
Genève, Suisse

Philip David Zelazo
Institute of Child Development, University of Minnesota
Minneapolis, Minnesota

PREFACE

Until recently, the body has been almost completely ignored in theories and empirical research in psychology in general, and in developmental psychology in particular. This neglect is partly due to the Cartesian split between mind and body, which has held sway over philosophy and psychology for the last centuries. As a consequence of Cartesian dualism, psychologists and developmental psychologists, in particular, have considered emotions, sociality, and cognition independently of the body, analogous to the software program of a computer that should be studied apart from its hardware.

Recently, increasing dissatisfaction with Descartes' dualism has been expressed in different scientific disciplines, including biology and neuroscience, philosophy, anthropology, and psychology. Common to this movement is the conviction that Descartes' dualist conception of body and mind is inadequate. Hence, several alternative conceptions of the relation between body and mind have been developed. Common among these conceptions is the idea that the body plays an important role in human emotional, social, and cognitive life.

This volume is largely based on the 32nd Anniversary Symposium of the Jean Piaget Society: The Study of Knowledge and Development, entitled, *The embodied mind and consciousness: Developmental perspectives*. The intent of the symposium was (a) to illustrate different ways in which the concept of embodiment can be used in developmental psychology; (b) to show that the concept of embodiment has important implications for theoretical and empirical work in different areas of psychology; and (c) to demonstrate that the concept of embodiment is a bridge concept that spans biological, psychological, and socio-cultural approaches to development.

The chapters in this volume explore the role of the body in the development of meaning, consciousness, and psychological functioning. In chapter 1, Overton discusses the concept of embodiment from a meta-theoretical perspective. Johnson (chapter 2) examines the role of embodiment in grounding conceptual meaning. Colombetti and Thompson (chapter 3) discuss the embodiment of emotions. Vonèche's chapter 4 and Thelen's chapter 5 examine the place of embodiment in cognitive development in general. In chapter 6, Csordas suggests that embodiment is the source of religious experience. Chapter 7 by Racine and Carpendale approaches social development from an embodiment perspective. Liben (chapter 8) elaborates on the role of the body in spatial cognition. Gao and Zelazo's chapter 9 describes the role of language in the development of increasingly complex forms of consciousness that entail a distancing from overt bodily activity. Chapter 10 by Scholnick and Miller, as well as chapter 11 by Fegley, Spencer, Goss, Harpalani, and Charles, examine the impact of culture on the conceptualization of the embodied self. In the final chapter, Müller and Newman place the contributions to the current volume within the historical context of the mind–body dualism.

In general, the chapters in this volume thematisize embodiment in two different and complementary ways. First, embodiment is examined as being a condition of and influencing the particular shape of psychological experience. This sense of embodiment, which may either refer to the body as physical structure or to the lived body—that is, the body as experienced and actively engaged in the world—reflects the effort to put the mind back into the body. Second, embodiment is examined as a reflective experience in the sense that the mind forms particular images about the body. This sense of embodiment reflects the effort to put the body into the mind. The different chapters in this book demonstrate that the concept of embodiment deepens our understanding of development by suggesting new possibilities of integrating biological, psychological, and socio-cultural approaches to development.

This volume represents ideas from philosophy, anthropology, and psychology. In the absence of any book on the development of embodiment, this volume is unique in that several chapters discuss the concept of embodiment from a developmental perspective. The content of this volume will be of interest for developmental psychologists, cognitive psychologists, social psychologists, philosophers, anthropologists, biologists, and sociologists. The chapters in this volume should be suitable for upper-level undergraduate courses and graduate seminars on cognition, development, and culture.

—Willis F. Overton
—Ulrich Müller
—Judith Newman

1

EMBODIMENT FROM A RELATIONAL PERSPECTIVE

Willis F. Overton

Temple University

The chapters in this book explore the role of the body as lived experience and the body as physical object in the development of meaning, consciousness, and psychological functioning. Body as lived experience and body as physical object—understood as coequal and indissociable complementarities—constitute the fundamental notion of *embodiment*. Behavior emerges from the embodied person actively engaged in the world. Thus, embodiment is the claim that perception, thinking, feelings, and desires—that is, the way we behave, experience, and live the world—are contextualized by our being *active agents* with this particular kind of body (Taylor, 1995). In other words, the kind of body we have is a precondition for our having the kind of behaviors, experiences, and meanings that we have. As Johnson (1999) stated, "Human beings are creatures of the flesh. What we can experience and how we make sense of what we experience depend on the kinds of bodies we have and on the ways we interact with the various environments we inhabit" (p. 81). The chapters in this book explore embodiment from several theoretical orientations and focus on diverse functions of embodiment. Vonèche's chapter 4 and Thelen's chapter 5 examine the place of embodiment in cognitive functioning and development as a whole. Liben's chapter 8

focuses on spatial cognition and development. Johnson's chapter 2 and
Scholnick and Miller's chapter 10 explore embodiment and conceptual meaning and the impact of culture, as does Fegley, Spencer, Goss,
Harpalani, and Charles' chapter 11. In addition, Gao and Zelazo's chapter 9 considers language and the development of levels of consciousness
as this process entails a distancing of the conceptual from overt bodily
activity, described as a move *toward* disembodiment. The chapters also
extend beyond cognition *per se*. In chapter 7, Racine and Carpendale
examine the development of social understanding from an embodied perspective. In chapter 3, Colombetti and Thompson discuss the
embodiment of the emotions, and Csordas, in chapter 6, describes the
embodiment of religious experience.

THE METATHEORIES OF SPLITTING AND RELATIONISM

To fully understand the notion of embodiment, it is necessary to appreciate the idea of disembodiment, not as an increasing distancing of the sensorimotor and the conceptual (see Gao & Zelazo's chapter 9 and Thelen's
chapter 5 of this volume), but as conditioned by Descartes' 17th-century
proposal concerning the nature and relation of mind and body. In the
concluding chapter of this volume (chapter 12), Müller and Newman discuss Descartes' role in detail. Here, it is sufficient to simply reiterate the
basic Cartesian argument. This is the familiar splitting of mind and body
into segregated, pure forms. Descartes not only distinguished between,
but also sharply contrasted and segregated, *res extensa* (extended substance; the physical, the body) and *res cogitans* (unextended substance; the
mental, consciousness). This splitting, this disembodiment, has remained
a basic metatheoretical background assumption for many areas of psychological inquiry to the present day (see Müller & Newman, chapter 12
of this volume, for several extended examples). Following Descartes, the
problem for all who have accepted his premises has been that of finding
a means of reconciling the chasm between the physical and the mental.
Numerous attempts have been made to resolve this dualism, the most
contemporary being a materialistic monism, which either suppresses the
mental or renders it epiphenomenal (Searle, 1992). Within this framework, however, any notion of the lived body and the physical necessarily
reduces the lived body to the physical.

If metatheoretical background assumptions establish the framework
for the disembodied mind, then other metatheoretical assumptions must
be found as a ground for framing an understanding of embodiment in
which the lived body and the physical are indissociable complements,
and not competing alternatives forever segregated into pure forms of

reality. Such a set of assumptions is described by a perspective termed *relationism* (Latour, 1993; Overton, 2006). Latour described this perspective as a move away from the extremes of Cartesian splits to a center or "Middle Kingdom" position where all objects of knowledge are represented not as pure forms, but as forms that flow into each other across fluid boundaries. From this perspective, mind does not cause body, nor does body cause mind, nor do two entities interact; rather, mind and body are coconstituted, and as such, form indissociable complements. Within the context of this metatheoretical grounding, Hilary Putnam (1987) has argued from a philosophical point of view that it is not the case that the mind makes up the world, nor that the world makes up the mind, but that "the mind and the world jointly make up the mind and the world" (p. 1). From a similar philosophical perspective, John Searle (1992) pointed out that, "The fact that a feature is mental does not imply that it is not physical; the fact that a feature is physical does not imply that it is not mental" (p. 15). Finally, from an anthropological perspective, Ingold (2000), who made an explicit commitment to a relationism—"What we need . . . is a quite different way of thinking about organisms and their environments. I call this 'relational thinking'" (p. 295)—stated, "Body and mind . . . are not two separate things but two ways of describing the same thing—or better, the same process, namely the activity of the organism-person in his or her environment" (p. 291).

Relationism is the claim that objects and events derive their meaning from their relations as parts of a whole, and not as split-off elements of nature. Mind without a human living body engaged in the world is inconceivable, as is the engaged human living body inconceivable without a mind. From this relational stance, embodiment is not about a split-off, disengaged agent defined by its movements. Nor is it about a moving agent peeking at a preformed world and drawing meaning directly from that world. Nor is embodiment about a set of genes causing behavior, or a split-off brain causing or being the mind (e.g., brain-in-a-vat), or a split-off culture imprinting itself on mind and behavior. Embodiment is a concept of synthesis, a bridge that joins broad areas of inquiry into a unified whole (e.g., the biological, the phenomenological, the sociocultural and environmental) as relative standpoints that together constitute the whole. Thus, embodiment references not merely physical structures, but *the body as a form of lived experience, actively engaged in and with the world of sociocultural and physical objects.* The *body as form* references a biological standpoint, the *body as lived experience actively engaged* references a phenomenological or psychological person standpoint, and the *body actively engaged in and with the world* points to a contextual social, cultural, and environmental standpoint.

RELATIONAL SYNTHESIS:
THREE STANDPOINTS ON EMBODIMENT

A relational synthesis of standpoints is broadly unfamiliar to those raised in a Cartesian scientific culture; as a consequence, the following sections will briefly explore each and present examples.

Biological Standpoint on Embodiment

The biological standpoint on embodiment stands in contrast with typical Cartesian biological reductionism, which places explanation at, and only at, the level of brain mechanisms, genes, and DNA. The neurobiologists Antonio Damasio (e.g., 1994) and Joseph LeDoux (1996), exploring the neurological dimension of emotions, as well as Gerald Edelman (e.g., 1992), exploring the neurological dimensions of consciousness, all support an embodied approach to biological-psychological inquiry. In addition, all argue that the cognitive, affective, and motivational meanings that define the mind can no longer be thought of as the direct expression of genetic modularities (as nativists such as Steven Pinker, 1997, would claim). Nor can they be thought of as a functionalist piece of software, nor even as merely a function of brain processes. Rather, they argue, these meanings must be considered in a fully embodied context. As Damasio said, "Mind is probably not conceivable without some sort of embodiment" (p. 234), and further, commenting on contemporary perspectives on mind,

> This is Descartes' error: the abyssal separation between body and mind. . . . The Cartesian idea of a disembodied mind may well have been the source, by the middle of the twentieth century, for the metaphor of mind as software program. . . . [and] there may be some Cartesian disembodiment also behind the thinking of neuroscientists who insist that the mind can be fully explained in terms of brain events, leaving by the wayside the rest of the organism and the surrounding physical and social environment—and also leaving out the fact that part of the environment is itself a product of the organism's preceding actions. (pp. 249–250)

Similarly, Edelman (1992) argued,

> The mind is embodied. It is necessarily the case that certain dictates of the body must be followed by the mind. . . . Symbols do not get assigned meanings by formal means; instead it is assumed that symbolic structures are meaningful *to begin with*. This is so because categories are determined by bodily structure and by adaptive use as a result of evolution and behavior. (p. 239)

In the present volume, several authors discuss issues related to biological embodiment; these include the chapters by Johnson; Colombetti and Thompson; Thelen; and Vonèche.

Sociocultural and Environmental Standpoints on Embodiment

Broadly moving to the sociocultural and the environmental (e.g., objective world), the Cartesian framework privileges these as split-off elements, and thus argues that, for example, social discourse is "prior to and constitutive of the world" (Miller, 1996, p. 99), or claims a "Primacy of Cultural Mediation," (Cole & Wertsch,1996, p. 251). Increasingly, however, social constructivists such as Harre (1995), Csordas (1999), Ingold (2000), and Sampson (1996) have argued for embodied action as a relational anchoring to the relativism of any split-off discourse and cultural analyses. Sampson, for example, has argued for "embodied discourses," as these "refer to the inherently embodied nature of all human endeavor, including talk, conversation and discourse itself" (p. 609; see also Overton, 1997). Perhaps the most fully articulated contemporary employment of embodiment in a developmentally oriented cultural psychology is found in Boesch (1991). Boesch's presentation of "the I and the body" is a discussion of the centrality of embodiment for a cultural psychology. Thus, he stated "The body, obviously, is more than just an object with anatomical and physiological properties: *it is the medium of our actions* [italics added], it is with our body that we both conceive and perform actions" (p. 312).

The idea of situated cognition or situated learning—when freed from its Cartesian contextualist moorings, which splits object from subject and privileges the former—is tightly intertwined with the environmental and sociocultural embodied standpoint. Muller and Newman, in chapter 12 of this volume, spell out in detail the situated nature of embodiment and point to its examination in several other chapters of this volume (Liben, chapter 8; Scholnick & Miller, chapter 10; Racine & Carpendale, chapter 7). Here, it can simply again be reasserted that the relational meaning of embodiment as a *body actively engaged in and with the world* necessitates that not only cognition and learning, but all emotions and motivations and all psychological functions are coconstituted by the sociocultural and environmental context.

With respect specifically to the environment (e.g., objective world), Sanders (1999) described a framework for transforming the Cartesian split between subject and object into a relational embodied joining through an understanding of the environment as a system of "affordances"

(Gibson, 1979). Sanders began from a relational perspective on the contrast between organism and environment:

> For *any* way of characterizing the contrast, the important feature to be noted is that neither contrasted pole [or "point-of-view"] can be characterized independently of the other. "Environments" just *are* organism-indexed parts of the world. "Organisms" are just part of the world distinguished, for particular purposes (whatever they may be), from what they are embedded in. (p. 133)

Defining 'affordances' as "opportunities for action in the environment of an organism" (p. 129), Sanders went on to argue,

> The perceptual readiness or theoretical set with which we frame particular experiences varies not only from time to time and from culture to culture, it varies from moment to moment in any individual's life as a function of interest, purpose, desire, and the like. It is relative to this changing background that the world gets cast in terms of opportunities and risks—in terms, that is, of affordances. (p. 135)

Sanders completed his affordances argument by describing the role they play in embodiment:

> Affordances serve . . . as analytical units of embodiment. This is not an embodiment that is merely physical—the language of affordances relativizes ontology not simply to the physical body, but to what an agent *can do*. The "environment" within which affordances may be deployed is not only the perceptual environment, but also the entire universe of potential action. What it is comprised of and how it is parsed will be a function of affordances. The embodied agent is "embodied" precisely insofar as the agent's capacities and functions are understood as deriving in vital part from activity, rather than from an a priori gift of passive assimilation of external messages. . . . Affordances thus help to elucidate both the theoretical insight and the dynamic implications of the idea of embodiment and engaged agency. (p. 135)

Phenomenological and Person-Centered Developmental Standpoint on Embodiment

If embodiment entails, in part, the *body as lived experience actively engaged*, then a phenomenological and person-centered standpoint of relational synthesis becomes a necessary vantage point for understanding embodiment as a whole. This point of synthesis maintains a theoretical and empirical focus on the psychological processes and changes that constitute the psychological subject and the development of the psychological subject. The single most important value of recognizing a person-centered standpoint as a necessary point of synthesis—along with the biological and sociocultural points of synthesis—is that it rescues psychology generally, and developmental psychology specifically, from becoming a mere adjunct to biology, or to culture, discourse, narrative, or computer science. *Psyche* initially referenced "soul," and later, "mind;" if psychology is not to again lose its mind—as it did in the days of the hegemony of behaviorism—keeping the psychological subject as the center of action is a necessary guard against explanatory reduction to biology, culture, discourse, and so forth.

The person-centered point of view entails five interrelated concepts: (a) person, (b) agent, (c) action, (d) experience, and (e) person-embodiment.

Person-agent. Person and agent are complementary levels of analysis of the same whole. The person level is constituted by genuine psychological concepts (e.g., thoughts, feelings, desires, wishes) that have intentional qualities, are open to interpretation, and are available to consciousness (Shanon, 1993), or in other words, have psychological meaning. The agent level—called the "subpersonal" level by some (Dennett, 1987; Russell, 1996; Hurley, 1998)—here refers to action systems or dynamic self-organizing systems. "Schemes," "operations," "ego," "attachment behavioral system," and "executive function" are some of the concepts that describe these action systems.

Taken as a whole, the person-agent, when framed by a relational context, entails engaged human agency (Taylor, 1995) and forms the nucleus of a psychological metatheory of mind. From this perspective, mind is defined as a self-organizing dynamic system of cognitive (knowings, beliefs), emotional (feelings), and conative or motivational (wishes, desires) meanings or understandings, along with procedures for maintaining, implementing, and changing these meanings. Importantly, it must be noted—and underlined—that a person-centered metatheory of mind is not an encapsulated cognition, but rather, a perspective that includes emotions, wishes, and desires as well as cognition. Further, there is no question about where mind is "located." Mind emerges from a relational biosociocultural activity matrix. In the present context, mind is a person-centered concept because the approach being described takes the *person standpoint*. As a person-centered concept, mind bridges naturally to both the biological and the sociocultural.

Action, intention, behavior. Person-agent is the source of action, which is itself a necessary feature of engaged human agency. Action is a fundamental for what have traditionally been termed "action theories of psychological functioning and development" (Brandtstädter, 1998; Brandstädter & Lerner, 1999; Müller & Overton, 1998; Overton & Ennis, 2006). At the *agent level*, where it is not necessary to limit a definition to the human organism, action is defined as the "characteristic functioning of any dynamic self-organizing system." For example, a plant orients toward the sun. Weather systems form high- and low-pressure areas and move from west to east. On the other hand, engaged human systems organize and adapt to their biological, sociocultural, and environmental worlds. At the *person level*, action is defined as "intentional activity" (e.g., meaning giving activity). Intentionality, however, is not to be identified with consciousness. While all acts are intentional, only some intentions are conscious or self-conscious. In a similar fashion, intention is not to be identified solely with a symbolic level of reflection. Following Brentano (1973) all acts, even those occurring at early sensorimotor levels of functioning intend some object.

Action is often distinguishable from *behavior*, as the action of the person-agent implies a *transformation* in the intended object of action, while behavior often simply implies movement and states (e.g., the classically defined "response" was understood as specific movement in space and time, a behavior; see von Wright, 1971, p. 199). As action, when the infant chews (act)—something that from a *sociocultural standpoint* is called a "basket"—the infant, from a *person-centered standpoint*, is transforming this part of her known world into a practical action, "chewable." Piaget's cognitive developmental theory is a good example of a child-centered developmental action theory, where the metatheoretical "action" becomes translated into specific theoretical concepts. Thus, Piaget's basic theoretical concepts of "function," "assimilation," "accommodation," "operation," and "reflective abstraction," all reference action. Piaget repeatedly affirms the centrality of action throughout his writings: "I think that human knowledge is essentially active. To know is to assimilate reality into systems of transformations. To know is to transform reality. . . . To my way of thinking, knowing an object does not mean copying it—it means acting upon it" (Piaget, 1967, p. 15); "To know an object . . . is to act on it so as to transform it" (Piaget, 1977, p. 30); "Nothing is knowable unless the subject acts in one way or another on the surrounding world" (Piaget, 1974/1980, p. 43).

Action serves at least three major functions in the development of mind. First, *action of engaged human agency expresses cognitive/affective/ conative meaning*. Here, it is important to recognize that "meaning," like many other basic concepts, has relational complementary definitions that are determined by the standpoint being taken (Overton, 1994). "I mean" and "it means" operate in a relational matrix. The former is concerned with person-centered meanings, the latter with sociocultural meanings and reference. From a person-centered standpoint, the focus of analysis is on "I mean," and secondarily, on how "I mean" becomes associated with "it means." Considered as *expressive,* action entails the projection of person-centered meanings, thus transforming the "objective" environmental world (e.g., an object point of view) into an "actual" world as known, felt, desired. "World" here is another relational bipolar concept. The *actual* world is the world of meanings constructed by the person: the known world. The *environmental or objective* world is the world of reference, examined from a sociocultural or environmental standpoint.

The second function that action serves is the *instrumental function of communicating and adjusting person-centered meanings.* Communication, dialogue, discourse, and problem solving all call attention to the relational to-and-fro movement between the expression of the self-organizing system and instrumental adaptive changes. Completely adapted (e.g., successful) action entails only the *projection* of meaning onto the world (e.g., If I intend this object before me to hold water as a "cup," and I successfully drink from it, no change occurs in my conceptual system). Partially adapted (e.g., partially successful) action results in exploratory action, or *variations* (e.g., If the intended "cup" leads to water leaking onto my shirt, I vary my actions, such as putting my finger across a crack in the object). Exploratory action that is adaptive (e.g., The finger placement permits successful drinking) entails reorganization of the system (transformational change) and hence, new meanings (e.g., A cup is an object without cracks).

Experience and action. This general cycle of projected action, and exploratory variational action in the face of encountered resistances, constitutes the third and most general function of action: *Action defines the general mechanism of all psychological development.* From a person-centered developmental action standpoint, *all development is explained by the action of the subject.* Again, however, this metatheoretical concept will be translated into specific theoretical concepts at the level of theory itself (e.g., Piaget's concepts of "assimilation-accommodation" and "equilibration" identify action mechanisms of development).

In claiming that action is the general mechanism of all development, it is necessary to recognize that within an action based perspective, *action and experience are identical concepts.* Consequently, the claim that action is the mechanism of development is identical to the claim that experience is the mechanism of development. All development occurs through experience. In this definition, however, it should be clear that experience as action excludes neither the biological nor the sociocultural and environmental. In fact, experience understood as action of the person-agent represents a synthesis of these points of view.

Experience is itself, however, yet another concept that acquires complementary meanings depending on whether the focus is from the person-agent or the objective environmental standpoint. From each perspective, experience is identified as the coconstitution of the act and the environment, but each has a distinct emphasis regarding the locus of this coconstitution. From the person-agent standpoint, *experience is the action of exploring, manipulating, and observing the world,* while from an environmental standpoint, *experience is an objective event or stimulus present in the context of the act.* Further, as understood from the person-agent standpoint, when experience is described as feeling or qualia, the reference here is the person-centered felt meaning of the observational, manipulative, and exploratory action. In a similar fashion, to speak of "perceptual experience" is to speak of the felt meanings of the observational, manipulative, and exploratory action.

When experience is understood as entailing the developmental *action cycle* of projection and transformation (of the known world) and exploration-transformation (of the system), experience also becomes the psychological bridge between biological and cultural systems. There is no sense here of an isolated, cut off, solitary human psyche. Person-centered experience emerges from a biosociocultural relational activity matrix (see, for example, Gallese 2000a, 2000b; Suomi, 1999), and this experience both transforms the matrix and is transformed by the matrix. Person development is neither a split-off nativism, nor a split-off environmentalism, nor a split-off, additive combination of the two. The neonate is a dynamic system of practical action meanings. These meanings represent the outcome of nine months of the coconstituting action of biology-environment, and this coconstituting stretches all the way down to DNA (Gottlieb, 2002; Lewontin, 2000). Finally, it is important to repeat that to say that development is explained by experience does not deny that development is explained by biology *and* that development is explained by the sociocultural *and* by the environment. What is denied is the absolute exclusivity of any of these standpoint explanations.

Development of person-agent. Psychological development of the person-agent—and hence, engaged human agency—entails the epigenetic stance that novel forms emerge through the coconstituting actions of the target system, as well as the resistances the target system encounters in both the actual and objective sociocultural and physical environment. It is through coconstitutive actions that the system changes and, hence, becomes differentiated; however, differentiation of parts implies a novel coordination of parts, and this coordination itself identifies the emergence of novelty. Thus, as suggested earlier, the neurological action system becomes differentiated through the coconstitutive actions of neurological-environmental functioning. This differentiation leads to a novel coordination or reorganization, and through continuing transformations to the adapted level of conscious practical action found in the neonate. Consciousness is a person-level systemic property of this emergent action system as it operates in the world. The initial adapted practical consciousness entails a minimum awareness of the meaning constituted by an act (Zelazo, 1996; Gao & Zelazo, chapter 9, this volume). Consciousness cannot be reduced to or "squeezed" out of lower stages; it is the result of organism-environment transformations. Similarly, further developmental differentiations and coordinations of actions—described as "higher" levels of consciousness—emerge through the coconstitution of conscious action and the sociocultural and physical worlds it encounters. Symbolic meaning and the symbolic representational level of meanings (Müller & Overton, 1998) describes forms of consciousness that arise from the coordination of practical actions. Reflective and trans-reflective (reflective symbolic understandings of reflective symbolic understandings) meanings describe further developmental advances in the coordination of action systems.

To summarize, to this point, the nucleus of a relationally informed, person-centered, developmental action metatheory of mind has been described, where mind is conceptualized as a dynamic, self-organizing system of cognitive (knowings, beliefs), emotional (feelings), and conative or motivational (wishes, desires) meanings or understandings, along with procedures for maintaining, implementing, and changing these meanings. Mind, through expressive projections, transforms the world as known, and through adaptive exploration, transforms itself (e.g., develops); however, this remains a nucleus and only a nucleus, because it lacks the critical necessary feature of embodiment.

Person-agent engaged embodied actions.   Person-agent is the source of action, and action is the source of meaning; but this action itself is embodied. As described earlier, embodiment is defined, in part, as "the body as lived experience actively engaged." Embodiment is the claim that the person's perception, thinking, feelings, desires—that is, the way the person experiences or lives the world—is contextualized by persons being active agents with this particular kind of body. At the agent level, embodiment specifies the characteristic nature of the activity of any living system (e.g., the world of the fly is necessarily shaped by the nature of the fly's embodied acts). At the person level, embodiment affirms that from the beginning, bodily acts constrain and inform the nature of intentionality (Margolis, 1987). Intentionality is not limited to a symbolic, reflective, or trans-reflective system of psychological meanings; intentionality also extends to a system of psychological meanings that characterize practical, embodied actions operating at the most minimum level of consciousness (see Müller & Newman, chapter 12, this volume). These most basic meanings and all others "come from having a body with particular perceptual and motor capabilities that are inseparably linked" (Thelen, Schoner, Scheier, & Smith, 2001, p. 1)—that is, they arise, as Piaget repeatedly insisted, from the sensorimotor functioning that represents a concrete instantiation of embodied actions engaged with the world.

Varela, Thompson, and Rosch (1991) have sketched a general outline for an embodied theory of cognition (see Colombetti & Thompson, chapter 3, this volume). Sheets-Johnstone (1990) and Ingold (2000) provide an evolutionary anthropological perspective on human embodiment and thought, and Santostefano (1995) has detailed the emotional and cognitive dimensions of practical, symbolic, and reflective embodied meanings. Further, many who have studied psychopathology, from R. D. Laing, (1960) to Donald Winnicott (1965) and Thomas Ogden (1986), argue that disruptions in the embodied actions of the person-agent are central to an understanding of the development of severe forms of psychopathology (see Overton & Horowitz, 1991).

At the level of practical actions, Bermudez's (1998) work on the development of self-consciousness is central to an understanding of the impact of an embodied person conceptualization. Bermudez's fundamental argument is that late emerging forms of meaning found in symbolic and reflective consciousness develop from—and are constrained by—embodied self-organizing action systems available to the infant. Most importantly, these early systems entail person-level somatic proprioception and exteroception. As these person-centered processes coconstitute the physical and sociocultural worlds, proprioception operates as the differentiation mechanism for the emergence of a self-consciousness action system, and exteroception operates as the differentiation mechanism for the emergence of an object-consciousness system. Hence, over the first several months of life, a basic practical action associated with "me" and "other" develops, which in turn becomes transformed into the symbolic "me" and "other" of early toddlerhood.

Thelen's (chapter 5, this volume) work on the role of movement generally, and specifically "body memory" in infant cognitive functioning, is another closely related area that illustrates the importance of embodiment at the level of practical actions.

Langer's (1994) empirical studies represent important demonstrations of the intercoordination of embodied action systems as these intercoordinations move development from the practical to the symbolic plane of meaning. Earlier work by Held and colleagues (e.g., Held & Bossom, 1961; Held & Hein, 1958), on the other hand, illustrates the significance of *voluntary* embodied action at all levels of adaptation. Goodwyn and Acredolo's (1993) research on the use of bodily gestures as signs expressing practical meanings in older infants suggests the expressive and instrumental value of embodied practical gesture. Other work has elaborated on the significance of bodily representations at the symbolic and reflective levels of meaning. For example, while the use of fingers for counting is well-documented (Gelman & Williams, 1998), Saxe's (1981, 1995) research has shown cross-culturally that other bodily representations enter into counting systems. Further, earlier research by Overton and Jackson (1973) and more recently, by Dick, Overton, and Kovacs (2005) has demonstrated that bodily gestures support emerging symbolic representations at least until the level of reflective meanings.

At the level of symbolic, reflective, and trans-reflective conceptual functioning, the writings of Lakoff and Johnson (1999; see also Johnson, chapter 2, this volume) are well known for their detailed exploration of the significance of person embodiment. For Lakoff and Johnson, embodiment provides the fundamental metaphors that shape meanings at all levels of functioning. In a parallel but distinct approach, Kainz (1988) has described how the basic laws of ordinary logic (e.g., the law of identity, the law of contradictions, and the law of the excluded middle) can be understood as emerging from the early-embodied differentiation of self and other. Finally, Liben's (1999; chapter 8, this volume) work on the development of the child's symbolic and reflective spatial concepts presents a strong argument for viewing this development in the context of an embodied child rather than in the context of the disembodied eye that traditionally has framed this domain.

CONCLUSION

In conclusion, a coherent understanding of human embodiment necessitates a relational context. Moving from a split Cartesian to a relational context makes intelligible the idea of embodiment as physical structures and a form of lived experience, actively engaged in and with the world of sociocultural and physical objects. Because the concept of embodiment as a form of lived experience is foreign to those whose vision has been shaped by Cartesian background assumptions, we have placed greater emphasis here on the lived body than on physical structures. There is a danger here, however, of creating a new split that marginalizes the significance of physical structures themselves. We guard against this danger to the extent that relational categories are forefronted in all analytic venues when the concept of embodiment is explored.

By establishing the intelligibility of these two faces of embodiment, a relational context facilitates a concretization of, and makes intelligible, the very notion of engaged human agency. Further, within this context, engagement and disengagement come to represent two sides of the same coin, and not radically opposed alternatives. Consequently, development from sensorimotor action to symbolic and reflective thought entails no rupture in the action base of engaged human agency. Symbolic and reflective thought represent a relative disengagement or differentiation, sometimes termed a "distancing," of subject from object (see Müller and Newman, chapter 12, this volume) and not the kind of radical split that would be entailed by a classic Cartesian disembodiment. Thus, instrumentalities such as social imitation and language (see, Fegley et al., chapter 11, this volume; Gao & Zelazo, chapter 9, this volume; Müller & Newman, chapter 12, this volume) come to be interpreted as just that, instruments that facilitate subject-object differentiation or distancing, and not as mechanisms of Cartesian disembodiment.

As a final point, along with making intelligible the two faces of embodiment and the nature of engaged human agency, relationism establishes the potential ground for a truly interdisciplinary scientific research program designed to explore all facets of engaged human agency. This program begins from a recognition that embodiment is a concept of synthesis that can join relationally committed research scientists from a wide variety of disciplines. This program develops through empirical studies that begin from the premise that disciplinary affiliation is about point of view or standpoint, and not about competing alternatives on the ultimate nature of truth. Finally, the program grows to maturity through an explicit articulation of the fact that truth is found at the intersection of points of view or standpoints, and not in a Cartesian reductionism to a foundationally fixed certainty.

REFERENCES

Bermudez, J. L. (1998). *The paradox of self-consciousness*. Cambridge, MA: The MIT Press.

Boesch, E. E. (1991). *Symbolic action theory and cultural psychology*. Berlin, Germany: Springer-Verlag.

Brandtstädter, J. (1998). Action perspectives on human development. In W. Damon (Series Ed.), & R. M. Lerner (Vol. Ed.), *Handbook of child psychology: Vol. 1. Theoretical models of human development* (5th ed., pp. 807–863). New York: Wiley.

Brandtstädter, J., & Lerner, R. M. (Eds.) (1999). *Action and self-development: Theory and research through the life span*. London: Sage Publications.

Brentano, F. (1973). *Psychology from an empirical standpoint*. (A. C. Rancurello, D. B. Terrell, & L. McAlister, Trans.). London: Routledge. (Original work published 1874)

Cole, M., & Wertsch, J. V. (1996). Beyond the individual-social antinomy in discussions of Piaget and Vygotsky. *Human Development, 39*, 250–256.

Csordas, T. J. (1999). Embodiment and cultural phenomenology. In G. Weiss & H. F. Haber (Eds.), *Embodiment: The intersection of nature and culture* (pp. 143–162). New York: outledge.

Damasio, A. (1994). *Descartes' error: Emotion, reason, and the human brain*. New York: Avon Books, Inc.

Dennett, D. (1987). *The intentional stance*. Cambridge MA: The MIT Press.

Dick, A. S., Overton, W. F., & Kovacs, S. L. (2005). The development of symbolic coordination: Representation of imagined objects, executive function and theory of mind. *Journal of Cognition and Development, 6*, 133–161

Edelman, G. M. (1992). *Bright air, brilliant fire: On the matter of the mind*. New York: Basic Books.

Gallese, V. (2000a). The acting subject: Towards the neural basis of social cognition. In T. Metzinger (Ed.), *Neural correlates of consciousness* (pp. 325–334). Cambridge: MIT Press.

Gallese, V. (2000b). The 'shared manifold hypothesis': From mirror neurons to empathy. *Journal of Consciousness Studies, 8*, 33–50.

Gelman, R., & Williams, E. M. (1998). Enabling constraints for cognitive development and learning: Domain specificity and epigenesis. In D. Kuhn & R. Siegler (Eds.), *Handbook of child psychology: Vol. 2. Cognition, perception, and language* (5th ed., pp. 575–630). New York: Wiley.

Gibson, J. J. (1979). *The ecological approach to visual perception*. Boston: Houghton-Mifflin.

Goodwyn, S. W., & Acredolo, L. P. (1993). Symbolic gesture versus word: Is there a modality advantage for onset of symbol use? *Child Development, 64*, 688–701.

Gottlieb, G. (2002). Developmental-behavioral initiation of evolutionary change. *Psychological Review, 109*, 211–218.

Harre, R. (1995). The necessity of personhood as embodied being. *Theory & Psychology, 5,* 369–373.

Held, R., & Bossom, J. (1961). Neonatal deprivation and adult rearrangement: complementary techniques for analyzing plastic sensory-motor coordinations. *Journal of Comparative Physiological Psychology, 54,* 33–37.

Held, R., & Hein, A. (1958). Adaptation of disarranged hand-eye coordination contingent upon re-afferent stimulation. *Perceptual-Motor Skills, 8,* 87–90.

Hurley, S. L. (1998). *Consciousness in action.* Cambridge, MA: Harvard University Press.

Ingold, T. (2000). Evolving skills. In H. Rose & S. Rose (Eds.), *Alas, poor Darwin: Arguments against evolutionary psychology* (pp. 273–297). New York: Harmony Books.

Johnson, M. (1999). Embodied reason. In G. Weiss & H. F. Haber (Eds.). *Embodiment: The intersection of nature and culture* (pp. 81–102). New York: Routledge.

Kainz, H. P. (1988). *Paradox, dialectic, and system: A contemporary reconstruction of the Hegelian problematic.* University Park: The Pennsylvania State University Press.

Laing, R. D. (1960). *The divided self.* New York: Pantheon Books.

Lakoff, G., & Johnson, M. (1999). *Philosophy in the flesh: The embodied mind and its challenge to western thought.* New York: Basic Books.

Langer, J. (1994). From acting to understanding: The comparative development of meaning. In W. Overton & D. Palermo (Eds.), *The nature and ontogenesis of meaning* (pp. 191–214). Hillsdale, NJ: Erlbaum.

Latour, B (1993). *We have never been modern.* Cambridge, MA: Harvard University Press.

LeDoux, J. (1996). *The emotional brain: The mysterious underpinnings of emotional life.* New York: Touchstone.

Lewontin, R. C. (2000). *The triple helix. Inside and outside: Gene, organism, and environment.* Cambridge, MA: Harvard University Press.

Liben, L. S. (1999). Developing an understanding of external spatial representations. In I. E. Sigel (Ed.), *Development of mental representation: Theories and applications* (pp. 297–321). Mahwah, NJ: Lawrence Erlbaum Associates.

Margolis, J. (1987). *Science without unity: Reconciling the human and natural sciences.* New York: Basil Blackwell.

Miller, J. G. (1996). Theoretical issues in cultural psychology. In J. W. Berry, Y. H. Poortinga, & J. Pandey (Eds.), *Handbook of cross-cultural psychology: Theory and method* (pp. 85–128). Boston: Allyn and Bacon.

Müller, U., & Overton, W. F. (1998). How to grow a baby. A re-evaluation of image-schema and Piagetian action approaches to representation. *Human Development, 41,* 71–111.

Ogden, T. H. (1986). *The matrix of the mind: Object relations and the psycho-analytic dialogue*. Northvale, NJ: Jason Aronson.

Overton, W. F. (1994). Contexts of meaning: The computational and the embodied mind. In W. F. Overton & D. S. Palermo (Eds.), *The nature and ontogenesis of meaning* (pp. 1–18). Hillsdale, NJ: Lawrence Erlbaum Associates.

Overton, W. F. (1997). Beyond dichotomy: An embodied active agent for cultural psychology. *Culture and Psychology, 3*, 315–334.

Overton, W. F. (2006). Developmental psychology: Philosophy, concepts, methodology. In R. M. Lerner (Ed.), *Handbook of child psychology: Vol. 1. Theoretical models of human development* (6th ed., pp. 18–88), New York: Wiley.

Overton, W. F., & Ennis, M. (2006). Cognitive-developmental and behavior-analytic theories: Evolving into complementarity. *Human Development, 49*, 143–172.

Overton, W. F., & Horowitz, H. (1991). Developmental psychopathology: Differentiations and integrations. In D. Cicchetti & S. Toth (Eds.), *Rochester symposium on developmental psychopathology: Vol. 3* (pp. 1–41). Rochester, NY: University of Rochester Press.

Overton, W. F., & Jackson, J. (1973). The representation of imagined objects in action sequences: A developmental study. *Child Development, 44*, 309–314.

Piaget, J. (1967). *Six psychological studies*. New York: Random House.

Piaget, J. (1977). The role of action in the development of thinking. In W. F. Overton & J. M. Gallagher (Eds.), *Knowledge and development* (pp. 17–42). New York: Plenum.

Piaget, J. (1980). *Adaptation and intelligence: Organic selection and phenocopy*. Chicago: The University of Chicago Press.)

Pinker, S. (1997). *How the mind works*. New York: Norton.

Putnam, H. (1987). *The many faces of realism*. Cambridge, England: Cambridge University Press.

Russell, J. (1996). *Agency: Its role in mental development*. Erlbaum: Taylor and Francis.

Sampson, E. E. (1996). Establishing embodiment in psychology. *Theory and Psychology, 6*, 601–624.

Sanders, J. T. (1999). Affordances: An ecological approach to first philosophy. In G. Weiss & H. F. Haber (Eds.), *Embodiment: The intersection of nature and culture* (pp. 121–142). New York: Routledge.

Santostefano, S. (1995). Embodied meanings, cognition and emotion: Pondering how three are one. In D. Cicchetti & S. L. Toth (Eds.). *Rochester symposium on developmental psychopathology: Vol. 6. Emotion, cognition and representation* (pp. 59–132). Rochester, NY: University of Rochester Press.

Saxe, G. B. (1981). Body parts as numerals. A developmental analysis of numeration among the Oksapmin of New Guinea. *Child Development, 52*, 306–316.

Saxe, G. B. (1995, June). *Culture, changes in social practices, and cognitive development.* Paper presented at the annual meeting of the Jean Piaget Society, Berkeley, CA.

Searle, J. (1992). *The rediscovery of the mind.* Cambridge, MA: The MIT Press.

Shanon, B. (1993). *The representational and the presentational: An essay on cognition and the study of mind.* New York: Harvester Wheatsheaf.

Sheets-Johnstone, M. (1990). *The roots of thinking.* Philadelphia: Temple University Press.

Suomi, S. J. (1999). Attachment in rhesus monkeys. In J. Cassidy & P. R. Shaver (Eds.), *Handbook of attachment: Theory, research, and clinical applications* (pp. 181–197). New York: Guilford Press.

Taylor, C. (1995). *Philosophical arguments.* Cambridge, MA: Harvard University Press.

Thelen, E., Schoner, G., Scheier, C., & Smith, L. (2001). The dynamics of embodiment: A field theory of infant perseverative reaching. *Behavioral and Brain Sciences, 24*, 1–86.

Varela, F. J., Thompson, E., & Rosch, E. (1991). *The embodied mind: Cognitive science and human experience.* Cambridge, MA: The MIT Press.

von Wright, G. H. (1971). *Explanation and understanding.* Ithaca, NY: Cornell University Press

Winnicott, D.W. (1965). *The maturational process and the facilitating environment.* New York: International Universities Press.

Zelazo, P. D. (1996). Towards a characterization of minimal consciousness. *New Ideas in Psychology, 14*, 63–80.

2

THE MEANING OF THE BODY

Mark Johnson

Department of Philosophy
University of Oregon

We humans are incarnate. Our embodiment shapes both *what* and *how* we experience, think, mean, imagine, reason, and communicate. This claim is a bold one, and it flies in the face of our received wisdom that what we call "mind" and "body" are not one and the same but rather are somehow fundamentally different in kind. From a philosophical point of view, one of the hardest tasks you will ever face is coming to grips with the fact of your embodiment. What makes this task so very difficult is the omnipresent idea of disembodied mind and thought that shows itself throughout our intellectual tradition, from claims about pure logical form, to ideas of noncorporeal thought, to spectator views of knowledge, to correspondence theories of truth. Everywhere you turn, the mysterious exotic snail of disembodied mind leaves its shiny, slippery trail through our views of thought, language, and knowledge.

My modest efforts to counteract this tradition of conceiving of mind as disembodied consist primarily in trying to show some of the ways that meaning, concepts, logic, and inferential patterns are grounded in our bodies and in bodily activities. In a nutshell, to say that reason is embodied means that what reason is and does depends directly on how our bodies and brains work and on the patterns of our bodily interactions with the world. This is not merely the obvious claim that we need brains and bodies in order to think. *It is the much stronger claim that the ways our bodies work and the nature of our bodily encounters with our environments shape the nature of reason itself.*

In this chapter, I argue that meaning emerges in our sensory-motor experiences, where recurring patterns of bodily perception and action known as image schemas organize it. Image schemas support body-based thinking and inference, but this occurs mostly beneath the level of conscious awareness. Imaginative processes like conceptual metaphor extend this body-based meaning to structure our abstract concepts. Conceptual metaphors allow us to understand and reason about abstract entities and domains, without losing the bodily grounding of meaning. I will suggest that our bodily experience thus provides a prereflective fund of meaning that makes it possible for us to think abstractly and to carry out all forms of meaningful human symbolic interaction, expression, and communication.

WHERE DOES MEANING COME FROM?

Human beings are embodied organisms engaged in ongoing patterned interactions with their ever-changing environments. Those environments are not just physical—not just earth, air, fire, and water—but are also always social, economic, moral, political, and spiritual. Experience is therefore never just bodily or just mental, but rather both at once. Experience is neither merely subjective nor merely objective, but rather is a more continuous process out of which what we call "subjects" and "objects" emerge. Experience does not separate itself into emotional versus rational components; rather, our rationality is at once embodied and emotional, full of eros.

Our experiences are always structured by a large number of recurring interactional patterns that make up our intercorporeal communal experience. Such flesh and blood patterns are the bodily basis of our shared world, given our present state of evolutionary development. What these patterns are and how they blend depends on a massive number of factors: the nature and limits of our perceptual systems, the character of the environments we inhabit (including the "affordances" available to us for our experience), the kinds of motor programs we can execute, the needs we have, the purposes we seek to realize through our actions, the range of emotions we are capable of experiencing, and the values we have as a result of our overall makeup and evolutionary history. Thus, the characteristics of our bodies, our neural makeup, and our environments constrain not only *what* it is possible for us to think about, but also, more importantly, *how* we think about it.

If you think, as I do, that there is no mind without a body—a body in continuous interaction with ever-changing environments—then you have to explain how this bodily activity gives rise to all our glorious abstract thought and symbolic interactions. I want to give a sketch of certain key aspects of this account of embodied meaning and thought, in particular, (a) image schemas, (b) controller executing schemas, and (c) primary conceptual metaphors.

IMAGE SCHEMAS

Let us start with the fact that our experience is permeated with hundreds of recurring sensory-motor patterns, known as "image schemas," that give shape, connection, and significance to what we experience (Johnson, M., 1987; Lakoff, 1987; Lakoff & Johnson, M., 1999). To illustrate this kind of meaningful structure, consider the *Container* schema. Thousands of times each day we perceive, manipulate, and interact with containers, such as cups, boxes, briefcases, rooms, vehicles, and even our own bodies. Via these recurrent vital interactions, we come to learn the meaning and logic of containment. The Container schema consists of the following minimal structure:

1. A boundary
2. An interior
3. An exterior

To get schemas for concepts like *in* and *out,* you must add structure that profiles various parts of the Container schema. The concept *in* profiles (highlights or activates) the Interior of the Container schema, whereas the concept *out* profiles the Exterior that surrounds the Boundary. *In* and *out* also requires identification of a figure/ground (or trajector/landmark) structure relative to the Container schema. When we say, "The horse left the barn," the horse is the trajector relative to the barn (landmark).

Even for image schemas as elementary and simple as the Container schema, there is already a definite spatial or bodily logic that we learn from our sensory-motor experience and that constrains our inferences about containers:

1. If an object X is in container A, then that object is not outside that container.
2. If an object X is within container A and container A is within container B, then object X is within container B.

3. If an object X is outside of container B and container A is inside container B, then object X is outside of container A.

To emphasize just how much internal structure, and thereby how much constraint on spatial logics there can be for even our most elementary image schemas, consider the Source-Path-Goal schema, with at least the following minimal structure:

1. A source point from which the path begins
2. A path leading in some direction
3. A goal, that is, an endpoint for the path

Described in this minimal way, it might seem as though the image schema does not have enough internal structure to support extensive inferences. However, actual Source-Path-Goal schemas typically have considerable additional structure that can serve as the basis for a wide range of inferences, for example,

- A trajector that moves
- A source location (the starting point)
- A goal (the intended destination for the trajector)
- A route from the source to the goal
- The actual trajectory of motion
- The position of the trajector at a given time
- The direction of the trajector at that time
- The actual final location of the trajector when the motion terminates, which may be different from the intended destination

Typically, there is even more structure available within this image schema since the above list leaves out other possible dimensions that might play a role in various events, including the speed of the trajector, the trail left by the moving object, obstacles to motion, aids to motion, forces that move the trajector, multiple trajectors, and so on.

An important feature of image schemas is their topological character, in the sense that they can undergo a wide range of distortions or transformations while still retaining their image-schematic structure and logic. For example, a path can be straight, it can twist and turn back upon itself, or it can involve stop-and-go motion without losing its characteristic Source-Path-Goal structure and without violating its characteristic spatial logic.

Another crucial property of image schemas is their compositionality, that is, their ability to combine to produce other image schemas. Via such composition, vast expanses of our experience and understanding of our mundane bodily experience are image schematically structured.

For example, as Lakoff and Nunez (2001) showed the concepts *into* and *out of* are blendings of the Container schema with the Source-Path-Goal schema.[1] The Into schema is a composition of the In schema and the To schema, whereas the Out Of schema combines the Out schema and the From schema.

Into Schema

- The In schema: consisting of a Container schema, with the Interior profiled and taken as Landmark
- The To schema: consisting of a Source-Path-Goal schema, with the Goal profiled and taken as Landmark
- Correspondences: (Interior; Goal) and (Exterior; Source)

Out-of Schema

- The Out schema: consisting of a Container schema, with the Exterior profiled and taken as Landmark
- The From schema: consisting of a Source-Path-Goal schema, with the Source profiled and taken as Landmark
- Correspondences: (Interior; Source) and (Exterior; Goal)

A full accounting of the image-schematic structure of our experience and understanding might extend to thousands of structures. However, most of these would be complex combinations of a smaller number of more basic image schemas.

In summary, there are four major points to keep in mind concerning the nature and activation of image schemas:

1. Image schemas characterize the recurring structure of much of our sensory-motor experience, and they are the basis for much of our embodied prereflective meaning.
2. We learn image schemas automatically and usually unconsciously through our bodily interactions with aspects of our environment, given the nature of our brains and bodies in relation to the possibilities for experience that are afforded us within different environments. Image schemas are meaningful to us even when, as is typical, they operate beneath the level of conscious awareness.
3. Image schemas have highly determinate "spatial" or "bodily" logics that support and constrain inferences.
4. Image schemas are compositional in that they combine and blend, yielding even more complex embodied meaning and inference patterns.

Originally, experts hypothesized image schemas to explain the bodily basis of meaning, language, and inference structure, and they were often illustrated via phenomenological descriptions of various dimensions of our sensory-motor experience (Lakoff, 1987; Johnson, M., 1987). Subsequently, empirical studies have supplied evidence of the existence of cross-modal connections of the sort that we have claimed for image schemas. A recent survey of research on the role of motor and kinesthetic capacities in the processing of mental images (Gibbs & Berg, 2002) includes the following striking examples of cross-modal representational capacities:

Motor processes in mental imagery. Wexler, Kosslyn, and Berthoz (1998) argued that certain motor programs are part of our capacity to rotate mental images. In one experiment, participants first learned to rotate a handheld joystick at different speeds (45 or 90 degrees/second), in both clockwise and counterclockwise directions, without being able to see their hands. Wexler et al. then directed participants to perform a dual task that consisted of rotating the joystick at the same time as they were performing image-rotation tasks of the sort Shepard and Cooper (1982) studied. These experiments showed that clockwise rotation of the joystick facilitated clockwise rotation of mental images, while rotating the hands in the opposite direction from that in which the mental image rotates hinders the image rotation task. If there was no motor dimension to the mental image rotation task, then there should be no differential interference evident when the hands and mental images were rotating in opposite directions.

Various studies of congenitally blind peoples' abilities to perform a range of mental image manipulation tasks also support the idea that motor and kinesthetic processes are involved in mental imagery. Although blind people are typically slower at performing these tasks, they are able to rotate and scan mental images (Marmor & Zaback, 1976; Carpenter & Eisenberg, 1978). The explanation of this ability, given the absence of certain types of visual processing in blind people, is that they use their tactile, proprioceptive, and kinesthetic abilities to perform tactile analogues of visual inspection and rotation.

Sensory and motor coactivations (mirror neurons). Over the past few years, a number of experiments indicate that people weakly activate parts of the sensory-motor cortex when they observe others performing motor tasks or imagine themselves doing those tasks. For example, when a person merely observes another person move his hand in a certain way (e.g., grasping a specific object), he or she activates the same areas of the motor cortex that he or she also uses when that person performs that same grasping motion with his or her own hand (DiPellgrino, Fadiga, Foggassi, Gallese, & Rizzolatti, 1992). These are remarkable findings because they reveal connections between various perceptual, kinesthetic, and motor capacities. Cross-domain connections of this sort are exactly what are required for image schemas to be cross modal.

These experimental results also suggest that simulation is a key part of our capacity to understand situations and events. Part of the meaning of seeing another person perform an action depends on our own simulation of that same action in the appropriate motor cortex. Moreover, when we merely imagine ourselves performing a certain bodily movement or object manipulation, we activate the sensory-motor areas that would be involved in our actually performing those actions. Gibbs and Berg (2002) summarized key implication of such research:

> Most scholars agree that the motor processes activated during perception and imagination are always a limited subset of those activated during overt movement (Ellis, 1995; Ramachandran & Hirstein, 1997). More generally, though, the various behavioral and neuroimagery findings highlight that motoric elements are recruited whenever the perceived or imagined object is conceptualized in action-oriented terms. (p. 13)

Representational momentum. Freyd and colleagues, in a series of experiments, argued that people have body-based models of physical momentum (which Freyd & Finke, 1984, called "representational momentum") that they use in reasoning about visual and auditory images. In one example of the experimental design, researchers presented three static images of some simple object, such that the object appeared either to move along a linear path or else to rotate in one direction. Then, researchers presented a final target position of the image and asked the subject whether that target image location coincided with the earlier third image they just saw. In several such experiments, researchers found a tendency for people to misremember the final (e.g., third) location as being farther along the trajectory than it actually is. If the trajectory is a linear path, they will think that the third position was farther in the direction of motion than it was. If there is rotational motion, they will tend to remember the third object location as rotated beyond where it actually was. Kelly and Freyd (1987) claimed that representational momentum of this sort "reflects the internalization in the visual system of the principles of physical momentum" (p. 369). These effects occur in linear motion, rotation, centripetal force, and spiral paths, and they are relative to object speed, acceleration, and size. Moreover, there appears to be momentum experienced in the auditory domain, such as when a third tone in an ascending pitch contour will be remembered as higher than it actually was and lower than it was in a descending pitch contour (Kelly & Freyd, 1987). Although there is no settled explanation of such representational momentum phenomena, they indicate the role of embodied structures of perception, motion, and object manipulation in our representation of events.

In general, then, experiments of the sort described above give evidence for the existence of cross-modal representations in mental imagery and image-schematic structure. The key point is that sensory-motor correlations lie at the heart of our abilities to form mental images and to recognize corresponding structures of imagination across different perceptual and motor representations. Gibbs and Berg (2002) concluded,

> To the extent, then, that people's mental images reflect the operation of various modalities and kinesthetic properties of the body, the experimental findings on mental imagery support the idea that image schemas play a significant role in certain aspects of perception and cognition. (p. 26)

In addition to linguistic, phenomenological, sensory-motor, and cognitive evidence for the existence of image schemas, there are now neural models of how such image schemas might be realized in known neural architectures. Terry Regier (1996), for instance, designed and built so-called "structured connectionist" models capable of computing a number of basic image schemas. "Structured" connectionism uses neural structures and capacities known to exist in humans (e.g., orientation-sensitive cell assemblies, center-surround architecture, "filling-in" mechanisms, and spreading activation) to model the topological features of selected image schemas. Such modeling is important because it suggests how creatures with brains, bodies, and environments like ours might neurally realize image schemas.

EMBODIMENT OF ABSTRACT THOUGHT

Anyone who is convinced by the evidence for the embodiment of mind must face the vexing problem of how abstract thought is tied to the body. The general form of the answer appears to be something like this: The body must recruit neural structures central to sensory and motor processing to carry out the inferences that make up our abstract patterns of thinking. Structures of *perceiving and doing* must serve as structures of *thinking and knowing*.

At present, we have only speculations and some preliminary neural models of how this process might work, but they are highly instructive. David Bailey (1997) developed a model that learns how to categorize and name verbs of hand motions from various languages around the world. His model could also give orders to produce the appropriate hand motions for these verbs in a computer model of the body that researchers could use in robotics. Bailey's model involved high-level motor control schemas (called "X-schemas," for executing schemas) that operate dynamically to control and organize various motor synergies. Thus, for example, there would be a specific X-schema for a simple action like picking up a glass and drinking. The X-schema for this particular action would be a controller schema with particular kinds of bindings to certain motor synergies that are part of picking up and moving a glass (e.g., opening the fingers, forming them into an appropriate grasping configuration, closing the hand around the glass, lifting the glass to your lips, etc.).

Srini Narayanan (1997) worked with Bailey to model motor schemas of this sort. They soon recognized that all of the motor schemas they were modeling shared a common high-level control structure with the following dimensions:

- Readiness: Prior to initiating a particular action, your body must satisfy certain readiness or preparatory conditions. For example, in order to lift a chair, you might have to reorient your body posture and stop doing some other bodily task.
- Starting up: You have to begin the specific action process in an appropriate way (e.g., to lift a chair you must grasp it with your hands in a way that will allow you to exert force in an upward direction).
- Main process: You then undertake the typical motor movements that constitute the particular kind of action you are performing.
- Possible interruption and resumption: While engaged in the main process, you might be interrupted and have to stop, and you can then consider whether to resume the same action.
- Iteration: Having completed one iteration of the main activity, you might choose to repeat that structure over again.
- Purpose: In cases where there is a goal or purpose for one's action, you monitor your progress toward the fulfillment of that purpose.
- Completion: You may then decide to terminate the action, recognizing it as completed (with perhaps the purpose or goal achieved).

- Final state: At this point, you then enter the final state with whatever results and consequences it brings.

These dimensions of motor schemas together constitute what linguists call "aspect." They define the semantic structure of events in general, and so they are not specific only to particular motor schemas. Any action a person undertakes—from picking up a cup to preparing a salad to planning a trip—will manifest this general aspectual structure. Because even our most abstract acts of thought are *acts*, they, too, have these dimensions. Languages around the world have syntactic and semantic devices for coding these aspectual dimensions for all kinds of actions and events.

Notice also that once we have one or more actions that manifest both this generic X-schema structure and some more specific X-schema structures (such as lifting a chair), we can then build up an indefinite number of larger event and action structures by means of compositional processes of the following sort:

- Iteration: We can repeat an action, or some subroutine within an action, over again. You can swing a golf club, swing it again, and then swing it seven times more.
- Sequences: The stringing together of a series of events or actions can build up large-scale event structures. You can go to the store before preparing dinner, which you can follow with a walk in the park before coming back home to read a book.
- Embedding: One part of an X-schema can embed some other action or part of an action. For example, the *goal* of the action of packing your camping gear might become the *starting point* for your extended action of going backpacking in the mountains.
- Conditional relations: One action can provide the condition for the performance or occurrence of another, as in "If you pick up your dirty clothes, your girlfriend won't leave you."

In short, via structures like these for combining, embedding, and sequencing actions, we are able to construct the large-scale actions and narrative structures that make it possible for us to make sense of our actions. Moreover, insofar as the structure of motor programs can also perform abstract inferences, our abstract conceptualization and reasoning manifests sequencing, embedding, iteration, and other structures for building up actions.

Narayanan (1997) hypothesized that controller X-schemas might exist in the premotor cortex, which co-ordinates various motor synergies into organized actions and action sequences. What Narayanan then proceeded to show is that his neural models for X-schemas are capable of performing inferences about events and actions. For example, let us say that you read in the *Wall Street Journal* that Germany fell into a deep economic depression but that it was slowly climbing out thanks to improved international trade. Narayanan developed a model of conceptual metaphor that could recruit structure from various sensory-motor domains to perform inferences for some abstract domain (e.g., economics). Narayanan then showed that certain models of metaphoric thinking based on motor schemas could perform the appropriate abstract inferences for the domain of international economics.

We do not yet know whether the human brain actually works in precisely the same way as these neural models specify. That is, we do not yet have sufficient evidence that the human brain recruits motor schemas for abstract reasoning. What we do have so far are some examples of neural models that can both perform appropriate motor actions within a model of the body and that can also perform appropriate inferences about abstract conceptual domains. And we have evidence, as previously noted, of the existence of cross-modal neural connections. There is a certain evolutionary economy to such a picture of human cognitive functioning. Instead of developing a second set of inferential operations for abstract concepts—a kind of *doppelgänger* of sensory-motor inference structure—it would be more efficient to recruit sensory-motor programs for so-called higher level cognitive functions. However, the details of how this might work remain to be developed, and we await neuro-imaging evidence that would be relevant to the assessment of this hypothesis.

PRIMARY METAPHORS

It is not surprising that all of our perceptual, spatial relations, and bodily movement concepts are intimately tied to our embodiment. Even though this may seem obvious to many people, it is nonetheless a difficult task to explain just how this meaning arises and achieves symbolic expression. Image schemas are but one key part of how this happens. The most difficult problem facing any proponent of the embodied thought hypothesis is to explain how abstract conceptualization and reasoning are possible. How can we move from embodied meanings tied to our sensory-motor experience all the way to abstract concepts like love, justice, mind, knowledge, and freedom? How can we move from embodied spatial logic and inferences all the way to abstract logical relations and inferences?

There is no simple answer to these questions, but I believe that the general answer is that various imaginative structures and processes allow us to extend embodied meaning and thought to the highest level of abstraction possible for us, all the way up to science, philosophy, mathematics, and logic. Let us begin with a simple but suggestive example of how this works. Recall our earlier description of the structure and logic of the Container schema. There is a commonplace conceptual metaphor, *Categories Are Containers*, that is pervasive in our culture and has its grounding in embodied Container logic. The conceptual metaphor *Categories Are Containers* consists of a systematic mapping of entities and relations from the domain of spatial containment onto our understanding of conceptual categorization, as shown in Table 2.1.

Via this conceptual mapping, we can understand categorization as metaphorical placement within a container. The *Categories Are Containers* metaphor underlies linguistic expressions of the following sort:

> The biologist identified the newly discovered object as being *in* the category of "living thing," while other mysterious objects fall *outside* that category. A subcategory is *part of* a larger category. Logically, several subcategories can be *contained within* one larger category. Developing scientific research can *move* one organism from the "plant" category *into* the "animal" category.

Via the mapping for *Categories Are Containers*, the spatial logic of Containment that we described earlier can carry over directly into the logic of abstract categories. This gives rise to a series of correspondences between the logic of spatial containment and that of metaphorical containment for abstract entities of the following sort:[2]

- "Every object is either within a container or outside of it" (Source Domain inference) yields "Every entity is either within a category C or outside of it" (Target Domain inference) = the *Law of the Excluded Middle*
- "Given two containers A and B and an object X, if container A is in B and X is in A, then X is in B" (Source Domain inference) yields "Given two categories A and B and an entity X, if A is in B, and X is in A, then X is in B" (Target Domain inference) = *Modus Ponens*
- "Given three containers (A, B, C), if A is in B and B is in C, then A is in C" (Source Domain inference) yields "Given three cat-

Table 2.1 The Categories are Containers Metaphor

Source Domain Containers		Target Domain Categories
Bounded regions in space	>>>>>	Categories
Objects inside bounded regions	>>>>>	Category members
One bounded region inside another	>>>>>	Subcategory

egories (A, B, C), if A is in B and B is in C, then category A is in
C" (Target Domain inference) = the *Hypothetical Syllogism*
- "Given two containers A and B and an object Y, if A is in B and
  Y is outside B, then Y is outside A" (Source Domain inference)
  yields "Given two categories A and B and an entity Y, if A is in
  B and Y is outside of B, then Y is outside of A" (Target Domain
  inference) = *Modus Tollens*

What this metaphorical logic of containment illustrates is the general principle that there are metaphorical and other imaginative structures that make it possible for us to understand abstract concepts and to reason about them using the spatial logics of various body-based source domains. For example, when we hear someone say, "Penguins fall *outside* the category of birds," *outside* activates the source-to-target mapping of the conceptual metaphor *Categories Are Containers*, and we thereby enlist the logic of containers as we process the next utterances of the speaker.

One of the most pressing questions raised by the existence of conceptual metaphors is why we have the ones we do and how we acquire them. When Lakoff and M. Johnson (1980) first described conceptual metaphors of this sort, they did not have satisfactory answers to such questions about grounding. However, over the past two decades a substantial and growing body of empirical research has shed increasing light on the experiential grounding issue.

Joe Grady (1997) proposed a theory of "primary metaphors" that offered a way of explaining how systems of conceptual metaphors that are more complex arise and are built from body-based metaphors that are more primitive. Grady's work drew on C. Johnson's (1997) study of metaphor acquisition in young children. C. Johnson hypothesized that young children go through a *conflation stage* in which certain sensory-motor experiences conflate, and therefore do not differentiate, subjective experiences and judgments. An infant, whose mother is holding it in her arms, for instance, will simultaneously experience affection and warmth. During this conflation period, the young child will automatically acquire a large number of associations between these two different domains of affection and warmth, since they are coactive domains. Later, the child enters a *differentiation stage,* in which she can conceptually distinguish the different domains, even though they remain coactivated and associated. These cross-domain associations are the basis of mappings that define a large number of primary metaphors, such as *Affection Is Warmth.* The *Affection Is Warmth* metaphor underlies such expressions as "She was *cool* toward me all afternoon," "The ambassador was *warmly* greeted by her new staff," "He shot her an *icy* glare,"

"She's *warming* to me slowly," and "Relations between the two nations have *thawed* since the Cold War ended." Prior to the differentiation stage, a child would use terms like *warm, cool, hot,* and *cold* only for cases where there is an actual temperature change for some object or person. After the differentiation stage, terms like *warm* and *cool* have metaphoric applications to states of temperament and character.

Grady (1997) analyzed a large number of primary metaphors that result from basic cross-domain correlations in our shared bodily experience. What follows are some representative examples of primary metaphors, along with their grounding and examples of linguistic manifestations of the underlying mapping.[3]

Affection Is Warmth

Subjective Judgment: Affection
Sensory-motor Domain: Temperature
Experiential Basis: Feeling warmth while being held affectionately
Examples: "I received a *warm* reception in Norway." "Our relationship has *cooled off* recently."

Intimacy Is Closeness

Subjective Judgment: Intimacy
Sensory-motor Domain: Physical closeness
Experiential Basis: Being physically close to people you are intimate with
Examples: "We've been *close* for years." "Now we seem to be *drifting apart.*"

Bad Is Stinky

Subjective Judgment: Evaluation
Sensory-motor Domain: Smell
Experiential Basis: Being repelled by foul-smelling objects and pleased by good-smelling things
Example: "This whole affair *stinks!*" "Something *smells fishy* with this contract."

More Is Up

Subjective Judgment: Quantity increase or decrease
Sensory-motor Domain: Vertical orientation
Experiential Basis: Observing rise and fall of levels of piles and fluids as more is added or taken away
Examples: "Prices are *sky-rocketing!*" "The number of crimes *rose* precipitously this year."

Organization Is Physical Structure

Subjective Judgment: Abstract form or relationships
Sensory-motor Domain: Perceiving and manipulating physical objects.
Experiential Basis: Interacting with physical objects and recognizing their functional structure (correlation between observing part-whole structures of physical objects and forming cognitive representations of functional and logical relationships)
Examples: "The *pieces* of his theory don't fit together." "I can't see how the premises are *connected to* the conclusion in your argument."

Linear Scales Are Paths

Subjective Judgment: Degree
Sensory-motor Domain: Motion along a path
Experiential Basis: Observing the amount of progress made by an object in motion (correlation between motion and scalar notion of degree)
Example: "She's *way beyond* Bill in intelligence." "The temperature hasn't *moved* very far over the past few minutes."

Time Is Motion

Subjective Judgment: Passage of time
Sensory-motor Domain: Motion
Experiential Basis: Experiencing the "passage" of time as one experiences the motion of an object
Examples: "The time *is coming* when typewriters will all be in museums." "Time *flies* when you're having fun."

Purposes Are Destinations

Subjective Judgment: Achieving a purpose
Sensory-motor Domain: Reaching a destination
Experiential Basis: Correlation of reaching a destination and thereby achieving a purpose
Examples: "You've finally *arrived*, baby." "She's got *a long way to go* to the completion of her graduate degree."

Knowing Is Seeing

Subjective Judgment: Knowledge
Sensory-motor Domain: Vision
Experiential Basis: Gaining knowledge through visual perception

Examples: "I finally *see* the answer to our problem." "That's an *obscure* part of your theory."

Grady (1997) surveyed a large number of such primary metaphors and argued that they are blended together to produce the more complex metaphors that form large systems in our abstract thinking. It is not always clear precisely how to decide what is and is not primary. For example, is the *Categories Are Containers* metaphor, previously discussed, primary or complex? While it appears to be primary, based on the correlation of bounded spaces or containers with kinds of objects located in a bounded space, one might also view it as a specification of the primary metaphor *Organization Is Physical Structure*. On this interpretation, the container is a specific type of physical structure that characterizes a source domain. This domain is the basis for our understanding of categorization as a matter of perceiving abstract organization that defines a *kind*.

In spite of difficulties of this sort, the C. Johnson (1997) and Grady (1997) hypotheses together give us an account of how mostly unconscious correlations in our experience could be the basis for primary conceptual metaphors, which are then combined into complex metaphors. Their views are consistent with neural models of the sort developed by Srini Narayanan (1997) that can "learn" certain types of metaphors.

Over the past decade, Raymond Gibbs carried out a number of experiments to test for the existence of conceptual metaphors in our thinking and to probe the alleged bodily grounding of such metaphors. In his book *The Poetics of Mind*, Gibbs (1994) summarized his early work, and he continued to explore various experimental techniques to test hypotheses about the workings of conceptual metaphor. One recent study (Gibbs, Lima, & Francuzo, 2004; Gibbs, 2003) focused on the bodily and experiential basis of conceptual metaphors for desire that underlie expressions in English and in Brazilian Portuguese. Consider the question of whether there exists a bodily based conceptual metaphor *Desire Is Hunger*. How could we show this using psychological testing methods? In the following passage, an American university student describes her romantic attraction to a boy she knew in high school.

Back in high school, I had this HUGE crush on this guy, James, who was a total hunk. He would flirt with me when we'd talk, but I didn't get a chance to know him very well, nevermind ever be alone with him. I was dying to get closer to him, and felt starved for his attention. I walked around for over five months feeling silly and empty because I wanted him so bad. I wanted to eat him alive! He was yummy! (Gibbs, 2003, p. 17)

Is this embodied way of talking about her desire as hunger merely a way of talking, or is it a conceptual metaphor grounded in her bodily experience of hunger? In other words, is *Desire Is Hunger* a primary metaphor that underlies specific ways we conceptualize and talk about desire, or do we just sometimes coincidentally happen to use linguistic expressions about aspects of hunger when we talk about desire? An initial inspection of the language of desire in English and Brazilian Portuguese revealed that both languages extensively use the concepts of *hunger* and *thirst* to talk about a broad range of abstract desires. For instance, we can *hunger* or *thirst* for attention, promotion, righteousness, justice, power, revenge, or equality. But what evidence could there be that this is more than just *talk*—that it is *conceptual* and guides our *reasoning*?

What Gibbs and his colleagues did was first to determine how their American and Brazilian subjects understood hunger, or, one might say, what their cognitive model of hunger was. For example, both cultures associate hunger with *local symptoms* like grumbling stomach, having one's mouth water (salivating), and stomachache, with *general symptoms* like feeling discomfort, feeling weak, becoming dizzy, and with *behavior symptoms* like feeling anxious and feeling out of balance. Now, if one strongly associates such symptoms with hunger, and if he or she thus forms a shared cultural model of hunger that intimately links to our shared bodily experiences, then these cognitive models should show up in manifestations of the *Desire Is Hunger* metaphor, assuming, of course, that there really is such a conceptual mapping activated when we think about desire.

One way in which this hypothesis was tested was to formulate a number of linguistic expressions in the two languages concerning lust, love, and other desires. Researchers constructed some of these expressions using the knowledge of the idealized cognitive model of hunger that they elicited in the earlier study. Researchers made up the other expressions from a range of symptoms judged in the first study to be only weakly associated with hunger or not associated at all. They used expressions of the following sort: "My whole body aches for you," "I have a strong headache for knowledge," "My hands are itching for you," and "My knees ache for information about my ancestry." Participants read such statements, in either English or Portuguese, and researchers asked them to rate how acceptable each of these ways of talking would be in their culture. As one would expect, if there actually exists a Desire Is Hunger metaphor, then subjects would rate the sentences with expressions tied to the local, general, and behavioral symptoms of hunger (as specified in their cognitive models of hunger) much higher (as more appropriate) than those that conceptualized desire only with very weakly (or nonassociated) bodily experiences. Indeed, that is precisely what they found. Gibbs (2003) concluded,

> The data demonstrate how knowing something about people's embodied experiences of hunger allows one to empirically predict which aspects of desire will, and will not, be thought of, and talked about, in terms of our complex embodied understandings of hunger. This evidence is generally consistent across two different languages and cultural communities. People use their embodied knowledge as the primary source of metaphorical meaning and understanding. In this way, the answer to the question "where does metaphor come from?" is given by understanding how embodiment provides the foundation for more abstract concepts. (p. 10)

The "prediction" Gibbs (2003) referred to here is an experimental prediction about what expressions our shared embodied knowledge of hunger properly motivated. He does not claim that we can predict which primary metaphors will exist; rather, we can explain how bodily experience grounds and motivates various conceptual metaphors, and we can explain why we have the specific inferential structure in our conception of desire that we do.

What makes the theory of primary metaphor so potentially important is that it suggests answers to two crucial questions: (a) Why do we have the conceptual metaphors we do? and (b) How can the meaning of abstract concepts be grounded in our bodies and our sensory-motor experience? The answer to the first question is that we have certain primary metaphors because of the way our brains, bodies, and environments are structured. Because of the specific kinds of cross-domain neural connections that we acquire through our mundane experience, we will naturally acquire a shared set of primary metaphors. The nature of our bodies and environments determines what precisely those metaphors will be. This explanation does not *predict* which metaphors will be activated for a particular person and thus show up in their symbolic interaction and expression; rather, it shows how the kinds of cross-domain associations that are possible for creatures embodied like us motivate and make sense of the conceptual metaphors that we actually have in a given culture at a given time.

The second crucial question that the theory of primary metaphor allows us to answer is how it might be possible for creatures embodied in the way we are to use their embodied meaning to develop abstract concepts and to reason with them. The key to all of this imaginative activity is the coactivation of sensory-motor areas along with areas thought to be responsible for so-called "higher" cognitive functions. Primary metaphors are thus cross-domain mappings based on correlations between sensory-motor maps and structures in domains involved in judgment and reasoning about abstract domains. In other words, there is a directionality to the mapping—*from* the source domain *to* the target domain—and this is instantiated in the flow of activation *from* a sensory-motor area *to* a neural assembly responsible for what we regard as "higher" cognitive activity. Grady (1997) called this second area a domain of "subjective judgment," but we really do not have a good account yet of how to describe these neural regions. The key point is that sensory-motor areas actually perform the inferences and that they carry over these inferences to the target domain via the cross-domain correlations that define the primary metaphors.

METAPHORS STRUCTURING ABSTRACT CONCEPTUAL SYSTEMS

Once we have primary metaphors, we are off and running, so to speak. Through various types of blending and composition, we develop vast coherent systems of metaphorically defined concepts. Researchers have performed detailed analyses of such complex metaphorical concepts in domains such as events, states, causes, purposes, desire, thought, mind, reason, knowledge, values, morality, and politics (Lakoff & Johnson, M., 1999). All of our most impressive intellectual achievements—in physics, chemistry, biology, anthropology, sociology, mathematics, logic, philosophy, religion, and art—involve irreducible and ineliminable conceptual metaphors. In other words, multiple, often inconsistent, metaphors define all of the key concepts in all of these disciplines, and we reason using the internal logic of those metaphors.

As an example of the constitutive nature of conceptual metaphor in science, Fernandez-Duque and M. Johnson (1999; 2003) analyzed the metaphors used by cognitive psychologists to define attention and to frame their experimental programs. What we found appears to be characteristic of all fundamental metaphors in science. That is, the metaphors defined what phenomena count as part of attention and what counts as an adequate scientific explanation of attention phenomena. Consider, for example, the *Attention Spotlight* metaphor that guides a great deal of scientific research. Table 2.2 shows the cross-domain mapping for the Spotlight metaphor.

Table 2.2 The Attention Spotlight Metaphor

Source Domain Spotlight		Target Domain Attention
Spotlight	>>>>>	Mechanism of attention (Attentional system)
Agent who controls spotlight	>>>>>	Executive system
Agent who sees	>>>>>	Awareness system
Potential field of vision	>>>>>	Representational space
Area illuminated by spotlight	>>>>>	Attended area

Notice how precisely the logic and knowledge structure of the source domain carries over into our understanding of, and reasoning about, the target domain. In the source domain,

(a) There is a field with (b) objects in it. (c) The spotlight sheds (d) light over some part of the field, thereby illuminating objects, (e) so that they can be seen by the person (f) who is looking.

This source-domain knowledge guides our understanding of the target domain as follows. In the target domain (attention), (a') there is a mental field with (b') unconscious ideas in it. (c') The attentional system directs (d') attention over the brain areas (or mental field), and this facilitates processing of certain ideas (or mental representations) in that part of the mental field, so that (e') they are accessible by our awareness system (f'), and the idea becomes conscious.

Fernandez-Duque and M. Johnson (1999; 2003) showed, for the *Spotlight* metaphor and for other key metaphors in the cognitive psychology of attention, how tightly the details of the mapping control the completed empirical research. For instance, visual spotlights have characteristics that determine the basic research problems for attention studies. Here are four cases:

1. Certain areas of the visual cortex have retinotopic maps of regions of the external world, such that objects adjacent to each other in the world activate adjacent areas in the visual cortex. Now, if attention "sheds light" over sensory areas, then cueing attention to a peripheral part of a visual field should increase blood flow in areas that map such a peripheral part of the visual field. Brefczynski and DeYoe (1999) tested this hypothesis and found empirical support for it.

2. In the source domain, the controlling agent is an entity distinct from the spotlight and from the field upon which the spotlight

directs the light. This logic dictates that there should be a distinct Executive System that controls attentional focus and that is physically separate from the orienting system and from the sensory areas where they express attention. The concept of an executive system, as defined by the *Spotlight* metaphor, led to the discovery of a network of cortical areas that participate in the control and movement of attention (Corbetta, Kincade, Ollinger, McAvoy, & Shulman, 2000; Hopfinger, Buonocuore, & Mangun, 2000). What is important here is that the *Spotlight* metaphor entails an Executive System; however, other metaphors (which are part of what some call "effect" theories of attention) have no controller of the spotlight and hence no distinct executive for attention. In other words, the metaphor structures the ontology of the phenomena. It is not simply a fact that attention requires a control mechanism, but rather this is an entailment only for certain metaphors and not others.

3. Since a spotlight moves in an analog fashion, the target domain inference would be that attention would move in an analog fashion. Woodman and Luck (1999) confirmed that electrophysiological enhancement associated with the processing of attended stimuli did indeed move in an analog fashion.

4. It takes a finite period to move a spotlight from one location to another. Müller, Teder-Salejärvi, and Hillyard (1998) interpreted the delay between a cue and the enhancement of the electrophysiological response at the cued location as an analog result of the time it takes the attentional spotlight to move to the cued location.

There is considerable (and growing) evidence for the central point I wish to emphasize. Multiple metaphors that use various body-based source domain knowledge and inference structures to generate target-domain knowledge define our theoretical concepts. This holds generally for our most basic theoretical concepts in all disciplines and fields of inquiry. The metaphors define what the relevant phenomena are, what counts as evidence, and what makes for an adequate explanatory framework. Moreover, the body-based character of such theory-defining metaphors makes them understandable to us and gives them their internal logic.

As Lakoff and Nunez (2000) showed, body-based conceptual metaphors and other imaginative blending devices link even logic and mathematics, the traditional bastions of allegedly pure, disembodied, universal reason, to embodied structures of meaning and are built up.

I cannot here survey the evidence for the pervasiveness of conceptual metaphor. However, there is a virtual cottage industry built around studying the role of conceptual metaphor in every area of human thought. Over the past 20 years, research has come up with at least nine types of empirical evidence for the existence of conceptual metaphor in all aspects of our symbolic expression. There is evidence, for example, such as polysemy generalizations, inferential generalizations, extensions to novel cases, sign language, gesture studies, psychological priming experiments, and discourse analysis (Lakoff & Johnson, M., 1999).

The implications of the constitutive nature of conceptual metaphors are quite far reaching. We come to see that even our most abstract theories are webs of body-based metaphors. This discovery does not denigrate theory. On the contrary, it humanizes it and shows us why it is even possible for us to understand a theory and to use it to organize our inquiries into experience. Such analyses give us new cognitive tools for exploring the internal logic of our theories, seeing how they are experientially grounded, and tracing out their insights and limitations. And, most importantly, this view gives us a way of understanding how embodied creatures like us can come to think what and how we do.

CONCLUSION

The task of explaining how our embodiments ground abstract conceptualization and reasoning is daunting. Perhaps it is helpful to end by reminding ourselves that we are not without plentiful resources as we set out to explore this new and dangerous territory. The territory is dangerous, I think, because what we are finding, and are likely to find, challenges many foundational assumptions of our received philosophical picture of how the mind works. It calls into doubt some of our inherited prejudgments about the universal, disembodied nature of mind and thought. It also challenges certain deeply rooted views about the origin of values. Yet, this territory is well worth the risks of exploration, insofar as it holds out the promise of revealing how we do what we do without the aid of disembodied spirit.

I want to conclude by suggesting that the picture of embodied mind, meaning, and symbolic expression that is emerging, and that remains to be extensively developed, will include at least the following dimensions of embodied meaning that are crucial for our abilities to think abstractly and to come up with new ideas:

- Image Schemas: Recurring patterns of sensory-motor experience that provide spatial and bodily logic and inferences that can become the basis of abstract inference

- X-Schemas: Executing schemas for motor programs that manifest the generic structure of events and actions known as "aspect"
- Force Dynamics: Structures of our bodily experience of force, such as forced motion, attraction, diversion from a path, speeding up and slowing down, and so on
- Primary Metaphor: Unconscious cross-domain correlations based on coactivations of neural maps in different parts of the brain
- Complex Conceptual Metaphor: Large-scale systematic metaphors, built up from complex blendings of primary metaphors, that define our most important abstract concepts
- Other Grammatical Structures: Additional aspects of grammar based on our bodies and brains (e.g., agentive manipulation)
- Blending: There are a large number of forms of conceptual blending (e.g., superimposition, blending from two or more input spaces) by which we establish frames, scenarios, and narrative structures (Fauconnier & Turner, 2002)

These are some of the more impressive resources available to those who are trying to frame a theory of embodied mind, meaning, and thought. Obviously, we do not yet have fully adequate accounts of the bodily grounding of all of these types of imaginative structure. We have but a small part of the neural side of this story. We have some phenomenological evidence for many of these structures. And we are developing a growing body of several types of empirical evidence from recent work in the cognitive sciences. This is only the beginning, but if you contrast it with where we were 20 years ago, it looks like we are well on our way into the search for the meaning of the body in human thought.

ENDNOTES

1. The following account of image schema composition is taken directly, in an abbreviated form, from Lakoff and Nunez (2001), p. 39.

2. See Lakoff and Nunez (2001), p. 44, for a complete mapping that shows how the abstract inference patterns are based on the spatial logic of containers.

3. This list is a selection from a longer list found in Lakoff and Johnson (1999), pp. 50-54, which, in turn, is a slightly revised analysis of a subset of the primary metaphors listed in Grady (1997).

REFERENCES

Bailey, D. (1997). *A computational model of embodiment in the acquisition of action verbs.* Unpublished doctoral dissertation, University of California, Berkeley, California.

Brefszynski, J. A., & DeYoe, E. A. (1999). A physiological correlate of the 'spotlight' of visual attention. *Nature Neuroscience, 2,* 370–374.

Carpenter, P., & Eisenberg, P. (1978). Mental rotation and the frame of reference in blind and sighted individuals. *Perception and Psychophysics, 23,* 117–124.

Corbetta, M., Kincade, J. M., Ollinger, J. M., McAvoy, M. P., & Shulman, G. L. (2000). Voluntary attention is dissociated from target detection in the human posterior parietal cortex. *Nature Neuroscience, 3,* 292–297.

DiPellgrino, G., Fadiga, L., Foggassi, L., Gallese, V., & Rizzolatti, G. (1992). Understanding motor events. *Experimental Brain Research, 91,* 176–180.

Ellis, R. (1995). *Questioning consciousness.* Amsterdam: Benjamins.

Fauconnier, G., & Turner, M. (2002). *The way we think: Conceptual blending and the mind's hidden complexities.* New York: Basic Books.

Fernandez-Duque, D., & Johnson, M. (1999). Attention metaphors: How metaphors guide the cognitive psychology of attention. *Cognitive Science, 23*(1), 83–116.

Fernandez-Duque, D., & Johnson, M. (2002). Cause and effect theories of attention: The role of conceptual metaphor. *Review of General Psychology, 6,* 153–165.

Freyd, J., & Finke, R. (1984). Representational momentum. *Journal of Experimental Psychology: Learning, Memory, and Cognition, 10,* 126–132.

Gibbs, R. (1994). *The Poetics of mind: Figurative thought, language, and understanding.* Cambridge, U.K.: Cambridge University Press.

Gibbs, R. W. (2003). Embodied experience and linguistic meaning. *Brain and Language, 84,* 1–15.

Gibbs, R., & Berg, E. (2002). Mental imagery and embodied activity. *Journal of Mental Imagery, 26,* 1–30.

Gibbs, R., Lima, P., & Francuzo, E. (2004). Metaphor in thought and language is grounded in embodied experience. *Journal of Pragmatics, 36,* 1189–1210.

Grady, J. (1997). *Foundations of meaning: Primary metaphors and primary scenes.* Unpublished doctoral dissertation, University of California, Berkeley, California.

Hopfinger, J. B., Buonocuore, M. H., & Mangun, G. R. (2000). The neural mechanisms of top-down attentional control. *Nature Neuroscience, 3,* 284–291.

Johnson, C. (1997). Metaphor vs. conflation in the acquisition of polysemy: The case of SEE. In M. K. Hiraga, C. Sinha, & S. Wilcox (Eds.), *Cultural, typological and psychological issues in cognitive linguistics: Current issues in linguistic theory* (pp. 154–169). Amsterdam: John Benjamins.

Johnson, M. (1987). *The body in the mind: The bodily basis of meaning, imagination, and reason.* Chicago: University of Chicago Press.

Kelly, M., & Freyd, J. (1987). Explorations of representational momentum. *Cognitive Psychology, 19,* 369–401.

Lakoff, G. (1987). *Women, fire, and dangerous things: What our categories reveal about the mind.* Chicago: University of Chicago Press.

Lakoff, G., & Johnson, M. (1980). *Metaphors we live by.* Chicago: University of Chicago Press.

Lakoff, G., & Johnson, M. (1999). *Philosophy in the flesh: The embodied mind and its challenge to Western thought.* New York: Basic Books.

Lakoff, G., & Nunez, R. (2001). *Where mathematics comes from: How the embodied mind brings mathematics into being.* New York: Basic Books.

Marmor, G., & Zaback, L. (1976). Mental rotation by the blind: Does mental rotation depend on visual imagery. *Journal of Experimental Psychology: Human Perception and Performance, 2,* 515–521.

Müller, M. M., Teder-Sälejärvi, L. W., & Hillyard, S. A. (1998). The time course of cortical facilitation during cued shifts of spatial attention. *Nature Neuroscience, 1,* 631–634.

Narayanan, S. (1997). *Embodiment in language understanding: Sensory-motor representations for metaphoric reasoning about event descriptions.* Unpublished doctoral dissertation, University of California, Berkeley, California.

Ramachandran, V., & Hirstein, W. (1997). Three laws of qualia: What neurology tells us about the biological functions of consciousness. *Journal of Consciousness Studies, 4,* 429–457.

Regier, T. (1996). *The human semantic potential: Spatial language and constrained connectionism.* Cambridge, MA: MIT Press.

Shepard, R., & Cooper, L. (1982). *Mental images and their transformations.* Cambridge, MA: MIT Press.

Shepard, R., & Metzler, J. (1971). Mental rotation of three-dimensional objects. *Science, 171,* 701–703.

Wexler, M., Kosslyn, S., & Berthoz, A. (1998). Motor processes in mental rotation. *Cognition, 68,* 77–94.

Woodman, G. F., & Luck, S. J. (1999). Electrophysiological measurement of rapid shifts of attention during visual search. *Nature, 100,* 867–869.

3

THE FEELING BODY: TOWARD AN
ENACTIVE APPROACH TO EMOTION

Giovanna Colombetti
University of Exeter

Evan Thompson
University of Toronto

For many years, emotion theory has been characterized by a dichotomy between the head and the body. In the golden years of cognitivism, during the 1960s and '70s, emotion theory focused on the cognitive antecedents of emotion, the so-called "appraisal processes." Some saw bodily events largely as by-products of cognition, and as too unspecific to contribute to the variety of emotion experience. Cognition was conceptualized as an abstract, intellectual, "heady" process separate from bodily events. Although current emotion theory has moved beyond this disembodied stance by conceiving of emotions as involving both cognitive processes (e.g., perception, attention, and evaluation) and bodily events (e.g., arousal, behavior, and facial expressions), the legacy of cognitivism persists in the tendency to treat cognitive and bodily events as separate constituents of emotion. Thus, the cognitive aspects of emotion are supposedly distinct and separate from the bodily ones. This separation indicates that cognitivism's disembodied conception of cognition continues to shape the way emotion theorists conceptualize emotion.

During the last two decades, this disembodied conception of cognition has been seriously challenged by the rise of embodied and situated approaches in cognitive science (see Clark, 1997; Varela, Thompson, & Rosch, 1991). The dynamical systems approach has challenged the idea that cognition is the manipulation of abstract representations according to syntactic rules, and has proposed instead that cognition emerges from the coupled interactions of the brain, body, and environment (Beer, 2003; Kelso, 1995; Port & van Gelder, 1995; Thelen & Smith, 1994; Thelen, Schöner, Scheier, & Smith, 2001). Other theorists have stressed, in a variety of ways, the embodied and situated nature of cognition (Clancey, 1997; Clark, 1997; Johnson, 1987; Varela et al., 1991).

Nevertheless, most emotion theorists have not embraced the embodied view of the mind. This reticence is surprising, given the important roles played by the body in early emotion theory. Well-known examples are Darwin's (1872/1998) interest in the bodily expression of emotion, and James' (1884/1968) and Lange's (1885/1967) claim that emotions *are* bodily processes. The body already played an important role in the theories of emotion of Aristotle, Descartes, Spinoza, and Hume, to mention only a few. As we will see, the importance these authors accorded to the body does not mean that they denied or neglected other aspects of emotion, such as their cognitive and evaluative characters. Rather, these authors all conceived of emotions as psychosomatic states, and each focused on different aspects of emotion according to their specific theories.

Whereas emotion theorists have kept their distance from the embodied approach in cognitive science, theorists of embodied cognition have tended to treat cognition as if it were a "cold," nonemotional process. This attitude is also surprising. Given the intimate link between emotions and the body, emotions should be privileged phenomena for attempts to reintegrate mind and body.

Our aim in this chapter is to bring emotion theory and the embodied view of cognition closer to each other. We first present an overview of classical (pre-Jamesian) theories of emotion and show that they were all psychosomatic. We then turn to the disembodied stance of cognitivism and trace how and why emotion theory came to lose the body. We argue that cognitivism not only neglected the body, but also tended to classify previous theories of emotion as *either* cognitive *or* physiological. This tendency has fostered a tension between these two features of emotion that exists to this day. The main manifestation of this tension in current emotion theory is the tendency to see cognitive and bodily processes as separate aspects or constituents of emotions. Finally, in the remainder of the article, we sketch an embodied approach to emotion, drawing especially on the "enactive approach" in cognitive science (Noë, 2004; Varela et al., 1991).

CLASSICAL PSYCHOSOMATIC ACCOUNTS OF EMOTION

Unlike more recent cognitivist theories of emotion, classical (pre-Jamesian) accounts of emotion were thoroughly psychosomatic. These accounts acknowledged that emotions have both cognitive and bodily components. Let us mention some of the most influential examples.

In *On the Soul* (*De Anima*), Aristotle (version, 1981) claimed that it is necessary to analyze both the *form* (the function) and the *matter* (the bodily aspects) of emotion. For example, anger can be seen as the desire to avenge an insult, as well as the "boiling of the blood." For Aristotle, there is no doubt that the body plays a crucial role in emotion: "It seems that all the *attributions* of the soul, e.g., temper, good temper, fear, pity, courage, also gladness and love and hate, exist with the body, for the body is being affected simultaneously with these" (403a). If the body plays this role, Aristotle continued, then the emotions are *logoi en hyle*, which could be translated as "embodied ideas."[1]

It is true that in *The Art of Rhetoric,* Aristotle (version, 1991) did not mention bodily processes. Rather, he described (a) the temperament typical of people in emotional states, (b) the situations that typically arouse these states, and (c) at whom or what these emotions are directed. This text is considered the first "cognitive theory of emotion," yet there is no need to think that a tension (if not an explicit contradiction) exists between the claims of the *Rhetoric* and those of *On the Soul*. The fact that emotions have a cognitive aspect does not mean that the body plays *no* role in emotion (unlike what 20th-century cognitive theorists of emotion will maintain). In addition, to take Aristotle's *Rhetoric* as giving a definition of the nature of emotion would be misleading. The aim of the *Rhetoric* is to teach the orator how to arouse emotions in the audience by depicting real or fictional situations, so as to influence and change their judgment. It is not an attempt to describe the *ousìa* (essence) of emotion.

Descartes' (1644/1988) treatise *The Passions of the Soul* is a detailed account of the role of the body in emotion and emotion experience. For Descartes, the passions are mental states or processes "caused, maintained and fortified" by the body (art. 27). According to Descartes, the body acts on the mind through the movements of the animal spirits that reach the pineal gland. In his treatise on the passions, Descartes referred to this theory to account for the variety of our emotional feelings: Each specific movement of the spirits gives a specific impulse to the pineal gland, which in turn causes a specific feeling.

Descartes was also interested in explaining the bodily *manifestations* of emotion. He observed, for example, that redness accompanies joy because the opening of the orifices causes the blood to flow more rapidly and to become thinner and hotter; this, in turn, fills the face and renders it smiling and joyful (art. 115). On the other hand, paleness and coldness of the limbs is a manifestation of sadness; in sadness, the orifices are closed and blood is retained around the heart. These ideas are particularly important in the history of emotion theory. Darwin (1872/1998) assumed that the perception of the behavioral and bodily manifestations of emotion constitutes feelings, and James (1884/1968) claimed that each emotional feeling depends on a specific pattern of bodily arousal.

In addition to careful physiological descriptions, Descartes (1644/1988) provided definitions of emotions that relate them to "cognition." He claimed, for example, that the recognition that one possesses some good causes joy, whereas sadness is caused by the recognition that one possesses some fault (art. 93). These definitions do not occupy much of the treatise. Nevertheless, they reveal that, for Descartes, bodily events are strictly related to mental ones. Emotions depend on the interaction of mind and body, in both directions—from the body to the mind, and from the mind to the body.

Descartes' (1644/1988) account of the passions also influenced Hume (1739/2003) and Spinoza (1677/2000), whose theories are sometimes defined as "cognitive" because they analyze emotions in relation to *ideas*. But this categorization is misleading if taken to imply that, in these theories, the body plays no role in emotion.

On the one hand, one cannot disembody Spinoza's (1677/2000) theory because of his overall account of the mind-body relation. According to Spinoza, mind and body are two of the infinite attributes of the same divine entity (which is also no other than nature). They are not two separate substances that interact causally, but are coordinated properties of the same substance. In this framework, emotions are defined as modifications of both attributes, "affections of the body by which the body's power of acting is increased or diminished, helped or hindered, and at the same time the ideas of these affections" (p. 163).

On the other hand, Hume (1739/2003), in his *Treatise on Human Nature,* defined the passions as sensations arising in the soul from the body. He eventually ended up analyzing the passions in relation to ideas. Once again, this does not mean he held that emotions are disembodied. Rather, he stated that illustrating the activity of the body occurring in emotional episodes would take him too far astray from his main concerns in the *Treatise* (see *Treatise*, Book 2, Part 1, Section 1).

COGNITIVISM AND THE DISEMBODIED STANCE: HOW EMOTION THEORY LOST THE BODY

Our interpretation of classical accounts of emotion as psychosomatic is different from the one offered by philosophers of emotion, such as Kenny (1963), Solomon (1976), and Lyons (1980). These authors tended to classify classical theories as *either* "cognitive" *or* "physiological," and they emphasized either one of these two aspects to the detriment of the other. Their readings of the classical accounts are thus consistent with their own disembodied view of emotion: Cognition (e.g., beliefs, desires, judgments, and evaluations) is an intellectual—not a bodily—process, and bodily events (e.g., physiological arousal and behavior) are contingent by-products of cognitive processes.

According to these authors, "physiological" and "behavioral" accounts of emotions cannot capture the fact that emotions depend on what we know and believe about the world. The same criticism is made of theories that focus on the experiential aspects of emotions (feelings) and that explain these aspects in terms of the awareness of one's bodily processes (as did Descartes, Hume, Darwin, and James). Such theories are described as "mere feeling theories." This (mis)characterization assumes that such theories simply identified emotions with feelings, to the neglect of other aspects of emotion, and that feelings are epiphenomena.

From the cognitivist viewpoint, only cognitive theories can capture what really matters about emotions—namely, their world-relatedness and meaningfulness. "Cognition," in this view, has nothing to do with the body. It is an abstract, intellectual process that is not influenced by the state of the body. Experiential aspects of emotion, when acknowledged, depend uniquely on such abstractly characterized cognitive states. The tendency is to either deny their bodily aspect or reduced it to a by-product. We can call this attitude "the disembodied stance."

The manifesto of the disembodied stance is Kenny's 1963 book *Action, Emotion and Will*. Kenny spent a whole chapter arguing that experimental psychology cannot say anything fundamental about the relation between emotion and behavior. The reason is that psychology as an empirical discipline provides only causal accounts of the link between emotion and behavior. Such a link, in Kenny's view, is merely contingent. For example, there is no necessity for anger to cause aggressive behavior (or a specific pattern of bodily arousal); it is logically possible to conceive of anger as associated with some opposite action (e.g., buying flowers).

For Kenny (1963), to unveil the essence or necessary features of emotions, we need to analyze their *intentional objects,* that is, what we take each emotion to be distinctively about. Kenny did a remarkable job both in specifying the various objects of emotion and in distinguishing subtleties in our use of the words *feeling, pleasure,* and *desire.* On the one hand, this kind of analysis provides a rich and sophisticated account of what we think emotions are about, and of how we use certain terms. On the other hand, it discourages empirical observations by suggesting that the necessary features of mental states can be defined solely through introspection and logical analysis. As Griffiths (1997) complained, Kenny's attitude is the heritage of the "Wittgensteinian distinction between the 'criteria' which logically define a mental state and the inessential 'symptoms' that can be studied empirically" (p. 23).

Other theorists, such as Solomon (1976), similarly disregarded empirical research, behavioral data, and neurophysiological studies. Lyons (1980) seemed willing to adopt a more moderate and empirically minded view, but he was still entrenched in Kenny's concerns and reduced bodily processes in emotion to by-products of evaluations. Overall, it seems fair to say that, for philosophical accounts of emotion at this time, "[m]ental states are *defined* by the rules which ordinary speakers use when applying mental states terms" (Griffiths, 1997, p. 23).

We can point to two main reasons why emotion theory lost the body. First, the disembodied stance of the 1960s and '70s was an extreme reaction to the equally extreme attitude of the activation and behavioral theories of the 1940s and '50s. According to activation theory (e.g., Duffy, 1941), emotions are motivational states defined in terms of different degrees of "energy" of the organism. According to behavioral theory, emotions are tendencies to behave in a certain way (Skinner, 1953). Both of these accounts entirely neglected the cognitive and/or evaluative aspects of emotion.

Second, in the 1960s, many scientists thought that the role of the body in emotion was limited to autonomic activity. For James (1184/1968), the body was richly differentiated, and there was an "immense number of parts modified in each emotion" (p. 21);[2] the muscles, heart, and the circulatory system all contribute to the generation of different emotional feelings (note the similarity with Descartes' theory). Cannon (1927), however, argued that only the sympathetic activity of the autonomic nervous system is appropriate to account for the rapidity with which feelings arise in certain situations. Moreover, during Cannon's time, most viewed this activity as uniform. Accordingly, for Cannon, differences in emotional feelings had to depend on something other than autonomic processes.[3] This view marked a crucial step toward the disembodiment of emotion. The role of the body in emotion started to be that of a mere *enhancer*—an affectively neutral support whose activation would, at best, influence the intensity of emotional feelings.

The well-known study of Schachter and Singer (1962) reinforced this idea, who concluded that the process of *labeling* one's bodily arousal is what confers affective specificity to emotion experience. This process is not driven by the body, but depends on how the subject interprets the surrounding environment. Interpretation, in turn, is not influenced by the state of the body; it is abstract, intellectual, and thus "purely cognitive." Schachter and Singer's view is sometimes seen as a hybrid between a cognitive and a physiological theory of emotion (e.g., Calhoun & Solomon, 1984). Whatever its status, there is no doubt that it influenced subsequent disembodied theories of emotion, according to which cognition (conceived in a disembodied way) is a necessary and sufficient condition for emotion (see Lazarus, 1966; Valins, 1966).

Thus, consider what Solomon (1976) wrote about Schachter and Singer's (1962) study: "[W]hat was 'discovered' was that the physiological changes and their accompanying sensations had nothing to do with the differentiation of emotion, a conclusion reached by Cannon thirty years before" (p. 95).[4] Lyons (1980, p. 121) interpreted Schachter and Singer's study as showing that people do not consider themselves in an emotional state unless they are provided with suitable cognitions. In this view, arousal does not contribute in any way to one's emotional state.

The disembodied stance has been highly influential. Schachter and Singer's (1962) theory was later refined by so-called "causal attribution" theories (London & Nisbett, 1974; Ross, Rodin, & Zimbardo, 1969), according to which arousal needs to be attributed to a specific cause to acquire affective specificity. Other theorists, such as Reisenzein (1983) and Chwalisz, Diener, and Gallagher (1988), supported a weak form of arousal theory according to which somatic feedback, including that from autonomic arousal, is not necessary for emotional experience, but can only enhance it in certain circumstances.

Ironically, cognitive theories of emotion in the 1960s and '70s were more Cartesian than Descartes himself. The disembodied stance assumed a thorough head/body distinction, and tried to deny any role to the body in the differentiation, or even elicitation, of emotions. The experiments designed in those years to show that emotions are "cognitive" were based on a disembodied notion of cognition—one that placed cognition all on the head side of the head/body distinction.

CURRENT EMOTION THEORY: REEMBODIED
EMOTIONS OF A DISEMBODIED MIND

More recent accounts of emotion have abandoned the disembodied stance of cognitivism. For example, Frijda (1987) acknowledges the cognitive aspect of emotion, but also the role of the body in feelings and the differentiation of emotion, as well as the body's relation to appraisal and action tendencies. De Sousa (1987) has no doubt that emotion is where mind and body "make contact." Sue Campbell (1997) argues that feelings are formed through expression, including bodily expression. Griffiths (1997) criticizes philosophers of emotion such as Kenny, Solomon, and Lyons for their neglect of empirical studies and for their related contempt for the role of the body in emotion. Goldie (2000), in his discussion of feelings, also considers bodily feelings. Solomon (2004), discussing his earlier work, admits that, with respect to "physiological disturbances," he was "as dismissive as could be, relegating all such phenomena to the causal margins of emotion, as merely accompaniments or secondary effects" (p. 85). He now believes that "accounting for the bodily feelings . . . in emotion is not a secondary concern and not independent of appreciating the essential role of the body in emotional experience" (p. 85). A strong claim in favor of the embodiment of emotion comes from Prinz (2004), who argues that emotions are *embodied appraisals*—that is, bodily states that track meaning in the environment. Fear, for example, is the embodied evaluation that some aspect of the environment is dangerous.

In addition, some psychologists have recently adopted the tools of dynamical systems theory to model emotions (see Lewis & Granic, 2000). Scherer (2000), for example, argues that emotion is a system comprising five continuously interacting subsystems: (a) the cognitive subsystem with appraising functions; (b) the autonomic nervous system responsible for internally regulating the organism and generating energy resources for action; (c) the motor subsystem involved in the expression of emotion; (d) the motivation subsystem governing the preparation and execution of actions; and (e) the monitoring subsystem controlling the states of the other subsystems, and supporting feeling states. Importantly, Scherer explicitly acknowledges that arousal can affect the cognitive subsystem: "Feedback of increasing arousal from the physiological system or changes in the motivational system can affect attention deployment or change perception and judgment thresholds" (p. 76).

Similarly, Lewis (2005) argues that emotion, with its arousal and action constituents, constantly interacts with appraisal; in particular, he claims that emotion and appraisal merge in what he calls an *emotional interpretation*, a rapid convergence of a cognitive interpretation of a situation and an emotional state on a timescale of seconds and minutes. According to Lewis' model, the emergence of an emotional interpretation begins as a fluctuation in the ongoing stream of intentional action; this fluctuation is triggered by a perturbation (external or internal), which eventually disrupts the orderliness of the current emotional interpretation. Rapid processes of self-amplification through positive feedback ensue, followed by self-stabilization through negative feedback and entrainment, leading to the establishment of a new orderliness in the form of a new momentary emotional interpretation and global intention for action. This self-stabilization phase is the precondition for learning, the consolidation of long-term emotion-appraisal patterns.

Lewis (2005) likens the whole process to a bifurcation from one attractor to another in an emotion-cognition state space, and presented a neuropsychological model of some of the brain areas and large-scale neural-integration processes involved. A crucial feature of his model is that the processes that subsume emotion and appraisal during an emotional interpretation are integrated in such a deep and complex way that it becomes impossible to disentangle the moment of emotion from the moment of appraisal. Thus, Lewis describes an emotional interpretation as an "emotion-appraisal amalgam."

These rediscoveries of the body by emotion theory mainly consist in reevaluating the role of the body in *emotion*, but without abandoning the disembodied conception of *cognition* (evaluation, appraisal) inherited from cognitivism. Emotions are reembodied in the sense that their bodily aspects are rediscovered, but not necessarily in the sense that they are reinterpreted in relation to embodied approaches to cognition. For example, the dynamical approaches to emotion just mentioned still tend to see bodily constituents of emotion (arousal and behavioral) as separate and distinct from the cognitive components (appraisal).

Thus, Scherer (2000) implements the functions of appraisal, arousal, and behavior in distinct subsystems. Appraisal, although distributed over different stimulus-check components, and although influenced by arousal and motor systems, remains in charge of interpreting, monitoring, and controlling the body. Lewis' (2005) view is similar. Although he introduced the new concept of an emotional interpretation and acknowledges the complexity of its constituent processes, he sees appraisal and emotion as distinct psychological functions with their own constituents.[5] In particular, he considers arousal, action tendencies, and feelings as constituents of emotion, but not of appraisal.

We can contrast these views of cognition with the approach to cognition taken by dynamical cognitive science. According to Thelen and colleagues (2001) and Beer (2003), for example, cognitive capacities are emergent from a complex web of reciprocal influences among the brain, body, and environment. Here, the notion of emergence implies giving up the idea that one can identify specific cognitive functions with specific constituent subsystems whose role is to control the body. Rather, cognitive abilities are global and emergent capacities of bodily self-regulation that cut across the brain/body/world divisions.

Despite their appeal to dynamical systems, neither Scherer (2000) nor Lewis (2005) seems willing to go this far. Scherer's partition of the emotional agent into five component subsystems seems reminiscent of cognitivist models. In his model, cognition (appraisal) is a separate subsystem of emotion that cannot overlap with the arousal and motor subsystems. Lewis' model is more complex and allows for considerable overlap among the processes subserving appraisal and emotion. Nevertheless, emotion constituents (arousal, action tendencies, and feelings) and appraisal constituents (perception, attention, and evaluation) remain conceptually distinct at the psychological level and subserved by distinct subsystems at the neural level. As a result, we would argue, the integrated, dynamical form of the model is compromised, such that it leaves less room for a concept of *embodied appraisal* (Colombetti & Thompson, 2005; Colombetti, 2005).

Recent philosophical accounts of emotion also do not link their reevaluation of the role of the body in emotion to embodied views of the mind and cognition. Thus, Prinz (2004) revives the James-Lange theory, supported it with reference to recent empirical research, and thoroughly criticizes cognitive theories of emotion for downplaying the role of the body. In particular, his view of emotions as "embodied appraisals" aimed at undermining the traditional and unquestioned appraisal/arousal dichotomy.[6] Nevertheless, his theory of emotion does not encompass the theory of embodied cognition. Thus, he distinguishes judgments from embodied appraisals, and presented judgments as good old-fashioned cognitive appraisals—as abstract and intellectual, and as causing bodily states in a linear way (see pp. 74, 98–100). Although Prinz reevaluated the body's role in emotion and claims that this role is one of appraisal, he did not replace the traditional notion of appraisal with an embodied one. Rather, he replaces it with a similar notion of judgment, thus, in effect, reproposing an old view in new words.

In our view, there is something missing in the rediscovery of the body in emotion theory. The common separations of appraisal and arousal, and appraisal and action (and judgments and embodied appraisals) suggest that, for much of current emotion theory, the body still plays the role of an *objective concomitant* of emotion. It is the appraisal component that is seen to be in charge of providing personal significance, and thus, of accounting for individual differences in emotional responses.[7] Whereas appraisal is seen in this way as the subjective element of emotion, arousal and behavior are seen as objective.

This subjective/objective division is another aspect of the head/body division inherited from cognitivism. Although current emotion theory aims to move beyond the disembodied stance, it holds onto a disembodied conception of cognition (appraisal), and takes cognition so understood to be the source of the meaning of an emotion. The head is where mind and intelligence reside, while the body is mainly a channel for inputs to and outputs from the head. The body can influence appraisals, but only by "interacting" with them in a manner reminiscent of the Cartesian conception of mind and body as "making contact" at some particular location in the brain.

THE ENACTIVE APPROACH

In the remainder of this paper, we wish to sketch an enactive approach to emotion. In this section, we will outline the main features of the enactive approach in cognitive science, and then in the next section develop the approach in relation to emotion.

The name "the enactive approach" and the associated concept of *enaction* were introduced by Varela and colleagues (1991) in order to describe and unify under one heading several related ideas. The first idea is that living beings are autonomous agents that actively generate and maintain their identities, and thereby enact or bring forth their own cognitive domains. An autonomous system, instead of processing preexisting information "out there" brings forth or enacts information in continuous reciprocal interactions with its environment. "Inner" and "outer" are not separate spheres, connected only through a representational interface, but mutually specifying domains enacted in and through the structural coupling of the system and its environment.

The second idea is that the nervous system does not process information in the computationalist sense. Information does not flow through a sequence of processing steps in a hierarchically organized architecture (typically divided into a perceptual, a cognitive and a motor layer). Rather, the nervous system is an autonomous system. It actively generates and maintains its own coherent and meaningful patterns of activity according to its operation as a circular and reentrant sensorimotor network of interacting neurons.

The third idea is that cognition is a form of embodied action. Cognitive structures and processes emerge from recurrent sensorimotor patterns of perception and action. Sensorimotor coupling between organism and environment modulates, but does not determine, the formation of endogenous and dynamic patterns of neural activity. This activity, in turn, informs sensorimotor coupling, so that the whole embodied organism can be seen as a self-organized autonomous system that creates meaning

The fourth idea is that a cognitive being's world is not a prespecified, external realm, represented internally by its brain, but a relational domain enacted or brought forth by that being's autonomous agency and mode of coupling with the environment. This idea links the enactive approach to phenomenological philosophy, for both maintain that cognition bears a *constitutive relation* to its objects. Stated in a classical phenomenological way, the idea is that the object, in the precise sense of that which is given to and experienced by the subject, is conditioned by the mental activity of the subject. Stated in a more existential, phenomenological way, the idea is that a cognitive being's world—whatever that being is able to experience, know, and practically handle—is conditioned by that being's form or structure. Such "constitution" on the part of our subjectivity or being-in-the-world is not subjectively apparent to us in everyday life, but requires systematic analysis—scientific and phenomenological—to disclose.

This point brings us to the fifth and last idea, which is that experience is not an epiphenomenal side issue, but central to any understanding of the mind, and needs to be investigated in a careful, phenomenological manner. For this reason, the enactive approach has from its inception maintained that cognitive science and phenomenology need to be pursued in a complementary and mutually informing way (for detailed discussion of this point, see Thompson, 2005).

In summary, according to the enactive approach, the human mind is embodied in our entire organism and embedded in the world, and hence is not reducible to structures inside the head. Meaning and experience are created by, or enacted through, the continuous reciprocal interaction of the brain, the body, and the world.

Within this web of reciprocal interaction, we can distinguish three permanent and intertwined modes of bodily activity: (a) self-regulation, (b) sensorimotor coupling, and (c) intersubjective interaction (Thompson & Varela, 2001). Self-regulation or organismic regulation of the internal milieu is essential to being alive and sentient. It is evident in conditions such as being awake and asleep, alert or fatigued, hungry or satiated. It is also evident in emotion and feeling, in Damasio's (1999) sense of distinctive patterns of brain-body activity (emotions) and the felt experience of such patterns (feelings). Sensorimotor coupling with the world is expressed in perception and action. According to the enactive approach to perception as recently developed by Noë (2004), perception is not something that happens to us or in us; it is something we do. Perceiving is a kind of action, and involves tacit, skilful knowledge of how sensory stimulation varies as a function of movement (see O'Regan & Noë, 2001). Intersubjective interaction is the cognition and affectively charged experience of self and other. Our bodily structure and sensorimotor skills ground our ability to make sense of the other, and vice versa (Thompson, 2001, 2005). The human brain is crucial for these three modes of activity, but it is also reciprocally shaped and structured by them at multiple levels throughout the lifespan.

One of the ideas from phenomenological philosophy especially relevant to the enactive approach is the idea that one's body is not simply another physical entity, but rather, a subjectively *lived body* (*Leib*). To experience one's own embodiment is to be a bodily subject of experience, a lived body. Phenomenological investigations of the lived body are investigations of the various aspects of bodily subjectivity—one experiences oneself as a subject of voluntary movement, as a subject of ownership (as aware of oneself as the one who is undergoing certain experiences), as a situated subject, as a perceiving and acting subject, as an affective subject, as a social subject, and so on (Gallagher & Marcel, 1999).

Cognition is thus embodied in both a structural and a phenomenological sense. Cognition is structurally embodied in the sense that it is subsumed by neural, bodily, and environmental processes (including other embodied agents). This idea is related to the so-called "extended-mind" viewpoint, according to which environmental resources play a necessary, constitutive role in cognition (Clark & Chalmers, 1998; Clark, 2003). Cognition is phenomenologically embodied, because cognition—as a subjectively experienced mental activity—involves one's experience of oneself as a bodily subject situated in the world.

In the next section, we look at the implications of this conception of embodied cognition for the way appraisal and feeling are characterized by emotion theory.

A SKETCH OF AN ENACTIVE APPROACH TO EMOTION

The enactive approach implies that we need to move beyond the head/body and subjective/objective dichotomies that characterize much of emotion theory. Appraisal is not a cognitive process of subjective evaluation "in the head," and arousal and behavior are not objective bodily concomitants of emotion. Rather, bodily events are constitutive of appraisal, both structurally and phenomenologically.

This enactive proposal can be developed by drawing on Lewis' (2005) concept of an emotional interpretation, mentioned in a previous section. According to Lewis, during an emotional interpretation, emotion and appraisal are amalgamated in a complex, self-organizing pattern, such that it is impossible to disentangle the moment of emotion from the moment of appraisal. One way to think about this idea is by comparison with enactive or dynamic sensorimotor approaches to perception and action (Hurley, 1998; Noë, 2004; O'Regan & Noë, 2001). According to these approaches, perception is as much a motor process as a sensory one. At the neural level, there is common coding of sensory and motor processes (e.g., Prinz, 1997; Rizzolatti, Fadiga, & Fogassi, 1996). At the psychological level, action and perception are not simply instrumentally related, as means-to-end, but are constitutively interdependent (Hurley, 1998). Perception is thus enactive; it is a kind of action (Noë, 2004; Varela et al., 1991).

If we set aside Lewis' (2005) claim that emotion and appraisal are composed of distinct and separate constituents, then we can read him as presenting a logically analogous way of thinking about appraisal and emotion. At the neural level, brain systems traditionally seen as subserving separate functions of appraisal and emotion are inextricably interconnected. Hence, we cannot map appraisal and emotion onto separate brain systems. At the psychological level, appraisal and emotion are constitutively interdependent: One is not a mere means to the other (as in the idea that an appraisal is a means to the having of an emotion, and vice versa); rather, they form an integrated and self-organizing emotion-appraisal state, an emotional interpretation. Emotion is a kind of evaluation, and appraisal is part of emotion. In this enactive version of Lewis' proposal, there is no appraisal constituent that is not also an emotion constituent, and vice versa. Arousal and action tendencies can thus overlap with appraisal. On this view, the bodily aspects of emotion are constitutive of the sense of personal significance traditionally provided by a disembodied appraisal. They are not an objective index of one's emotional state, but rather, subsume the lived bodily experience of meaning and evaluation.

Consider also feelings. Lewis (2005) regarded feelings as constituents of emotion, and not of appraisal; when an emotional interpretation begins to emerge, feelings play an important role in modulating appraisals. This modulatory role is, in effect, a process of interaction between separate systems, because feelings are constituents of emotion, but not of appraisal. Our enactive revision of Lewis' account requires a different conception of feelings. Feelings do not belong uniquely to emotion, understood as separate from appraisal. Appraisals are not feelingless. There are "feelings of appraisal," and such feelings are constitutive of emotion experience (Frijda, 1987). More generally, feelings are not separate constituents of emotion, but emergent features of the whole complex system (animal or person) as it enacts an emotional interpretation. This view strikes us as more phenomenologically accurate than views that treat feelings as separate, constituent elements of emotion.[8]

From the enactive standpoint just sketched, emotions are simultaneously bodily and cognitive-evaluative, not in the familiar sense of being made up of separate-but-coexisting bodily and cognitive-evaluative constituents, but rather in the sense that they convey meaning and personal significance as *bodily meaning and significance*. To borrow Prinz's (2004) terminology,[9] emotions are *embodied appraisals*.

We can elaborate these ideas by considering some possible objections to the enactive approach. Someone might object that emotions do not require the body, but only brain processes that represent bodily states. If there are or can be such "merely brainy emotions," then emotions are not embodied in a strong sense, but really only or mainly in the head.

James (1884/1968) already considered this possibility. He noticed that there are cases of anxiety "in which objectively the heart is not much perturbed" (p. 29, footnote). He did not think, however, that this possibility provided evidence against his idea that emotions are perceptions of bodily processes. His point was that, in any given case, brain anxiety must involve brain areas that represent bodily processes. Similarly, Damasio (1994, 1999, 2003) claims that emotions can be activated through so-called "as-if body loops"—brain mechanisms that trick the brain into believing that the body is undergoing a change, when in fact it is not. Damasio, however, supported the idea that emotions and feelings are thoroughly embodied. He has argued that bodily representations in the brain need to be constantly updated by the body (the "body proper," as he calls it). In particular, biochemical activity is created anew in the body and cannot be fully represented neurally (see Damasio, 1994, p. 158).

For various reasons that concern both the functioning and possibility of as-if body loops, the possibility of merely brainy emotions poses no threat to the idea that emotions are embodied. Damasio's view is that as-if body loops are at play in emotion together with real bodily loops. The former tend to "overwrite" the latter in exceptional cases, such as spinal cord lesions and the so-called locked-in syndrome, in which subjects are conscious and have feelings, but remain locked in a totally paralyzed body (they are capable only of eye movements).[10] Even in these cases, as-if body loops are not likely entirely to replace "real emotions," because as-if body loops are entirely neural, and thus cannot simulate the biochemical activity of the body and the brain-body communication that takes place via the bloodstream. As-if body loops are thus only one player in the web of causal intricacies underpinning emotions.

Damasio's (1994, 1999) view, ultimately, is that feelings depend both on bodily representations in the brain and on activity in the body proper, and that feelings come in degrees, depending on how much bodily activity the brain can map. In normal conditions, brain and body are continuously interacting, and there are brain areas that correlate to parts of the body. Were the body proper to interrupt its communication with the brain, and were bodily representations in the brain to activate, emotional experience would then arise as if the body proper had really informed the brain about its state. Yet, because of the variety of ways in which the body proper and the brain are related, it is likely that the brain will not—or not always and not for a long time—be able to provide an entirely accurate map of the state of the body. Thus, a "brainy emotion" might feel some fractional amount of a bodily emotion, depending on how much of the bodily state it can represent and how much input from the body it receives.

Studies of the emotional lives of subjects with spinal cord lesions support this view. The intensity of their feelings seems to depend on the location of their lesion; the higher the lesion, the weaker the feelings (Hohmann, 1966; Chwalisz, Diener, & Gallagher, 1988). The fact that people with very high lesions still have feelings is no evidence for disembodied emotions. As Damasio (1999) pointed out, spinal cord lesions do not prevent feedback from cranial nerves, facial muscles, and facial viscera. Facial expressions can therefore still provide the feedback needed for the feeling. In addition, the vagus nerve, which enters and exits the brain at the level of the brain stem, carries much information about the viscera; in other words, this nerve functions at a much higher level than the ones damaged by spinal cord lesions. The brain and body are also still connected through the bloodstream, which may allow hormones and other peptides to support background moods and rather slow, long-term emotional changes. Even when the vagus nerve is lesioned, cranial nerves and the bloodstream continue to provide bodily feedback to the brain.

Finally, and more generally, bodily representations in the brain depend on the coevolution and codevelopment of brain and body. The possibility of bodily representations in the brain is intelligible only in a framework that assumes embodiment and embeddedness as the default case. A bodily representation would eventually cease to represent in its normal way were it not embedded in a web of processes linking it to the world and to the possibility of action in the world (see Hurley & Noë, 2003).

Given these points, it should come as no surprise that the possibility of merely brainy emotions also does not negate the phenomenological dimension of embodiment. Brain anxiety, for example, is still accompanied by the feeling that the body is upset. It was for this reason that James (1884/1968) did not see the possibility of brain anxiety as a threat to his theory.

Let us now consider alleged cases of "purely cognitive" and/or "disembodied" feelings, often discussed in the cognitivist era and still assumed in current emotion theories. In our view, such feelings are not a real empirical and phenomenological possibility, but only seem to be given the assumption that mind and body (and/or brain and body) are distinct, as well as the disembodied stance toward cognition.

Valins' (1966) study of the effect of "bogus bodily feedback" on feelings is sometimes used to support the idea that emotions and feelings do not require bodily processes, but only cognitive ones.[11] Valins addressed Schachter and Singer's (1962) view that feelings depend on both physiological arousal and cognitive interpretations of one's surroundings; the former determines the *intensity* of feelings, whereas the latter determines specific *emotional qualities* (e.g., anger, joy, fear, etc.). Valins wanted to test a more radical hypothesis, according to which it is possible to have emotions without physiological arousal altogether.[12] According to this view, cognition alone (understood according to the disembodied stance) would be sufficient for emotion. In his experiment, Valins showed pictures from *Playboy* magazine to male subjects while they listened to what they thought was their own heartbeat. In fact, the pictures were paired with prerecorded sound tracks and provided what Valins called "bogus internal feedback." The study showed that the pictures paired with faster heartbeats were judged to be more attractive. Valins concluded that bogus internal feedback is sufficient to trigger a feeling ("liking," in this case).

What exactly does this study show with respect to the embodiment of feelings? Notice first that, as Valins himself admitted, the bogus feedback might modify the state of the body, either by increasing or decreasing its arousal. Hence, the study does not rule out the possibility that feelings of attraction depend on real bodily arousal. Nevertheless, even if bogus feedback had no effect on the body, Valins' study would not support the idea that feelings are disembodied. We can make this point with respect to both the phenomenological and structural embodiment of emotion.

On a phenomenological level, the experience involved in Valins' study is the experience of a concretely perceived sound. To be embodied, an experience does not need to be an experience of internal bodily processes. A perceptual experience is an embodied experience because it is an experience of the body in the act of perceiving. From this perspective, the study merely shows that the preferences of the subjects can be influenced by sensory stimulation. Film directors and advertisers know this fact well.

What about structural embodiment? According to LeDoux (1996), Valins' study validates the existence of as-if body loops, because it shows that the elicitation of emotion does not require real bodily loops. This analogy is misleading. The bogus feedback is a real sound that activates brain centers through actual sensory systems. For the experiment to take place, there must obviously be a source of sound and a perceiving body. We believe that a better way to interpret the study is as supporting the idea that emotional experience can depend on structures that extend beyond the boundary of the skin. We can use technology to modulate our emotions. From this "extended mind" perspective (see Clark & Chalmers, 1998; Clark, 2003), the biological brain and body can incorporate other external players in the web of processes subserving emotions and feelings.[13]

Here is another example of extended embodiment. Damasio (2003) stated that "mirror neurons" are an as-if body mechanism. Mirror neurons are activated both when one sees a goal-oriented action, and when one performs the same action (Rizzolatti et al., 1996). Mirror neurons are thus activated as if the individual seeing the movement were actually performing the movement. The existence of mirror neurons suggests that perception and action share a common neural substrate, and that this shared substrate evolved as a means to make sense of the actions of others (Gallese, 2001). Gallese, Keysers, and Rizzolatti (2004) argued that mirror-neuron mechanisms are at play in empathy or the understanding of the emotions of others. For example, studies with humans have shown that increased activity in the insula occurs both when one feels and manifests disgust, and when one perceives someone else expressing disgust. Gallese and colleagues speculate that analogous mirror mechanisms provide the neural basis for emotional contagion, as well as for empathy. There is evidence that the anterior insula activates during both the observation and the imitation of facial expressions of basic emotions.

Overall, such mirror mechanisms reveal the mutual interdependence of the three aspects of embodiment mentioned earlier—self-regulation of the internal milieu, sensorimotor coupling, and intersubjective interaction. Our face-to-face understanding of one another involves a similarity of bodily structure and sensorimotor skills, the capacity for visceral reactions, and bodily proximity.

CONCLUSION

Since the enactive approach was proposed in the early 1990s (Varela et al., 1991), the sensorimotor aspect of embodiment has received increasing attention in cognitive science, thanks to important advances in dynamic sensorimotor approaches to perception (Hurley, 1998; Noë, 2004; O'Regan & Noë, 2001). The intersubjective aspect of embodiment, including its ties to sensorimotor processes, is also currently of great interest (e.g., Gallese, Keysers & Rizzolatti, 2004; see also Thompson, 2001, 2005). Emotion and feeling, however, have received much less attention in cognitive science, even from advocates of the embodied approach to cognition. In this chapter, we have tried to correct this imbalance by using the enactive approach to bring emotion theory and embodied cognitive science closer together.

We have argued that the enactive approach has important implications for emotion theory. Emotion theory is still largely caught in the head/body dichotomy inherited from cognitivism and often looks at the body as an objective, impersonal structure, rather than as a subjectively lived body. We have argued that emotions are simultaneously bodily and cognitive-evaluative: They convey meaning and personal significance as bodily meaning and significance.

Our proposal at this point is only a sketch, not a detailed account. Much work remains to be done, both in theoretical and experimental psychology, and in phenomenology (where there is still no detailed phenomenological analysis of specific emotions and their relation to the lived body). In particular, dynamic systems theorists of emotion can benefit from revising their accounts of appraisal and feeling to incorporate embodied accounts of cognition, while enactive theorists can benefit from expanding their accounts of cognition to include emotion and feeling. Only through this joint effort can emotion take its rightful place in an integrated view of mind in body and body in mind.

ENDNOTES

1. Rather than with the obscure expressions "material notions" (proposed by Jon Solomon; see Calhoun & Solomon, 1984, p. 49), or "formulae in matter" (proposed by H. G. Apostle; see Aristotle, [version, 1981], 403a).

2. All quotations from James (1884/1968) refer to the reprinted version.

3. Today we have a different view of bodily arousal and of its role in emotion. We know that there are more than 70 different types of peptides, each of which has a different function (Panksepp, 1998; Pert, 1997). LeDoux (1996) speculates that each emotion might depend on a specific peptide.

4. Note that Schachter and Singer (1962) explicitly stated that their study did *not* rule out the possibility of physiological differences among emotional states (p. 397).

5. Nor is he willing to give up the idea that emotion and appraisal are made up of distinct components. See our commentary (Colombetti & Thompson, 2005), and Lewis' reply (Lewis, 2005).

6. He wrote that the notion of embodied appraisal "marks . . . a major reconciliation. The tradition that associates emotions with appraisals is generally presumed as at odds with the tradition that identifies emotions with changes in physiology" (Prinz, 2004, p. 78).

7. For example, Lazarus (2001) claimed that appraisal has to do with "personal meaning," and he writes that "an *appraisal* connotes evaluation of the personal significance of what is happening in an encounter with the world" (p. 40). Roseman and Smith (2001) stated that "[d]*ifferences in appraisal can account for individual and temporal differences in emotional response. . . .* Because appraisal intervenes between situation and emotions, *different individuals who appraise the same situation in significantly different ways will feel different emotions*" (p. 6).

8. For an account of feelings along there lines see Watt (1998) and Varela and Depraz (2000).

9. But not his theory, which, as we discussed in a previous section, maintains a traditional disembodied conception of judgment.

10. See Damasio (1994, pp. 155–158; 1999, p. 281; 2003, pp. 115–116).

11. LeDoux (1996) also mentioned the study as providing evidence for the existence of as-if body loops as characterized by Damasio. See below for a criticism of this interpretation.

12. Schachter and Singer's (1962) conclusion reflects a disembodied stance, because they concluded that arousal does not contribute in any way to affective specificity. Nevertheless, some still considered arousal necessary for a nonspecific sense of relevance and for determining the intensity of feelings.

13. See Clark (2003, pp. 189–195) for a defense of the idea that the "extended mind" view does not imply disembodiment.

REFERENCES

Beer, R. D. (2003). The dynamics of active categorical perception in an evolved model agent. *Adaptive Behavior, 11,* 209–243.

Calhoun, C., & Solomon, R. C. (Eds.). (1984). *What is an emotion? Classic readings in philosophical psychology.* New York: Oxford University Press.

Campbell, S. (1997). *Interpreting the personal: Expression and the formation of feelings.* Ithaca: Cornell University Press.

Cannon, W. B. (1927). The James-Lange theory of emotions: A critical examination and an alternative theory. *American Journal of Psychology, 39,* 106–124.

Chwalisz, K., Diener, E., & Gallagher, D. (1988). Autonomic arousal feedback and emotional experience: Evidence from the spinal cord injured. *Journal of Personality and Social Psychology, 54,* 820–828.

Clancey, W. J. (1997). *Situated cognition.* Cambridge: Cambridge University Press.

Clark, A. (1997). *Being there: Putting brain, body, and world together again.* Cambridge MA: MIT Press.

Clark, A. (2003). *Natural-born cyborgs: Minds, technologies, and the future of human intelligence.* Oxford: Oxford University Press.

Clark, A., & Chalmers, D. (1998). The extended mind. *Analysis, 58,* 7–19.

Colombetti, G. (2005). Enactive appraisal. *Phenomenology and the Cognitive Sciences.*

Colombetti, G., & Thompson, E. (2005). Enacting emotional interpretations with feeling. *Behavioral and Brain Sciences, 28,* 200–201.

Damasio, A. R. (1994). *Descartes' error: Emotion, reason and the human brain.* New York: Putnam.

Damasio, A. R. (1999). *The feeling of what happens: Body and emotion in the making of consciousness.* New York: Harcourt Brace.

Damasio, A. R. (2003). *Looking for Spinoza: Joy, sorrow, and the feeling brain.* Orlando: Harcourt.

Darwin, C. (1998). *The expression of the emotions in man and animals.* London: Harper Collins. (Original work published 1872)

De Sousa, R. (1987). *The rationality of emotion.* Cambridge, MA: MIT Press.

Descartes, R. (1988). The passions of the soul. In J. Cottingham, R. Stoothoff, & D. Murdoch (Eds.), *Selected philosophical writings of René Descartes.* Cambridge: Cambridge University Press. (Original work published 1644)

Duffy, E. (1941). An explanation of "emotional" phenomena without the use of the concept "emotion." *Journal of General Psychology, 25,* 283–293.

Frijda, N. H. (1987). *The emotions.* Cambridge: Cambridge University Press.

Gallagher, S., & Marcel, A. J. (1999). The self in contextualized action. *Journal of Consciousness Studies, 6,* 4–30.

Gallese, V. (2001). The "shared manifolds" hypothesis: From mirror neurons to empathy. *Journal of Consciousness Studies, 8,* 33–50.

Gallese, V., Keysers, C., & Rizzolatti, G. (2004). A unifying view of the basis of social cognition. *Trends in Cognitive Sciences, 8*, 397–403.

Goldie, P. (2000). *The emotions: A philosophical exploration.* Oxford: Oxford University Press.

Griffiths, P. E. (1997). *What emotions really are: The problem of psychological categories.* Chicago: University of Chicago Press.

Hohmann, G. W. (1966). Some effects of spinal cord lesions on experienced emotional feelings. *Psychophysiology, 3*, 143–156.

Hume, D. (2003). *A treatise of human nature.* (J. P. Wright, R. Stecker, & G. Fuller, Eds.). London: Everyman. (Original work published 1739)

Hurley, S. L. (1998). *Consciousness in action.* Cambridge, MA: Harvard University Press.

Hurley, S. L., & Noë, A. (2003). Neural plasticity and consciousness. *Biology and Philosophy, 18*, 131–168.

James, W. (1968). What is an emotion? In M. B. Arnold (Ed.), *The nature of emotion: Selected readings.* London: Penguin. (Reprinted from *Mind, 9*, 188–205, 1884)

Johnson, M. (1987). *The body in the mind: The bodily basis of meaning, imagination, and reason.* Chicago: University of Chicago Press.

Kelso, J. A. S. (1995). *Dynamic patterns: The self-organization of brain and behavior.* Cambridge MA: MIT Press.

Kenny, A. J. P. (1963). *Action, emotion and will.* London: Routledge and K. Paul.

Lange, C. G. (1967). The emotions. In C. G. Lange & W. James (Eds.), *The emotions.* New York: Hafner. (Original work published 1885)

Lazarus, R. S. (1966). *Psychological stress and the coping process.* New York: McGraw Hill.

Lazarus, R. S. (2001). Relational meaning and discrete emotions. In K. R. Scherer, A. Schorr, & T. Johnstone (Eds.), *Appraisal processes in emotion.* Oxford: Oxford University Press.

LeDoux, J. (1996). *The emotional brain: The mysterious underpinnings of emotional life.* New York: Simon and Schuster.

Lewis, M. D. (2005). Bridging emotion theory and neurobiology through dynamic systems modeling. *Behavioral and Brain Sciences, 28*, 169–194.

Lewis, M. D., & Granic, I. (Eds.) (2000). *Emotion, development, and self-organization: Dynamics systems approaches to emotional development.* Cambridge: Cambridge University Press.

London, H., & Nisbett, R. E. (1974). Elements of Schachter's cognitive theory of emotional states. In H. London & R. E. Nisbett (Eds.), *Thought and feeling.* Chicago: Aldine.

Lyons, W. E. (1980). *Emotion.* Cambridge: Cambridge University Press.

Noë, A. (2004). *Action in perception.* Cambridge MA: MIT Press.

O'Regan, K. J., & Noë, A. (2001). A sensorimotor account of vision and visual consciousness. *Behavioral and Brain Sciences, 24*, 883–917.

Panksepp, J. (1998). *Affective neuroscience: The foundations of human and animal emotions.* New York: Oxford University Press.

Pert, C. B. (1997). *Molecules of emotions: Why you feel the way you feel.* New York: Scribner.

Port, R. F., & van Gelder, T. (Eds.) (1995). *Mind as motion: Explorations in the dynamics of cognition.* Cambridge MA: MIT Press.

Prinz, J. J. (2004). *Gut reactions: A perceptual theory of emotion.* Oxford: Oxford University Press.

Prinz, W. (1997). Perception and action planning. *European Journal of Cognitive Psychology, 9,* 129–54.

Reisenzein, R. (1983). The Schachter theory of emotion: Two decades later. *Psychological Bulletin, 94,* 239–264.

Rizzolatti, G., Fadiga, L., & Fogassi, L. (1996). Premotor cortex and the recognition of motor actions. *Cognitive Brain Research, 3,* 131–141.

Roseman, I. J., & Smith, C. A. (2001). Appraisal theory: Overview, assumptions, varieties, controversies. In K. R. Scherer, A. Schorr, & T. Johnstone (Eds.), *Appraisal processes in emotion.* Oxford: Oxford University Press.

Ross, L., Rodin, J., & Zimbardo, P. G. (1969). Toward an attribution therapy: The reduction of fear through induced cognitive-emotional misattribution. *Journal of Personality and Social Psychology, 12,* 279–288.

Schachter, S., & Singer, J. E. (1962). Cognitive, social, and physiological determinants of emotional state. *Psychological Review, 69,* 379–399.

Scherer, K. R. (2000). Emotions as episodes of subsystem synchronization driven by nonlinear appraisal processes. In M. D. Lewis & I. Granic (Eds.) (pp. 70–99).

Skinner, B. F. (1953). *Science and human behavior.* New York: Free Press.

Solomon, R. C. (1976). *The passions.* Garden City, NY: Anchor Press/ Doubleday.

Solomon, R. C. (2004). Emotions, thoughts, and feelings. In R. C. Solomon (Ed.), *Thinking about feeling: Contemporary philosophers on emotions.* Oxford: Oxford University Press.

Spinoza, B. (2000). *Ethics.* (G. H. R. Parkinson, Ed. & Trans.). Oxford: Oxford University Press. (Original work published 1677)

Thelen, E., & Smith, L.B. (1994). *A dynamic systems approach to the development of cognition and action.* Cambridge MA: MIT Press.

Thelen, E., Schöner, G., Scheier, C., & Smith, L. B. (2001). The dynamics of embodiment: A field theory of infant perseverative reaching. *Behavioral and Brain Sciences, 24,* 1–86.

Thompson, E. (Ed.) (2001). *Between ourselves: Second-person issues in the study of consciousness.* Charlottesville: Imprint Academic. (Special issue, *Journal of Consciousness Studies, 8* [5–7].)

Thompson, E. (2007). *Mind in life: Biology, phenomenology, and the sciences of mind.* Cambridge, MA: Harvard University Press.

Thompson, E., & Varela, F. J. (2001). Radical embodiment: Neural dynamics and consciousness. *Trends in Cognitive Sciences, 5*, 418–425.

Valins, S. (1966). Cognitive effects of false heart-rate feedback. *Journal of Personality and Social Psychology, 4*, 400–408.

Varela, F. J., & Depraz, N. (2000). At the source of time: Valence and the constitutional dynamics of affect. *Arobase: Journal des Lettres et Sciences Humaines 4*, 143–166.

Varela, F. J., Thompson, E., & Rosch, E. (1991). *The embodied mind: Cognitive science and human experience.* Cambridge MA: MIT Press.

Watt, D. F. (1998). Emotion and consciousness: Implications of affective neuroscience for extended reticular thalamic activating system theories of consciousness. Retrieved January 20, 2002, from http://server.philvt.edu/assc/watt/default.htm.

4

ACTION AS THE SOLUTION TO THE MIND-BODY PROBLEM IN PIAGET'S THEORY

Jacques Vonèche
University of Geneva

In his *Introduction à l'épistémologie génétique*—which has not yet been translated into English—Piaget (1950) maintained that the scientific method prohibits psychologists from choosing among the classic metaphysical solutions to the mind-body problem (e.g., interactionism, epiphenomenalism, idealism, and monism). Instead, Piaget argued, the solution to the mind-body problem must be found in the principle of psychophysical parallelism, which unites mental implication (e.g., the truth . . . of $2 + 2 = 4$ 'implies' that of $4 - 2 = 2$) and physical causality (e.g., a cannon causes the movement of two billiard balls; Piaget, 1963/1968, pp. 187–188). While other solutions entail either a privileging of causality (e.g., interactionism, epiphenomenalism) or a privileging of implication (e.g., idealism, monism), psychophysical parallelism unites the two in a nondichotomous relational matrix.

The solution to the mind-body problem, according to Piaget (1963/1968), begins in taking a genetic (e.g., developmental) perspective. From this perspective, mental implication and physical causality originate from a common source—action—and become differentiated through the process of development. In Piaget's system, action and movements are virtually identical. Movements can be miniaturized in micromovements (e.g., eye-movements) and they can be internalized (e.g., representations). First and foremost, however, movements are intentional actions—that is, movements or actions constitute regularity-seeking mechanisms across all developmental levels from rhythms to regulations, and ultimately to rules and norms. At the beginning of the organism's development, all action is fundamentally rhythmical. Through action in the world, these rhythms become transformed into regulations, and then to rule-following behaviors, and ultimately, to the awareness of norms.

The awareness of norms itself implies a distinction between facts and norms, causes and meanings, and thus, a distinction between body and mind. In Piaget's relational system (see Overton, 2004), however, these distinct concepts are always understood as indissociable complementarities. In human knowledge, there can be no values without facts and vice versa, no causes without reasons, and no body without mind. In a similar fashion, there is no known reality without possibility, no object without a subject, and no externality without internality. Within Piaget's theory of cognitive development, the equilibration process, a process that regulates the potential isomorphism between opposites and regulates their development, accounts for the complementarity of these and other concepts. It is in this context that the concept of embodiment becomes central, as we shall now see.

The centrality of embodiment for Piaget reflects the phenomenological origins of his thinking. It was indeed no accident that Piaget succeeded Maurice Merleau-Ponty at the Sorbonne, and it was Merleau-Ponty who most clearly articulated the significance of embodiment for the phenomenological dimension of psychology. Piaget's and Merleau-Ponty's colleagues at the Sorbonne were philosophers, and they were well aware of what separated Piaget from most psychologists of his time. In French-speaking countries there were two opposing traditions concerning the mind-body problem: (a) the spiritualistic school, which followed Descartes and favored a strict separation of mind and body, and (b) the positivistic movement, which reduced mind to body. This latter movement had such a strong impact on psychology that the Genevan Carl Vogt conceived of thinking as the secretion of the brain in the same way that gall is a secretion of the liver.

At the University of Neuchâtel, where Piaget was educated, the positivistic movement was dominant in biology, but not in philosophy. Given his interest in both biology and philosophy, Piaget was exposed to the two currents of ideas concerning the mind-body problem. Early on, Piaget's own solution to the mind-body problem was oriented toward pragmatism: The central nervous system is kept informed by the periphery. But by the time he was 20, the influence of the philosopher Bergson became dominant. Under this influence, Piaget rejected the naïve realism of experimental psychology and came to understand that the world became an intentional object of the mind. The choice of the term "intentional" was Piaget's own, but it clearly demonstrated the influence of Brentano as well as Bergson.

In coming to this solution, Piaget dealt with the idea of the "object" in a way similar to the approach taken by phenomenology. Merleau-Ponty (1942/1963), for example, understands the difference between a human and an ape to reside in the fact that humans can symbolically represent objects, while lower animals can only grasp objects as "things-in-action." For lower animals, "things" are literal. While things may become "signals" and, thus, stand for something other than themselves, they never rise to the level of symbol or sign, which requires both a "stand for" relation and a detachment of the symbol from the object being represented. There is no pretence in the world of lower animals, only literal, pragmatic, and concrete presence in the course of action. Invariance is achieved through habitual action, not through the development of systems of signs and symbols. There is no symbolic object permanence in this world.

In contrast to lower animals, humans construct symbolic permanent objects at an early age and construct symbolic spatial and temporal systems within which to operate on these objects. Why do humans and lower animals contrast in such a fashion? The answer lies in the idea of embodiment. The bodies—and, consequently, the actions in the world—of lower animals and humans significantly differ, and this difference becomes translated into the construction of different worlds. Take a simple and familiar example: Köhler's experiments with apes on the island of Tenerife. To reach bananas, an ape was required to build a tower of boxes. The apes, however, seemed incapable of building a solid construction of boxes, and thus, they fell from any tower. The reason for this is that for the ape, there is a disconnect between the visual features of the situation and the proprioceptive aspect of climbing the tower. Apes can deal with each aspect separately, but they do not relate the visual equilibrium of the boxes piled upon one another to the proprioceptive equilibrium of their own body climbing the boxes. To succeed in the equilibration of any symbolized object, one must establish a one-to-one correspondence between the spatio-temporal relations perceived visually and a series of body postures. To do this, it must be understood that (a) some visual stimuli and some proprioceptive stimuli are *representative* of one another, (b) a relation of proportionality exists between the visual and the proprioceptive, and (c) one dimension can be substituted for the other. Thus, the permanent symbolic object is constructed through the mediation of the body projected in space as a "visualizable" object, even in its nonvisible features.

An elaboration of this difference between the world of the human and the ape is found in a series of experiments on mirror self-recognition in apes (Povinelli, Gallup, Eddy, & Bierschwale, 1997). In these experiments, the experimental room contains a mirror, and a red dot is painted on the nose of a chimp while she is sleeping. It is expected that when she awakens, the animal will see herself in the mirror. If she has a symbolic representation of herself she should touch her nose on looking in the mirror. If she has no such representation, she should not. Touching the nose would represent a behavior intermediate between what would be required for a correct equilibration of the boxes in Köhler's work and the complete lack of any coordination between proprioceptive and visual stimuli. Touching the nose in this situation demonstrates the beginning of correctly locating the body in space which is complementary to the "delegation function" that Piaget described.

Delegation is a well-known phenomenon, and Piaget provided the following two examples (Bringuier, 1977). While riding a bike, one locates a pebble under the wheel, and not under the buttock where it is actually felt; or when one hits the ground with a cane, one feels the ground at the end of the cane that touches the ground and not in the hand, although the sensation is felt by the hand holding the cane.

As another intermediate form, I have anecdotal evidence that chimps of the Bonobo kind recognize themselves in photographs. When I grew up in the Congo during World War II, my parents raised a young Bonobo male called Marcel. This chimp evidently held the belief that he was so complete a member of our family that when my parents were in the process of sending—thanks to the Red Cross—pictures of their children that for reasons of censorship showed only faces without background, Marcel insisted on adding a picture of himself to the set of other pictures.

Another example illustrating the incomplete coordination between proprioceptive movement and visual perception in great apes involves the act of aiming at a target. As a child, I was repeatedly puzzled by the inability of great apes to aim correctly at a target. When disturbed, gorillas in the Virunga Mountains often responded by throwing young trees they had uprooted at the invader of their privacy; however, the gesture was surprisingly inaccurate. The same was true of chimpanzees throwing stones at each other, although they were quite capable of positioning a flat stone on the ground, positioning a coconut on the stone, and using a sharp pebble to break the nut. Here, it becomes evident that when the spatio-temporal distances between tool-objects and target-objects is not too great, apes are able to succeed. When that distance increases, however, thus requiring a more representational coordination between the proprioceptive and the visual, success is elusive.

The situation using tools and a target should be distinguished from that of an animal jumping from branch to branch, or capturing prey at the correct moment. These latter situations involve only the positioning of the body in space and time, without the use of any intermediary between body and target. Nonhuman animals can use tools, but only momentarily—they do not keep tools for another opportunity—and only when the spatio-temporal distances are small. What is lacking here is the kind of intentionality well-illustrated in the art of archery, as a representational projection of oneself as a bodily based, acting object among objects; an embodied subject who thinks by acting and acts through thought as well as external movements.

Thus, the active body constitutes a mediator between self and environment and conversely this mediation constitutes the self. This is exactly what Piaget (Piaget & De La Harpe, 1928) claimed when drawing on the writing of Jean de la Harpe. He argued that "Experience shapes thinking as well as thinking experiencing" (p. 33). This reciprocal process is at the heart of Piaget's position on the embodiment of mind, and in taking this embodied position, he has avoided both idealism and empiricism in favour of constructivism; a reciprocal relation between physical movement and logical thought. The body is conceived as the locus of action and, more specifically, of movements, and the dual process of assimilation (bodily organized action that constructs the known world) and accommodation (feedback from the known world that serves to change categories of the known world) are mediated by the body.

ACTION AS MOVEMENT AND MOVEMENT AS ACTION

To understand the central role that embodied action plays in Piaget's (1936/1952) theory of the development of mind, a further elaboration of the concepts of action and movement is important. Here, two examples provided by Piaget—one concerning his daughter Lucienne, and one concerning himself—are significant. Both examples involve invention and symbolic representation. Lucienne is one year and four months old when the first observation was made.

Observation 179. The example of the watch chain to be put into an aperture 16×34 mm. is more complex. Here again we remember Jacqueline's gropings (Obs. 173 and 173 repeated). But Lucienne has solved the problem by sudden invention:

At 1;4(0) without ever having contemplated this spectacle, Lucienne looks at the box which I bring nearer and return without her having seen the contents. The chain spreads out on the floor and she immediately tries to put it back into the box. She begins by simply putting one end of the chain into the box and trying to make the rest follow progressively. This procedure which was first tried by Jacqueline, Lucienne finds successfully the first time (the end put into the box stays there fortuitously), but fails completely at the second and third attempts.

At the fourth attempt, Lucienne starts as before but pauses, and after a short interval, she places the chain on a flat surface nearby (the experiment takes place on a shawl), rolls it up in a ball intentionally, takes the ball between three fingers, and puts the whole thing in the box.

The fifth attempt begins by a very short resumption of the first procedure. But Lucienne corrects herself at once and returns to the correct method.

Sixth attempt: immediate success.

Thus one sees the difference between the behavior patterns of Jacqueline and of Lucienne. What was, in the former, the product of a long apprenticeship, was suddenly invented by the latter. Such a difference is surely a question of the level. So it is that at 2;6 (25) Jacqueline, with whom I repeat the experiment, solves the problem unhesitatingly. By grasping the chain in both hands she puts it in with her left hand while holding the remaining part in her right, to prevent it from falling. In the event that it gets caught, she corrects the movement.

Observation 180. Another mental invention, derived from a mental combination and not only from a sensorimotor apprenticeship, was that which permitted Lucienne to rediscover an object inside a matchbox. At 1;4 (0), that is to say, right after the preceding experiment, I play at hiding the chain in the same box used in Observation 179. I begin by opening the box as wide as possible and putting the chain into its cover (where Lucienne herself put it but deeper). Lucienne, who has already practiced filling and emptying her pail and various receptacles, then grasps the box and turns it over without hesitation. No invention is involved of course (it is the simple application of a schema, acquired through groping) but knowledge of this behavior pattern of Lucienne is useful for understanding what follows.

Then I put the chain inside an empty matchbox (where the matches belong), then close the box leaving an opening of 10 mm. Lucienne begins by turning the whole thing over, then tries to grasp the chain through the opening. Not succeeding, she simply puts her index finger into the slit and so succeeds in getting out a small fragment of the chain; she then pulls it until she has completely solved the problem.

Here begins the experiment which we want to emphasize. I put the chain back into the box and reduce the opening to 3 mm. It is understood that Lucienne is not aware of the functioning of the opening and closing of the matchbox and has not seen me prepare the experiment. She only possesses the two preceding schemata: turning the box over in order to empty it of its contents, and sliding her finger into the slit to make the chain come out. It is of course this last procedure that she tries first: she puts her finger inside and gropes to reach the chain, but fails completely. A pause follows during which Lucienne manifests a very curious reaction bearing witness not only to the fact that she tries to think out the situation and to represent to herself through mental combination the operations to be performed, but also to the role played by imitation in the genesis of representations. Lucienne mimics the widening of the slit.

She looks at the slit with great attention; then, several times in succession, she opens and shuts her mouth, at first slightly, then wider and wider! Apparently Lucienne understands the existence of a cavity underneath the slit and wishes to enlarge that cavity. The attempt at representation which she thus furnishes is expressed plastically, that is to say due to inability to think out the situation in words or clear visual images, she uses a simple motor indication as "signifier" or symbol. Now, as the motor reaction which presents itself for filling this role is none other than imitation, that is to say, representation by acts, which, doubtless earlier than any mental image, makes it possible not only to divide into parts the spectacles seen but also to evoke and reproduce them at will. Lucienne, by opening her mouth thus expresses, or even reflects, her desire to enlarge the opening of the box. This schema of imitation, with which she is familiar, constitutes for her the means of thinking out the situation. There is doubtless added to it an element of magico-phenomenistic causality of efficacy. Just as she often uses imitation to act upon persons and make them reproduce their interesting movements, so also it is probable that the act of opening her mouth in front of the slit to be enlarged implies some underlying idea of efficacy.

Soon after this phase of plastic reflection, Lucienne unhesitatingly puts her finger in the slit and, instead of trying as before to reach the chain, she pulls so as to enlarge the opening. She succeeds and grasps the chain.

During the following attempts (the slit always being 3 mm. wide), the same procedure is immediately rediscovered. On the other hand, Lucienne is incapable of opening the box when it is completely closed. She gropes, throws the box on the floor, etc., but fails. (pp. 336–338)

And now Piaget's (1936/1952) interpretation:

From this point of view let us again take up Observations 177–182, comparing them to the mechanism of empirical gropings. As before, the point of departure of these behavior patterns consists in the impetus given by the schema assigning an end to the action; for instance, in Observation 180, sight of the chain in the matchbox sets in motion the schema of grasping. This schema of the goal immediately arouses a certain number of schemata which the child will utilize as initial means and which he must accommodate, that is to say, differentiate according to the variations of the new situation. In Observation 180, Lucienne tries to turn the box over or to slide her finger into the slit in order to extract the chain. But in utilizing these schemata the child perceives at the same time the difficulties of the present situation. In other words, there occurs here, as in the course of empirical groping, an encounter with the foreseen fact which creates an obstacle (the slit is too narrow to admit the finger). Now in both cases, this encounter entails a new intervention of earlier schemata. It is due to the latter that these unforeseen facts acquire meaning. The only difference is that, henceforth, such encounters with the obstacle no longer take place in the course of discovery (since the latter is no longer groping and consists in sudden invention) but beforehand, at the moment when the first procedures tried out as hypotheses fail, and when the problem is clarified by virtue of that very failure. In Observation 180, these auxiliary schemata which attribute a meaning to the facts are those that permit the child to understand what the slit is that he sees before him (= sign of a subjacent opening) and how it is troublesome (because it is too narrow). The child often opens and closes boxes, wants to put his hand through very small openings, etc. Those are the schemata which confer a meaning on the present situation and which at the same time direct the search. They intervene, therefore, as secondary means and hence are subordinated to the initial procedure. It is then that invention comes in, in the form of sudden accommodation of the ensemble of those schemata to the present situation. How does this accommodation work?

It consists, as always, in differentiating the preceding schemata according to the variations of the present situation, but this differentiation, instead of operating through actual groping and cumulative assimilation, results from a spontaneous assimilation, hence more rapid and operating by means of simply representative attempts. In other words, instead of exploring the slit with his finger and groping until he has discovered the procedure which consists in drawing to him the inner side (of the box) in order to enlarge the opening; the child is satisfied to look at the opening, except for experimenting no longer on it directly, but on its symbolic substitutes. Lucienne opens and closes her mouth while examining the slit of the box, proving that she is in the act of assimilating it and of mentally trying out the enlargement of the slit; moreover, the analogy thus established by assimilation between the slit perceived and other openings simply evoked leads her to foresee that pressure put on the edge of the opening will widen it. Once the schemata have thus been spontaneously accommodated on the plane of simple mental assimilation, Lucienne proceeds to act and succeeds right away.

An interpretation of this sort applies to each of our observations. In Observation 179, for example, if Lucienne rolls the chain up into a ball to put in into the box after having noted the failure of the direct method, it is because the schemata acquired in putting the chain into a pail or a necklace into a watering can (Obs. 172) or again in squeezing materials, putting her pillow or handkerchief in her mouth, etc., afford her sufficient assimilation of the new situation. Instead of groping she mentally combines the operations to be performed. But this mental experience does not consist in mnemonic evocation of already manufactured images; it is an essentially constructive process, the representation of which is only a symbolic adjuvant, since genuine invention exists and it never perceived a reality identical to the one it is in the process of elaborating. In Observations 180 and 180 there also exists spontaneous functioning of the schemata of displacement, by analogy, to be sure, with the experiments the child was able to make in reality, but this analogy entails imagination of new combinations. Finally, in Observation 182, we see how an initial schema can be differentiated, without progressive groping, through sudden dissociation and assimilation. (pp. 343–345)

Now Piaget's observation (1936/1952) of himself as an adult:

In order to better understand the mechanism of this assimilation which has become deductive while remaining on the plane of sensorimotor operations, let us again analyse a case of elementary practical invention observed in an adult and consequently capable of correct introspection. While driving an old automobile I am bothered by oil on the steering wheel which makes it slippery. Lacking time to stop, I take out my handkerchief and dry the spots. When putting it in my pocket I observe that it is too greasy and look for a place to put it without soiling anything. I put it between my seat and the one next to me, as deeply as possible in the crevice. An hour later the rain forces me to close the windshield but the resulting heat makes me try to open it a little. The screws being worn out, I cannot succeed; it only stays wide open or completely shut. I try to hold the windshield slightly open with my left hand, but my fatigue makes me think that some object could replace my hand. I look around me, but nothing is in evidence. While looking at the windshield I have the impression that the object could be put, not at the bottom of the windshield (one pushed it at the bottom to open it), but by wedging it in the angle formed by the right edge of the windshield and the vertical upright of the body of the car. I have the vague feeling of an analogy between the solution to be found and a problem already solved before. The solution then becomes clarified. My tendency to put an object into the corner of the windshield meets a sort of motor memory of having just a few minutes before placed something into a crevice. I try to remember what it was, but no definite representation comes to mind. Then suddenly, without having time to imagine anything, I understand the solution and find myself already in the act of searching with my hand for the hidden handkerchief. Therefore the latter schema directed my search and directed me toward the lateral corner of the windshield when my last idea was a different one.

This trite observation demonstrates very well how a sensorimotor search can arouse schemata previously acquired and make them function independently of internal language and clear representation. The tendency to introduce an object into a slit, in this example, is modelled exactly on a schema remaining in an almost purely motor state, and the conjunction thus produced suffices to insure discovery of a solution. One therefore understands how a sensorimotor deduction is possible in the small child through simple practical evocation of the schemata and independently of a well-defined system of representations. (p. 345)

And again, Piaget's (1936/1952) interpretation:

But how can we account for the mechanism of this spontaneous reorganization of schemata? Take, for example, the construction of the schema of "rolling into a ball" in Observation 179, or that of "widening the slit" in Observation 180; does this construction consist in a sudden structurization of representations or of the perceptual field, or is it the result of assimilatory activities prior to invention? As we have just recalled, a certain number of already acquired schemata direct the search at the moment of invention without, however, any one of them containing in itself the correct solution. For example, before rolling the chain up into a ball to put it in the narrow opening, Lucienne has already: (a) squeezed the material, (b) put the chain in a wide opening, and (c) compared large objects to inadequate openings (as when she tried to bring objects through the bars of her playpen). In Observation 180 she also possesses the earlier schemata we have already emphasized. The question raised is therefore to find out how these schemata will intercoordinate in order to give rise to invention: Is it by a structuring independent of their genesis or due to the very activity which engendered them and which is now pursued without any longer depending on the external circumstances in which it began? One might as well ask whether ideas organize themselves in the course of theoretical invention or whether they are organized as a function of implicit judgments and of the potential intelligent activity they represent. We do not doubt that the second of these two theses is in both cases (in sensorimotor intelligence as well as in reflective thought) much the most satisfying to the mind, the first only consisting in a manner of speaking which veils the dynamism of the facts with static language. (pp. 345–346)

From the perspective of the present essay, these observations and their interpretation by Piaget lead to several relevant conclusions. In Observations 179 and 180, as well as in Piaget's memory of what happened in his old car during a rainy day, we witness the same bodily movements spontaneously prompted by a visual situation.

Lucienne opens and closes her lips to understand how to put a chainlet into a box. The "idea" of the body as a microcosm of the macrocosm and the fact that what is first tested on, the body can be successfully extended to the world of objects, are significant for the mutual assimilation of schemata for Piaget. They also indicate, however, that the body is functioning as the metaphor of reality par excellence, both before the emergence of the semiotic function and after. What is relevant for our purpose here is the fact that the body is, in Piaget's case as well as in that of his daughter, the mother of invention. Even more interesting is the fact that movement works as the trigger of innovative behavior. Once external reality is embodied in the body literally (could there be a more perfect embodiment?), the innovation occurs so much so that one seems to be entitled to consider the body as the workshop of thinking or the tool of invention. This is made possible in Piaget's theory thanks to the concept of *scheme*. This concept, which psychologists tend to consider as either strictly Piagetian or Kantian, is—in my opinion, at least—Bergsonian. Indeed Kantian schematism has a lot in common with Piaget's. For instance, the paragraph that starts with the words "In der that liegen unsern reinen sinnlichen Begriffen . . ." (Kant, 1781, pp. 140–141), which has a very Piagetian ring. For both authors, the notion of schema establishes the link between the pure concepts of understanding and the objects of experience. In Kant, however, a schema is just a means to give content to a concept; which is not the case with Piaget.

Consider now Bergson's (1896/1994) concept of *schéma moteur* (motoric schema): "So would unroll itself, in the shape of nascent muscular sensations, what we call the motoric schema of the heard word" (p. 115, my translation). It seems much more similar to Piaget's notion of "scheme." In addition, Bergson's influence upon the young Piaget is well-documented, especially by Piaget himself. The quote from Bergson is reminiscent of Lalande's (1893) notion of *schème opératoire*. According to Lalande (1893), a *schème opératoire* is something like the rhythm of a verse of which one cannot find the words or like the empty motion of a press going on automatically after having printed its page.

The similarities are rather striking. Schemas seem to be the structures of a procedure or, at least, their algorithmic form; they are motoric in origin. Thus, movement is the heart of action; however, the argument holds in reverse: Action is the motor of movement because of its schematic properties. Any movement is animated by a schematic procedure that originates in its repetition or exercise, but also gradually becomes the core of further movements, so much so that there is a circular relation between the two.

ACTION AS THE SOURCE AND FORM
OF REPRESENTATION

To the extent that action is not only bodily movements, but also mental intention, it is also the source of movement, if only in terms of its planning by animals and humans. For the cat to jump from the cupboard, across the table, and to the window in order to get out of the house, there is a need to compute, in one way or another, the total distance between the cupboard and the window, and also to measure the quantity of energy required if such a jump is to be successful. In other words, a visual distance has to be transformed into a motoric act or movement. This situation is analogous with, but not identical to, that of the chimp, who must balance the boxes correctly in order to climb up and get the bananas hanging from the ceiling of the cage. Here, the cat deals with a single, simple jump. The situation does not require an elaborate equilibration of several boxes on top of each other. Mutatis mutandis, the two situations, boxes versus jump, are similar to the development of object permanence in human babies: at nine months, they can remove one screen without any real problem, but they fail to remove several screens. Gruber, Girgus, and Banuazizi (1971) have shown that cats do not reach the final stages of object permanence and stay at inferior levels of object permanence as measured by the Hunt-Uzgiris' scale of infant development.

What is important to note, in this example, is the relationship between perception and movement. In empiricist psychology, movements and perception are kept separate. Perception is on the sensory receptive side of the nervous side, while movement is on the motoric effective side. The division is clear and neat. Within Piagetian psychology, things are quite different: perceptual and motoric activities are the two sides of the same coin. Perception is not the mere registration of external stimuli, but the result of the activity of the eye-movements in vision, the structuring of tones, pitches, and so forth in audition, and the organization of smells and odors, as well as the movements needed for kinesthetic sensation, not to speak of the inner sensations of proprioception, which are also coordinated in a system of actions.

It would require too much space to discuss here each sensory modality in detail. So let us concentrate on eye-movements (Piaget, 1961/

1969). Piaget does not consider perception to be a passive registering of sensory impressions. For him, visual perception is the result of the constant activity of eye-movements. Eye-movements consist of the bipolar activities of centration and decentration. *Centration* means focusing on a specific element in the visual field. Every centration is relative to another centration, so much so that the total balance of relative centrations yields a form of decentration, or of balancing out of all the centrations involved in scanning the visual field. This bold theory of perception leads to the formulation of a law of relative centrations that is not of interest for our present purpose. What is relevant here is that visual perception is a form of action by which the eye and the brain "imitate" the shape of the perceived object. Now, if we consider, with Piaget and Guillaume, that imitation is always an imitation of what the subject understands of the object, we have a neat explanation for visual illusion and deformations. But we have, in addition, a better understanding of the embodiment of knowledge. The act of perceiving amounts to actively scanning the visual field in the same way that the open space becomes known only by roaming through it. Perception gives rise to constancies, spatial displacements to permanence.

The fact that eye-movements "imitate" forms and shapes indicates that the passage from the sensorimotor movements and actions to their internalization as representation is, once again, mediated by bodily action. Anticipating what would be discovered later by electromyographic studies (Kosslyn, 1994), Piaget proposed that the mental imagery of an action was similar to real action and moreover, that simply observing actions performed by others stimulated the same areas of innervation in brain and body with a double emphasis on both, the motoric component and on the spatial indices over the strictly sensory visual ones (see Gallese, 2000a, 2000b).

For memory, Piaget (Piaget & Inhelder, 1968/1973) assumed the same centrality of action within a top-down information-retrieving structure. In addition, Piaget proposed that the position of the body in space and the different recollections of the sequences of actions performed during learning improved the recording and retrieval of information and revived the emotional states that occurred during learning (especially a strong level of emergency and urgency).

Piaget (Piaget & Inhelder, 1948/1967) also argued that in drawing, the movements involved in the graphic act play the most important role in representing reality. What is important here, for our purpose, is that drawing as a motoric *and* representational process reflects an exactly equivalent mental level of development.

In dream contents, actions are also central as they are in any narrative. In play, what I do with my body gives symbolic meaning to the usual common object that is transformed by playing. It is because I sit on my chair facing its back and because I imitate with my legs the ups and downs of horseback riding, that my chair can be assimilated to a horseback.

THE PROBLEM OF INTERNALIZING ACTIONS

Thinking has something to do with truth-values. Actions have only to be efficient. This is the reason why most philosophical epistemologies root thinking in language either metaphorically or actually. Language has a grammar, obeys certain rules at different levels and in different forms: (a) semantic, (b) pragmatic, and (c) syntactic. Actions seem to be only factual and not normative. Consequently, when Piaget roots thinking in action by means of operations, he accomplishes a revolutionary reversal of common beliefs among epistemologists, because he seems to make room for a passage from performance to norm. How is this possible?

Indeed, every system of values is composed of two different parts. On one hand, it is composed of rules that are perceived as necessary and independent of any factual observation. On the other hand, it is composed of a set of empirical sense-data seemingly independent of any prescription. Normative sciences such as logic and mathematics have truth-values that claim to be strictly independent of experience, be it empirical testing of reality or feelings, beliefs, or any other arbitrary human state of affairs. Norms seem to be objective and universal.

Reciprocally, empirical sciences claim to be as objective and universal as normative ones but their truth-value rests upon a procedure called experimental method based upon the behavior of real objects. Therefore they are called "experimental sciences."

The question, then, becomes, "How are these two forms of knowledge related?" "How do mind and the objective world come together?" Experimental truths such as physical constancies depend on observation and measurement. Normative truths such as an N-dimensional geometry cannot be grasped by any form of physical experimentation. Physical phenomena, however, *can* be modelled by mathematical means. Riemann's geometry was a purely physically useless mathematical object, until Einstein took hold of it to elaborate his physical theory of relativity. On the basis of this abstract model, several deductions and predictions regarding the nature of the universe could be made and tested experimentally by physicists.

In contrast to Gestalt theory, neither Popper (1928) nor Piaget (1968) considered this sort of harmony between mind and universe to be the result of a general law of totality making the universe isomorphic to the mind and vice versa, (e.g., the idea that both mind and universe belong to the same universal system of physical rules). Nor do they consider this harmony to be the result of a pragmatic convention or agreement as in Winston Churchill's conception of democracy, "the worst of all systems, except for all the others." They also do not accept materialistic reductionism, according to which this harmony is caused by the simple fact that the mind is as material as the universe and, as such, is a mere reflection of the universe as manifest in Lenin's theory of empirio-criticism or in crude empiricism.

What Popper (1928) and Piaget (1932) have in common, despite their differences in other matters, is a belief in the rule-seeking capacity of the human mind. Thus, the agreement between facts and norms is explained by Piaget in terms of what Popper and Bühler (1908) called "*Regelbewustsein*"—that is, a search for regularities, or better, what Popper calls "*Gesetzerlebnis*," or experience of rules. This is a developmental explanation in terms of interactions between the self and the world. The external stimulus is a stimulus only to the extent that it corresponds to an active receptor being ready to assimilate. In other words, the stimulus is the *material* condition of the subject's action, but the response is the *formal* condition for the triggering of the action. The search for rules spans from the early and primitive detection of regularities in nature to the most abstract scientific theories. Piaget developed this position in a paper that is roughly entitled, "Rhythms, Regulations, and Operations, the Three Basic Cognitive Processes" (Piaget, 1942).

For Piaget, living and knowing continue each other; the action cognitive adaptation is biological adaptation by other means. Biological balance is made possible by the activity of metabolism, cognitive adaptation by the activity of self-regulation—via the three basic processes mentioned above. Rhythms are the most elementary form of self-regulation, since, as chrono-bio-psychology has abundantly demonstrated, the alternation of day and night, as well as that of seasons, have strong effects on the biological clock. But rhythms also have an impact on our understanding of a sentence, our motor behavior, our perception of pain, and so forth.

Rhythmic alternation is the most primitive norm; operation is the most abstract one. But both appear on the same continuum of regulations. Regularities become rules and norms when they become logically necessary. So there is a passage from causality to necessity through the various forms of regulations, because self-regulation is nothing other than circular causality by retroaction (or feed-back) only. Once this circular causality becomes *internalized* as an abstract system of compensations regulating itself either by feed-back (as in homeostatic systems) or by feed-forward (as in homeorrhesis), the integration of all three structures becomes possible. The mind can move from the simple detection of regularities that are never completely reversible (as in regulations) to a complete reversibility, typified in mental operations. This is only possible when there is no resistance of the object, no friction, no time delay, no entropy, but strict reversibility by ideal compensation as in thought. This progressive freeing from material conditions into a strictly formal structure leads to pure norms. But, at any level, the previous norms are absorbed, as a special case, into higher order norms. This special case is called *normative fact* by Piaget. Thus, genetic epistemology studies norms as facts and not as such—for instance, as norm, law or rule. This raises an important question.

By describing the entire normative system in terms of normative facts, Piaget "levels off the difference between logical and natural thought," to use an expression by Husserl (1913, p. 209). Before Piaget, Durkheim (1968) attempted to explain Australian totemism in terms of social expression of the sacred (e.g., in terms of normative facts). He confused religion as an idea with religion as a cultural form and took the rite for what it stands. Indeed, Piaget has given the impression that his sociohistorical and psycho-genetic study of the growth of knowledge solves the problem. Since scientific theory (normative science) is constructed by the same means (common mechanisms) as children's knowledge, the identification of common mechanisms between the two is enough to end Piaget's questioning. In addition, because this isomorphism corresponds to a certain logic, Piaget seems satisfied with his solution: The growth of knowledge obeys a law of development that consists of a hierarchy of embedded logical levels from the least to the most powerful. This is a form of logicism that does not solve the problem of internalization of actions, for the same reasons that Durkheim could not explain totemism. As Durkheim mistook religion as a cultural form of behaviour for religion as an idea, Piaget too often takes the things of logic for the logic of things ("les choses de la logique pour la logique des choses"). This is taking the instruments of something for the thing itself or the means for the meaning.

Husserl (1913) answered this question not in terms of logicism (as he is too often accused of), but in terms of a sort of law of equilibrium typified in *Gestaltheorie* as emerging out of the inner and most intimate nature of things, a sort of *Wesenschau*, or intuition of essences, that reproduces itself under the same circumstances as an invariant in the midst of transformations and variations. The essence is what remains constant in spite of the flux of experience. It is a principle of conservation and, to that extent, it is similar to Piaget's notion of conservation. Piagetian conservation evolves from the activity of a general or epistemic subject, however, whereas Husserl's subject is transcendental and, as such, intuits the essence from the beginning; it is a *terminus a quo* and not a *terminus ad quem*. It is an a priori form of knowledge; however, by the same token, it is also something as contingent as a fact. Hence, it is a dialectical principle, both factual and essential. Here we are very close to the Piagetian notion of a normative fact, but with the fundamental difference that it is there in principle (or more precisely, *in principio*, with the double meaning of the Latin word: "from the beginning" *and* "in principle"). It is both genetically and logically there, whereas a normative fact is by definition ever changing; it is a stage, a moment soon to be overtaken by another moment, another more advanced state of affairs and, as such, historically contingent and thus relative. For Piaget, each and every norm is valid for a moment soon to be changed by a more complex one, more advanced, that builds its own perfection upon the remnants of the previous one. Thus, there is *no* absolute truth; all truth-values are transient, whereas Husserl's sort of essential and automatic restructuration gives a transcendental "place to values in a world of facts," to use Köhler's (1938) phrase.

All this is very well, but we reach here a very difficult point. If every truth is true *en passant,* there must necessarily be a *Veritas perennis* from which to judge this. In other words, the veracity of relativism must be based, in the end, on some sort of absolute in order to be true. This is the paradox of absolute relativism. It is Piaget's theoretical paradox. It is, more generally, the paradox of every form of genetic structuralism. It is the combination of the two aspects that raises the problem. Either one takes the perspective of structuralism and assumes that every structure is a sort of monad to itself and, as such, should not be judged from any external point of view; or one adopts a genetic perspective from which any novelty in development is considered as more advanced, hierarchically higher or more mature, than earlier stages of development. But this evaluation *must* necessarily be made from an external point of view providing an orthogenetic principle or invariant from which criteria for development, advance, or evolution are deductible. Falling back on external empirical criteria is fallacious. Often, in developmental psychology, the criterion of time has been used as an ordering principle, however, it leads to the erroneous conclusion that anything that appears later is necessarily more advanced: Recency is mistaken for progress.

Evolution cannot be demonstrated by any natural objective criterion. This can be illustrated by the concept of maturity as used in social sciences, and particularly, in psychology. At first glance, maturity is a concept imported from biology, and it refers to a fruit's degree of edibility, for instance. It seems a perfectly sound, solid, common-sense observation that can be made rather easily by anyone in her right mind. But, once this concept is translated into psychology, it becomes strangely ideological; it serves to designate those behaviors that are irreproachable to the researcher's eye. Immaturity is rarely less than a stigma in such contexts. By such a bias, parochial values get an absolute and universal value. Justice becomes the interest of the strongest and the history of the world becomes the world court of justice (die Weltgeschichte ist das Weltgericht, Hegel, 1821, §340), all of which is unacceptable for Piaget.

There seems to be no way to avoid norms that transcend the structure under scrutiny in order to be operative. Only such norms allow for a classification of behavior into categories such as "underdeveloped," "degenerate," "stagnant," "deviant," or "pathological," without which no education, no treatment, nor remediation would be possible. This demand for transcendence is in contradiction with the structuralist claim that there should be no cross-cultural, extrasystemic, or universal criteria outside of the structure under consideration. Clearly, the solution of normative facts is no solution at all, because it naturalizes something that should remain logical, normative, and transcendent, and it fails to maintain the dialectical process between naturalistic observation and ideal τελος (telos).

Indeed, Piaget is aware of this difficulty. Nevertheless, instead of facing it head-on, he prefers to rely on a tangential strategy, that of the circle of sciences. If any science relies upon its neighbour to exist as an explanatory system, then psychology relies upon logic to provide guidelines for action and natural thought, and logic relies upon psychology to explain the origins and the development of such guidelines. Once again, however, such a view is strictly adaptive. Furthermore, it heads toward evolutionary psychology and fails to answer the criticism levelled toward the evolutionary view that truth is not necessarily a well-adapted means of survival. Survival and truth-values are two different things. Otherwise, mistakes and errors would be deadly. How does Piaget get around these two difficulties, (a) the strife of systems between geneticism and structuralism, and (b) the relationships between norms and facts, as well as between truth-values and adaptive action?

In order to understand Piaget's attempt at solving this problem, the reader has to keep in mind that the double difficulty of the strife of systems between geneticism and structuralism and that of the articulation of values (be it truth or moral values) with actions, arose late in his life and career. At the time Piaget became aware of these difficulties, he had already solidified his system in many ways and he could no longer recognize the necessity of a transcendental τελος to justify geneticism, since he had been involved in immanentism and relativism since the mid-1920s at least. It would have meant a contradiction in his system that he could not tolerate. Hence, the recourse to a principle that he considered still immanent but, in addition, telos-oriented: *équilibration majorante*. Equilibration is, by definition, immanent to the system considered. Once Piaget asserts, however, that, in the end, every equilibration becomes "majorante," he really means that the system constantly optimizes its balance with the passage of time. This is a dangerous position to hold, because there is no reason internal to the system itself that motivates this directional change; therefore, Piaget is really begging the question here.

If we now look at the relationship between action and values, we are confronted with another variety of the same difficulty: there is no continuity between the two. This is reflected in Piaget's writings as the duality between causal action and meaningful thought (e.g., psychophysical parallelism), as we shall now examine.

THE MIND-BODY PROBLEM

As discussed, the relation between mind and body is explained by Piaget in terms of a parallelism between the psyche and physical processes. On the one hand, body is an integral part of the world of material objects and, as such, abides to the rule of causality. On the other hand, mind is a formal unity and, as such, obeys the law of formal necessity, which is implication. Thus, body and mind seem to belong to two different universes of discourse: (a) material causality and (b) formal implication. Events taking place in the body are explained by causality, mental events by logical necessity or implication. So there seems to be two parallel systems governed by two different rules. What, then, is the relationship between them?

For Piaget, there are two series of events: (a) material ones and (b) mental ones co-occurring and being explained in different terms (causality and implication). During the course of action, any human act is intentional, purposive, and meaningful. It is commanded by a logic of meanings. A causal explanation of human action becomes possible only a posteriori, once the course of action is explicitly terminated, by opposition to a formal explanation which anticipates action considered as a goal-directed behavior.

Such a position is somewhat surprising because it supposes two things that are not obvious within Piaget's thinking. One is the assumption of dualism in the most classical sense, which does not seem congruent with the idea of a continuity between biology and psychology or between physiological and cognitive processes, which is also characteristic of Piaget's theory. The second surprise is closely related to and follows from this assumption: If there is a psychophysical parallelism, how does Piaget reconcile this idea with that of a continuity from biology to psychology? There must be, both logically and genetically, a moment when causal concatenation becomes logical implication. Hence, there should be a reason for this transformation.

Unfortunately, there is no reason to be found in Piaget writings, as if parallelism did not raise any questions within his perspective. Does the passage happen during phylogeny, since it does not show up during ontogeny? There is no hint to that, either. The only way in which Piaget deals with the problem is by assuming that mental operations transform ideas in the same way that actions transform objects—or, more precisely, things—in the physical world. All of this is well, but once again, it supposes the preexistence of parallelism. The only light shed on the genesis of the parallelism comes from Piaget's biological writings. There, Piaget (1967/1971) shows how cognitive adaptation continues biological adaptation:

> Cognitive processes seem, then, to be at one and the same time the outcome of organic autoregulation, reflecting its essential mechanisms, and the most highly differentiated organs of this regulation at the core of interactions with the environment, so much so that, in the case of man, these processes are being extended to the universe itself. (p. 26)

But this statement, in turn, raises a host of questions. First, considering cognitive processes as organs has a ring of idealism in the sense that such a statement grants material reality status to ideas and, as such, fuses materiality with ideality and begs all the questions raised by parallelism. Second, if one pursues the analogy further, how can processes become structures, since organs are structures by definition? Processes are on the genetic, developmental side of things; organs are on the structural one. We have already noticed that a certain strife of systems exists between these two notions. In this way, the analogy seems fuzzy in every respect and confuses instead of helping.

A second reading of the passage above in addition to the following one might elucidate what Piaget (1967/1971) meant in this context:

Cognitive autoregulation makes use of the general systems of organic regulation such as are found at every genetic, morphogenetic, physiological, and nervous level, and forthwith adapts them to their new situation. . . . This situation constitutes the exchanges with the environment that form the basis of behavior. (p. 34)

Thus, it means that cognition cannot be said to occur in any one of the conventionally defined organ systems of the body, but draws upon them all and reorganizes them in a new set of functional relations. This reorganization leads to some important differences between organic and cognitive functioning. The most crucial ones are the completeness, stability, and flexibility of cognitive structures compared to organic ones, as expressed in the following passage:

Here, then, is the conclusion of this summary of our guiding hypotheses. The living organization, is an equilibrated system (even if one avoids the term and substitutes Bertalanffy's "stable states in an open system"). But this organic equilibrium only represents a relative sort of stability in those very fields where it is best protected. The genome is isolated to the maximum degree from its environment, although it cannot be so completely; its equilibrium is nevertheless upset by mutations, etc., despite these ideal conditions. The epigenetic system is more open, but it finds its equilibrium by means of a number of processes, among them homeorrhesis. Physiological systems are even more "open," and yet they react by homeostasis of the interior environment—an environment all the more remarkably stable as the various animal groups are evolved and differentiated. The role of the nervous system is to be open to external stimuli and to react to them by means of its effectors; its increasing mobility does not prevent there being remarkably mobile equilibrium in the overall reactions. Finally, behavior is at the mercy of every possible disequilibrating factor, since it is always dependent on an environment which has no fixed limits and is constantly fluctuating. Thus, the autoregulatory function of the cognitive mechanisms produces the most highly stabilized equilibrium forms found in any living creature, namely, the structures of the intelligence, whose logico-mathematical operations have been of inescapable importance ever since human civilization reached the stage of being consciously aware of them. (Piaget, 1967/1971, pp. 36–37)

One further difference between biological and cognitive adaptation ought to be mentioned here: "The outstanding characteristic of cognitive organization is the progressive dissociation of form and content" (Piaget, 1967/1971, p. 153). This difference will be discussed in the following.

The matter becomes even more complicated with the introduction of the social dimension into cognition. Up to 1928, Piaget used to believe that interactions with others helped the child in moving out of egocentrism and developing increasing decentration (e.g., considering the self as part of the world instead of its center). But, at the annual meeting of the French Philosophical Society in 1928, the French developmental psychologist, Henri Wallon (1928), in his comments on Piaget's paper, advised him,

> "Instead of making of sociability, the agent and the factor of relational thinking, I would reverse the terms, I would say that, when, due to organic development, the child has become capable of holding together two different points of view, that is to say capable of those (extremely complicated) mental operations consisting of retaining from a given situation only certain elements, in other words of inhibiting, somehow, the representation of everything else, so that the child can constitute systems of relationships that are no longer those continuous wholes, those dynamic situations from which the child started, then (and only then) could his sociability be transformed into relational thought" (p. 133).

The discussion with Wallon (1928) demarcates an important reversal in Piaget's thinking. After this 1928 conference, Piaget replaced the idea that socialization is the causal factor of mental development with the idea that mental development is the causal factor of socialization. But, in the meantime, he leaned on the empiricist approach according to which the milieu is the cause of mental development. As Wallon said toward the end of his discussion, "Instead of explaining the emergence of our logic (adult logic) in the child by a progress in sociability, I would explain sociability by advances in mental abilities," (p. 136) which is a genetic rationalistic perspective that Piaget developed in the '40s and '50s.

As the discussion up to this point has made clear, Piaget's (1963/1968) position on the mind-body problem is very confusing up to his last chapter in the first volume, "History and Methods," of his *Traité de psychologie expérimentale*, jointly edited with the French Paul Fraisse, in which he presents his own version of the psycho-physical parallelism. This version, however, is not coherent with his general views on the continuity between cognitive mental processes and organic adaptation. The locus of mind is neither in society, as in Vygotsky's (1978, 1986) position, nor in the body, as in most psychological theories for which mind and brain are one and the same. There is only a transformation in the coordination of organs such as to create a differentiation of form from content that emerges gradually from various increasingly open forms of equilibrium between the organism and its environment.

This differentiation of form from content involves three interrelated claims: (a) there are three levels of consciousness; (b) there is a movement from practical success to conceptual understanding; and (c) there exists a psychophysical parallelism. The three levels of consciousness are distinguished from one another in the extent to which the subject becomes aware of one's own functioning. The first level, or *practical consciousness*, appears during the sensorimotor period and is unreflective. It is the mere awareness of the success or failure of an action (means-ends coordination). The second level (which is characteristic of the period of concrete operations) can be defined as *conceptual consciousness*. It is a form of reflection that increases the mobility and the reversibility of intelligence. The third level marks the passage to *reflective consciousness*. It involves not only the capacity to coordinate, but also that of taking one's own functioning as an object of consciousness, which is an operation upon an operation. This can only be achieved with the advent of formal operations.

The movement from practical success to conceptual understanding is necessary, within Piaget's system, to explain the distinction between practical intelligence aiming at success only, and conceptual intelligence aiming at understanding. For Piaget, practical intelligence develops prior to and forms a necessary condition for conceptual intelligence, but stays behind in the understanding of success because its consciousness is more directed toward the external object than toward its inner mechanism. Therefore, the grasp of consciousness inverts the order of construction and is a rather late by-product of formal operations and their complete reversibility and reflexivity. As such, it is necessarily based upon (a) a differentiation of form and content, and (b) an augmented anticipation of possible states of affairs due to the optimizing principle of equilibration.

MINDING THE BODY

This long detour through the mind-body problem and the question of consciousness was necessary to understand how, for Piaget, the passage from action to thought is made possible. It is the after-effect of the means-ends distinction at the very sensorimotor level, as we shall now see. This very first form of consciousness determines the passage from action to thought in many different ways: (a) the attachment of truth-values; (b) the intermalization of actions into symbols by mental imitation; (c) mental imagery; and (d) the notion of self as "corps propre" (Körper-Leib distinction in German adapted to French).

The attachment of truth-values to actions is made possible by the means-ends distinction typical of the first level of consciousness. This practical level of consciousness is marked by the awareness of success and failure of an action, on the one hand, and by the constitution of functional invariants on the other. That is to say that the child is capable of making distinctions between instances in which the same object is seen twice (repetition) and instances in which two similar objects are seen once (equivalence). These invariants can be considered as innate, learned, or constructed. If they were innate, they would be triggered by an external stimulus during an internally determined period of sensitivity to this stimulus (as in the case of the red dot or the male stickleback, during spawning-season), aptly called the "critical period." Actual observations tend to demonstrate that this is never the case in mental development.

If the invariants were learned, they would appear according to a schedule of reinforcements and exercises (which has not yet been demonstrated) and not according to a logic progressing from the simple to the complex, such as they appear to follow.

A movement from simplicity to complexity would be the best evidence in favor of logical construction of these invariants. This is because going from simple to complex is, indeed, logical; it is also a construction as something is simple or complex relative to a subject. The fact that something is simple for the subject means that something mobilizes readily available resources and knowledge in the subject effortlessly, whereas something complex requires considerably more resources and knowledge both quantitatively and qualitatively (e.g., more elaborate structures). This also means that more advanced forms of reasoning and thinking presuppose only logically and not actually physically verified forms of inferior complexity. This logical argument takes care of the biological "missing link" or the sociological "lost tribe." In logic, all links and articulations should be present.

According to this hypothesis, universals are the expression neither of an innate structure nor of reinforcements of an empirical sequence, but the outcome of an increasing coordination of actions not only as witnessed in counting, but also in the domain of giving meaning to space and time, classes and series, and causality and implication. Object permanence is the practical result of the group of displacements representing a complex coordination of the movements of the self (body), the object, and the screens covering up the object with their ensuring consequences. It also requires the distinction between bodily movements made significant as self-actions and object movements.

Thus, symbolic development consists in the child's construction of more consistent and more complete systems of procedures to transform sensorimotor signification into symbolic operations. This transformation consists in the gradual internalization of bodily actions. But the body here is what the German language calls "LEIB" by opposition to "KÖRPER." *Leib* is the body animated by the self, whereas *Körper* is the objective external body. Since this distinction does not exist in French, which has only one word (*corps*), Piaget (following others) called this "inner" body "*corps propre*" (one's own body). Given the symmetry of the human body both in sensory (two eyes, two ears) and motor (two arms, two legs, two hands) action, human universals tend to rely on symmetrical structures of thought such as reversibility at the most abstract level. This is not the place to dwell on these axes of symmetry, both bilateral, but also vertical, as witnessed by the opposition between head and feet with the waist as the central point of this axis. But it should be noted that our universals would have probably been entirely different if we had different bodies.

Nevertheless, what is important to notice is the fact that symbols are the product of the relation between self-regulated actions and physical object. Action feeds into predication. This process is the semantic side of the logic of action. It accounts for surprises. A child is surprised whenever the world does not behave according to the child's expectations. A number of rhythmic regulations and operations are expected from a meaningful environment predicated as a unique object; however, a child also has many procedures at hand to test the hypotheses made about the environment, such as removing a screen, counting, and so forth. Action is no longer efficient only; it becomes informative. That information is, in turn, coded in symbols, mental images, and so forth. It should be noted here, however, that each of these symbols represents a transformation from a previous state in a sort of Boolean algebra of opposites: tall is opposed to short on the figurative[1] side of things, just as standing is opposed to lying on the operative[2] side. Figurativity is the sedimentation of former forms of operativity that have become automatized. In every instance, however, the *corps propre* (one's own body) plays the essential of a standard according to which everything is measured; therefore, thinking, in the end, means minding the body.

From this perspective, the body plays the most central role, because it is the place where the mind is articulated in interaction with the environment. The body is part of the environment or the world, but it is also the place where the mind comes to the world. This can be shown developmentally, since, at first, the baby lives in a state of adualism as J. M. Baldwin (1896) first noticed. Self and other, self and world are one without boundaries or limits. Then, the body becomes the model of all actions and capable of all actions upon the environment by progressive differentiation. The distinction between the realm of action of the body upon the environment, which results in the differentiation of means and ends at the practical level, comes later. With symbol formation, the deepening of the gap between self and its inner world and the outside reality becomes qualitatively different. With representation, the child enters the world of make-believe, tales, dreams, plays, drawing, and imitation that all make present in the mind what is absent in reality. By the same token, self-awareness becomes possible, and that is the starting point of reflection, which will be so important for further developments, because every step further in the direction of external reality becomes, at the same time, a step further in the direction of internal self, as is demonstrated in Piaget's (1937/1954) drawing in the last chapter of his book, *The Construction of Reality*.

In this process of complementary assimilation and accommodation, however, reality and self become more and more differentiated in the sense that accommodation no longer remains at the surface of experience, but instead penetrates more and more into the inner structure of matter seeking regularities under the chaos of experience. At the same time, that assimilation, instead of remaining egocentric, seeks to embody external phenomena to the inner, most intimate structures of intelligence—that is to say, a deductible arbitrary system of signs whose meaning was given during evolution (both ontogenetic and phylogenetic) in social coaction and cooperation with other sign-users and exchangers.

CONCLUSION

As the analysis of Piaget's view on the mind-body problem has shown, his position is far away from positions such as "The Synaptic Self" of Joseph Le Doux (2002), according to which you are what your synapses tell you to be, or that of computational psychology, for which the psychophysical parallelism is equivalent to the software-hardware division in computers; however, it is also different from the Vygotskyan tradition. Piaget's position encompasses both the social dimension of bodily productions (including language) and the biological one, whereas the Vygotskyan approach accounts for the internalization of the communicative value of linguistic signs only, and not for the fact that society and culture are the continuation (by other means indeed) of species and nature. According to Vygotsky (1987), as well as Saussure (1972), the arbitrariness of signs makes them radically different from nature.

By contrast, Piaget's approach—by its very focus on the sensorimotor origin of all forms of knowledge and their gradual transformation in indices, symbols, and signs from the mere initial sensorimotor implication involved in action—demonstrates beyond any doubt the existence of a lineal ascent from action to concept (through representation and semiotic functioning) by the processes of reflective abstraction and optimising equilibration. This equilibration is made possible by two processes of transformation: (a) equilibration, properly speaking, and (b) the intra-inter-trans mechanism of transition. In equilibration, the growth of knowledge goes from (a) reequilibration after perturbation to (b) reequilibration by integration of the perturbation and (c) reequilibration by anticipation of possible variations. In the second process, it goes from intraobjectal to interobjectal and transobjectal. Thus, it goes from knowledge in the course of bodily action (sensorimotor object analysis) to interrelations between a present action and a represented one (semiotic relations and transformations) to transrelations at the most abstract level (formal structures).

ENDNOTES

1. Figurative Knowledge: Knowledge that focuses on the external, figural aspect of an event in a static manner, closely tied to a particular accommodation and as illustrated in perception, imitation, image, memory. Figurative knowledge is conceivable only within a framework of operative knowing.

2. Operativity: Contrasted with figurative knowledge, it implies the action aspect of intelligence at all periods, including sensorimotor intelligence. Operativity is the essential, generalizable structuring aspect of intelligence insofar as knowing means constructing, transforming, incorporating, and so forth.

REFERENCES

Baldwin, J. M. (1896). *Mental development in the child and the race.* New York: McMillan.

Bergson, H. (1994). *Matter and memory.* New York: Zone Books. (Original work published 1896)

Bringuier, J. C. (1977). *Conversations libres avec Jean Piaget* [Free conversations with Jean Piaget]. Paris: R. Laffont.

Bühler, K. (1908). Tatsachen und Probleme zu einer Psychologie der Denkvorgänge [Facts and problems of a psychology of thought]. *Archiv für die Gesamte Psychologie, 12,* 1–92.

Durkheim, E. (1968). *Les formes élémentaires de la vie religieuse* [The elementary forms of religious life] (5th ed.). Paris: Presses Universitaires de France.

Gallese, V. (2000a). The acting subject: towards the neural basis of social cognition. In T. Metzinger (Ed.), *Neural correlates of consciousness* (pp. 325–334). Cambridge: MIT Press.

Gallese, V. (2000b). The 'shared manifold hypothesis': From mirror neurons to empathy. *Journal of Consciousness Studies, 8,* 33–50.

Gruber, H. E., Girgus, J., & Banuazizi, A. (1971). The development of object permanence in the cat. *Developmental Psychology, 4,* 9–15.

Hegel, G. W. F. (1821). *Grundlinien der Philosophie des Rechts* [Basic principles of the philosophy of law]. Frankfurt am Main: Ullstein.

Husserl, E. (1913). *Prolegomena zur reinen Logik* [Prolegomena to pure logic]. Halle: Niemeyer.

Kant, I. (1781). *Kritik der reiner Vernunft* [Critique of pure reason]. Leipzig: Reclam.

Köhler, W. (1938). *The place of value in a world of facts.* New York: Liveright.

Kosslyn, A. (1994). *Image and brain: The resolution of the imagery debate.* Cambridge, MA: MIT. Press.

Lalande, A. (1893). *Lectures sur la philosophie des sciences.* Paris: Alcan.

Le Doux, J. E. (2002). *Synaptic self: How our brains become who we are.* New York: Viking.

Merleau-Ponty, M. (1963). *The structure of behavior.* Boston: Beacon Press. (Original work published in 1942).

Overton, W. F. (2004). A relational and embodied perspective on resolving psychology's antimonies. In J. Carpendale, & U. Müller (Eds.), *Social interaction and the development of knowledge* (pp. 19–44). Mahwah, NJ: Lawrence Erlbaum Associates.

Piaget, J. (1932). *The moral judgment of the child.* London: Kegan Paul Trench Trubner.

Piaget, J. (1942). Les trois structures fondamentales de la vie psychique: Rythme, regulation et groupement [The three fundamental structures of psychic life: Rhythm, regulation, and grouping]. *Revue Suisse de Psychologie et de Psychologie Appliquée, 1–2,* 9–21.

Piaget, J. (1950). *L'épistémologie génétique. Tome 1: La pensée mathématique* [Genetic epistemology. Volume 1: Mathematical thinking]. Paris: Press Universitaires de France.

Piaget, J. (1952). *The origins of intelligence.* Neuchâtel, New York: International University Press Inc. (Original work published 1936)

Piaget, J. (1954). *The construction of reality in the child* (M. Cook, Trans.). New York: Basic Books. (Original work published in 1937)

Piaget, J. (1968). Explanation in psychology and psychophysiological parallelism. In P. Fraisse & J. Piaget (Eds.), *Experimental psychology: Its scope and method: Vol. 1. History and method* (pp. 153–191). London: Routledge & Kegan Paul. (Original work published 1963)

Piaget, J. (1968). *Structuralism.* (C. Maschler, Trans.). London: Routledge & Kegan Paul. (Original work published 1968)

Piaget, J. (1969). *The mechanisms of perception* (G. N. Seagrim, Trans.). New York: Basic Books. (Original work published 1961)

Piaget, J. (1971). *Biology and knowledge.* Chicago: The University of Chicago Press. (Original work published 1967)

Piaget, J., & De La Harpe, J. (1928). *Immanence et transcendance: Deux types d'attitudes religieuses* [Immanence and transcendence: Two types of religious attitudes]. Genève: Association chrétienne d'étudiants de Suisse romande.

Piaget, J., & Inhelder, B. (1967). *The child's conception of space* (F. J. Langdon & J. L. Lunzer, Trans.). New York: W. W. Norton & Company. (Original work published in 1948)

Piaget, J., & Inhelder, B. (1973). *Memory and intelligence* (A. J. Pomerans, Trans.). London: Routledge & Kegan Paul. (Original work published 1968)

Popper, K. (1928). *Die methodenfrage der denkpsychologie.* Unpublished doctoral dissertation. Vienna.

Povinelli, D. J., Gallup, J., Eddy, T. J., & Bierschwale, D. T. (1997). Chimpanzees recognize themselves in mirrors. *Animal Behavior, 53,* 1083–1088.

Saussure, F. de (1972). *Cours de linguistique générale.* Paris: Payot.

Vygotsky, L. S. (1978). *Mind in society: The development of higher psychological processes.* Cambridge MA: Harvard University Press.

Vygotsky, L. S. (1986). *Thought and language.* Cambridge: MIT Press.

Vygotsky, L. S. (1987). *The collected works of L .S. Vygotsky: Problems of general psychology: Vol. 1.* New York: Plenum.

Wallon, H. (1928). Discussion d'une communication de Piaget: Les trois systèmes de la pensée de l'enfant [Discussion of a speech of Piaget: The three systems of infant thought]. *Bulletin de la Société Française de Philosophie, 28,* 97–141.

Wertsch, J. (Ed.) (1985). *Culture, communication and cognition.* New York: Cambridge University Press.

5

GROUNDED IN THE WORLD: DEVELOPMENTAL ORIGINS OF THE EMBODIED MIND

Esther Thelen

Indiana University

Piaget's (1952) question of how the adult mind emerges from the sensorimotor infant is still the framing issue for developmental psychology. Here I suggest that real-life skill is better understood if the sensorimotor origins of cognition are not abandoned. Skilled people are not only better at both abstract and logical thinking but also at processing the world "online" and, most important, seamlessly and rapidly shifting between the two modes. I illustrate the tight coupling between action, perception, and cognition in early life and propose that this coupling remains but becomes more flexibly adaptive. Further, I show that the language of dynamics is appropriate to capture these mind–body–world interconnections.

Contemporary developmental psychologists are still asking the same questions that have intrigued philosophers and scientists since ancient times: How does the human mind, in all its power and imagination, emerge from a squiggly, crying, drooling creature, the infant? How can people do mathematics, paint pictures, write poetry, play music, create laws, and build cities when we start out so unformed and helpless? From where can these immense talents come?

We owe our contemporary framing of the question most directly to Jean Piaget. Piaget's epistemological goal was to understand how abstract, formal, logical thought—a hallmark of human cognition— could arise from the here-and-now sensorimotor activities of infants. When contemporary developmentalists talk about the shift from perceptual to conceptual processing (e.g., Mandler, 1988), infants as theorists (e.g., Gopnick & Meltzoff, 1996), innate knowledge modules (e.g., Spelke, Breinlinger, Macomber, & Jacobson, 1992), representational redescription (Karmiloff-Smith, 1992), or hierarchies of skills (Fischer, 1980), they are echoing Piaget's agenda: How does human mental activity rise above the immediacy of the senses? How does human cognition go beyond simple associations between stimulus and response? How do children form categories, learn language, make plans, manipulate numbers, remember stories, and understand the actions of other people?

One of our legacies from Piaget is a highly elaborated theory of how this transformation from infant to thinker comes about. Many of the details of his theory have been debated for several decades. It is no matter. I believe that another aspect of Piaget's legacy is equally fundamental. This is Piaget's foundational assumption that the goal of development is for human thought to be increasingly abstract and distanced from its precursors, perception and action. The abstract concept of *object,* for instance, is only fully realized once infants can be freed of their immediate actions on the world (Piaget, 1954). Likewise, logical operations are only fully elaborated when children can ignore the direct evidence of their senses, moving beyond their initial egocentrisms. In the strictest sense, Piaget asked that children rise above what James (1890/1950) called "a teeming multiplicity of objects and relations" (p. 224) into the realm of pure and formal relations. In Piaget's view, sensorimotor operations are critical as the transducers of the logic of the world into the logic of the mind, but once children possess such formal means, perceiving and acting are but bystanders in the structure of behavior.

In our time, most researchers in cognitive development accept Piaget's assumptions and his hierarchy of mental values. Behavior that can be explained as "merely perceptual" or "only motor" is sometimes disdained as simple and primitive. Developmental progress, in turn, is measured by the diminishing distance toward abstract conceptual knowledge and rich theories. Some theorists believe that perception and action are too impoverished to lead to abstract thought and language, which must instead be embedded in the brain by evolution as specially dedicated modules (e.g., Pinker, 1994). In many cases, the contemporary agenda is to describe the content and structure of mind in its most pure and abstract forms.

There is little disagreement on the importance of Piaget's (1952) issue, that is, how the adult mind emerges from early perception and action. Many, including myself, also accept his epigenetic, developmental account of how more can come from less. However, I want to question the equally pervasive acceptance of Piaget's assumption that the endpoint of development is increasingly abstract reasoning, formal logic, or elaborated knowledge structures and that, as a consequence, perceiving and acting become mere bystanders. I instead argue for the grounding of mental activity in continually perceiving the world and acting in it, not just in the initial state but throughout life. I follow in the tradition of James (1890/1950), Merleau-Ponty (1963), Gibson (1969), and a growing group of psychologists, philosophers, linguists, and cognitive scientists who seek to understand how human cognition is truly embodied (e.g., Almássy, Edelman, & Sporns, 1998; Ballard, Hayhoe, Pook, & Rao, 1997; Brooks, 1991; Chiel & Beer, 1997; Clark, 1997; Damasio, 1994; Edelman, 1987; Fogel, 1993; Glenberg, 1997; Johnson, 1987; Lakoff, 1987; Talmy, 1988; Thelen, 1995; Thelen & Smith 1994; van Gelder, 1998; Varela, Thompson, & Rosch, 1991).

To say that cognition is *embodied* means that it arises from bodily interactions with the world and is continually meshed with them. From this point of view, therefore, cognition depends on the kinds of experiences that come from having a body with particular perceptual and motor capabilities that are inseparably linked and that together form the matrix within which reasoning, memory, emotion, language, and all other aspects of mental life are embedded. The developmental issue, as I argue in this article, becomes not so much to describe the purely abstract structures of the mind but to understand the emergence of a dynamic and flexible coupling between direct and online cognition and cognition that is less tightly coupled to the input.

BEING SKILLED

One of the recurring criticisms of Piaget is that he was only concerned with a limited part of human existence, the abstract, logical, and rational part (e.g., Shweder, 1984). If true, the post-Piagetian challenge is to find a theory of development that can account for the range of human activity as people do what they do in everyday life. So what do we do? We jump out of bed, take a shower, make breakfast, pack lunches for the children, drive to work, discuss the game with our colleagues, shop at the supermarket, read the newspaper, and go to the gym. We go on vacations and visit family, swim, ski, look at old buildings, or read bad novels. As academics or researchers, if we are lucky, we may spend several hours sitting before a computer screen filled with numbers or words. Occasionally, life demands from us very difficult decisions such as whether to buy a house, where to send our children to school, or whether our parents need to go into a nursing home. Some of our activities are thus abstract and logical, but many are not. Even those of us privileged to work with data and ideas spend much of our time just doing: monitoring, planning, conversing, and moving.

Now consider what it takes to be skilled, not just at the abstract tasks, but in the whole range of things that people actually do all day. What are the general characteristics of skilled people whether they are doing manual labor, making policy decisions, engaged in a musical or sport performance, or taking care of children? Here are some general characteristics of skilled actions:

1. Skilled people are adept at assessing the current situation or noticing the relevant stimuli in the physical and social environment.
2. Skilled people are adept at recalling from memory similar but not identical situations, using their past experience, and choosing an action that fits their current situation. The fit in this case requires a flexible and generative response, perhaps similar to, but not identical with, the category of responses used in the past.
3. Skilled people thus have consistent behavior in similar situations but are good at changing their actions rapidly and appropriately when the situation changes.

Note that, by this definition, being skilled is a question not only of how abstract or logical one's thoughts are but of how responsive and adaptive one's behavior is.

By this definition, infants and young children are not very skilled. They may not yet have learned how to perceptually discriminate what a particular context affords and demands. Their processing of information may be a bit slow. They do not have a large store of memories, or knowledge, of similar situations. They may be poor at extracting a category of responses from their memories, or they may rely on a previously used solution that may be close but not good enough. So the developmental question centers on how infants and children acquire this whole range of talents we call skill.

AN ABSTRACT THEORY OF SKILL

How can we begin to think about the development of real-world skill, not just formal, abstract thinking but also graceful, adaptive acting? We need to revise some old views first. In strict information-processing and engineering views, our interactions with the environment proceed as in the top panel of Figure 5.1. The world is out there, provides information to our senses, which is processed by our central nervous system, which then commands the body to act in particular ways. The mind mediates between the world and the body. We become more skilled, in this view, as the mind develops a bigger store of control devices, modules, and representations. We can attempt to describe these structures of mind, but having such a catalog does not inform us about the processes people use for their fluid, everyday skills.

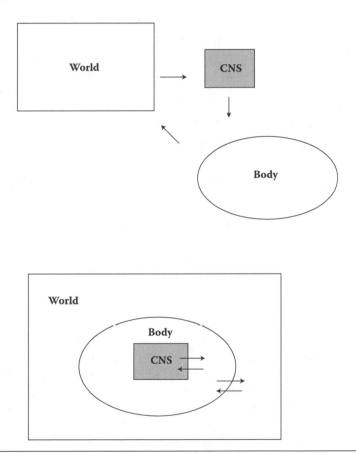

FIGURE 5.1 Two views of the relations among the nervous system, the body, and the world. Top panel: The world delivers information to the nervous system (NS), which directs the body, which interacts with the world. Bottom panel: The three components as nested and coupled dynamic systems, where the interactions are continual and bidirectional. Adapted from *Trends in Neuroscience, 20,* H. J. Chiel & R. D. Beer, "The brain has a body: Adaptive behavior emerges from interactions of nervous system, body, and environment," 553–557, Copyright 1997, with permission from Elsevier Science.

For a different way of thinking, let us rearrange the boxes and the arrows as in the bottom panel in Figure 1, a depiction first used by Beer (e.g., Chiel & Beer, 1997). Here the components are not serial or hierarchical elements but deeply embedded and continuously coupled dynamic systems. The nervous system is a dynamic system embedded in and coupled to the body, a dynamic system, and together they are embedded in and coupled to the environment (Chiel & Beer, 1997).

There are three critical features of such an embedded and coupled system that together distinguish it from the traditional input–output model. First, the system is multiply causal and self-organizing. This means that behavior is an emergent pattern of multiple cooperating components, all of which count and none of which are privileged. It is the relation of the multiple parts that gives the system order and pattern. This is what is meant by self-organizing. The mind simply does not exist as something decoupled from the body and the environment in which it resides. Second, a dynamic system exists as patterns in time, such that the current state is a function of previous states (both in the immediate and more distant past) and, in turn, is the basis of future states. Our view of cognition and development changes profoundly when we consider everything as processes in time rather than as static structures and modules. Third, the time-based system can vary in its relative stability. The stability is determined by how tightly the components cohere. For change to occur, the system needs to lose stability so that the elements are free to form new patterns. Development involves continual shifts in the pattern stability: times when the system is quite stable and other times when new combinations arise.

The critical implication of this dynamic conceptualization is that nervous system, body, and environment are always embedded and coupled dynamic systems. They start out that way, and there is no point in development and no context when they are not embedded and coupled. What can change is the nature of the coupling. In skilled behavior, the coupling is highly flexible and is dynamically responsive to the task. For instance, there are times when mental activity and body are very tightly linked to the environment, such as when driving down a winding mountain road at night in a rainstorm, cooking an elaborate meal, or being engaged in a social discussion. At times like these, you cannot easily isolate your thinking from the immediate task at hand; you may risk missing the turn, scorching the sauce, or making an embarrassing social mistake. However, there are also times when the mind-to-environment coupling is very tight and the body coupling is less; for example, I think of watching an engrossing movie and being oblivious to my foot falling asleep. Then, of course, there are those moments when contemplation takes over and we try shut out both world and body, such as in states of concentration, meditation, or daydreaming, often even closing our eyes to avoid distractions from the sights around us. Again, being skilled is not just having these moments of more protected mental activity but being able to rapidly and appropriately change the coupling strengths. Imagine driving down the freeway on a nice day, mentally planning your next lecture when a large deer suddenly bounds in front of the car. Too much contemplation might be fatal! What is adaptive one second is not necessarily adaptive the next. Similarly, social skill completely depends on an intricate ability to sense your partner's vocal and postural changes as they happen at the same time you plan your responses in the social dialogue.

A second implication is that, in the initial state, the components of the system are coupled in a particular and obligatory way and that development consists of the progressive ability to modulate the coupling so as to meet different and changing situations. Development means acquiring not only better offline processes but also better online ones and, most important, the ability to seamlessly shift between them. So the critical skills are being able to categorize the world to flexibly and rapidly recruit useful categories of activities within it and, thus, to make mental plans based on prior experience before actually acting when required but also acting very quickly without a lot of hesitation when that is necessary.

It is precisely the continuity in time of the embedded and coupled dynamic systems essential for fluid, adaptive behavior that gives meaning to the notion of an *embodied cognition*. There is no point in time when these dynamic processes stop and something else takes over. Thus, there are good reasons to believe in not only the sensorimotor origins of cognition but in the intimate and inextricable mesh between thinking and acting throughout life. Thinking begins in perceiving and acting and retains the signatures of its origins forever. The goal of development is not to rise above the mere sensorimotor but for cognition to be at home within the body.

DISTRIBUTED AND EMBODIED PROCESSES IN THE BRAIN

I argue for a distributed, multiply determined cognition, where the lines between perceiving and acting and between remembering and planning are blurred and shifting like drops of oil on a puddle. Before discussing the behavioral evidence for my claims, I ask about their biological plausibility: Does what we know about the brain support such a picture? If you read the literature in the new discipline of cognitive neuroscience or even pick up the local newspaper, you will see beautiful pictures of local areas of the brain "lighting up" as people do various tasks. There is an equally interesting and large literature in neuropsychology that relates particular cognitive and emotional deficits to specific regions in the brain. Taken together, this work depicts the brain as many functionally and anatomically specific connected local areas or modules, each dedicated to processing information for an encapsulated domain: areas for language, spatial vision, numerical reasoning, remembering faces, and so on. Some have also argued that this anatomical specificity is innate and the specific means by which evolution has provided for some uniquely human qualities (Fodor, 1983; Pinker, 1994).

However, there is also another picture of brain structure and function, one that is perfectly consistent with a coupled and embedded, time-based dynamic system. First, the evidence for locality from imaging studies and brain lesions, largely garnered from well-practiced adults, must be viewed in light of equally important evidence for the graded, distributed, and interactive nature of human information processing (Farah, 1994). Anatomical specialization of function is just one side of the picture. The other is represented by Figure 5.2, which is one example of the dense interconnectivity of the brain: a simplified depiction of connectivity in the visual system.

The nature of these complex connections, in the terminology used by Edelman (1987, 1993), is that they are *reentrant* and *degenerate*. *Reentry* means that the stream of processing is not one way, or even parallel, but densely interwoven such that the output of one tract is fed back on itself—output is also input. *Degeneracy* means that neural processing is multiply determined: There is no one dedicated pathway to do anything. Any network may participate in multiple tasks at the same time that a single task may be accomplished by many different routes. Figure 5.3 illustrates how connections can be reentrant and degenerate. (The boxes and arrows are often the best we can do, but they are inadequate representations for these continuously active, shifting patterns of neural activity. Perhaps a better metaphor would be a landscape of undulating waves and basins.) Most important, it is impossible in such a system to identify serial or hierarchical causality or even "first principles" that motivate behavior.

A second feature of this densely interconnected brain is that major portions are dedicated to the reason we have a brain—to move the body (Georgopolous, 1995). Consider any planful decision to act—what we actually do nearly all of the time; we think to move. However deliberative the process, the ultimate job of the central nervous system is to move the body, including the muscles of speech. The issue is how the multiple

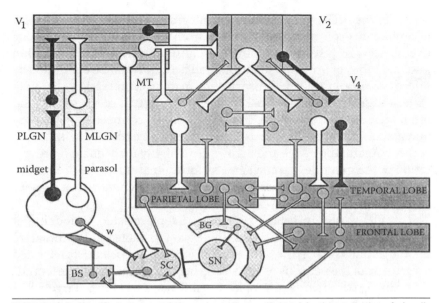

FIGURE 5.2 Simplified diagram of the major pathways invloved in the generation of visually guided saccadic eye movements, illustrating widely distributed multiple excitatory and inhibitory connections. For details, see Felleman and van Essen (1991). V1, V2, and V4 = areas of visual cortex; PLGN and MLGN = parvocellular and magnocellular portions of the lateral geniculate nucleus; SC = superior collicular; BG = basal ganglia; SN = substantia nigra; BS = brainstem. Redrawn from *A Dynamic Systems Approach to the Development of Cognition and Action* by E. Thelen and L. B. Smith, 1994, Cambridge, MA: MIT Press. Copyright 1994 by MIT Press. Reprinted with permission. Original courtesy of Peter Schiller.

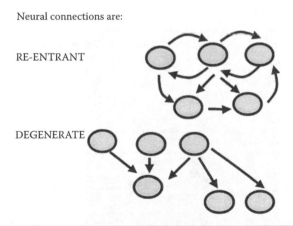

FIGURE 5.3 Neural connections are reentrant (many-to-one) and degenerate (one-to-many; terms used by Edelman, 1987).

inputs to the decision to act become integrated so that the muscles get unambiguous commands. Figure 5.4, from Edelman (1987), gives one overall view of just how this integration of current task information and memories of previous situations and actions could be continuously and dynamically cycled. Sensory information, from vision, hearing, taste, and so on, is continuously integrated with that of the sensed and moving body. The processing stream is multiply connected to memory and association areas as well as those primarily concerned with motor control. Again, the boxes and arrows are a highly inadequate representation of the multiple, parallel, and reciprocal nature of the process. In fact, even the most elementary distinctions between what is a sensory area and what is a motor area are blurred and overlapping.

This view of brain function can best be appreciated by looking at activity in multiple sites during a single task. In Table 5.1, I summarize 20 studies published in the last 5 years in which neuroscientists recorded directly from the neurons of awake and behaving monkeys. These studies all involved versions of simple reaching tasks where the targets had particular visual properties, the monkeys received specific instructions, or when the monkeys relied on memory over a short delay. The researchers then measured when particular neurons were active during

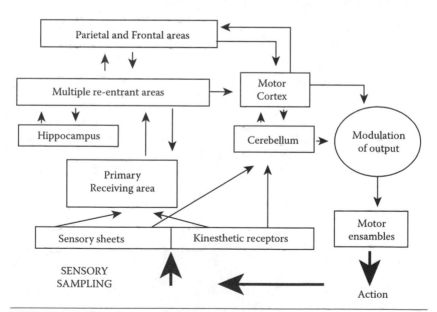

FIGURE 5.4 Multiple influences and parallel pathways form a continuous perception–action loop. Adapted from *Neural Darwinism,* by Gerald M. Edelman. Copyright © 1987 by Basic Books, Inc. Adapted by permission of Basic Books, a member of Perseus Books, L.L.C.

TABLE 5.1 Neural Activity in Four Brain Areas Related to Reaching Tasks

Neurons Encoding	Motor	Premotor	Parietal	Prefrontal
Visual stimulus				
Cue-based	12, 16	4, 10, 17	1, 11	4, 5, 13
Set-based	16	4, 17	1, 11	4, 5
Location-specific	16	10, 17	1, 11	5
Object matching				13
Look				
Eye position or saccades		2	1	5, 13
Delay				
Cue held over delay	12	4, 10, 12, 17	1, 11	4, 5, 13
Plan				
Active before movement onset	7, 8, 16	3, 4, 17	1, 11	4, 5
Reach				
Direction	6, 16	3, 17	1, 11	5
Force	9	15		
Arm posture	5, 17	10, 15	11, 15	
Somatosensory		10, 17		
Remember				
Memory of previous acts	16	17		13

Note: 1 = Anderson. Snyder, Bradley, and Xing (1979); 2 = Boussaoud (1995); 3 = Caminiti, Johnson, Galli, Ferraina, and Burnod (1991); 4 = diPelligrino and Wise (1993); 5 = Fuster (1989); 6 = Georgopoulous, Kettner, and Schwartz (1988); 7 = Georgopoulous, Crutcher, and Schwartz (1989); 8 = Georgopoulous, Lurito, Petrides, Schwartz, and Massey (1989); 9 = Georgopoulous, Ashe, Smyrnis, and Taira (1992); 10 = Graziano, Hu, and Gross (1997); 11 = Kalaska and Crammond (1995); 12 = Kettner, Macario, and Port (1996); 13 = Miller, Erickson, and Desimone (1996); 14 = Scott and Kalaska (1997); 15 = Scott, Sergio, and Kalaska (1997); 16 = Shen and Alexander (1997b); 17 = Shen and Alexander (1997a).

the various parts of the task: looking at the target, deciding where to move, remembering the instructions, and so on. Note that this kind of information cannot be obtained from imaging studies, which rely on subtractive techniques and thus report relative rather than absolute activity. The recorded areas were two classically motor areas, the primary motor cortex and premotor cortex; the parietal cortex, long thought to be an area of visual integration; and the prefrontal cortex, involved in many aspects of memory, planning, and higher cognitive functions.

The results of these studies show that traditional motor areas are not just coding movement. Likewise, in visual and association areas, neurons have both specialized and multiple sensitivities. Indeed, the very same neuron frequently responded to multiple aspects of the task: It fired when the visual stimulus was presented and fired again during the memory or motor decision time. Is this a visual neuron or a motor neuron or one representing the stimulus in memory? It does all of these things. The line between what is perception, what is action, and what is cognition is very hard to draw. Indeed, maybe we experience our existence in the world as seamless and integrated because the brain is everywhere processing that existence as seamless and integrated.

DEVELOPMENTAL IMPLICATIONS

Although the evidence of diffuse neuronal mapping comes from adult monkeys with thousands of trials of practice in the tasks involved, there are important developmental implications. Indeed, a cornerstone of Edelman's (1987, 1993) theory of neuronal development is that these networks of vastly interconnected areas are laid down very early in life as part of the epigenetic processes of neural development. These networks then form the matrix for experience-dependent changes and, in particular, synaptic strengthening and growth as part of a process whereby pathways that are simultaneously activated are selectively retained. The critical process is illustrated in the diagrams of Figure 5.5. Normal awake infants are continually looking and moving. Because of the dense overlapping networks in place from the beginning, simultaneous visual input and motor kinesthesia is mutually mapped; that is, pathways are selectively strengthened and retained (Figure 5.5a). At a second instance in time, another correlated experience of moving and looking forms another map, perhaps partially overlapping with the first because they hold some elements in common (Figure 5.5b). A third dynamic moment of experience is recorded in these overlapping networks, again with some pathways in common with the first two (Figure 5.5c). In time, a map of maps of similar experiences will emerge by itself, just from the infants' ordinary recurrent activities in the world, which are different from each other and also share things in common (Figure 5.5d). Following Edelman (1987), we can call this mapping of maps an *emergent perceptual motor category*. Like all categories, it is

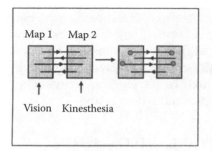

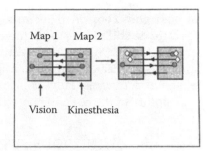

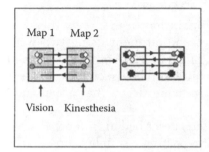

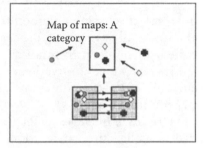

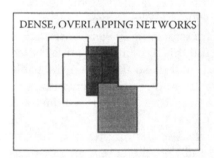

FIGURE 5.5 Multiple mapping leads to dense, overlapping, and higher order networks, which can be accessed by partial elements, a characteristic of categories.

both more abstract than the specific experiences that contributed to it and more general in that it can be accessed by only partial fragments, perhaps only aspects of the visual stimulus or the memory of the movement that were originally coded.

As infants' perceptual–motor experiences increase and become more varied, the nest of overlapping categories becomes both larger and more dense, as well as more abstract and general (Figure 5.5e). Because the system is dynamic and processes occur in parallel, people may seamlessly shift between mental activity that is abstract and "offline" and that which is tightly coupled to the immediate perceptual input. It is precisely this ability to shift that is the hallmark of skill. In this way, more abstract mental activity is not only constituted from perception and action but remains dynamically coupled to it. The important metric is not whether the mental activity is truly "conceptual" or merely "sensorimotor" but the flexibility of the coupling between thinking and acting.

BODY/NERVOUS-SYSTEM/ENVIRONMENT COUPLING IN INFANTS

So far, my discussion about embodiment has been largely theoretical. Now I illustrate this process of embodiment using two well-studied phenomena in infancy. The first is a 3-month-old's use of leg kicks to move an overhead mobile, and the second is Piaget's venerable A-not-B error, evidenced in babies when they are about 8 to 12 months of age.

In *Origins of Intelligence*, Piaget (1952) described his infants' discovery of so-called circular reactions, or repeating a simple action on the world to produce an interesting result: kicking the side of the crib to make a celluloid toy jiggle. In the 1970s, Carolyn Rovee-Collier initiated a landmark series of studies by transforming Piaget's observations into an experimental paradigm. She did this by connecting infants' legs by means of a ribbon to an overhead mobile so that when the babies kicked their legs, the mobile would move and provide them with interesting sights and sounds. Using this task, Rovee-Collier demonstrated remarkable abilities in infants of only 2½ to 3 months of age. At this young age, babies learn the task quickly. Within minutes they discover that their kicks activate the mobile, and they increase their rate of leg movements. Moreover, they remember what they have learned for a week or more and for a very long time if their memory is reactivated by the sight of the training mobile. In addition, babies can perceptually distinguish elements on the mobile and the environmental contexts under which they were trained, and they can, under the right circumstances, form simple categories and generalize the functional context to novel situations, given varied training (see reviews in Rovee-Collier, 1990, 1995, 1997). These experiments have given us remarkable insight to what infants can do and reveal what seem to be quite astonishing mental feats in babies who in everyday life seem to do very little in terms of voluntary actions.

Why is this experimental paradigm so potent? Why is there such good evidence of learning, memory, recognition, recall, categorization, and so on with this task and with no other?

I suggest here that the mobile task works because it is uniquely embodied. In particular, feats of seeming cognitive precocity emerge dynamically because of biomechanics and dynamics of leg kicking, a seemingly trivial and commonplace behavior. Early in my research career, I looked at the kinematic and neuromuscular organization of leg kicks in young infants. I discovered that these everyday infant movements indeed have considerable organization and pattern. First, the joints of the leg often move in a very coordinated fashion together. Second, kicking has a very beautiful temporal organization with the flexion and extension phases often being quite regular and each constrained to about half a second or a little longer, and the kicks themselves are patterned in rhythmical bouts. Third, this organization seems to arise from very minimal neuromuscular control (Thelen & Fisher, 1983b). All the baby needs to do is to contract a rather diffuse set of muscles at the onset of flexion and the anatomical and elastic qualities of the legs produce the rest, very much like stretching and releasing a spring.

The consequence of this intrinsic patterning is that the degree of freedom in leg movements is quite reduced, compared to say, arm movements. The hip joint has a much more reduced effective range of motion than the shoulder, and in young infants, arm movements rarely show the stereotyped rhythmicity and interjoint coordination characteristic of leg movements. What does this mean for the baby? First, it means that, in the kind of kinesthetic mapping I described earlier, the maps of legs may be much more well circumscribed than those of arms or other parts of the body: The input from the legs is much more patterned, regular, and vigorous in the first months. Thus, in the months before infants get the opportunity to control an overhead mobile, their frequent spontaneous but patterned movements have strengthened pathways associated with these movements and the other perceptual experiences associated with them. Second, because of the relative ease of controlling leg movements, such movements can be recruited by babies quite flexibly in service of the interesting result of moving the mobile. Indeed, when Donna Fisher and I (Thelen & Fisher, 1983a) studied how infants changed their movements to move the mobile, we discovered that they indeed used the simple patterns in a variety of adaptive ways. First, they kicked more frequently. This requires more frequent pulses of energy to activate the muscle. Second, they kicked harder to make the mobile move more. When they acquired the contingency, their movements were faster and more forceful. Again, this was a consequence of pumping more force into the muscles. However, they could also modulate activation between the legs. In a more recent experiment (Thelen, 1994), I tethered infants' legs together loosely with a piece of elastic, making it more efficient to switch from kicking with one leg or both legs alternately to in-phase, simultaneous kicking. Three-month-old infants were able to effectively change the timing and coordination of their bursts of activation to switch to more predominantly in-phase movements. Finally, they could also change the relative balance of flexor and extensor activation to discover and maintain a posture that was rewarding. Angulo-Kinzler, Ulrich, and Thelen (2002) designed a "high-tech" version of the mobile task by replacing the usual ribbon connecting the baby to the mobile with an "electronic" ribbon. Electronic sensors on the baby's legs detected the rotations of the joints and fed the information into a computer. The experimenter could thereby arrange the contingency so that the mobile only rewarded very specific patterns of movement or postures of the infants' legs, in this case highly flexed or very extended joints. Indeed, when given this task, 3-month-olds learned within several minutes to hold their legs in a highly flexed position or a more extended position, and some babies even learned the reversal. Moreover, preliminary results suggest that these learned postures may be remembered for several days.

Infants do so well in the mobile task because it takes advantage of a set of predictable, well-established, and easily modified movements. The mapping between vision and proprioception is highly facilitated, leading to an enhanced memory and categorization. Wonderful experiments by Rochat and Morgan (1995) provided additional support. In these experiments, infants were allowed to look at videos of their kicking legs either as they would actually see and feel them, that is where vision and proprioception were congruent, and videos where the spatial or temporal aspects of the movements were distorted, say where the left and right legs were reversed so that infants would kick the right leg, but the video would show the left leg extending. Infants demonstrated by their preferential looking that they could easily tell the difference. Months of perfectly coherent vision and movement strengthened those neural pathways where vision and proprioception overlap to establish a memory of what these movements should feel and look like, and infants were surprised when their expectations are violated. Again, I believe it was the very biomechanical and anatomical constraints on leg movements—their regular and rhythmic patterning—that facilitated these maps.

Such a dynamic view allows us to conceptualize the mobile-kicking experiments in a somewhat different light. Conventionally, we would think of the leg kicking as merely the manifestation of mental structures and processes inherent in the baby, a convenient way to demonstrate what the infants can and will do under these experimental conditions, an operant conveniently conditioned, like bar pressing in rats. A more embodied view is that recognition, long-term memory, recall, categorization, and generalization are absolutely created by our experiments themselves because of established multimodal perception–action maps already in place. Because these early areas are already primed through patterned spontaneous movement, accesses to higher order memory and association processes are enormously facilitated. These so-called higher processes are not just sitting there developing autonomously, waiting for connections to whatever output device gets hooked up. Rather, these processes themselves develop only through the reiterative mapping and remapping that is the emergent result of coherent experience. The seemingly happy choice of independent variables in infant experiments, looking times or kicking or sucking, are not accidental. Looking, kicking, and sucking are all actions that infants spontaneously do all the time and that have some regularities associated with them. When we bring infants into the laboratory and put them in situations where we "ask" them to demonstrate that they "know" something about visual displays or that they "remember" something about what happened in the last few moments or the last few days, we are truly conducting microgenesis experiments, creating with the task moments of knowing or moments of remembering. This is possible only because—by good luck or by trial and error—we happened upon perception–action loops with a history of patterned activation. This is why leg kicks, and not arm movements, are successful creators of higher order cognition at 3 months of age. Because arm movements are much less patterned, infants have less well-defined maps. In a few months, however, the situation changes: Legs become used less for free expression and manipulation and more for weight support and locomotion. Their mapping changes. At the same time, with the onset and improvements in reaching and grasping, these movements and their perceptual consequences become represented in a more general and more stable fashion. Again, not by accident, researchers switch independent variables to assess infant cognition from looking and kicking to reaching and grasping. It is an interesting and unexplored issue if, for example, 7- to 10-month-old infants would learn the mobile task using leg kicks with the same intensity and speed as 3-month-olds or whether with the remapped representations of the legs, the connections are less easily called forth.

The radical idea here is that the sophisticated skills shown by infants in the mobile task are created by the performance and not just reflected in the performance. I am suggesting that cognition is literally acquired from the outside in and depends on the strength and nature of the perceptual–motor pathways that access higher functions. The consequences are that, at least initially, cognitive skills are tightly linked with these modalities such that we cannot really assess the pure contents of mind. Nor can we say that infants can discriminate or categorize or remember abstracted from the way that they demonstrate these skills to us. Each time we ask infants to demonstrate what they "really know," we must also confront the real-time dynamics of the specific task, which include perceiving and moving limbs, head, and eyes.

EMBODIMENT IN PERSEVERATIVE REACHING

I have contended that the remarkable cognitive abilities discovered in early infancy are created online, so to speak, in the context of the perceptual–motor history of the infant and the experimental task itself, which links these well-used pathways with current perceptual input. I now turn to some experiments that give further insight into how this process of integration of perceptual–motor memory and visual task may actually occur. These come from a long series of studies done in collaboration with Linda Smith, Fred Diedrich, Bob Titzer, Melissa Clearfield, and others at Indiana University inspired by Piaget's classic A-not-B error, reinterpreted from a dynamic systems viewpoint.

As is well known, the A-not-B error occurs when infants, usually 8 to 10 months of age, after uncovering a hidden toy at one location, A, return to the original hiding place even after the toy is hidden at a second, close-by location, B. Although there have been so many experiments on the A-not-B error that one would think there is not a word left to say about it, it continues to intrigue and attract researchers. Another take on this simple baby trick is warranted because it illustrates in very clear form my argument about embodiment.

The heart of our reinterpretation is to discard the traditional ideas that the A-not-B task taps some kind of knowledge that the infants have about object permanence or that it reveals singular abilities or disabilities of spatial coding, search strategy, or object representation. Rather we focus entirely on the dynamics of the task: what infants do and what they have done. We believe we can explain both the typical versions of the task and the many contextual effects by coupled dynamic processes that are amenable to experimental manipulation.

In brief, we explain the error as emerging from repetitive perceptual–motor activity in novel or difficult contexts. By our account, repetitive activity strengthens the memory for a particular action, thereby increasing the likelihood that the action will be repeated again. The more consistent and repetitive the initial perceptual–motor acts, the more likely the perseverative behavior. The identical targets, we believe, constrain the movements and lead to more consistent reaching than in more familiar situations. In the manner that I described earlier, pathways are established as the infant reaches repeatedly that, in dynamic terms, act as an attractor, and the infant effectively gets "stuck" in the previously performed action. The heart of the explanation, therefore, is the multiple contributions of perception, action, and memory to the error and the importance of considering these behaviors over time (Smith, Thelen, Titzer, & McLin, 1999; Thelen, Schöner, Scheier, & Smith, 2001).

The flavor of the dynamic theory of the A-not-B error may best be communicated with a qualitative version of the formal model developed in collaboration with Gregor Schöner, Christian Scheier, and Linda Smith, followed by a few critical experimental results that echo the theme of cognitive embodiment.

We begin with a simple task analysis. As is well known, the A-not-B error occurs when infants reach to the wrong location to uncover a hidden object. Typically the task proceeds as follows (although there are numbers of variations). The baby sees a table or box with two, identically covered hiding wells. The experimenter calls attention to an attractive toy and hides it in Location A while the infant watches. Then there is a short delay of a few seconds, and the baby is allowed to reach for the toy. After a number of repetitions to the A side, the experimenter, again while the baby watches, hides the toy at Location B. Typically, under these standard conditions, 8- to 10-month-old infants, although they watched the toy being hidden at B stubbornly reach back to A, where they have reached before.

In our theory and model, we focus on what happens in the time when infants must decide whether to move their arms to the A side or B side, that is, after the toy is hidden or another cue is given and before the reach is initiated, typically with the imposed delay of a few seconds. In adult experiments where a movement is cued, this decision time, with or without a delay, is traditionally called the reaction time. Uniquely, however, we contend that this is a decision in so-called movement parameter space, where infants must activate whatever movement parameters that actually move the arm to one side or another. (By *movement parameters,* we mean the particular combination of muscles or balance of forces that infants have learned will activate their arms in a particular direction.) Many factors impact on this decision, as I detail in the following. However, as in any human behavior, the final common pathway for mental activity must be in this decision to move parts of the body, whether it be the arms and hands for manipulation, the gaze, or motor apparatus of speech. Thus, all of the perceptual inputs are represented in their corresponding action dimension.

We represent this movement space as a continuous field, with the relative activation as the height of the curve, as shown in the top of Figure 5.6. The activation represents the movement parameters needed to get the hand to the particular location of the target, which is represented as A or B, but could span the continuous distance between them. That is, they could be further or closer apart. For movement to actually occur, this activation must reach some threshold. Here I have shown what the field looks like when the infant faces the two identical covers and no toy has been hidden. If nothing else happens here, this would result in an equal probability to activate a reach to either A or to B, but neither is very compelling, and the threshold has not been reached. Indeed, when infants are just given the two covers and they have not been trained to reach to one side, they reach randomly and sometimes do not reach at all. In such a situation, there is a weak tendency to reach, and if a reach did occur, it would be equally likely to either direction.

The important feature of this decision field is that it evolves over time. This means it takes time to reach a decision, during which the activations change. The bottom graph in Figure 5.6 shows what the field

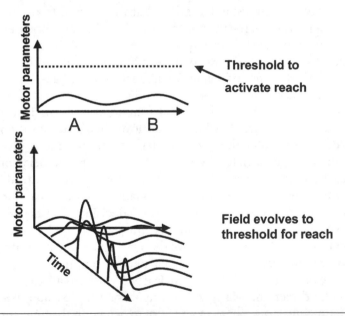

FIGURE 5.6 Top panel: A and B targets represented in a continuous movement space, showing probability of reaching to two identical, not very interesting targets. The activation must reach the threshold (dotted line) for the movement to occur. Bottom panel: Evolution of a decision to reach to A. The decision takes time and has a continuous evolution. Figures 5.6 through 5.9 are based on theory and simulations in Thelen et al. (2001).

looks like after the infant has been trained or cued to reach to the A side. With time, the field evolves to reach a decision threshold, and here the reach parameters are activated to the A side. The probability of a reach actually happening to A, therefore, is time dependent.

As I mentioned earlier, there are many factors that come together to generate this final motor decision. In the A-not-B model, we have considered three particular aspects of the task, the tonic and transient visual input provided to the baby and the infants' memories of their actions reaching to a location. These contributions can take on different values, depending on the experimental conditions. For example, the targets can be particularly bright and salient or they can blend into the background, the cue to move to one location to another can be highly attention grabbing or fleeting and weak, and the memory of previous reaches can have different strengths. The important feature of the model is that the particulars of the visual input and memory are integrated together to contribute to the dynamics of the decision field. Because the multiple contributions to this decision can take on different values and are time based, gradual, and coupled together in a dynamic way, a small change in one or more of these parameters can influence the decision of where to reach. Indeed, context dependency is the hallmark of the A-not-B task, and the model beautifully accounts for these contextual changes (see Thelen et al., 2001, for details and simulations).

In the model, the box and the hiding places are called the *task input*. This provides a continuous field of decision possibilities depending on the location and differing salience of the two targets at A and B. If the two covers are different, for example, one exerts a stronger pull to one location than the other even before any toy is hidden. In Figure 5.7, the task input is depicted as in the canonical A-not-B task, that is, as two equally activated locations. The second input is the cue to either target specified by hiding the toy, or by simply pointing out the location or waving the cover, and it is called the *specific input*. This is a transient input, which must be remembered once the event is over. Figure 5.7 shows the specific input to the A side. Thus, the first time the baby is cued to the A side, the decision field evolves under the perceptual influence of both the task environment and the cue, as shown in the bottom of Figure 5.7. As I stated earlier, these can take on different values; the A target can be more salient or the targets can be further apart, the cue can be more or less potent and so on, and these values change the probabilities that infants will reach to either target.

Once infants have generated a reach, we assume that the time-based system retains a memory of the act just performed, again in the movement parameter space of reaching. At the second reach to A this memory

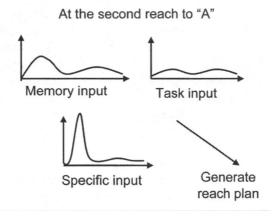

At the second reach to "A"

Memory input

Task input

Specific input

Generate
reach plan

FIGURE 5.7 Visual inputs to the decision to reach to A or B at the first reach. Top left panel: The two identical targets present a tonic input specifying either A or B. Top right panel: The cue (hiding the toy or waving the lid) gives the infant a transient specification of where to reach, which must be remembered over the delay. Bottom panel: The two inputs combine, here generating a reach to A.

joins in with the continuing task input and the cue to again contribute to the decision dynamics. The three sources of input to the decision are shown in Figure 5.8. As the second reach to A is generated, the memory of the action builds. After many reaches to A, the memory input is quite strong. Now, even if the cue is to the B side, after the transient effect of the B cue subsides, the field is dominated by the A memory, giving rise to the well-known reach back to A. This is illustrated in Figure 5.9. The action happens because the processes are continuous and take time.

The decision to move is thus a cognitive act. It is based on motivation, recent and longer term memory, and the qualities of the immediate visual input. It is also an embodied act. In particular, we suggest that the memory of actions that are built up during this experiment contain the felt and stored perceptions of the movements of the reaching for the target, as well as the visually specified locations. These become part of the next plan for action. Here is some experimental evidence for my claim.

First, in an experiment reported in Smith et al. (1999), infants were given six trials to uncover objects at the A side. Then, before the B trials, parents simply changed the babies' postures by standing them up on their laps. With this slight motor perturbation, perseveration was interrupted and infants reached correctly to B. The memory of each action included a body memory of a specific felt posture. The perceptual motor attractor that led to perseveration on the B trials was a result of the repetition of similar body movements that presumably

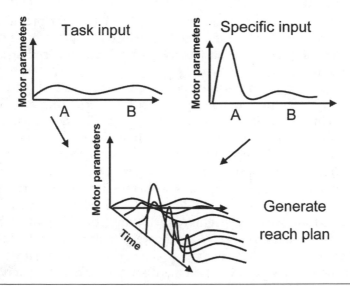

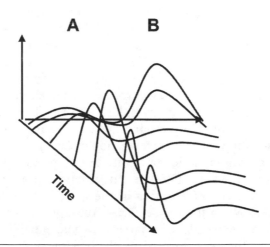

FIGURE 5.8 Inputs to the decision to reach to A or B after the first reach. Here there is also an input that represents the memory of the just-completed reach to A, combined with the task and specific inputs as in Figure 5.7.

FIGURE 5.9 The A-not-B error evolves over the delay. Competition between the transient cue to B and the more persistent, built-up memory to A resolves over the day to a perseverative reach back to A.

strengthened constrained neural ensembles. We might predict from this, for instance, that infants would be less likely to perseverate on B if their A training had motor variability, say by alternating trials of sitting and standing.

A second experiment also demonstrated the embodied nature of a decision to reach for one item or another (Diedrich, Thelen, & Smith, 1999). As in the previous study, our reasoning was that, if posture and movement memory were incorporated into successive reaching acts and were part of the perceptual motor attractor that produced perseveration, then disrupting this memory by a new motor perception should reduce perseveration. Thus, as before, infants were trained to reach for an A target, with no hidden toys, and before the usual cue to B, we added a sleeve with weights to their arms (control infants received cotton batting in the sleeve). When the weights were 75% of body mass, infants continued to perseverate at above chance rates. However, at 100% of body mass, perseveration was disrupted, and infants were more likely to be correct. Conversely, when infants were trained to the A side wearing the sleeve with 100% of body mass and when the weights were removed before the B trials, perseveration was also disrupted. Infants carry with them the feel of the movements they just made.

Indeed, we can actually detect the signatures of infants' spatial–motor memories in the traces of their hand movements during an A-not-B task (Diedrich, Thelen, & Smith, 2000). As is well known, young infants' reaches are not smooth and straight as are adults' (von Hofsten, 1991). Rather each reach has a distinctive profile: The hand path meanders, and the speed of the hand shows bumps where it speeds up and slows down. In Figure 5.10, on the left panel, you can see examples of such signature trajectories recorded from one infant as the baby reached for a single object on a table. Under these task conditions, each reach is different from the last one in its motor configuration. Compare this with the right panel, which was recorded from another infant in an A-not-B situation but without any hidden objects. The infant was cued to reach to A or B simply by waving the appropriate lid to the hiding well. This situation produces perseveration in exactly the same proportion as when a toy was hidden, a result our group has replicated many times (see also Munakata, 1997). In this circumstance, infants' trajectories often converge in form; that is, the speed bumps become more and more alike. When their trajectories converge, infants perseverate. We suggest that the two identical targets are perceptually confusing for infants because they are novel. This challenging situation constrains the infants' reaching solutions such that the memory of a preceding action is retained and influences subsequent actions.

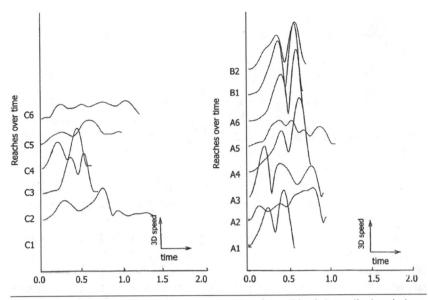

FIGURE 5.10 The A-not-B error evolves over the delay. Competition between the transient cue to B and the more persistent, built-up memory to A resolves over the day to a perseverative reach back to A.

These are important findings, I believe, for a theory of embodiment. Speed bumps in reach trajectories result from changes in the pulses of energy delivered to the arms. Thus, for the first time, we showed that infants remember the particular patterns of force impulses that underlie their reaches and that this memory may be strong enough to be incorporated into the execution of the next reach. We believe that this mechanism is fundamental in the learning and memory of skill. Indeed, there are analogous experiments in adults. Adult participants were trained to reach in a novel external force field (Shadmehr & Mussa-Ivaldi, 1994). At first, their reaches were poorly done, not straight to the target. After several hundred practice trials, adults learned the properties of the novel field and produced straight and smooth reaches. Then the experimenters turned off the novel forces and asked the participants to reach for targets in the normal environment. Now adults looked a bit like baby reachers again, showing inappropriate trajectories and sometimes missing the targets. Their motor memories for reaching had been biased to the solutions in the novel fields. In some ways the baby's problem of controlling arms in an ordinary environment is like a novel force field for an adult. What the baby must learn is the appropriate patterns of forces to negotiate the environment. What is critical is that this kind of learning and memory becomes part of the cognitive act of deciding what to do.

CONCLUSION

In many ways, we have returned to Piaget's explanation of the A-not-B error as infants being unable to divorce themselves from where they have just acted, and we also echo Adele Diamond's (1990) suggestion that babies are unable to inhibit a dominant response. In the terminology of the nested and coupled dynamic systems that I introduced earlier, infants, when placed in the A-not-B situation, cannot flexibly adjust the body/nervous-system/environment couplings to isolate their mental plan of where to reach from the memory of their previous action. Possibly, (a) the memory dynamics in infants are somewhat sluggish so that the trace of some actions is retained for a longer time; (b) the decision to act—like a reaction time—is also slower, giving the memory trace time to exert its influence; (c) the target cue memory is not retained in as potent a form; or (d) all of these mechanisms are present. The overall effect is that infants get stuck; although adaptive, flexibility is the mark of skill.

Where a dynamic theory of embodiment differs from Piaget and from others, however, is to see the A-not-B error and other perceptual–motor processes of infancy not as only stages or waystations to higher forms of cognition but truly as the dynamic grounding of cognition throughout the life span. If such integrated dynamics apply to the act of reaching in the A-not-B task, how can there be a time or a stage when such dynamics do not apply to human actions and all that is behind them? How can there be a time when human actions are something other than these multiple time-based processes, that include, with every act, body sense and body memory? Can the so-called cognitive aspects of our actions be carried out in some other processing language, a shift into symbol manipulation, for example, or into purely formal structures? What indeed is pure knowledge when every act of knowing is constituted by such dynamics?

The argument for life-span embodiment is thus predicated on two kinds of continuity: continuity of time and continuity of levels. Continuity of time means that the integrated sensorimotor processes that are at work at birth do not stop or change in a fundamental way, although they become more refined, faster, more flexible, and more general. Continuity of levels means that the currency of mental events must be the same as that of perception and action because the two are so tightly and completely interwoven. The traditional view of logical or knowledge structures is as abstract entities, disconnected from the world, static, discrete, and context independent. However, such constructs as the object concept or the theory of mind or even conservation do not have within them the means to do any real work for the person in which they putatively reside. The real work is applying such structures to real-life problems, which come with perceptual dynamics, memories, and motor demands just like the A-not-B task. Objects are lost and then found. Social interactions are events in time with complex and subtle dynamics. Real leftovers must be stored in the right size containers. Skill in these endeavors is not marked by whether one really knows what to do but by what one does, and this requires the seamless melding of mental events with the changing cues of the here and now.

ACKNOWLEDGMENTS

This research was supported by Grant NIH RO1 HD22830 from the National Institutes of Health and a Research Scientist Award.

My research would not have been possible without the collaboration of many wonderful graduate, undergraduate, and postdoctoral students, extraordinary colleagues, and a dedicated staff over more than 20 years. And it would not have been much fun either. I am very grateful for their intellectual and social contributions.

This chapter is a reprint from *Infancy* (2000), *1*, 3–28.

REFERENCES

Almássy, N., Edelman, G. M., & Sporns, O. (1998). Behavioral constraints in the development of neuronal properties: A cortical model embedded in a real world device. *Cerebral Cortex, 8*, 346–361.

Anderson, R. A., Snyder, L. H., Bradley, D. C., & Xing, J. (1997). Multimodal representation of space in the posterior parietal cortex and its use in planning movements. *Annual Review of Neuroscience, 20*, 303–330.

Angulo-Kinzler, R., Ulrich, B. D., & Thelen, E. (2002). Three-month-old infants can select specific leg motor solutions. *Motor Control, 6*, 52–68.

Ballard, D. H., Hayhoe, M. M., Pook, P. K., & Rao, R. P. N. (1997). Deictic codes for the embodiment of cognition. *Behavioral and Brain Sciences, 20*, 723–767.

Boussaoud, D. (1995). Primate premotor cortex: Modulation of preparatory neuronal activity by gaze angle. *Journal of Neurophysiology, 73*, 886–890.

Caminiti, R., Johnson, P. B., Galli, C., Ferraina, S., & Burnod, Y. (1991). Making arm movements within different parts of space: The premotor and motor cortical representation of a coordinate system for reaching to visual targets. *Journal of Neuroscience, 11*, 1182–1197.

Chiel, H. J., & Beer, R. D. (1997). The brain has a body: Adaptive behavior emerges from interactions of nervous system, body, and environment. *Trends in Neuroscience, 20,* 553–557.

Clark, A. (1997). *Being there: Putting brain, body, and world together again.* Cambridge, MA: MIT Press.

Damasio, A. R. (1994). *Descartes' error: Emotion, reason, and the human brain.* New York: Putnam.

Diamond, A. (1990). Developmental time course in human infants and infant monkeys and the neural bases of inhibitory control in reaching. In A. Diamond (Ed.), *The development and neural bases of higher cognitive functions* (pp. 637–669). New York: New York Academy of Sciences.

Diedrich, F. J., Thelen, E., & Smith, L. B. (1999). Motor memory is a factor in infant perseverative errors. *Developmental Science, 3,* 479–494.

Diedrich, F. J., Thelen, E., & Smith, L. B. (1999). *Infant spatial location memories include perceptions of limb mass.* Manuscript submitted for publication.

diPelligrino, G., & Wise, S. P. (1993). Visuospatial versus visuomotor activity in the premotor and prefrontal cortex of a primate. *Journal of Neuroscience, 13,* 1227–1243.

Edelman, G. M. (1987). *Neural Darwinism: The theory of neuronal group selection.* New York: Basic Books.

Edelman, G. M. (1993). *Topobiology: An introduction to molecular embryology.* New York: Basic Books.

Farah, M. (1994). Neuropsychological inference with an interactive brain: A critique of the "locality" assumption. *Behavioral and Brain Sciences, 17,* 43–104.

Felleman, D. J., & van Essen, D. C. (1991). Distributed hierarchical processing in the primate cerebral cortex. *Cerebral Cortex, 1,* 1–47.

Fischer, K. W. (1980). A theory of cognitive development: The control and construction of hierarchies of skills. *Psychological Review, 87,* 477–531.

Fodor, J. A. (1983). *The modularity of mind.* Cambridge, MA: MIT Press.

Fogel, A. (1993). *Developing through relationships: Communication, self, and culture in early infancy.* Cambridge, England: Harvester.

Fuster, J. M. (1989). *The prefrontal cortex: Anatomy, physiology, and neuropsychology of the frontal lobe* (2nd ed.). New York: Raven.

Georgopoulos, A. P. (1995). Motor cortex and cognitive processing. In M. S. Gazzaniga (Ed.), *The cognitive neurosciences* (pp. 507–517). Cambridge, MA: MIT Press.

Georgopoulos, A. P., Ashe, J., Smyrnis, N., & Taira, M. (1992). Motor cortex and the coding of force. *Science, 256,* 1692–1695.

Georgopoulos, A. P., Crutcher, M. D., & Schwartz, A. B. (1989). Cognitive spatial–motor processes: III. Motor cortical prediction of movement direction during an instructed delay period. *Experimental Brain Research, 75,* 183–194.

Georgopoulos, A. P., Kettner, R. E., & Schwartz, A. B. (1988). Primate motor cortex and free arm movements to visual targets in three-dimensional space: II. Coding of the direction of movement by a neuronal population. *Journal of Neuroscience, 8,* 2928–2937.

Georgopoulos, A. P., Lurito, J. T., Petrides, M., Schwartz, A. B., & Massey, J. T. (1989). Mental rotation of the neuronal population vector. *Science, 243,* 234–236.

Gibson, E. J. (1969). *Principles of perceptual learning and development.* Englewood Cliffs, NJ: Prentice Hall.

Glenberg, A. M. (1997). What memory is for. *Behavioral and Brain Sciences, 20,* 1–56.

Gopnick, A., & Meltzoff, A. N. (1996). *Words, thoughts, and theories: Learning, development and conceptual change.* Cambridge, MA: MIT Press.

Graziano, M. S. A., Hu, X. T., & Gross, C. G. (1997). Coding the locations of objects in the dark. *Science, 277,* 239–241.

James, W. (1950). *Principles of psychology* (Vol. 1). New York: Dover. (Original work published 1890)

Johnson, M. (1987). *The body in the mind: The bodily basis of meaning, imagination, and reason.* Chicago: University of Chicago Press.

Kalaska, J. F., & Crammond, D. J. (1995). Deciding not to GO: Neuronal correlates of response selection in a GO/NOGO task in primate premotor and parietal cortex. *Cerebral Cortex, 5,* 410–428.

Karmiloff-Smith, A. (1992). *Beyond modularity: A developmental perspective on cognitive science.* Cambridge, MA: MIT Press.

Kettner, R. E., Marcario, J. K., & Port, N. L. (1996). Control of remembered reaching sequences in monkey: II. Storage and preparation before movement in motor and premotor cortex. *Experimental Brain Research, 112,* 347–358.

Lakoff, G. (1987). *Women, fire, and dangerous things: What categories reveal about the mind.* Chicago: University of Chicago Press.

Mandler, J. M. (1988). How to build a baby: On the development of an accessable representational system. *Creative Development, 3,* 113–136.

Merleau-Ponty, M. (1963). *The structure of behavior* (C. Smith, Trans.). London: Routledge & Kegan Paul.

Miller, E. K., Erickson, C. A., & Desimone, R. (1996). Neural mechanisms of visual working memory in prefrontal cortex of the macaque. *Journal of Neuroscience, 16,* 5154–5167.

Munakata, Y. (1997). Perseverative reaching in infancy: The role of hidden toys and motor history in the *AB* task. *Infant Behavior and Development, 20,* 405–416.

Piaget, J. (1952). *The origins of intelligence in children.* New York: International Universities Press.

Piaget, J. (1954). *The construction of reality in the child.* New York: Basic Books.

Pinker, S. (1994). *The language instinct.* New York: Harper.

Rochat, P., & Morgan, R. (1995). Spatial determinants in the perception of self-produced leg movements by 3- to 5-month-old infants. *Developmental Psychology, 31,* 626–636.

Rovee-Collier, C. (1990). The "memory system" of prelinguistic infants. In A. Diamond (Ed.), *The development and neural bases of higher cognitive functions* (pp. 517–536). New York: New York Academy of Sciences.

Rovee-Collier, C. (1995). Time windows in cognitive development. *Developmental Psychology, 51,* 1–23.

Rovee-Collier, C. (1997). Dissociations in infant memory: Rethinking the development of implicit and explicit memory. *Psychological Review, 104,* 467–498.

Scott, S. H., & Kalaska, J. F. (1997). Reaching movements with similar hand paths but different arm orientations: I. Activity of individual cells in motor cortex. *Journal of Neurophysiology, 77,* 826–852.

Scott, S. H., Sergio, L. E., & Kalaska, J. F. (1997). Reaching movements with similar hand paths but different arm orientations: II. Activity of individual cells in dorsal premotor cortex and parietal area 5. *Journal of Neurophysiology, 78,* 2413–2426.

Shadmehr, R., & Mussa-Ivaldi, F. A. (1994). Adaptive representation of dynamics during learning of a motor task. *Journal of Neuroscience, 14,* 3208–3224.

Shen, L., & Alexander, G. E. (1997a). Neural correlates of a spatial sensory-to-motor transformation in the primary motor cortex. *Journal of Neurophysiology, 77,* 1171–1194.

Shen, L., & Alexander, G. E. (1997b). Preferential representations of instructed target location versus limb trajectory in dorsal premotor area. *Journal of Neurophysiology, 77,* 1195–1212.

Shweder, R. A. (1984). Anthropology's romantic rebellion against the enlightenment, or there's more to thinking than reason and evidence. In R. A. Shweder & R. A. LeVine (Eds.), *Culture theory: Essays on mind, self, and emotion* (pp. 27–64). New York: Cambridge University Press.

Smith, L. B., Thelen, E., Titzer, R., & McLin, D. (1999). Knowing in the context of acting: The task dynamics of the A-not-B error. *Psychological Review, 106,* 235–260.

Spelke, E. S., Breinlinger, K., Macomber, J., & Jacobson, K. (1992). Origins of knowledge. *Psychological Review, 99,* 605–632.

Talmy, L. (1988). Force dynamics in language and cognition. *Cognitive Science, 12,* 49–100.

Thelen, E. (1994). Three-month-old infants can learn task-specific patterns of interlimb coordination. *Psychological Science, 5,* 280–285.

Thelen, E. (1995). Time scale dynamics and the development of an embodied cognition. In R. Port & T. van Gelder (Eds.), *Mind as motion: Explorations in the dynamics of cognition* (pp. 69–99). Cambridge, MA: MIT Press.

Thelen, E., & Fisher, D. M. (1983a). From spontaneous to instrumental behavior: Kinematic analysis of movement changes during very early learning. *Child Development, 54*, 129–140.

Thelen, E., & Fisher, D. M. (1983b). The organization of spontaneous leg movements in newborn infants. *Journal of Motor Behavior, 15*, 353–377.

Thelen, E., Schöner, G., Scheier, C., & Smith, L. B. (2001). The dynamics of embodiment: A field theory of infant perseverative reaching. *Behavioral and Brain Sciences, 24*, 1–86.

Thelen, E., & Smith, L.B. (1994). *A dynamic systems approach to the development of perception and action.* Cambridge, MA: MIT Press.

van Gelder, T. (1998). The dynamical hypothesis in cognitive science. *Behavioral and Brain Sciences, 21*, 615–628.

Varela, F. J., Thompson, E., & Rosch, E (1991). *The embodied mind: Cognitive science and human experience.* Cambridge, MA: MIT Press.

von Hofsten, C. (1991). Structuring of early reaching movements: A longitudinal study. *Journal of Motor Behavior, 23*, 280–292.

6

EMBODIMENT, ALTERITY, AND
THE THEORY OF RELIGION

Thomas J. Csordas

University of California San Diego

Some have implicated embodiment in the development of various psychological processes from perception to reasoning, but in this essay, I adopt a standpoint at the intersection of anthropology and philosophy in order to discuss the role of embodiment in the development of the religious experience. My broad thesis will be that the phenomenological kernel of religion resides in an embodied primordial sense of "otherness" or "alterity." This kernel becomes elaborated developmentally through an embodied process of objectification, which leads to the differentiation of self and other, thus making us human, and at the same time bestowing on us the inevitability of religion.

No matter how considerable is a person's self-knowledge, it is always possible to surprise oneself, and it is precisely this capacity that I want to draw attention to as an initial indication of my argument's direction. I can surprise myself, indeed I am never quite completely myself, I am always a bit outside myself, I am always outrunning or lagging a bit behind myself, and I am seldom in complete accord or in perfect identity with myself. If this already sounds too inward and individualistic, please bear with my insistence that I am not making an appeal to the unconscious, nor putting forward a description of consciousness. My point is about being in the world, our human condition of existence not only as beings with experience but also as beings in relation to others. And here we are inevitably surprised by others, given the impossibility of perfectly coinciding in thought or feeling, mood or motivation, with them. In this sense, the problem of subjectivity is that we are never quite completely ourselves, and the problem of intersubjectivity is that we are never completely in accord with others.

In a moment, I will formulate a thesis about religion that is foreshadowed in this observation about surprise. First, however, we must come to terms with just what is included in religion as a category of human activity and experience. In her distinguished lecture to the Society for the Anthropology of Religion, Edith Turner (2002) directly confronted this issue in her title, which included the question "What Does this Binding Word 'Religion' Mean?" With this, she alluded to the etymological source of the word *religion* in the Latin *religare* (from *ligare,* which means "to tie or bind"). This etymology has often been disputed—most recently, Derrida (1998), in his reflection on faith and knowledge as sources of religion, invoked the debate about whether the word derives from *religare* or *relegere* (from *legere,* which means "to harvest or gather"). But what or who is being bound or gathered, by whom, for what purpose, or as protection against what? Or to pose the question somewhat differently, when we use the adjective *religious* to qualify reference to institutions, ideas, rituals, experience, or imagination, what is being added that is unique? What is the difference between talking about "the religious imagination" and imagination tout simple? For that matter, to borrow Derrida's words, "All sacredness and all holiness are not necessarily, in the strict sense of the term, if there is one, religious" (pp. 8–9).

Moreover, as Derrida (1998) insistently pointed out, as soon as we adopt the word *religion* to designate our interest, "We are already speaking Latin" (p. 29). This means that we are already laden with a great deal of cultural and historical baggage, sedimented through the profound change involved in the succession of the Roman Empire by the Holy Roman Empire and the Roman Church and the Pax Americana. Indeed, it is simple enough to relativize the word with a few examples. In Japanese, the word that translates as *religion* applies only to so-called new religions and not to the established cults of Buddhism or Shinto. In Navajo, there is no generic word for *religion*, though there are words for *holy* and for *sacred ceremony.*

If the word *religion* carries too much baggage, neither can we depend on neologism, as in "numinous," a coinage of Rudolf Otto (1923) from the Latin *numen,* self-consciously on the model of how the word *ominous* is derived from *omen*. Neither does it feel safe simply to add together the entire vocabulary of relevant words such as religion, the numinous, the sacred, the holy, the supernatural, the divine, the transcendent, the occult, mystery, sacrifice, salvation, and faith—and declare that their sum constitutes our interest. The relations among these terms are endlessly nuanced. And we must be mindful of the dangers in attempting to construct a universalist definition of religion brought to the fore by Talal Asad (1993) in his critique of Clifford Geertz's (1973) widely cited definition. Yet, I am in favor of keeping religion as part of our conceptual repertoire: Asad's critique of the category was a necessary one, but no more does away with religion as an anthropological category than did the critique of *history* some years ago force historians to stop using that word (Wolf, 1982) or than did the critique of *culture* more recently (Abu-Lughod, 1991) force anthropologists to stop using that term. Such critiques do not force us to abandon our concepts, but constrain us to use the concepts more wisely.

In this respect, trying to outline the boundaries of religion as a category serves us less well than (taking a cue from cognitive science) searching for a prototype around which what we will provisionally call "religion" has been elaborated or built up. This prototype would be, in a particular sense, the origin of religion—its experiential source, its phenomenological kernel. My thesis concerning this problem is that religion is predicated on, and elaborated from, a primordial sense of otherness. Furthermore, because of this the religious sensibility exists sui generis; that is, it is not reducible to any other category. But let me say this more precisely:

Thesis: Alterity is the phenomenological kernel of religion.

Corollary: Insofar as alterity is part of the structure of being-in-the-world, religion is inevitable, perhaps even necessary.

In the remainder of this essay, I will elaborate, qualify, and illustrate this thesis and its corollary. To begin, alterity is neither objective nor absolute. In the sense in which I am using it, alterity is a constituent of subjectivity and intersubjectivity, and this is how it is part of the structure of being-in-the-world. Not only can it be elaborated into the monstrous as well as the divine, but also it can be transformed into identity, intimacy, or familiarity. Certainly, the mystics have discovered that the wholly other can be modulated into the wholly one, and that it is equally awesome either way. This mutability of alterity exists insofar as it partakes of indeterminacy, another element of the structure of being in the world, but I will not pursue that line of argument here.

ORIGINARY ALTERITY

Let us begin with William Blake (1790/1988), poetic master of alterity and imagination, from "The Marriage of Heaven and Hell":

> The ancient Poets animated all sensible objects with Gods or Geniuses, calling them by the names and adorning them with the properties of woods, rivers, mountains, lakes, cities, nations, and whatever their enlarged and numerous senses could perceive. And particularly they studied the genius of each city and country, placing it under its mental deity; Till a system was formed, which some took advantage of, and enslaved the vulgar by attempting to realize or abstract the mental deities from their objects: thus began Priesthood; Choosing the forms of worship from poetic tales. And at length they pronounced that the Gods had ordered such things. Thus men forgot that All deities reside in the Human breast. (p. 38)

Blake's (1790/1988) theory was evidently a theory of primal animism, but it was even more a theory of a poetic and corporal bringing to life made possible by the "enlarged and numerous senses" of the prelapsarian moment. For Blake, the fall was a flight from concreteness to abstraction and the slavery of mystification. Forgetting that all deities reside in the human breast was for Blake equivalent to saying that the "binding" achieved by religion was the binding, or binding off, of the human imagination. Blake's manifesto was thick with meaning, one strand having to do with the already braided historical-existential origin of religion, another having to do with the apparent "interiority" implied by the residence of deities in the human breast, and yet another having to do with the humanism in the poet's—and the scholar's—skeptical stance toward religion. Here, I will deal briefly only with the second issue evoked by Blake's argument, the apparent "interiority" implied by his reference to the residence of deities in the human breast. William James (1961) based his famous study of religion on the most acute and extreme interior, personal, solitary spiritual moments of religious geniuses, seeking the essence of religious experiences in those "which are most one-sided, exaggerated, and intense." Our reverse strategy of seeking the minimal criterion of religious experience, the phenomenological kernel that is the origin of religious symbol, sentiment, and institution, can be just as productive. Instead of examining the most religious moments of the most religious man, we want to know about the most marginally religious moments of the least religious person.

The most explicit clue as to what constitutes this minimal criterion, however, comes from the work of phenomenologists of religion. Here, I am thinking not so much of the more widely read Eliade (1958), but of the less familiar Rudolf Otto (1923) and Gerardus van der Leeuw (1938). Among anthropologists, van der Leeuw is virtually unknown, and Otto is often emblematic of anachronistic theories of religion. As a student in the 1970s, I learned about the study of religion from an anthropological standpoint that acknowledged precursors whose ideas were seminal but who were now to be understood as quaint and out-moded—Sir James George Frazier, Max Muller, Edward Tylor, Foustel de Coulanges, and Rudolf Otto were among these. I recall being sur-prised at some point to discover that Otto was relatively quite contem-porary, and some continued to read his work quite seriously in certain quarters of religious studies.

For Otto (1923), the object toward which the numinous conscious-ness was directed was a mysterium tremendum et fascinans, and he described its central characteristic as follows:

> Taken in the religious sense, that which is 'mysterious' is—to give it perhaps the most striking expression—the 'wholly other,' that which is quite beyond the sphere of the usual, the intelligible, and the familiar, which therefore falls quite outside the limits of the 'canny,' and is contrasted with it, filling the mind with blank wonder and astonishment . . . the essential characteristic . . . lies in a peculiar 'moment' of consciousness, to wit, the *stupor* before something 'wholly other'. . . (pp. 26–27)

The invocation of blank wonder, astonishment, and stupor are strik-ing, but I would call attention instead not to these reactions, but to the phenomenon of the "wholly other," pointing as well to the manner in which Otto (1923) cited the "limits of the 'canny,'" an issue to which we will return in a moment with reference to Freud's (1955) reflections on the uncanny. G. van der Leeuw (1938) had a corresponding observation about the object of religion:

> . . . the first affirmation we can make about the Object of Religion is that it is a highly exceptional and extremely impressive "Other." Subjectively, again, the initial state of man's mind is amazement; and, as Soderblom has remarked, this is true not only for philoso-phy but equally for religion. As yet, it must further be observed, we are in no way concerned with the supernatural or the transcen-dent: we can speak of "God" in a merely figurative sense; but there arises and persists an experience which connects or unites itself to

the "Other" that thus obtrudes . . . this Object is a departure from all that is usual and familiar; and this again is the consequence of the *Power* it generates. (p. 23)

This formulation was somewhat more sober than Otto's (1923), even in the way it identified amazement as the initial state of the human mind. It also, at least momentarily, spoke of God in a figurative sense, and the supernatural and transcendent as secondary to the encounter with otherness. Then, there was *power,* this single word being the title of van der Leeuw's (1938) first chapter, which he initially elaborated as a sublime potency using familiar ethnographic examples of mana and orenda. Otto (1923) too evoked the notion of power, but in his characteristically more dramatic fashion initially elaborated it as a powerful, indeed overpowering, "aweful majesty" (p. 20).

In looking to these quarters for an insight about alterity, it is well worth noting that vehement opposition to the phenomenologists of religion such as Otto (1923) and van der Leeuw (1938) persists. For example, as if William James (1961) had initiated some kind of degenerative process, the philosopher Giorgio Agamben (1998) identified Otto as the culmination of the psychologization of religious experience. Agamben argued that with Otto's

concept of the sacred that completely coincides with the concept of the obscure and the impenetrable, a theology that had lost all experience of the revealed word celebrated its union with a philosophy that had abandoned all sobriety in the face of feeling. That the religious belongs entirely to the sphere of psychological emotion, that it essentially has to do with shivers and goose bumps— this is the triviality that the neologism "numinous" had to dress up as science. (p. 78)

This critique indeed captured some of the flavor of Otto's (1923) text, but in its harsh dismissiveness, it squandered the embedded jewel of insight. Taking a different tack, Donald Wiebe (1999) identified the work of van der Leeuw (1938) as a religio-cultural quest, the effect of which was to depreciate and undermine the scientific study of religion. Wiebe (1999) cited van der Leeuw's interest in comprehending phenomena in accord with their spiritual content, and his claim that all comprehension was ultimately religious insofar as "all significance sooner or later leads to ultimate significance" (Wiebe, 1999, p. 180). But let us be aware that within religious studies the stakes in the battle between explanation and understanding are even higher than for the same battle in anthropology. There the scientific account is pitted against theological commitment, and to admit that religion has any existence sui generis implies the theological conclusion, whereas in anthropology the causal account is pitted against the interpretive one, and the issue is the relative merit of hard (I prefer *brittle*) and soft (or *flexible*) methods.

The problem with these formulations is not just that the phenomenologists were inordinately psychological in their approach. Neither is the problem simply that they were Christian theologians and hence both spiritually committed and ethnocentric. The problem is a theoretical one, or perhaps more accurately a methodological one that comes from reifying alterity—reifying the other as an object, rendering it "out there" in a way that we can be "in its presence." That is, the problem comes from rendering the other as an "it," a thing. If one can suspend this reification one finds, as Charles Long (1976) observed, "Otto [1923] is telling us that it is possible to experience apart from the categorical schema," that is, to have "experience of reality as a priori, as a datum that has not yet become a structure of the human project . . ." (p. 402)—in short, as simply other. I think that the basic insight can be given a theoretical grounding that is not theological, but accounts for the possibility and perhaps inevitability of religion. My argument is that alterity is a fundamental aspect of human being, an existential constituent of humanity as such—let us say an elementary structure of existence— and that misrecognition of this has resulted in both untold misery and boundless creativity in human life. This is no more than what Blake (1790/1988) said in "The Marriage of Heaven and Hell."

In sum, the phenomenologists' error was to make a distinction between the object and subject of religion, when the actual object of religion is objectification itself, the rending apart of subject and object that makes us human and in the same movement bestows on us—or burdens us—with the inevitability of religion. That is, the "object" of religion is not the other. The object of religion is the existential aporia of alterity itself. The difficulty in recognizing this is precisely the difficulty of distinguishing a psychological from an existential language, and the difficulty of moving from a language of interiority to a language of intersubjectivity. Saying this, our task is to rehabilitate the basic insight of these authors in light of anthropological interpretation and update it in light of contemporary theorizing about alterity.

INTIMATE ALTERITY

For Otto (1923), one could understand the numinous only "by means of the special way it is reflected in the mind in terms of feeling." Following Schleiermacher, he identified this feeling as a certain kind of dependence (or is it a feeling of contingency?), and the object of that dependence is the numinous. Curiously, he named this "creature-feeling . . . the emotion of a creature, submerged and overwhelmed by its own nothingness in contrast to that which is supreme above all creatures" (p. 10). Is this creature the infant or the animal, or the adult in prayer? I was listening to a commentator on National Public Radio who said that apes cannot swim, and indeed often panic and drown because they, unlike other mammals including dogs and horses who swim instinctually, are rational beings, and reason tells them they will drown if they breath in water. Humans cannot swim instinctually either, but the difference is that we have the capacity to imagine beyond reason and that allows us to transcend ourselves—to surprise ourselves—and to figure out how to move around in the water.

The image of water, of being submerged, the invocation of the creature, of dependence, most of all of our attempt to come to grips with alterity, leads us to the work of George Bataille (1992), for whose theory of religion animality and water figured heavily. Bataille's work invoked a profound alterity by inverting the expected relation between immanence and transcendence. In his view, the goal of religion is to recapture the intimacy of an immanence prior to all alterity, and he showed how very strange that is. The primary image was that of one animal eating another. "What is given when one animal eats another is always the fellow creature of the one that eats," in complete immediacy and without there being between the two any relation of subordination, difference, dependence, transcendence, objectification, discontinuity, consciousness, or duration—since for the animal nothing is given through time, the destruction of the eaten is "only a disappearance in a world where nothing is posited beyond the present" (Bataille, 1992, p. 18). Bataille might have responded to Otto (1923) that this is the original creature-feeling as opposed to the feeling of having been created that Otto implied. And far more than the feeling of being submerged, far more even than a feeling that is "oceanic," this ultimate intimate immanence of animality is a mode of being "in the world like water in water."

For Bataille (1992), the moment that renders us human is the moment in which we posit an object. The initial object is the tool, the "nascent form of the non-I," (p. 27), and the moment of alterity and discontinuity constituted by positing an object is what Bataille called "transcendence." From this moment, he demonstrated an inexorable unfolding of a consciousness that reduced the original immanence of the world to thingness and invented a supreme being that was also a kind of thing considerably impoverished from the animal sense of continuity. Discontinuity multiples as humans sequentially develop sacrifice, festivals, warfare, military order, universal empire, and industrial order, by means of processes including dualism, reason, transcendence, mediation, morality, clear consciousness, and sovereign self-consciousness.

> Man is the being that has lost, and even rejected, that which he obscurely is, a vague intimacy. Consciousness could not have become clear in the course of time if it had not turned away from its awkward contents, but clear consciousness is itself looking for what it has itself lost, and what it must lose again as it draws near to it. Of course, what it has lost is not outside it; consciousness turns away from the obscure intimacy of consciousness itself. Religion, whose essence is the search for lost intimacy, comes down to the effort of clear consciousness which wants to be a complete self-consciousness: but this effort is futile, since consciousness of intimacy is possible only at a level where consciousness is no longer an operation whose outcome implies duration, that is, at the level where clarity, which is the effect of the operation, is no longer given. (Bataille, 1992, pp. 56–57)

Insofar as we are human, we are always already in the world from the stance of alterity so that, paradoxically, it is identity and continuity that are alien to us and hence frightening and "vertiginously dangerous" (Bataille, 1992, p. 36). It is immanence and not transcendence that constitutes the true otherness of animal oblivion to which our consciousness aspires but which, asymptotically, "it must lose again as it draws near to it" (p. 57).

Put otherwise, "Intimacy is the limit of clear consciousness" (Bataille, 1992, p. 99). That is, consciousness as such cannot grasp intimacy because one cannot reduce intimacy to a thing. But consciousness can undo itself, reverse its reductive operations in order to reduce itself to intimacy, by dissolving and destroying utilitarian "objects as such in the field of consciousness," thereby returning "to the situation of the animal that eats another animal" (p. 103). The sovereign act of destroying objects is simultaneously the destruction of the subject as an individual, "[b]ut it is insofar as clear consciousness prevails that the objects actually destroyed will not destroy humanity itself" (p. 103). This is a form of violence, but it is necessary—and here I am again reminded of Blake (1790/1988)—"for anyone to whom human life is an experience to be carried as far as possible" (Bataille, 1992, p. 110), and it leads directly to the limit, the impossible. When we search for the existential structure of this final alterity, we must take our clue from Bataille's observation that humanity's first object is the tool, and combine it with Marcel Mauss's

(1950) insight that humanity's first tool is the body. But the body is also the site wherein this "internally wrenching violence that animates the whole . . . reveals the impossible in laughter, ecstasy, or tears," and this impossible is nothing other than "the sovereign self-consciousness that, precisely, no longer turns away from itself" (Bataille, 1992, p. 111).

We have more to do in specifying this embodied otherness, but let us pursue it by way of intimacy. The phenomenologists of religion had not only a too objectified understanding of the "wholly other," but one that was too grandiose. Instead of the wholly other projected onto cosmic majesty, I want to turn our attention to the intimately other. The intimate alterity that I will juxtapose to the wholly other is not the intimacy of animality but one that can be only an intimation of that intimacy, insofar as it begins necessarily from our human consciousness. Recall that one of the ways that Otto (1923) characterized the wholly other was that it was outside the canny, and indeed he equated the uncanny or unheimlich with the numinous (p. 40). Here we must fold Freud (1955) into our account, for the manner in which he captured a much more intimate alterity in this feeling. In his study of religious representations of the monstrous, Tim Beal (2002) compared the two authors' approaches to the unheimlich: "What Otto calls 'wholly other' Freud would call 'other' only insofar as it has been repressed. For Freud the unheimlich is only 'outside the house' (the house of the self, the house of culture, the house of the cosmos) insofar as it is hidden within the house" (p. 8). Yet the progression from self to cosmos within Beal's parentheses is itself a clue that we need not choose between the two, for the wholly other and intimately other are two sides of the same leaf.

One could find the image of otherness in Freud (1955), insofar as it relates to our topic, appears less in the notion of the sovereign id or the hidden unconscious than in the notion of the uncanny. My emphasis is not on uncanny as frightening but on uncanny as close to us, as intimately other. First, there is something uncanny about the word itself: not only can the *unheimlich* refer to both the wholly other and the intimately other, but the root word *heimlich* can, in certain contexts, mean its opposite. *Heimlich* can mean something that is familiar or agreeable, but also something hidden and kept out of sight. Although Freud was unclear about the precise relation between the two meanings, there appears to be a development along the lines that what is familiar becomes private, what is private becomes hidden, and what is hidden becomes spooky. In any case, there is in this word a semantic alterity such that "heimlich is a word the meaning of which develops in the direction of ambivalence, until it finally coincides with its opposite, unheimlich" (Freud, 1955, p. 226).

Freud's (1955) famous conclusion was that the uncanny eventuates in the recurrence of something that has been repressed, something originally familiar that by mean of this repression has become alienated and threatening, in the sense that although we may yearn to return to the womb we would be terrified to find ourselves there again, or in the sense that experience of having a double that is reassuring at a very young age becomes an uncanny harbinger of death much later on. For Freud, the factors that turn something merely frightening into something uncanny included the effacement of the distinction between imagination and reality found in animism, magic, and sorcery, the infantile omnipotence of thoughts, the human ambivalence toward death, involuntary repetition, and the castration complex (p. 243). Freud qualified his account as perhaps satisfying psychoanalytic but not aesthetic interest in the uncanny, and differentiated between the uncanny we actually experience and that which art and literature portrays. Although he said nothing explicitly about religion, he approached it in summarizing the two closely related phenomena that are the sources of the uncanny: "An uncanny experience occurs either when infantile complexes which have been repressed are once more revived by some impression, or when primitive beliefs [animism] which have been surmounted [by reason] seem once more to be confirmed" (p. 249). Freud too easily discounted, I think, the importance of a rival's theory that highlights uncertainty about whether something is living or not—a body ambiguously dead or alive, an automaton ambiguously animate or inanimate—because it did not quite fit the psychoanalytic account. It is also curious that, among the examples of uncanny experience he cited, one that Freud did not mention was the feeling of a presence that was not really there. This would be a feeling that we could contrast on the one hand to the feeling of invisible divine presence in religious experience and to the feeling of concrete intimacy in the caress of another person. But including these, and with a somewhat broader notion of alterity building on Freud's intuition, we can see one reason why religion can never go away, why it will always return in a myriad of forms. In the language that I have been developing here, the return of the repressed is the inevitable betrayal of identity by alterity, the reenchantment of the world that imposes itself as soon as the disenchanted world finally becomes so familiar as to begin to appear strange, that strange interchangebility or transposability of *heimlich* and *unheimlich* that Freud talked about. At least, such an analysis might make it easier to understand Eliade's (1958) notion of hierophany not as a manifestation of divinity but as an upwelling of alterity, a spontaneous epoché or lowering of the veil of cultural taken for grantedness that covers the illusion of self-identity.

The point again is that the other is much closer than we would be led to believe by the phenomenologists of religion, or at least that there is no understanding of the wholly other without the intimate other.

Let me specify this sense of intimate alterity with a concrete ethnographic instance. I observed it quite strikingly in my studies of Catholic Charismatic healing. In what I called imaginal performances, Jesus or the Virgin Mary would often appear or be evoked in healing prayer that took the form of visualization in which one of these divine presences would speak and engage the afflicted person in a healing embrace. Although these presences can be understood as internal transitional objects in a psychoanalytic sense, and even more generously as ideal objects or Others to which one can have a mature, intimate relationship that serves as a prototype on which to develop the capacity for intimacy as an aspect of a sacred self, I wanted to push the interpretation farther. I suggested that this experience is a genuine intimacy with a primordial aspect of the self that is the existential ground for both its fundamental indeterminacy and for the possibility of an intersubjective relationship—its own inherent otherness. In other words, the imaginal Jesus is the alterity of the self. In this sense to speak of intimacy with oneself is not to speak metaphorically. It is instead to say that the capacity for intimacy begins with an existential coming to terms with the alterity of the self, and that the presence of Jesus is an embodied metaphor for that condition of selfhood. This is the Jesus who speaks with a "still, small voice" within and whose presence is an act of imagination (Csordas, 1994, pp. 57–58).

This intimate alterity appears again in the Charismatic practice of "resting in the Spirit," in which a person is overwhelmed by divine power and presence and falls, typically from a standing position, into a sacred swoon. Although again we cannot fail to strike a psychoanalytic chord in noting the "oceanic" passivity before an omnipotent paternal deity that characterizes this experience, I also suggested that the experience is constituted in the bodily synthesis of preobjective self-processes. This is to say that the coming into being of "divine presence" as a cultural phenomenon is an objectification of embodiment itself. Consider the heaviness of limbs reported by people resting in the Spirit. Quoting Plugge, Zaner (1981) pointed out that "Within the reflective experience of a healthy limb, no matter how silent and weightless it may be in action, there is yet, indetectably hidden a certain 'heft'" (p. 56). This thing-like *heft* of our bodies in conjunction with the spontaneous *lift* of customary bodily performances defines our bodies as simultaneously belonging to us and estranged from us, and hence the alterity of self is an embodied otherness. While resting in the Spirit, the heft that is always there for us indeterminately and preobjectively becomes determinate and objectified. Its essential alterity becomes an object of somatic attention within the experiential gestalt defined as divine presence. The divine presence is an intimate presence in a way that, because it encompasses multiple modalities of the body-self, surpasses human companionship. Like the divine presence in imaginal performance, resting in the Spirit thus offers both a surrogate source of intimacy for the lonely and a prototype upon which human intimacy can be modeled (Csordas, 1994, p. 246).

One can take this alterity of the self in at least two senses. Following Zaner (1981), self-presence and presence to the other are the two foundational moments of self. Zaner understood self-presence as "situated self-reflexivity" and presence to the other as an "urgency . . . to reveal itself to other inwardly realized selves" (p. 153). This is tellingly reminiscent of the urgency or energy that Otto (1923) said was an element of religion's mysterium tremendum. Yet on the level of the intimately other rather than the wholly other, I think it appears more clearly as imagination and desire. The vivid presence of Jesus or Mary in Charismatic imaginal performance is a culturally specific way to complete the second foundational moment, providing an ideal Other to correspond to the moment of self-presence.

A second sense of the self's alterity is grounded in our very embodiment. Zaner (1981) again showed that the inescapableness of our embodied nature and the limitations it imposes contribute to the feeling that our bodies are in a sense "other" than ourselves. Our intimacy with our own bodies also implicates us in whatever happens to them, and realization that we are thus "susceptible to what can happen to material things in general" corresponds to experiencing the "chill" of mortality. In addition, our bodies are always "hidden presences" to us, both insofar as autonomic processes typically go on outside of awareness (see Leder, 1990) and insofar as the possibility persists of seeing ourselves as objects from the perspective of another. Our bodies are thus hidden presences to us at the same time as they are compellingly ours, and accordingly Zaner called the body intimately alien and strangely mine:

> My body is at once familiar and strange, intimate and alien: "*mine*" *most of all yet "other" most of all*, the ground for both subjective inwardness and objective outwardness. Whatever I want, wish, or plan for, I irrevocable "grow older," "become tired," "feel ill," "am energetic.". . . [T]he basis for *the otherness* (and thereby the otherness of everything else) *of the embodying organism is its having a*

life of its own, even when the person is most "at home" or "at one" with it . . . The otherness of my own body thus suffuses its sense of intimacy. (pp. 54–55; emphasis in original).

The necessity of this embodied alterity of the self even when one is most "at home" evokes the notion of the *heimlich*, homelike and *unheimlich* or uncanny. For the moment, let me emphasize that Zaner's (1981) discussion showed that the uncanny is not necessarily grounded in an abstract recognition of mortality but in the concreteness of everyday embodied existence in which the "chill" is present even "at home."

Elizabeth Grosz (1994) carried this line of thinking a step further, not only grounding alterity in embodiment but also making it the very precondition of embodiment:

> Bodies themselves, in their materialities, are never self-present, given things, immediate, certain self-evidences because embodiment, corporeality, insist on alterity, both that alterity they carry within themselves (the heart of the psyche lies in the body; the body's principles of functioning are psychological and cultural) and that alterity that gives them their own concreteness and specificity (the alterities constituting race, sex, sexualities, ethnic and cultural specificities). Alterity is the very possibility and process of embodiment: it conditions but is also a product of the pliability or plasticity of bodies which makes them other than themselves, other than their "nature," their functions and identities. (p. 209)

Grosz (1994) made these comments about alterity in the context of discussing sexual difference, and we will be obliged to return to this issue as well in order to complete our argument. In general, the insistence on alterity of which she spoke is a direct consequence of the indeterminate pliability and plasticity emphasized by much contemporary scholarship on embodiment, and which for our purpose can be identified with the body's spontaneity in contrast with its "natural" (regular and law-governed) functions and cycles.

EMBODIED ALTERITY

I must make this notion of alterity of the self as embodied otherness more precise. Blake (1790/1988) said that all deities reside within the human breast, and I want to take him literally, and say yes, the breast and the limbs and the genitals and the head and the manner in which all are synthesized into the same bodily existence. Merleau-Ponty

(1945/1962; 1968) got at the heart of the matter, and here it is worth pausing a moment to recognize the affinity between Merleau-Ponty and his colleague Piaget (1963). It is not only that in his university course on child psychology Merleau-Ponty drew heavily on the empirical work of Piaget. There is a thematic synergy especially between *Phenomenology of Perception* and *Origins of Intelligence*, insofar as both authors were uncomfortable with either empiricism or intellectualism, both were concerned with the problematic nature of the subject/object distinction, both had great respect for gestalt theory, and both recognized the implications of their work for a transformation of biology. In respectively asserting the primacy of perception and the primacy of assimilation as processes fundamental to the levels of analysis with which they were concerned, both recognized a basic indeterminacy at the core of existence, so that in one sense something can be more or less of an object, and in another sense the meaning of every object is inexhaustible. They also placed a parallel emphasis on the importance of the kinetic and motility in determining the manner in which we inhabit the world as intelligent, intentional beings. These last two features of human existence, indeterminacy and movement, are connected with the circumstance that we can never quite completely catch up with ourselves, always leaving both a surplus of meaning and of the unexplained, and hence an opening to alterity.

An aspect of this surplus is evident in Merleau-Ponty's (1968) discussion of the intertwining or the chiasmus between the sentient and sensible within our own bodies, using the example of "my hand, while it is felt from within, is also accessible from without, itself tangible, for my other hand" (p. 133). Furthermore, he observed that one could have the curious situation of one hand touching an object and, at the same time, the other hand touching it, such that there is a crisscrossing, and reversibility of the sentient and the sensible:

> There is a circle of the touched and the touching, the touched takes hold of the touching; there is a circle of the visible and the seeing, the seeing is not without visible existence; there is even an inscription of the touching in the visible, of the seeing in the tangible—and the converse; there is finally a propagation of these changes to all the bodies of the same type and of the same style which I see and touch—and this by virtue of the fundamental fission or segregation of the sentient and the sensible which, laterally, makes the organs of my body communicate and founds transitivity from one body to another. (Merleau-Ponty, 1968, p. 143)

Merleau-Ponty (1968) struggled for metaphors to describe this intimate alterity of embodiment, trying two leaves or layers, two halves of a cut orange that fit together perfectly but that are still separate, two lips of the same mouth that touch one another in repose, "two circles, or two vortexes, or two spheres, concentric when I live naively, and as soon as I question myself, the one slightly decentered with respect to the other . . ." (p. 138).

Slightly and, I might add, inevitably decentered, this "fundamental fission or segregation" is also overdetermined. We can see it in our mirror image, the encounter with which Lacan (1977/1998) argued is formative of the self at an early stage of development. We can see it in the bilateral symmetry of our bodies, which is moreover an imperfect symmetry, as any gentleman can observe who has attempted to grow nicely balanced sideburns on a face with one ear inevitably slightly higher than the other. In another sense, the phallus is other of the male as the fetus is the other of the female. Certainly, both the phallus and the pregnant female are images that one can find throughout human religion as symbols of the divine. But the other on the body's outside that is the phallus is different from the fetal other within precisely in relation to that profound dependence that Otto (1923) labeled creature-feeling, and may be one of its sources (the other being infantile neoteny, as La Barre, 1970, elaborated). That is, when the penis becomes the phallus it is sovereign, and the man who withdraws his allegiance in a moment of doubt can be punished by the disappearance of this other, the reversion of the phallus to a mere penis, leaving him to drown in the mirror of abandonment. In the case of the fetus, one reverses the valence of dependency, the fetus is profoundly dependent and cannot exist alone. Thus two gendered modes of intimate embodied otherness, with different valences of dependency and therefore different potentials for becoming vehicles of the divine. From this standpoint, the recurrence of the phallus and the pregnant female in religious symbolism does far more than to signal the veneration of potency or fertility.

To describe the kernel of embodied otherness Merleau-Ponty (1945/1962; 1968) used the French word *écart*, which one can translate as gap, interval, distance, difference, or lapse. Gail Weiss (1999) called attention to this term in a brief but important chapter, calling it a "space of non-coincidence that resists articulation . . . the unrepresentable space of differentiation . . . the invisible 'hinge' that both makes reversibility [between the sensible and the sentient] possible and, simultaneously, prevents it from being fully achieved" (pp. 120–121). Merleau-Ponty (1968) indeed took pains to emphasize that it is a reversibility always imminent and never realized in fact. My left hand is always on the verge of touching my right hand touching the things, but I never reach coincidence; the coincidence eclipses at the moment of realization, and one of two things always occurs: either my right hand really passes over to the rank of touched, but then its hold on the world is interrupted; or it retains its hold on the world, but then I do not really touch *it* [italics added]—my right hand touching, I palpate with my left had only its outer covering. (p. 148)

Weiss (1999) observed that *écart*, as the moment of disincorporation that makes all forms of corporeal differentiation possible, is also precisely what allows us to establish boundaries between bodies, boundaries that must be respected in order to respect the agencies that flow from them" (p. 128). Yet, it is not only the ground for boundaries but for intersubjectivity and intercorporeality. To reiterate the quote with which I began this section, the écart "founds transitivity from one body to another." Merleau-Ponty (1968) said, "If my left hand can touch my right hand while it palpates the tangibles, can touch it touching, can turn its palpation back upon it, why, when touching the hand of another, would I not touch in it that same power to espouse the things that I have touched on my own?" (p. 141). This écart of phenomenology describes the inevitable moment of embodied otherness as the kernel of the self's alterity (an inner reversiblity that corresponds to the reversibility between self and other) and hence of the alterity that is ultimately elaborated into the religious sentiment in all its plenitude of forms.

Luce Irigary (1993), in her sensuously intimate critique of Merleau-Ponty (1945/1962; 1968; she called him a male solipsist who ultimately privileges the visual over the tactile, and makes the diagnosis that his version of seeing "remains in an incestuous prenatal situation with the whole," p. 173), added to the stock of images. She asked how the feeling-felt relation of hand touching hand differs, with no subject or object, not passive or active, if one joins the two hands "palms together, fingers outstretched, constitut[ing] a very particular touching. A gesture often reserved for women (at least in the West) and which evokes, doubles, the *touching of the lips* silently applied on one another. A touching more intimate than that of one hand taking hold of the other" (p. 161). And as for the lips, in women there are two sets of two lips, those above and those below, touching each other in different ways and existing in relation to one another. "And this would be one of the differences between men and women, that these lips do not re-join each other according to the same economy" (p. 167).

There is a paratheological strain in the interplay between Merleau-Ponty (1945/1962; 1968) and Irigaray (1993), and this is not accidental since they were so close to discovering the origin of religion in embodied otherness. In sorting out the valences attributed to the interpenetration of vision and touch, Irigaray opened the question of God and how "God is always entrusted to the look and never sufficiently imagined as tactile bliss" (p. 162). Elsewhere, she chided Merleau-Ponty for espousing a form of animism. Indeed, he spoke of a flesh of the world that interpenetrates and is reversible with bodily flesh, as the general description of the more specific instances of the "coiling over of the visible upon the seeing body, of the touching on the tangible body" (Irigaray, 1993, p. 146) as well as the "double and crossed situating of the visible in the tangible and of the tangible in the visible" (p. 134).

This flesh that bridges or better enfolds the *écart* was for Merleau-Ponty (1945/1962; 1968) an element of Being in the sense that water, air, earth, and fire are elements. When he spoke of language as flesh in its sonorous being, there was a sense of the ultimate sacred postulate of the Bible being reversed to read "and the flesh was made word," and when he ended his essay with an ellipsis the preceding words were that reversibility "is the ultimate truth . . ." Neither is it a coincidence that when he wrote, "The world seen is not 'in' my body, and my body is not 'in' the visible world ultimately: as flesh applied to a flesh, the world neither surrounds it nor is surrounded by it" (p. 138), his articulation of the world as "flesh applied to flesh" was resonant with how for Bataille (1992) an animal's life is life "water in water." Could it be that both are referring to the same intimacy of immanence, that we are no more aware of flesh that the fish is of the water in which it swims, and that the difference in the animal's state of grace and ours is the existence of the *écart*, or alterity itself that includes the possibility of becoming self-aware of the element in which we move?

I will turn again to an ethnographic instance to capture this element of embodiment more precisely. A Navajo chanter of my acquaintance will declaim for extended periods against the contemporary travesty of tape recording sacred songs as a means of learning how to conduct ceremonies. Perpetrators go from ceremony to ceremony conducted by different healers instead of appropriately learning from one mentor over an extended period. They begin performing the ceremony without taking the trouble really to understand how they are supposed to use the songs. Worse, they use the material without either being authorized by the chanter from whom they took it or acknowledging the source. He told of having caught people in his ceremonies with a tape recorder concealed in their coats or in blankets and expelling them from the proceedings. He said that sometimes a person with a recorder will be sitting all the way on the other side of the hogan from the healer, sometimes such a person will be standing outside the hogan, and if the chanter is a powerful singer, the person might even be 100 yards away and still be able to record the song.

My initial understanding of why tape recording is unacceptable and inauthentic was in terms of the textuality of the songs and their appropriate treatment. It was a violent taking out of context, an *arrachement,* both as a tearing out of its setting within a moment of performance and as a wresting away from its legitimate owner. It was also the imposition of a nontraditional medium inscribing and preserving sacred material that should never be so fixed and frozen. Then the chanter told me something that changed my understanding of his objection. He said that the way it used to be, and the way it should be, was for the person learning the songs to be sitting *close enough to the chanter to see his lips move as he sang.* With the invocation of moving lips, the song emanating from the bodily portal, power passing by force of breath through the gap of the lips, the apprentice focusing on the action required to bring the chant into intersubjective being, my understanding shifted ground from textuality to embodiment. It shifted from context and technological medium to lived spatiality and physical proximity.

Somewhat later I came across the following passage written by Gladys Reichard (1950) about Navajo ceremonies: "Since power is to the Navaho like a wave in a pool, always effective though becoming weaker the farther it radiates from chanter and patient, each person in attendance derives benefit from what is done in proportion to his proximity to the ritual" (p. xxxvii). Previously I would not have taken the image of a wave in a pool quite as literally as I do, but I read this passage in light of the chanter's invocation of watching moving lips in immediate proximity, of recording from across the hogan, of recording from outside, and of recording from 100 yards away. Though perhaps attenuated, power is still power at 100 yards remove. But the optimal form of otherness as power is hardly grandiose, taking form in the *écart*—the narrow gap between the chanter's lips, and the narrow gap between healer and apprentice. This is the origin of religion, the sacred, and the holy: in the intimate alterity of power as a bodily secretion and not in the wholly other of abstract majesty.

CONTESTED ALTERITY

As I move to a close, let me anticipate several objections that might arise to my thesis that alterity is the phenomenological kernel of religion. The first is that it might appear to be an essentializing move, which would be highly suspect in the current theoretical climate. That depends on how you construe it. The relevant dichotomy is between the essential and the contingent, and the current theoretical bias is in favor of the contingent. The objection to positing an essence is when that essence has a specific content that is abstract and invariant. What I have called attention to, on the contrary, is an alterity that is experientially concrete, yet has no content prior to its elaboration in an ethnographic or historical instance. Alterity is not an essential thing, but an essential displacement; not a center of meaning but a duplicity (doubleness not deceit) of the kind that is recognized in the phenomenological *epoché*. This *epoché*, often referred to as a "phenomenological reduction" or "bracketing," is not a mystery but a method. To give a rudimentary example, it is the effect produced by uttering a word (try it with *egg*) 20 or 30 times without stopping. This effect is the bracketing off of the word's sonorous being from its semantic being. The point is not to wrench the word from its context but to allow it to become reduced to a "phenomenon" that can then be subject to precise existential description. The epoche is then a methodological elaboration of the alterity that is an elementary structure of existence. When one elaborates alterity in and for itself, what results is what we call religion. From this duplicity, this gap, this *écart* there develops an uncanny array of religious forms precisely because of the inevitable contingency and indeterminacy of existence. If there is an essence involved, it is an essence of the particular—that is, one is to describe it empirically where one found it among the *minute particulars* of existence, again to borrow a phrase from Blake (1790/1988).

A second objection might be that the alterity I have described is everywhere so therefore it is nowhere, and can thus account for nothing in particular, certainly not for religion in particular. Here an evaluation is needed, because if alterity is everywhere and nowhere, one may judge my thesis on that count either as quite trivial or as positing something equivalent in the domain of existence to the "dark matter" recently discovered by astrophysics in the cosmic domain. Alterity may be constituent of a "general atmosphere" pervading existence in a manner similar to the way Merleau-Ponty (1945/1962) described sexuality as pervading existence, a trace or dimension of it present in all our dealings with the world and others regardless of whether there is an explicit sexual reference in them. Yet if this is the case, alterity is hardly specific to religion. Recall that Freud (1955) framed his essay on the uncanny as a discussion of aesthetics, saying that the uncanny is a province of aesthetics that has to do with the frightening. If the uncanny is essential to religion and the aesthetic, how can we distinguish the two? I might want to say, again following Blake's (1790/1988) theory of imagination, that I do not want to distinguish the two—but it is more precise to say that they are distinguished in that, though alterity is important to both, alterity itself is the object of religion. To state this point in more general terms, when we elaborate alterity as oppression of the other, we are in the domain of politics; when we elaborate it as striking beauty, we are in the domain of art and aesthetics; when we elaborate it as competition, we are (perhaps) in the domain of athletics; but when we elaborate it as alterity in and for itself, we are in the domain of religion. What can one gain by this intimation of religion as diffused throughout social reality? It might suggest the need to translate or update van der Leeuw's (1938) and Otto's (1923) notions of power as divine majesty into Foucault's (1977) notion of power as inhabiting the very interstices and infesting the sinews of social life. It might suggest as well a reinterpretation of the thesis of disenchantment of the world that Marcel Gauchet (1985), following Weber's theory of religion's inevitable decline, has recently elaborated. For Gauchet, despite the persistence of belief, the human-social world has become reconstituted not only outside the religious domain, but also independently of the religious logic within which it originated. On the other hand, it is perhaps possible to interpret Gauchet's disenchantment as an escape of alterity from the domain of the strictly religious, such that the sacred does not disappear but becomes diffused through reality, rendering the human world even more rather than less a religious phenomenon.

These considerations raise a further question, if not an objection: If religion is inevitable, then how does the question of skepticism, the problem of belief and unbelief, enter this argument? Let us address this question by turning again to William James (1961) and another of his recent commentators, Charles Taylor (2002). Taylor showed that, for James, the choice between agnosticism and belief was a "forced option" and claimed that James's poignant formulation of this sometimes agonizing choice qualified him as "our great philosopher of the cusp" (p. 59) between the two great options. James challenged the "agnostic veto" on faith that requires skepticism "as a duty until 'sufficient evidence' for religion can be found" (James, as cited in Taylor, 2002, p. 48), on the grounds that it is not necessarily more irrational to risk erroneous belief than to risk hoping that what we desire to believe may be true. The cusp is precisely the choice of which form of risk to take, and as Taylor said, the choice must be made on "gut instinct" (p. 58). Yet although this gut instinct may be derived from originary embodied alterity, its content—including not only theistic principles but also the sense that a choice must be made and that this choice must be in the form of a commitment—consists of many layers of historical context and cultural meaning sedimented upon the phenomenological kernel. To be precise, Taylor observed that James predicated his notion of religious experience upon the development of a kind of personal religion made possible by Protestantism and evolved into a post-Durkheimian expressive individualism in which "a host of urban monads hover on the boundary between solipsism and communication" (p. 86), and in which the emphasis of religion "shifted more and more toward the strength and genuineness of the feelings rather than toward the nature of their object" (p. 99). The phenomenological kernel I have identified is at the opposite end of this continuum of elaboration from James' notion of religious "experience." It does not have to do exclusively with a personal religion experienced in solitude, for the alterity of self I have discussed is also the ground for intersubjectivity and by extension collectivity. It does not have to do with a personal religion that is an encounter with a personalized divinity, for the sense of alterity can be eminently impersonal. If my argument is accepted, one cannot be skeptical that there is a religious impulse that culture inevitably elaborates in a myriad of symbolic, institutional, and experiential forms, but must be skeptical of any particular elaboration as a product of its historical and social conditions. In this sense, the thesis I have developed here may contribute to the anthropological theory of religion but offers no help in resolving theological questions or dilemmas of faith.

A final objection may be that my understanding of alterity is too different from the way it is customarily used in anthropology, as referring to political, racial, ethnic, gender, class, and religious otherness—the otherness that is the occasion for identity politics, war, conflict, and violence (Corbey & Leersen, 1991; Taussig, 1993). But the implications of my argument are that embodiment also grounds these forms of alterity and that they too have a religious structure, and I agree with Jacques Derrida (1998) when he said, "In these times, language and nation form the historical body of all religious passion" (p. 4). And occasionally the religious dimension of political and ethnic alterity comes to the fore in discussions by anthropologists. Here, I am thinking of Taussig's (1993) intuition of "the marked attraction and repulsion of savagery as a genuinely sacred power for whiteness . . ." (p. 150). The colonial contrast between noble Indians and degenerate Blacks is not only a history of labor discipline, but "a Sacred History too, in which race-fantasy takes the place of heavenly fantasy" (Taussig, 1993, p. 150). This is the case because insofar as the Black phallus becomes a demonic figure of what Durkheim (1995) called the impure sacred, race "acquires the burden of carrying the emotive charge of men exchanging women across the colorless line of colonial proletarianization" (Taussig, 1993, p. 150). I cite these examples in order to suggest that, if there is something to my thesis that alterity is the phenomenological kernel of religion, then there is a sense in which we will be able to say that political alterity is a religious structure.

Let me pursue this line of argument via consideration of Derrida's (1998) account of religion in the contemporary world, which is riddled with reverberations of alterity at almost every level. At the level of metadiscourse, Derrida observed the apparent inevitablility of finding two sources of religion, an alterity in the form of "division and iterability of the source" (p. 65). In the title, Derrida identified these two sources as faith and knowledge, but they reappear as messianism and chora, experience of belief and experience of the unscathed (the latter is elsewhere called experience of sacredness (p. 62), *relegere* and *religare*, attestation and disenchantment (pp. 64–65), immunity and autoimmunity (p. 47), absolute respect for life and human sacrifice (p. 50), fiduciary and unscathedness (p. 58), and the works of Kant and Bergson (p. 33). These pairs roughly map on to one another at different levels of analysis, and I would want to add to them the intimate alterity of the self and the imposing alterity of the wholly other, but the one that is most salient at the moment is the image of immunity and autoimmunity.

Derrida (1998) asked, "Is not the unscathed <l'indemne> the very matter—the thing itself—of religion?" (p. 23). If "the thing itself" is the same object of religion identified by Otto (1923), then the wholly other is precisely then unscathed. But the most radically other for Derrida went beyond the positive Other represented in messianism; it is chora, nothing (no being, nothing present), "the very place of an infinite resistance, of an infinitely impassible persistence <restance>: an utterly faceless other" (p. 21). Indeed, for Derrida the *heilig* or holy was associated with unscathed, indemnity, and indemnification, and he made the move of associating these with immune, immunity, immunization, "and above all, 'autoimmunity'" (p. 70). The autoimmune response in not just the immune system reacting to itself, but "of protecting itself against its self-protection by destroying its own immune system" (this is a unique interpretation of immunology, I think). He said the more prevalent this becomes, "We feel ourselves authorized to speak of a sort of general logic of autoimmunization. It seems indispensable to us today for thinking the relations between faith and knowledge, religion and science, as well as the duplicity of sources in general" (p. 73, FN 27). But this is really a general logic of alterity in the form of an alterity of the self grounded in embodiment (that is, corporal immediacy), what I would call "raw existence" in contrast, or confrontation, with what Agamben (1995) called "bare life." Reaction to the machine (and one would add, its uncanny side, that of self as automaton) is at once immu-

nitary and autoimmune. It is a fear of self in the context of the disloca-
tion (alienation?) produced by what Derrida called "teletechnoscience,"
with which contemporary religion allies itself (thereby becoming it)
and reacts strongly against (thereby reacting against itself; p. 46).

Globalatinization (mondialatinization) is the term Derrida (1998)
coined to describe this "strange alliance of Christianity, as the experience of the death of God, and tele-technoscientific capitalism" (p. 13),
or again "the strange phenomenon of Latinity and its globalization"
(p. 29), where Anglo-American is the direct inheritor of Latin proper.
In this cultural regime,

> *Religion* circulates in the world, one might say, *like an English
> word <comme un mot anglais>* that has been to Rome and taken
> a detour to the United States. Well beyond its strictly capitalist
> or politico-military figures, a hyper-imperialist appropriation
> has been underway now for centuries. It imposes itself in a par-
> ticularly palpable manner within the conceptual apparatus of
> international law and of global political rhetoric. Wherever this
> apparatus dominates, it articulates itself through a discourse on
> religion. From here on, the word 'religion' is calmly (and vio-
> lently) applied to things which have always been and remain for-
> eign to what this word names and arrests in history. (Derrida,
> 1998, p. 29)

Globalatinization, the cultural dimension of the pax Americana, is
the language of "religion" pronounced with the accent of John Wayne.
But I bring in these considerations not so much to endorse Derrida's
(1998) argument per se, as to recognize in it one way in which religion
can be discussed as a cultural elaboration of alterity on the level of
global society at large rather than merely as an element of individual,
interior experience. This goes beyond saying that specific forms of religion are spreading globally, or even that religion has taken on global
significance, and suggests instead that there is a blurring of the very
boundary between alterity in its political and religious senses.

In this context, one can understand the contemporary return of
religion (of the repressed?) as a global upsurge of alterity that increasingly takes the form of autoimmunity. There is no need for a society
as organism metaphor here—I follow Rappaport (1999) in identifying the locus of the autoimmune response as an adaptive system rather
than an organism. Yet I want to say that this autoimmune response
"metastasizes" to places like Navajoland where it creates the religious
aporia encountered by the chanter I discussed above. Should I, asked
the chanter, risk the dangerous desecration of committing sacred mate-

rial to this technological medium that is an arm of global culture, or should I risk the disappearance of that knowledge altogether as the encroachment of global culture eats away the viability of my practices? This autoimmune response is even more virulent in those places less insulated from globalatinization, more open to the brute presence of technoscience and empire.

CONCLUSION: INEVITABLE ALTERITY

The theoretical move I have made to embrace alterity is not yet so much the presentation and defense of a thesis as the outline of a program of research. My intent has been to bring contemporary thinking about alterity to bear on rehabilitating the notion of otherness found in Otto (1923) and van der Leeuw (1938). My preliminary conclusion is that the latter provide insight into the proliferation of theorizing about alterity insofar as it coincides with the return of religion, the reenchantment of the world. Does this leave me on the verge of my own encounter with alterity, on the brink of a theological position, or at least with the desire to make what William James (1961) called a spiritual judgment rather than an existential judgment about religion? I can do no better than to cite Karl Jaspers, who said, "When the professor is told by the barbarian that once there was nothing except a great feathered serpent, unless the learned man feels a thrill and a half temptation to wish it were true, he is no judge of such things at all" (Jaspers, as cited in Smart, 1986, p. xi). For myself, I feel no need to declare any religion since from my standpoint we are in the realm of the religious whenever we encounter otherness in its own right, whether or not it is impressive, and whenever imagination sends a spark across the *écart*, animating the alterity that is the phenomenological kernel of our existence.

The task of elaborating the theoretical consequences of this approach remains. I have used the phrases "phenomenological kernel" and "elementary structure" interchangeably in this discussion to describe alterity. I have made no effort to account for how or why one elaborates different religious forms and institutions from this point. Yet should we be surprised that Levi-Strauss (1969; see also Geller, n.d.) found incest, conceivable as a primordial problematization of intimate alterity, to be critical to the elementary structure of kinship? Should we be surprised that Durkheim (1995) found totemism, conceivable as a primordial problematization of collective alterity and identity, to be critical as an elementary form of the religious life? Perhaps for now our advance is in the ability to refine the critique of Durkheim to say that, in arguing that society was the powerful other whose mystification leads to religion, his error was not one of reductionism, the attempt to explain religion in terms of society (cf., Csordas, 1997, p. 265). Instead, Durkheim's error was to mistake the specific instance for the general case—the alterity of the social for the general existential condition of alterity. Such a refinement allows religion, as a cultural elaboration of alterity sui generis, to maintain its status as sui generis vis-à-vis society, without granting it a right to turn the reductionist tables and reduce society to itself, and without the right to claim any content or meaning save that elaborated in the course of human life. It also allows us the possibility of examining the proposition that religion emanates from the core of existence in a way that goes far beyond what we typically label as religious. And, as long as we leave the possibility that we can still surprise ourselves, there is hope for us.

Note: I presented versions of this chapter as a Keynote Lecture at the 2002 annual meetings of the Jean Piaget Society and as the Presidential Lecture at the 2002 biennial conference of the Society for the Anthropology of Religion. The chapter is a modified and abridged version of an article published under the title "Asymptote of the Ineffable: Embodiment, Alterity, and the Theory of Religion" (2004) in *Current Anthropology*, 45, 163–185.

REFERENCES

Abu-Lughod, L. (1991). Writing against culture. In R. G. Fox (Ed.), *Recapturing anthropology: Working in the present* (pp. 137–162). Santa Fe, NM: School of American Research Press.

Agamben, G. (1998). *Homo Sacer: Sovereign power and bare life*. Stanford, CA: Stanford University Press.

Asad, T. (1993). *Genealogies of religion: Discipline and reasons of power in Christianity and Islam*. Baltimore, MD: The Johns Hopkins University Press.

Bataille, G. (1992). *Theory of religion*. New York: Zone Books.

Beal, T. K. (2002). *Religion and its monsters*. New York: Routledge.

Blake, W. (1988). *The complete poetry and prose of William Blake*. New York: Doubleday. (Original work published 1790)

Corbey, R., & Leersen, J. (Eds.). (1991). *Alterity, identity, image: Selves and others in society and scholarship*. Atlanta, GA: Rodopi.

Csordas, T. J. (1994). *The sacred self: A cultural phenomenology of charismatic healing*. Berkeley, CA: University of California Press.

Csordas, T. J. (1997). *Language, charisma, and creativity: The ritual life of a religious movement*. Berkeley, CA: University of California Press.

Derrida, J., & Vattimo, G. (Eds.). (1998). *Religion*. Stanford, CA: Stanford University Press.

Durkheim, E. (1995). *The elementary forms of religious life*. New York: Free Press.

Eliade, M. (1958). *Patterns in comparative religion*. Cleveland, OH: World Publishing.

Foucault, M. (1997). *Discipline and punish: The birth of the prison*. New York: Vintage Books.

Freud, S. (1955). The 'Uncanny.' In J. Strachey (Ed.), *The standard edition of the complete psychological works of Sigmund Freud* (Vol. 17, pp. 219–253). London: The Hogarth Press.

Gauchet, M. (1985). *Le desenchantement du monde: Une histoire politique de la religion* [The disenchantment of the world: A political history of religion]. Paris: Editions Gallimard.

Geertz, C. (1973). *The interpretation of cultures*. New York: Basic Books.

Geller, J. (n.d.). *Worked-over-matter-man ;eq chiasm*. Unpublished manuscript.

Grosz, E. (1994). *Volatile bodies: Toward a corporeal feminism*. Bloomington, IN: Indiana University Press.

Irigaray, L. (1993). The invisible of the flesh: a reading of Merleau-Ponty, The visible and the invisible, "The intertwining—the chiasm." In L. Irigaray (Ed.), *An ethics of sexual difference* (pp. 151–184). Ithaca, NY: Cornell University Press.

James, W. (1961). *The varieties of religious experience*. New York: Collier Books.

La Barre, W. (1970). *The ghost dance: the origins of religion*. New York: Dell Publishing Co., Inc.

Lacan, J. (1977). The mirror stage as formative of the function of the I. In J. Lacan, *Ecrits* (pp. 1–7). New York: Norton.

Leder, D. (1990). *The absent body*. Chicago: University of Chicago Press.

Levi-Strauss, C. (1969). *The elementary structures of kinship*. Boston: Beacon Press.

Long, C. (1976). The oppressive elements in religion and the religions of the oppressed. *Harvard Theological Review, 59*, 397–412.

Mauss, M. (1950). *Les techniques du corps: Sociologie et anthropologie* [The techniques of the body: Sociology and anthropology]. Paris: Presses Universitare de France.

Merleau-Ponty, M. (1962). *The phenomenology of perception*. New York: Humanities Press. (Original work published 1945)

Merleau-Ponty, M. (1968). *The visible and the invisible* Evanston, IL: Northwestern University Press.

Otto, R. (1923). *The idea of the holy*. Oxford, U.K.: Oxford University Press.

Piaget, J. (1963). *The origins of intelligence in children*. New York: Norton.

Reichard, G. A. (1950). *Navaho religion: A study of symbolism*. Princeton, NJ: Princeton University Press.

Smart, N. (1986). *Foreword*. In G. Van Der Leeuw (Ed.), *Religion in essence and manifestation* (pp. ix–xix). Princeton, NJ: Princeton University Press.

Taussig, M. (1993). *Mimesis and alterity.* New York: Routledge.

Taylor, C. (2002). *Varieties of religion today: William James revisited.* Cambridge, MA: Harvard University Press.

Turner, E. (2002, April). *Religion and connectedness: What does this binding word 'religion' mean?* Roy A. Rappaport Distinguished Lecture in the Anthropology of Religion at the 2002 meeting of the Society for the Anthropology of Religion, Cleveland, Ohio.

van der Leeuw, G. (1938). *Religion in essence and manifestation.* Princeton, NJ: Princeton University Press.

Weiss, G. (1999). *Body images: Embodiment as intercorporeality.* New York: Routledge.

Wiebe, D. (1999). *The politics of religious studies.* New York: Palgrave.

Wolf, E. R. (1982). *Europe and the people without history.* Berkeley, CA: University of California Press.

Zaner, R. M. (1981). *The context of self: A phenomenological inquiry using medicine as a clue.* Athens, OH: Ohio University Press.

7

THE EMBODIMENT OF MENTAL STATES

Timothy P. Racine

University of Manitoba

Jeremy I. M. Carpendale

Simon Fraser University

Wittgenstein (1958) famously asked, "What is left over if I subtract the fact that my arm goes up from the fact that I raise my arm?" (§621). Meltzoff, Gopnik, and Repacholi's (1999) answer to his question is "intention" (p. 24). Meltzoff and colleagues (1999) go on to assert that, "Intentions are mental states and bodily movements are physical events in the world. The two have an intimate relation because intentions underlie and cause bodily movements." Or, again, Meltzoff (2002) in writing again about the relation between action and mental states, asserted, "Wittgenstein (1953) makes it clear with a blunt question: 'What is left over if I subtract the fact that my arm goes up from the fact that I raise my arm?' Answer: intention" (p. 17). Although Meltzoff and his colleagues assume that the obvious answer is "intention," in fact, Russell (1996) pointed out that Wittgenstein's question was "intended to dramatize the absurdity of answers such as 'my intending to raise my arm' and thus the absurdity of the picture of a purely mental willing entity trapped, as it were, inside the body, able, if it pulls the right levers, to cause the body to move as it intends it to move" (p. 173).

This view of disembodied mental states underlying and causing behavior is embedded in our languages. It is not at issue in our everyday language use; it causes problems, however, when we take up this view unreflectively into our psychological theories. In this chapter, we contrast the various approaches to explaining the development of children's social understanding. In so doing, we discuss some of Wittgenstein's arguments against a disembodied view of language and mind, and we argue for an embodied view of mental states, which in turn leads to a different approach to the development of children's social understanding. According to the alternative view, minds are not a biological given, and they only arise through the social process of interacting with others (Mead, 1934, 1977). As case studies of the implications of taking these respective views of mental states, we consider recent research on infant and chimpanzee social cognition.

EMBODIED AND DISEMBODIED VIEWS OF MENTAL STATES AND CHILDREN'S SOCIAL UNDERSTANDING

The Causal-Psychological View of the Mind

In the social developmental literature, the view of mental states expressed by Meltzoff and colleagues (1999) is not unique. In fact, this common-sense view of mental states as inner mental entities that underlie and cause behavior is the generally accepted way of viewing mental states. This view of mental states is also evident in research on the relations between language and social development. When coding parents' and children's various uses of mental state terms, it is accepted practice to code the uses of such words as either "conversational" or "actual mental reference" (e.g., Bartsch & Wellman, 1995; Shatz, Wellman, & Silber, 1983). The assumption is that although people often use mental state terms in conversation as ways to influence interaction for example by expressing degree of certainty (e.g., "It is raining, I think"), at other times, such words actually do refer to inner entities that cause behavior. Although we could list many more clear statements of this common folk psychological view in the literature, we would like to point out simply that this is the position that Wittgenstein completely rejected. Yet, this commonsense view of the nature of the mind and mental states is embedded in our languages, and often recapitulates itself in our thinking. We take the commonsense view to be a disembodied view of mental states because, according to this way of thinking, attributes of persons, such as their beliefs, are thought of as independent of embodied lived experience and could be attributed to "brains in a vat."

Another way to broach this issue is to point out the role that "propositional attitudes" are assumed to play in mental states. For example, Joan having an attitude of belief toward the proposition "it might rain" is typically taken not only to be a description of what might be the case for a person named Joan, but also as a description of Joan's mental process of believing that it might rain. Namely, that Joan has a particular mental state (belief) about a particular contingency (that it might rain), which accordingly might cause her to bring an umbrella to work. This is assumed to constitute and define her belief, and Joan is understood to represent her attitude (a mental state) toward this proposition (a mental content) in order to bring the umbrella to work. Although this is again all well and good in ordinary language use, researchers seem to forget that this is a metaphorical view of mental activity. Agents are not mentally related to propositions but rather to what the supposed propositions are about (Bennett & Hacker, 2003; Hacker, 1992, 1996). Although observers of agents can construct these propositional relationships or describe beliefs in such a way, taking this metaphor literally results in a misguided view of mental states (e.g., Bickhard, 2001, 2004).

To us, the common conception of mental states and mental contents assumed by most researchers studying social development are characteristic of a causal-psychological view of mind according to which (a) mental states underlie and cause behavior; (b) mental representations are mental objects with semantic properties; (c) mental states are a series of relations between agents and mental representations (propositions or otherwise); and (d) what differentiates an intention from say a belief is the existence of a characteristic mental state occurring when one intends to x but not occurring when one believes y. Although multifarious problems have been identified with this approach from a diversity of perspectives (e.g., Button, Coulter, Lee, & Sharrock, 1995; Carpendale & Lewis, 2004; Fogel, 1993; Garfinkel, 1967; Racine, 2002, 2004; Savage-Rumbaugh, Shanker, & Talbot, 1998; Sinha, 1999; ter Hark, 1990; Turnbull, 2003; Wootton, 1997), our goal in subsequent sections is to trace this way of thinking across theorists who work in very different camps and to show that such problems do not come up in our approach. In contrast to the disembodied, dualistic, causal-psychological view of mental states, we argue instead for an embodied view of mental life. By embodied, we do not just mean a concern with isolated human bodies but rather with human embodied experience that is necessarily social. This embodied cultural and linguistic social experience, we argue, is the foundation for the development of children's understanding of the mind. Psychological talk is based on or redescribes activity.

This common view of mental states as inner mental entities becomes a problem when philosophers and psychologists take seriously the metaphors about the mind that our language is based on and use this as the basis for thinking, for example, about how children develop an understanding of the mind. It is normally not a problem when language is being used to do work in interaction. It is only when language, as Wittgenstein (1958) put it, *"goes on holiday,"* and is "idling" that this view begins to "bewitch" our thinking (§38). It is this commonsense way of thinking about mental states, we argue, that has resulted in serious problems in theorizing about children's social development in particular.

Why is this commonsense disembodied view such a taken-for-granted way of thinking about the mind? This current way of thinking may be due in large part to the well-discussed Cartesian dualistic split between mind and body (e.g., Bennett & Hacker, 2003; Lakoff & M. Johnson, 1999; Overton, 2004; Savage-Rumbaugh et al., 1998; Williams, 1999). Hacker (1997) summarized some of the many reasons why we have a view of the mind as inner so ingrained in our languages. According to Hacker (1997),

> [The view] that a human being is a composite creature consisting of body and soul (or mind, or spirit) is an ancient one. It is bound up with our fear of death, with the craving for an afterlife in a happier world, with our grief at the death of our loved ones and our longing to be reunited with them. . . . And it is deeply rooted in the grammar of our languages. . . . This conception, in different forms, was articulated in the religious and philosophical thought of antiquity and the Middle Ages. It was given its most powerful philosophical expression in our era by Descartes. According to Descartes, a human being is composed of two distinct substances, the mind and the body. (p. 14)

Our purpose here is not to trace the historical roots of this commonsense view but instead to examine the consequences of this way of thinking for a particular area of research literature on the development of children's understanding of the psychological world.

The current approach to this topic is known as children's "theories of mind." In this area, there are clear implications for the way in which developmental psychologists think about mental states that are made explicit in assumptions about the problem children face in learning about the psychological world. The problem is set up as one of inferring what is going on in the private and inaccessible reaches of the minds of others. How could young children solve this difficult problem? The commonly suggested solutions are that children either formulate a theory in their early years (e.g., Gopnik & Wellman, 1992, 1994), that they are born with such a theory in the form of a module or set of modules selected for the capacity to "compute" mental states (e.g., Baron-Cohen, 1995; German & Leslie, 2000), or, alternatively, that they solve the problem through simulation by introspecting on their own mind and reasoning by analogy about other minds (Harris, 1991, 1992). All of these attempts to explain children's social understanding are based on this same view of the mind. Wittgenstein, by contrast, in rejecting this view of the mind, completely changed the nature of the problem to be solved by children and hence the foundation for our theories of social development (Carpendale & Lewis, 2004; Montgomery, 2004; Racine, 2004).

Wittgenstein's overriding concern was to dispel the hold that our language has over our way of thinking. We think that we are carefully setting out to study the nature of thought, yet our language drives us to a particular view of the mind and thinking:

> The first step is the one that altogether escapes notice. We talk of processes and states and leave their nature undecided. Sometime perhaps we shall know more about them—we think. But that is just what commits us to a particular way of looking at the matter. For we have a definite concept of what it means to learn to know a process better. (The decisive movement in the conjuring trick has been made, and it was the very one that we thought quite innocent.) (Wittgenstein, 1958, §308)

As researchers, we believe that we have been very careful to avoid specifying the nature of mental states until we discover their nature, but we fail to notice that we have already made assumptions about mental states in the very language we use to talk about them. We have an idea about what it means to learn more about a physical process and we project this on to the case of mental processes. Wittgenstein (1958) discussed this as a confusion between the empirical and the conceptual.

Embodiment and Mental States

Embodiment has been variously discussed in philosophical, developmental, and cognitive science literatures (e.g., Lakoff & M. Johnson, 1999; Merleau-Ponty, 1945/1962; Overton, 1994; Varela, Thompson, & Rosch, 1991). Merleau-Ponty (1945/1962) cautioned that it is impossible to speak about the body and of life in general, but only, for example, the chimpanzee body and chimpanzee life or the human body and human life. This is compatible with the Wittgensteinian position that forms of life ground practices—that is, particular forms of activity emerge for particular species. Lakoff and M. Johnson (1999) drew on Merleau-Ponty's theorizing to argue that the human capability to understand or abstractly reason is attributable particularly to concrete human bodily experiences. They argued that capacities such as mental representation are parasitic on embodiment. Further, the form of our bodies is critical to the particular representations that humans develop and use for both our thought and our language. The notion of embodiment that we wish to develop in this chapter is more a Wittgensteinian one that, although in general agreement with the previously mentioned characterizations, focuses more on the role that distinctively human activities play in our embodied representations of our own minds and the minds of others. It is not just the form of our bodies but also our form of life. From this point of view, psychological concepts "emerge at the level of the whole person's context-embedded deeds" (McDonough, 1999, p. 179). We argue therefore that the meaning of psychological concepts is not only parasitic on embodiment, but is also intractably situated in particular social activities. Further, if psychological meanings are inherently situated and embodied, a disembodied mind is logically impossible (Dartnall, 1999).

Wittgenstein (1958, 1980) contended that intentions, desires, or beliefs do not refer to inner mental entities that are casually related to behavior. Rather, such notions are instantiated in and constituted by human language that is based on or redescribes activity. Such psychological talk should be thought of as embodied, because it is defined by and built into our concrete bodily activities in a social world rather than by particular discrete mental or neurological states that occur when, for example, one intends to write a letter, desires lunch, or believes (the proposition) that it might rain. From our point of view and in contradistinction to the commonsense causal-psychological view of mental states, what distinguishes intentions from say, beliefs, then, is not some disembodied state of mind or brain but rather the embodied role that such concepts play in our life. This is a view of the psychological world as built onto patterns of activity.

In contrast, the view of mental states as inner disembodied entities seems to follow from common assumptions about how language works. "If one thinks of words as names one will be prone to think of psychological expressions as names of psychological objects, events, processes, or states" (Hacker, 1996, p. 132). As a result, we end up with a picture of the mind in which inner processes such as thinking and remembering are thought of as objects. As Canfield (1993) pointed out, if we say of someone, "He has the intention to go to the store," it may appear that he possesses something. It suggests that he has something in the same way that a person might have an object. Although we talk about having intentions, we do not have an intention in the same way that we have a coin. According to Wittgenstein (1958), it is because we are in thrall of this "grammatical fiction" that we tend to think of the mind as inner and private.

However, it might seem to be less of a stretch to analogize having an intention with having a headache in that they are both ostensibly mental states. This analogy breaks down on closer inspection as well, though, when one considers an intention as a mental state. A headache has a clear beginning and an end. One could monitor the progress of a headache with a wristwatch; the awareness of a headache might fade when talking to a friend. Where, however, is the beginning and end to an intention when understood as a literal mental state? The same problem applies to desires and beliefs. Wittgenstein (1980) argued that because intentions, desires, and beliefs lack genuine duration and are not interrupted by attentional shifts, it is misleading to conceive of them as mental states (Racine, 2004). Although the foregoing may seem to some as an exercise in splitting hairs, we point out that many researchers base their theories on the assumptions about mental states that we have been questioning. If these assumptions about mental states are mistaken, their theories lack a coherent foundation.

It is instructive that Wittgenstein (1958) remarked, "An intention is embedded in its situation. If the technique of chess did not exist, I could not intend to play a game of chess" (§337). What does it mean to claim that an intention is "embedded in its situation?" Consider the following example taken from Racine (2004). Moving forward to stand at a bus stop as a bus pulls closer is an expression of an intention to get on the bus for which the criterion lies in mastery of the practice of waiting for a bus. Whether some neurons fired or some psychological events occurred during the execution of this intention is beside the point: If this particular practice did not exist and if this skill had not been mastered, these activities would not have constituted this intention. That is, these activities would not mean that a person had acted intentionally. Children need not "peer into other people's minds" in order to understand their intentions, desires, and beliefs but rather need to see these concepts in others' activities. That is, we say people have these mental states because we, as language-using agents who have mastered a multitude of shared embodied everyday practices, see the concepts that we do. These concepts are rooted in human activity—the human form of life—and are abstracted from the use of words (Bennett & Hacker, 2003). Although to an observer, children might apply these concepts appropriately (or not), the children themselves are not applying these concepts in a reflective sense, and in no way should their ability to attribute mental states to themselves or others be seen as theoretical, or that a child develops a "theory of mind." This is because children are not revising their understanding of psychological concepts based on disconfirming evidence that is argued to latently exist in social interactions (Gopnik & Wellman, 1992, 1994), but are rather developing expectations about the particular patterns of social activity that constitute intention, desire, or belief. In their interactions with others, children do not observe such a pattern of activity and then go about computing the underlying meaning; children instead come to see psychological concepts directly in such patterns of activity. As Hobson (1993) put it, "Perception is not a two-stage process of which the first stage is the perception of meaningless behavioral or other bodily forms (e.g., 'upturned mouth'), and the second is an intellectually based attribution of psychological meaning. Rather the perception is the meaning itself" (p. 40).

Another way to bring out problems with viewing mental state language as referring to inner causal entities is to consider the number of beliefs that a person can be said to have. Hacker (1996) noted, "There are indefinitely many things that I believe at a given time, but I am not in indefinitely many different mental states at a given time" (p. 419). Bickhard (2001, 2004) pointed out that most of us believe, for example, that stepping in front of an oncoming truck is dangerous, but we also believe that blue trucks, pink trucks, and even stripped trucks are dangerous. The point of this exercise is to demonstrate that it is possible to describe a seemingly unlimited number of beliefs that most of us hold. This shows that, just as beliefs cannot be particular mental states, they also cannot be particular mental contents. Children do not have the time to learn all of these beliefs nor the capacity to hold this unbounded number of beliefs. Instead, what is needed is an alternative view of mental states. To speak about beliefs and intentions is really just to talk about activity.

Wittgenstein's Private Language Argument

It is this commonsense causal-psychological and disembodied view of the mind just described that Wittgenstein argued against with his private language argument. What Wittgenstein meant by a private language is not a language that only one person speaks because he or she is the last living speaker or he or she has just developed a new language, but rather it is a language that is necessarily private and could not be taught to others because the meanings of the words are based on private inner referents. Thus, his private language argument is an argument against the view of mental states as private inner entities that we could introspect upon and label to form a language that is private and inaccessible to others. Although we will approach Wittgenstein's private language argument in the context of this general position on language, some authors focus on the "uncheckable checks" aspect of the private language argument (Williams, 1999). That is, if learning the meaning of mental state terms is learning a match between the word and an inner private referent, then how do we know if the child has it right and has learned the word correctly, because parents have no access to the private referent (i.e., the child's mental contents)? Further, because memory is not perfect, how does the child know from one situation to next that he or she has the right match? These are uncheckable checks, because it would be "as if someone were to buy several copies of the morning paper to assure himself that what it said was true" (Wittgenstein, 1958, §265).

However, if a word has a consistent use in a language, this problem is solved because the child can learn to use the word correctly. This is the point of Wittgenstein's (1958) "beetle box" story:

> Suppose everyone had a box with something in it: we call it a "beetle". No one can look into anyone else's box, and everyone says he knows what a beetle is only by looking at *his* beetle.—Here it would be quite possible for everyone to have something different in his box. One might even imagine such a thing constantly changing.—but suppose the word "beetle" had a use in these people's language?—If so it would not be used as the name of a thing. The thing in the box has no place in the language-game at all; not even as a *something*: for the box might even be empty.—No, one can "divide through" by the thing in the box; it cancels out, whatever it is. (§293)

This conclusion is the result of applying a view of language as based on naming objects to sensation and mental state terms. What this shows is that the assumed private inner referent is not necessary. "That is to say: if we construe the grammar of the expression of sensation on the model of 'object and designation' the object drops out of consideration as irrelevant." Williams's (1999) interpretation of the private language argument was that for Wittgenstein, "what lies at the bottom of this is a misguided application of the 'object and designation' model. It cannot apply to sensations. Sensations are not objects . . ." (p. 33). "It is not Wittgenstein who is denying the reality of sensations but the Cartesian who attempts to construe sensations as isolable entities, the objects of pure reference . . ." (p. 32). Wittgenstein (1958) claimed,

> [A sensation] is not a *something*, but not a *nothing* either! The conclusion was only that a nothing would serve just as well as something about which nothing could be said. We have only rejected

the grammar which tries to force itself on us here. The paradox disappears only if we make a radical break with the idea that language always functions in one way, always serves the same purpose; to convey thoughts—which may be about houses, pains, good and evil, or anything else you please. (§304)

The logical thrust of the private language argument applies to the formation of all mental state concepts. However, there are also important differences between sensations and, for example, intentions or beliefs. In Wittgenstein's (1980) analysis of psychological concepts, he argued that while mental states like sensations are neither nothings nor somethings, what social developmentalists canonically think of as mental states are neither nothings nor somethings in a different sense than sensations (or emotional states). As noted earlier, we can conceive of sensations and emotions as literal mental states, because they have clear beginnings and ends and attentional shifts can interrupt them. Thus, although it makes sense to say that one can be directly conscious in a one-to-one sense of a sensation, there is no such correlating state-like event of which to be conscious in the case of an intention, desire, or belief. It is a mistake then, a category error, to assume that what is true of sensations is equally true of all mental states (Racine, 2004). Of course, intentions and the like are still not nothings because they also clearly have their share of causally related psychological and neurological events. However, there are no one-to-one correspondences between these events and the execution of, for example, a belief or intention.

The private language argument can be thought of as a special case of Wittgenstein's (1958, §28–38) argument against language and meaning as being based on word-object relations and his argument against the possibility of ostensive definition (Montgomery, 2002). Wittgenstein began the *Philosophical Investigations* with this argument against what he referred to as Augustine's view of language, which he described in the following way: "[I]ndividual words in language name objects—sentences are combinations of such names.—In this picture of language we find the roots of the following idea: Every word has a meaning. This meaning is correlated with the word. It is the object for which the word stands" (§1).

Wittgenstein's (1958, §2–21) approach in evaluating this view of language was to try imagining a primitive language that might be consistent with Augustine's view. He began with a simple language used by a builder to tell his assistant what kind of building material is required, such as blocks, slabs, and pillars. This primitive language would require labels for these objects as well as numbers to indicate quantity. However, even this simple language immediately runs into problems. For example, what does the utterance "five slabs" mean? It could be a statement, a report, or an order (§21), or many other social acts. That is, the same utterance can be used in different social situations to convey different meaning. Therefore, its meaning cannot simply be due to a connection to a referent, because the same utterance can have different meanings. This is an argument against a mechanistic view of meaning and for an indexical view—that is, meaning depends on the location in a sequence of interaction, in a practice or a form of life.

An Alternative View of the Meaning of Mental State Terms

If this view of language in which meaning is based on word-object relations is problematic how should we think of language and what are the implications for the meaning of mental state terms? Wittgenstein (1958) considered this question:

> How does a human being learn the meaning of the names of sensations?—of the word "pain" for example? Here is one possibility: words are connected with the primitive, the natural, expressions of the sensation and used in their place. A child has hurt himself and he cries; and then adults talk to him and teach him exclamations and, later, sentences. They teach the child new pain-behavior. (§244)

Hacker (1997) gave further examples of this process: "A child cries out when he injures himself, grimaces, screams or groans, and assuages the injured limb. Here lie the roots of the language-game . . ." (p. 37). It is on such natural reactions that a language of sensations can be built.

Although Wittgenstein focused on sensations, this same argument also applies to a large degree for words such as *know, think*, and so on (Chapman, 1987). Hacker (1997) wrote,

> Something similar holds of other psychological terms—though not all, and not for the more developed forms of psychological states and conditions. A child who wants his teddy reaches for it and cries out in frustration—we teach him the use of "I want." In reaching for his teddy, he does not first introspectively identify his inner state as volitional, and he no more does so when he says, "I want Teddy." A child is frightened by a barking dog, he blanches with fear and shrinks back; he does not recognize his feeling as fear before he responds to the dog, and no more does he do so when he has learnt to say "I am frightened." (p. 37)

From a Wittgensteinian perspective, then, all psychological terms "either redescribe or else presuppose, *ways of acting.* . . . It is these ways of acting that provide the foundation for the psychological concepts" (Malcolm, 1991, p. 46). It is these more primitive activities that psychological terms are grafted onto. These natural reactions provide the foundation on which the uses of some mental state terms are added. "What is the natural expression of an intention?—Look at a cat when it stalks a bird; or a beast when it wants to escape" (Wittgenstein, 1958, §647). There are also, however, more complex ways to talk about intentions such as stating one's intentions or making promises that must be learned about in other ways but not by identifying and introspecting on a mental content (Hacker, 1997). Language is based on action: "The origin and the primitive form of the language-game is a reaction; only from this can the more complicated forms develop. Language—I want to say—is a refinement, 'in the beginning was the deed'" (Wittgenstein, 1998, p. 31). Words derive their meanings from the role they play in patterns of human action and interaction (Canfield, 1993); language is the refinement that gives us the ability to make finer distinctions. Language is not based on reasoning; it is based on and added onto patterns of interaction. Further, although a common assumption is that the purpose of language is communicating one's thoughts to other people, Wittgenstein and others pointed out that we do many more things with language, and he suggested that we think of language as a toolbox (Turnbull & Carpendale, 1999, 2001).

The use of words has to be built onto prior practices. Although Wittgenstein showed why this must logically be the case, he left the technical details of how this might work to the psychologist. To make psychological sense of Wittgenstein's arguments, we draw on Piagetian theory regarding infant development. Infants learn patterns of interaction by developing expectations about social situations; that is, they develop knowledge of their social world. In Piagetian terms, these are activity schemes. Many of these early routines have biological, and therefore, universal roots; they are based on the patterns of interaction involved in interacting with and caring for babies. Language is then added to this. For example, as Hacker (1997) noted, one pattern of interaction may develop around a child crying out in frustration after trying to grasp an out-of-reach teddy with parents teaching him or her the use of "I want." In a more complex case, a parent might say, "I'm going to pass you the ball," and then go about passing a ball to a young child. Within shared embodied practices such as these, the child would learn to say "I'm going to x" and then go about doing it. In so doing, the child learns that an intention is defined by the act that satisfies it. These notions of desire and intention are definitional rather than causal. The fact that intentions and desires can go unfulfilled does not imply that they are literal mental states. Rather, what we call intention and desire is presupposed in activities such as those just described and is defined therein. We see that a person or nonhuman animal has an unfulfilled intention or desire based on our shared understanding of these concepts.

From the foregoing, it might appear that Wittgenstein is denying mental states, and therefore he must be a behaviorist. And this is in fact how he is interpreted by some authors. If Wittgenstein is denying that a sensation is a mental object, it may appear that he is saying there is no sensation, in which case the child's understanding of the mind amounts to no more than learning to talk about mental states through enculturation. However, as noted earlier, this is not what he intended (Carpendale & Lewis, 2004; Racine, 2004). Wittgenstein (1958) pointed out that these concepts have the application that they do because humans (and other animals) act intentionally, want things, and are sometimes wrong about what they take to be the case. The proper application of these terms presupposes many capacities in the agent so described, some of which are often called mental. However, these are not particular mind or brain states that cause behavior. Wittgenstein realized that this claim might make it appear "as if we had denied mental processes. And naturally we don't want to deny them" (§308). "To deny the mental process would mean to deny the remembering; to deny that anyone ever remembers anything" (§306). Wittgenstein rejected labeling mental processes as private objects in the same way we label physical objects. His denial of pain as an inner object had to do with the grammar of sensation words—that is, how they are used. It is an argument about how our language makes us think about psychological processes—a clarification of mental processes, not a denial of them.

An implication of this discussion is that the mind is a social institution (Kusch, 1997); it is constructed to talk. However, we emphasize that this does not mean that we should think of the mind as completely culturally relative (Carpendale & Lewis, 2004; Racine, 2004). Although there are undoubtedly cultural differences, much of our basic understanding of persons is built onto aspects of our shared practices that must be universal due to our common experience of embodied interactions with others and the world. For example, Canfield (1993) suggested that, although cultures do differ in how they talk about intention, some way of talking about intentions is likely universal. Similarly, it is likely that basic social acts like making requests are universal and rooted in common biological constraints of human infants as born helpless but within the context of adults caring for them (Portmann, 1944/1990).

THE UNDERSTANDING OF MENTAL
STATES IN HUMAN INFANTS.

We will now attempt to show that the assumptions that we claim color the "theory of mind" landscape are laid bare in research on social understanding in infancy. Before we argue that theorists of diverse theoretical stripes work according to the same problematic view of mind, we set the scene by discussing the first year of a baby's life, and then we review theories of infant social development proposed by Baron-Cohen (1995), Tomasello (1995) and Moore (1996).

Infants begin to engage in activities toward the end of their first year of life that involve sharing attention with others. In so doing, the dyadic interactional relations between infants and others have the opportunity to become triadic, because as the infant and other begin to orient to the same object or event, the infant learns how to coordinate his or her activities with another in ongoing interaction. These emergent triadic forms of interaction (e.g., reliable gaze following, forms of pointing gestures, object-directed imitation, and social referencing; i.e., infants' response to ambiguous situations in terms of their parent's emotional reactions) are typically described as episodes of joint attention. Part of the controversy in the field concerns the debate about whether different forms of behavior that are thought to require an understanding of joint attention develop at different ages (e.g., Butterworth & Jarrett, 1991; Carpenter, Nagell, & Tomasello, 1998; Liszkowski, Carpenter, Henning, Striano, & Tomasello, 2004; Moore & D'Entremont, 2001; Morissette, Ricard, & Decaré, 1995; Slaughter & McConnell, 2003).

The controversy also spills over into the definition and conceptualization of the phenomenon. Butterworth (1998), for example, characterized joint attention as "simply . . . looking where someone else is looking" (p. 171), whereas Tomasello (1995) claimed that joint attention requires that "two individuals know that they are attending to something in common" (p. 106). In particular, Tomasello (1999) argued that although younger infants may share attention with others, 1-year-old human infants engage in joint attention with others in a manner suggesting that they "understand other persons as intentional agents like the self" (p. 68). These two definitions are both useful, but they clearly cannot be used interchangeably. Butterworth's definition gave a self-evident criterion as to why researchers and people more generally would say that two agents are jointly attending to the same object or state of affairs; namely, they are both looking at that self same object. Joint (visual) attention, by definition, involves two people looking at something in common, and infants and their parents should quite rightly be said to engage in joint attention when observers can see that their attention is visually coordinated in some shared pattern of activity. It would equally make sense to see this concept in the activities of two individuals of many other species; for it is we human adult observers who are seeing this concept in those activities. However, Butterworth's definition as it stands fails to distinguish the joint engagement a human might have with a dog and a stick from more complicated forms of joint attention.

Unlike Butterworth (1998), Tomasello (1995, 1999) was not content to use human concepts to describe activity; Tomasello wants to account for *the agents'* understanding of these concepts. We now need criteria that would justify first- and second-person knowledge claims and must accordingly have grounds for claiming that both individuals conceptualize their joint action as joint activity. Although we agree that it is humans, and only humans, who understand psychological concepts and variously see them in the activities of human and nonhuman species alike, explanations of joint attention need not be couched in commonsense causal-psychological terms (Carpendale & Lewis, 2004; Carpendale, Lewis, Müller, & Racine, 2005; Racine, 2004). Varying levels of complexity of joint relations between infants and adults are apparent in ongoing sequences of interaction and can be observed, for example, by noting infants' reactions to adults' responses within situations of shared attention.

Baron-Cohen (1995) articulated a biological account of human social understanding in infancy and beyond. He built upon Leslie's (1987, 1994) work by accepting the latter's suggestion that a Theory of Mind Module (ToMM) comes online toward the end of the second year of life that is responsible for coding the ostensible mental relations between agents and propositions. Baron-Cohen argued that an Intentionality Detector (ID), Eye-Direction Detector (EDD), and Shared Attention Mechanism (SAM) would, however, precede it. Baron-Cohen's claim was that early in life EDD and ID are jointly responsible for constructing dyadic intentional relations between self or other and some object— ID processes the directedness of the agent's behavior, EDD processes eye movement in particular. Later in the first year of life, SAM comes online and codes the fact that self and other are attending to the same event by using lower-level input from EDD or ID to generate triadic representations. The developing agent is said to understand the so-called propositional attitudes previously mentioned because ToMM adds the requisite psychological attitude to the lower-level representations generated by SAM.

Now, clearly biological factors play a critical role in infants' dawning appreciation of others' mental lives. For example, infants seem to be biologically primed to display early preferences for attending to social stimuli. The logic of Baron-Cohen's (1995) approach, however, goes beyond biological preparedness and ultimately entails that evolved algorithms could compute particular mental states. This places one of the key assumptions regarding the causal-psychological nature of mental states directly on the table. Namely, that it makes sense to conceive of beliefs or intentions as discrete attributes of mind that can be directly computed because their meanings are fixed. This is a disembodied view of mental states, because it is the internal machinery that is said to discriminate mental life rather than this occurring through our bodily engagements in a world of social activity. The problem here is that the social situation in which a gesture or a mental state utterance takes place determines its meaning—and this is in an ongoing sequence of interaction. Although meaning is indexical (i.e., dependent on a particular social situation), algorithms cannot be (Carpendale et al., 2005; Racine, 2002). Fixed a priori meanings are not possible from an embodied view of mental states. Further, if one wants an example of communication systems in which evolutionary pressures fix meaning, that is, of nonindexical meaning, looking at infants is ill advised. One might find better examples in the calls of vervet monkeys or the dances of honeybees because these seem to have fixed meanings indicating particular predators such as snakes, eagles, or leopards or directions to new sources of nectar. However, infants use the same gestures such as pointing to convey different meaning, such as to make a request or to direct attention.

In contrast to Baron-Cohen's (1995) mechanistic view of the meaning of mental states, Tomasello (1995, 1999) articulated what we take to be a top-down, more conceptual account of infant social understanding. His argument is that infants come to distinguish means and ends (i.e., as Tomasello noted, Piaget's sensorimotor period stage IV) and in so doing they experience their own intentional (goal-directed) mental states. That is, infants of 8–9 months of age "recognize that they have goals that are clearly separated from behavioral means" (Tomasello, 1999, p. 69). Because they perceive others as "like me," they automatically apply this understanding of their own intentionality to the behavior of others (Meltzoff et al., 1999). In so doing, they deduce that others also act on the world as a consequence of their internal intentional mental states. According to Tomasello, this insight into others' intentions therefore enables the multifarious manifestations of joint attention. More recently, Tomasello, Carpenter, Call, Behne, and Moll (2005) reconsidered the assumption of a simple identification with others based on neonatal imitation, and they speculated that identification with others must depend on the forms of emotional interpersonal engagement Hobson (2002) proposed.

In contrast to Tomasello (1995, 1999), although Piaget (1954) demonstrated the goal-directedness of 8-month-old infants as an emerging skill at coordinating means-ends relations, this does not mean that they understand their own intentions. It would seem that what distinguishes sensorimotor stages III and IV, from Tomasello's point of view, is the arrival of a capacity to experience the mental events that cause infants to act intentionally—that is, the experience of a mental state called an intention. Further, Tomasello predicated his account on a literal internal causal mental entity called an intention. However, as Wittgenstein argued, an infant or young child cannot introspect upon his or her mental world to conclude he or she is experiencing an intention because to do so presupposes that he or she already is familiar with the meaning of an intention. Thus, although human infants and members of many other species act intentionally—that is, it makes sense to talk about "intention" in their activities—we have to be careful about assumptions about what this means for the child's understanding. They are showing a practical competence in interacting with others and responding to their directedness toward aspects of the world and people's efforts to do things. However, understanding in the sense of thinking about intentions depends on the ability to talk about activity (Carpendale & Lewis, 2004; Mead, 1934; Racine, 2004; Sinha, 1999; Wittgenstein, 1958).

The difference between our position and Tomasello and colleagues' (2005) can be clarified by considering their statement: "What could it mean to say that language is responsible for understanding and sharing intentions, when in fact the idea of linguistic communication without these underlying skills is incoherent" (p. 690). Our differences turn on what "understanding" means. We agree with their view that "language is not basic, it is derived. It rests on the same underlying cognitive and social skills that lead infants to point to things and show things to other people declaratively and informatively" (Tomasello et al., 2005, p. 690). However, the question is how should we characterize these skills? From our perspective, if the word *understanding* is used, then it is sensorimotor or practical understanding. It is understanding in action or feeling, not reflective understanding (Hobson, 2002). It is competence in these forms of interaction that is the ground on which language is built. And this is consistent with Tomasello and colleagues' position that language involves directing others' attention. However, we have to talk about varying levels of complexity of language. Further complexity of language allows the conceptualization of and reflection upon attention and action. Thus, from our perspective, language is required to move from a practical or lived competence in interacting with others based on expectations about others' directedness and efforts to do things within shared practices to an ability to reflect on the intentions that are defined in patterns of shared activity.

Differing views of intentions can be further clarified by considering an ambiguity in the following statement:

> Understanding intentions is foundational because it provides the interpretive matrix for deciding precisely what it is that someone is doing in the first place. Thus, the very same physical movement may be seen as giving an object, sharing it, loaning it, moving it, getting rid of it, returning it, trading it, selling it, and on and on—depending on the goals and intentions of the actor. (Tomasello et al., 2005, p. 675)

Although this might be true in an everyday sense in that what we call intentions are defined in shared activities, such as the ones listed by Tomasello and colleagues (2005), another way to interpret their position is that to grasp the meaning of an action involves understanding the mental state that gave rise to it (Russell, 1921). This is a restatement of the commonsense causal-psychological view of (human) activity. From an embodied perspective, the meaning of the multifarious practices listed in the previous example are not defined by the mental state of an actor but by the mastery of these self-same practices. "Intention," in fact, is one such practice. To say that an agent has acted intentionally is to understand the concept intention as situated in particular activities. And we conceive of an agent's activities as intentional by virtue of the practices that Tomasello and colleagues list.

In contradistinction to biologically or conceptually driven accounts, Moore and his colleagues (Barresi & Moore, 1996; Corkum & Moore, 1995, 1998; Moore & Corkum, 1994; Moore, 1996, 1999; Moore & D'Entremont, 2001) articulated an approach to explaining infants' understanding of joint attention that attempts to ground social development in infancy in embodied practical activities. Their account proceeded as follows. Moore and Corkum (1994) claimed that various mechanisms are implicated in leading the infant to engage in matched activity with others and therefore to match attentional states with them. On this theory, such activities do not require social understanding; rather, they facilitate it. An instance of what Moore and colleagues conceive of as matching of attentional states would be set up, for example, by an infant learning that following a parent's head turn results in seeing interesting things. In this way, if the infant follows parental head turns, the infant will find rewarding objects or events in his or her line of sight (Corkum & Moore, 1995, 1998). Thus, Moore and colleagues suggested that a simple conditioning explanation could explain how a triadic exchange involving gaze following is set up. Moore and colleagues also accounted for other aspects of joint attention (e.g., social referencing) in the same manner. What is important about setting up such coordinated activities is that they are said to couple the infant's first-person psychological experience with a third-person experience of others' psychological states. The final component in their model is their claim that infants do not understand mental life outside of particular interactive contexts until they are able to construct multiple models of self, other, and some state of affairs. It is the development of this meta-representational capacity that is said to confer upon infants an understanding of joint attention (Perner, 1991).

From an embodied perspective on mental states, it is correct that once an infant finds him- or herself in this and other similar shared activities an opportunity has been afforded for the developing infant to learn about the mental life of others. However, there is an ambiguity in Moore and colleagues' account. Although it makes sense to claim an infant can coordinate attention—a legitimate mental state with a clear duration and other state-like attributes—with others, what might work for joint attention could not work for intention, desire, belief, and so on. Thus, even if Moore and colleagues are able to ground the development of an understanding of attention, no amount of "matching of psychological states with another" is going to facilitate the developing agent's understanding of these other aspects of mental life. Further, even if Moore and colleagues were to grant that mental states such as intention, desire, and belief are abstracted from language use, we will presently attempt to show that their account of joint attention is incomplete and seems to contain both embodied and disembodied elements.

From an embodied perspective, joint attention involves more than being able to reverse first-person and third-person perspectives on an object. This is because the ways in which infants come to perceive others as social agents necessarily involve the practices that are built on natural reactions and are rooted in the form of life of humans and many other higher animals. Whereas language and the embodied practices upon which it is based are a massively important part of the infant's interactional matrix, they are presupposed and are not elucidated in Moore and colleagues' account. We agree that it is important to underscore the role that information-processing abilities might play in distinguishing the infant who first shares attention with others from one who understands that another's attention is also focused in the exchange, but the strong implication in Moore and colleagues' account seems to be that an infant's increasing sophistication in coordinating his or her interactions is simply a matter of cognitive development given some shared activity. In their account, then, it would seem that any shared activity will do. However, from our embodied approach, particular social activities constitute and define intention, whereas others constitute and define desire. Where our account might diverge from Moore and colleagues' is that we argue that human language defines and creates the capacity to understand that agents intend, desire, or believe. It is not shared activity in general that matters, but rather particular activities on which particular words and concepts are grounded. If social understanding develops within such activities, Moore and colleagues' solution of an emerging metarepresentational capacity is only acceptable to the degree to which it reframes shared practices and the language by which they are defined.

THE UNDERSTANDING OF MENTAL STATES IN CHIMPANZEES

As has been the case when considering social understanding in human infants, a side effect of recent research with chimpanzees is that problems are raised that make the underlying assumptions about the commonsense causal-psychological nature of mental states in the "theories of mind" research tradition equally explicit. In the subsequent section, we will attempt to demonstrate that the alternative view of mind we have described in this chapter resolves the problems raised in chimpanzee research and in theorizing about the social development of human infants.

Research on chimpanzees' social cognition has important implications for our own biological inheritance concerning social cognition, because humans shared a common ancestor with chimpanzees about 5 to 6 million years ago. This research has been of continuing interest in social developmental research and theory, as exemplified by Premack and Woodruff's (1978) influential article on the question of whether chimpanzees have a "theory of mind", the commentaries upon which provided the impetus for the false belief test and in some ways spawned the "theory of mind" enterprise in the developmental literature. Initial optimism about chimpanzees' social cognitive abilities turned to pessimism after further research. For example, Tomasello and his colleagues discovered that chimpanzees can use others' head turns to follow gaze direction (Call, Hare, & Tomasello, 1998; Tomasello, Call, & Hare, 1998; Tomasello, Hare, & Agnetta, 1999). This would seem to indicate an understanding of others' attention. However, in a series of experiments, Povinelli and Eddy (1996) found that young chimpanzees do not seem to understand the psychological significance of seeing. They found that after chimpanzees were trained to beg for food from a research assistant and given the choice of two people to beg from, they were just as likely to beg from a research assistant with his or her eyes closed or with a bucket over his or her head as they were from someone looking directly at them. Povinelli and Eddy suggested that this sort of research showed that chimpanzees' abilities to follow gaze direction is due to a complex understanding of others' behavior rather than an understanding of their psychological states.

However, recent research by Tomasello, Call, and Hare (2003a) challenged this pessimistic view of chimpanzees' social cognition. These researchers found that in competitive situations a subordinate chimpanzee seemed to take into account what a dominant chimpanzee had seen when choosing which piece of food to select. In this paradigm, a dominant and a subordinate chimpanzee were both watching from separate rooms as pieces of food were placed in a central room. When their doors were opened, the outcome of interest was which piece of food the subordinate chimpanzee would move toward. The conditions varied in terms of whether the subordinate could see a piece of food that the dominant could not see. "The general finding was that subordinates took advantage of this situation in very flexible ways—by avoiding the food the dominant could see and instead pursuing the food she could not see (and even showing a knowledge that transparent barriers do not block visual access)" (Tomasello, Call, & Hare, 2003a, p. 154). In further studies using this paradigm, Tomasello and his colleagues found that chimpanzees also took into account whether the dominant had seen the food being hidden even if it was not currently visible to the dominant. That is, the subordinate chimpanzee took into account the past visual experience of a particular dominant chimpanzee when choosing which piece of food to pursue.

In another line of research, Tomasello and his colleagues (Call, Hare, Carpenter, & Tomasello, 2004) found that chimpanzees also seem to know something about others' intentional action. Across a series of conditions, chimpanzees behaved quite differently when an experimenter was *unable*, due to clumsiness or inability, to give them food, or was instead simply *unwilling* (e.g., teasing). The chimpanzees were more impatient and more likely to leave the area if the experimenter was unwilling to give them food than when the experimenter was simply unable to give them the food, suggesting that they understood something about the experimenters' intentions. This research has led Tomasello, Call, and Hare (2003a) to revise their earlier view of chimpanzee social cognition and to suggest instead that "chimpanzees can understand some psychological states in others—the question is only which ones and to what extent" (p. 156).

Tomasello, Call, and Hare (2003b) wrote, "Although chimpanzees almost certainly do not understand other minds in the same way that humans do (e.g., they apparently do not understand beliefs) they do understand some psychological processes (e.g., seeing)" (p. 239). Clearly, most people would agree that it is likely that chimpanzees do not understand others in the same way that humans do. However, in these particular examples, what is the difference between understanding seeing and understanding beliefs? Some experiments show that a subordinate chimpanzee is less likely to approach a piece of food that a dominant chimpanzee had previously seen being hidden, even though the dominant could not currently see the food (Hare, Call, Agnetta, & Tomasello, 2000; Hare, Call, & Tomasello, 2001). Further, the same chimpanzee adopts different strategies depending on whether it is the dominant or the subordinate in the pair (Hare et al., 2000). This suggests that chimpanzees have an understanding of the psychological implications of seeing. And these implications would often simply be stated as showing an understanding of the other's knowledge or beliefs (Savage-Rumbaugh et al., 1998).

Although this example nicely shows the continuity between activity and what is later referred to as the *mental world,* it also shows that Tomasello and colleagues are reluctant to use the concept of belief when describing the activities of chimpanzees. In one sense, there are no grounds for this reluctance, for certainly these agents actually act in ways in which it makes sense to talk about them believing such and such to be the case. However, what may have been at the heart of Tomasello's reluctance is that, although chimpanzees may understand the implications of seeing, it does not follow that chimpanzees have a conceptual understanding of their and others' beliefs or, put another way, that they understand the concept of belief.

The issue of whether chimpanzees' understand others in terms of psychological states or simply in terms of behavioral regularities is also addressed by Povinelli and Vonk (2003) in response to Tomasello, Call, and Hare (2003a). The question, as Povinelli and Vonk phrased it, was "Chimpanzees undoubtedly form concepts related to the statistical regularities in behavior. But do they also construe such abstractions in terms of mental states—that is, do they possess a 'theory of mind'?" (p. 157). Povinelli and Vonk assumed that chimpanzees form behavioral abstractions about the behavior of others from repeated experience. Their question was whether, in addition to this, chimpanzees also "construe behavior in terms of mental states?" (p. 157).

If a concept is taken to be an abstraction (an averaging across) from many experiences with a particular phenomenon, this might apply to chimpanzees developing a concept of, say, a stick based on what they can or cannot do with it. However, what is it to have a concept of a mental state? In this case, "*a concept is an abstraction from the use of a word*" and "*to have a concept is to have mastered the use of a word (or phrase)*" (Bennett & Hacker, 2003, pp. 339–340). Understood in these terms, although it makes sense to describe a chimpanzee's (or an infant's behavior) as, for example, intentional because it satisfies the criteria for an observer to apply the term in question, it would not make sense to say that these chimpanzees have a conceptual understanding of intention. Saying that chimpanzees construe behavior in terms of mental states would be parasitic upon our, not their, understanding of intention.

Our goal is to clarify what having a concept entails that can be obscured quite quickly when wondering whether chimpanzees construe behavior in terms of mental states. Tomasello and colleagues' research showed that chimpanzees take what conspecifics know into account in their own behavior and showed something about social cognition in the great apes. These types of activities are the ground upon which language-using agents develop an understanding (conceptualization) of what intentional verbs refer to and accordingly create an understanding of the concept "intention." However, to show that chimpanzees *understand* an agent's mental states, one has to show that they understand what the particular mental state concept means. This means understanding the application of the word in all of its nuances. Although humans come to appreciate these domains of application, chimpanzees do not. Thus, although our argument seems to converge somewhat at this point with Povinelli's (Povinelli & Vonk, 2003; Povinelli et al., 2003) reductive read of the chimpanzee data, it is for radically different reasons. We argue that it makes sense to talk about chimpanzee's beliefs. Belief is a way of talking about activity. Chimpanzees, like infants, have beliefs; they just do not understand that they do.

What can be said about the social cognitive capacities of chimpanzees? Empirical research has shown that these great apes have not only the type of practical transitional understandings characteristic of shared attention in young human infants, but they also seem to have an ability to follow gaze that rivals that of an 18-month-old human, can probably socially reference, and will use pointing gestures when given the opportunity to do so (Leavens, Hopkins, & Thomas, 2004). These are all relatively sophisticated forms of social interaction or uses of social knowledge. However, comparative psychologists and primatologists typically want to ask a different question, one that also seems equally empirical but is unfortunately not. They want to know whether chimpanzees understand other agents in terms of mental states, and these mental states are everyday concepts like intention (Tomasello, Carpenter, Call, et al., 2005). This question, when posed as a simple empirical matter amenable to naturalistic or even experimental methods, can never be answered because it conceals the need for a prior logical elucidation of the nature of mental states. We already have quite a bit of evidence as to what chimpanzees can and cannot do, but we still do not know how to make sense of it, because we are not clear about the criteria for the application of mental state term concepts.

So what is the basis for the social cognitive differences between humans and chimpanzees? To a large degree, it has to involve language. However, a bald statement like that is sure to be misunderstood, because it depends on what we mean by language. Language of varying levels of complexity is a refinement of the capacity to engage in triadic interaction with others, and this ability, although requiring particular individual capacities, is embedded in shared practices that are rooted in biological and social universal aspects of infant experience but which are also influenced by individual and cultural differences. Further, language of sufficient complexity is required to move beyond a practical competence in engaging with others to develop a conceptual understanding of human activity. What is required is a sufficiently complex social life, shared practices, and a language are built onto this. What about enculturated apes who acquire some language? We should not think of social understanding as an all-or-nothing ability. The language-trained bonobo, Kanzi, has the linguistic capacity of a 2-year-old but may lack sufficient linguistic complexity to talk about beliefs. This is similar to the finding that deaf children with hearing parents, who are not fluent in sign language, are delayed in their understandings of belief, perhaps because they lack exposure to sufficiently complex talk about human activity (Peterson & Siegal, 2000).

It is interesting that this work with chimpanzees makes the assumptions that also underlie the research known as "children's theories of mind" more explicit than is usually the case. As with young human infants, this may because these are nonlanguage using agents. When we strip away language, a causal privately determined world of mental states can seem so much more tenable, because we see that infants and great apes alike clearly have intentions, desires, and beliefs. However, as researchers, we sometimes forget that although infants and chimps are not language users, we still are and the view of mind we assume influences our interpretations. It is just these assumptions that we question. The problem arises because of our commonsense causal-psychological view of the mind, according to which mental states such as beliefs and intentions are inner mental entities that causally underlie observable behavior.

AN ALTERNATIVE TO DISEMBODIED VIEWS OF MENTAL STATES IN HUMAN INFANTS AND CHIMPANZEES

We offer an approach to social development that dissolves the apparent problems raised in the previous two sections. We do not assume an unbridgeable gap between mere behavior and hidden psychological states that underlie and drive that observable behavior. From our perspective, minds are not biologically given. Rather, minds arise through communicative interaction (Mead, 1934).

We argue that infants' first form of social understanding is sensorimotor or practical. This early social knowledge is based on activity; infants gradually develop a set of sequential expectations through a history of interaction with others. Tomasello and colleagues observed this form of understanding in chimpanzees. Although we mean something quite different by a concept, we could redescribe Povinelli and Vonk's (2003) notion of behavioral abstraction as the ability to form sequential expectations about others' behavior, and we suggest that this is a requirement for engaging in social interaction. Engagement with others, which involves important emotional dimensions, is essential for experiencing the sort of interaction that results in further social development (Hobson, 2002).

How is it that humans develop more complex forms of understanding? Our proposal has been that when language is added onto previously shared practices, children can begin to talk about the psychological world. The development of sequential expectations surrounding shared practices makes language possible. Children can then begin to talk about human activity, and this leads to the development of an understanding of the psychological world. Children can then acquire the ability to think, reason, and reflect on the psychological world of others as well as the self. Thus, from our perspective, what is added to what Povinelli and Vonk (2003) referred to as "systems for behavioral abstraction" is language, which makes possible the ability to represent human action that is not immediately present and thus to reason about such activity. This allows for the abstraction of the concepts that are defined by word use, thereby giving a set of tools not available to non-human primates. This ability is referred to as "theory of mind." We, however, prefer the more general phrase, social understanding, because from our perspective, the term *theory* is misleading.

Our approach provides a developmental way to avoid the discontinuity faced by Povinelli and colleagues between chimpanzees relying on either behavioral abstractions or attributing mental states. We offer a naturalistic and continuous view of social development. Of course, we do have to account for the evolution of the ability to develop social understanding and language. The route we take here is not by postulating innate mechanisms or modules, such as Baron-Cohen (1995), and neither Tomasello nor Povinelli take this approach. Instead, we consider the ingredients required in order to set the human infant up in the type of social engagement necessary for further social development. Here we would speculate that the adaptations would include emotional and motivational factors that encourage the infant to engage in emotional social interaction. Further, humans' extended period of infancy guarantees close interpersonal interaction. This "social gestation" means development that in other animals would occur in isolation in the womb occurs within social interaction (Portmann, 1944/1990). This also sets up the problem space in which an infant is helpless and depends on an adult caregiver (Leavens et al., 2004). And, of course, the infant must have the capacity to benefit from such interaction. Although clearly there is a great deal of neurological capacity that must be in place, social engagement is also essential (Carpendale et al., 2005; Müller & Carpendale, 2000, 2004).

The currently influential position on how it is that children come to understand the mind is that false belief understanding indicates a major conceptual revolution in a child's thinking indicating that he or she has formed a "theory" about the mind and this involves the child's acquisition of the concept of metarepresentation—an understanding of the process of representation (e.g., Perner, 1991). However, we would argue that there is a more gradual transition between infants' development of an understanding of attention and preschoolers' later understanding of beliefs. That is, we do not think that children's understanding of social situations involving false beliefs is driven by the formation of a "theory" but rather through the gradual build up of practical skills in understanding when their attention toward aspects of the world is or is not shared by others (Carpendale & Lewis, 2004). From our perspective, children's understandings of beliefs and the psychological world is rooted in their practical understanding of interacting with others and their awareness of when attention is or is not shared with others.

As we have previously demonstrated, it is important to remember that not all mental states are the same. Attention can be shared (that is, coordinated) with another in a literal sense; intention cannot be.

However, a person can share intentions with another in a metaphorical sense if both people literally know each other's intentions (which is not the same thing as knowing each other's literal mental states). This is not possible for infants and great apes because, even though they may have developed a practical ability to interact with others, they lack a language-based conceptual understanding. Even though intentions and desires are not literal mental states, they, like pain, are grounded on and replace more primitive behavior. Belief has a more complicated grammar that includes actions that involve the psychological significance of visual access or the qualification of certainty about some state of affairs. Although the former function is grounded in practical activity, the latter is more removed from nonlinguistic practice.

CONCLUSION

We have argued that the dominant view of mental states as inner entities is disembodied in the sense that such mental states are thought of as separate mental entities that cause behavior and are independent of lived socially embodied experience. We have reviewed problems with this approach by drawing on Wittgenstein's arguments suggesting that talk about beliefs and intentions is not in reference to inner mental entities that underlie and cause outer behavior. Instead, from our perspective, understanding the beliefs that developmental and comparative psychologists are most interested in requires a focus on how talk about belief is built onto more practical embodied experience involving sharing attention with others and the practical experience of the consequences of whether or not attention is shared. However, Wittgenstein did not address the details of how infants develop the ability to engage in shared practices with others; for this aspect of development, we drew on a Piagetian approach. As parents begin to talk about their children's activities, children learn to talk about what they are doing. This is one form of talk about intentions. Thus, talk about mental states is built onto natural reactions and shared activity. Intentions and beliefs are not causal mental states that infants must learn about through inference or introspection. Instead, these are ways of describing activity. Once children can talk about this psychological world with sufficient complexity, they can then reflect on their own and others' activity and talk about their intentions, desires, and beliefs (Mead, 1934, 1977). Of course, one should not take this to herald the development of an ability to reflect on one's mental state of belief.

ACKNOWLEDGMENTS

Work on this chapter was supported by doctoral fellowships from the Social Sciences and Humanities Research Council of Canada and the Michael Smith Foundation for Health Research to the first author and by grants from the Social Sciences and Humanities Research Council of Canada and the Human Early Learning Partnership to the second author.

REFERENCES

Baron-Cohen, S. (1995). *Mindblindness: An essay on autism and theory of mind.* Cambridge, MA: MIT Press.

Barresi, J., & Moore, C. (1996). Intentional relations and social understanding. *Behavioral and Brain Sciences, 19*, 107–154.

Bartsch, K., & Wellman, H. M. (1995). *Children talk about the mind.* Oxford, U.K.: Oxford University Press.

Bennett, M. R., & Hacker, P. M. S. (2003). *Philosophical foundations of neuroscience.* Oxford, U.K.: Blackwell.

Bickhard, M. H. (2001). Why children don't have to solve the frame problems: Cognitive representations are not encodings. *Developmental Review, 21*, 224–262.

Bickhard, M. H. (2004). Why believe in beliefs? *Behavioral and Brain Sciences, 27*, 100–101.

Butterworth, G. E. (1998). What is special about pointing in babies? In F. Simion & G. Butterworth (Eds.), *The development of sensory, motor and cognitive capacities in early infancy: From perception to cognition* (pp. 171–190). Hove, UK: Psychology Press.

Butterworth, G., & Jarrett, N. (1991). What minds have in common is space: Spatial mechanisms serving joint visual attention in infancy. *British Journal of Developmental Psychology, 9*, 55–72.

Button, G., Coulter, J., Lee, J. R. E., & Sharrock, W. (1995). *Computers, minds, and conduct.* Cambridge, U.K.: Polity Press.

Call, J., Hare, B. A., & Tomasello, M. (1998). Chimpanzee gaze following in an object-choice task. *Animal Cognition, 1*, 89–99.

Call, J., Hare, B., Carpenter, M., & Tomasello, M. (2004). 'Unwilling' versus 'unable': Chimpanzees' understanding of human intentional action. *Developmental Science, 7*, 488–498.

Canfield, J. V. (1993). The living language: Wittgenstein and the empirical study of communication. *Language Sciences, 15*, 165–193.

Carpendale, J. I. M., & Lewis, C. (2004). Constructing an understanding of mind: The development of children's social understanding within social interaction. *Behavioral and Brain Sciences, 27*, 79–96.

Carpendale, J. I. M., Lewis, C., Müller, U., & Racine, T. P. (2005). Constructing perspectives in the social making of minds. *Interaction Studies, 6*, 341–358.

Carpenter, M., Nagell, K., & Tomasello, M. (1998). Social cognition, joint attention, and communicative competence from 9 to 15 months of age. *Monographs of the Society for Research in Child Development, 63*(Serial No. 255).

Chapman, M. (1987). Inner processes and outward criteria: Wittgenstein's importance for psychology. In M. Chapman, & R. A. Dixon (Eds.), *Meaning and the growth of understanding: Wittgenstein's significance for developmental psychology* (pp. 103–127). Berlin, Germany: Springer-Verlag.

Corkum, V., & Moore, C. (1995). Development of joint visual attention in infants. In C. Moore, & P. Dunham (Eds.), *Joint attention: Its origins and role in development* (pp. 61–83). Hillsdale, NJ: Lawrence Erlbaum Associates.

Corkum, V., & Moore, C. (1998). The origins of joint visual attention in infants. *Developmental Psychology, 34*, 28–38.

Dartnall, T. (1999). Normative engines: Stalking the wild Wittgensteinian machine. *Idealistic Studies, 29*, 215–230.

Fogel, A. (1993). *Developing through relationships: Origins of communication, self and culture.* Exeter, U.K.: Harvester Wheatsheaf Press.

Garfinkel, H. (1967) *Studies in ethnomethodology.* Englewood Cliffs, NJ: Prentice-Hall.

German, T. P., & Leslie, A. M. (2000). Attending to and learning about mental states. In P. Mitchell, & K. J. Riggs (Eds.), *Children's reasoning and the mind* (pp. 229–252). Hove, U.K.: Psychology Press.

Gopnik, A., & Wellman, H. M. (1992). Why the child's theory of mind really is a theory. *Mind and Language, 7*, 145–171.

Gopnik, A., & Wellman, H. M. (1994). The theory theory. In L. Hirschfeld, & S. Gelman (Eds.), *Mapping the mind: Domain specificity in cognition and culture* (pp. 257–293). New York: Cambridge University Press.

Hacker, P. M. S. (1992). Malcolm and Searle on 'intentional mental states.' *Philosophical Investigations, 15*, 245–275.

Hacker, P. M. S. (1996). *Wittgenstein, mind and will.* Cambridge, U.K.: Blackwell.

Hacker, P. M. S. (1997). *Wittgenstein: On human nature.* London: Phoenix.

Hare, B., Call, J., Agnetta, B., & Tomasello, M. (2000). Chimpanzees know what conspecifics do and do not see. *Animal Behavior, 59*, 771–785.

Hare, B., Call, J., & Tomasello, M. (2001). Do chimpanzees know what conspecifics know? *Animal Behavior, 61*, 139–151.

Hark, M. T. (1990). *Beyond the outer and the inner: Wittgenstein's philosophy of psychology.* Dordrecht, The Netherlands: Kluwer.

Harris, P. L. (1991). The work of the imagination. In A. Whiten (Ed.), *Natural theories of mind* (pp. 283–304). Oxford, U.K.: Blackwell.

Harris, P. L. (1992). From simulation to folk psychology: The case for development. *Mind & Language, 7*, 120–144.

Hobson, R. P. (1993). *Autism and the development of mind.* Hillsdale, NJ: Lawrence Erlbaum Associates.

Hobson, R. P. (2002). *The cradle of thought.* London: Macmillan.

Kusch, M. (1997). The sociophilosophy of folk psychology. *Studies in History and Philosophy of Science, 28*, 1–25.

Lakoff, G., & Johnson, M. (1999). *Philosophy in the flesh: The embodied mind and its challenge to Western thought.* New York: Basic.

Leavens, D. A., Hopkins, W. D., & Thomas, R. K. (2004). Referential communications of chimpanzees (pan troglodytes). *Journal of Comparative Psychology, 118*, 48–57.

Leslie, A. M. (1987). Pretense and representation: The origins of "theory of mind." *Psychological Review, 94*, 412–426.

Leslie, A. M. (1994). Pretending and believing: Issues in the theory of ToMM. *Cognition, 50*, 211–238.

Liszkowski, U., Carpenter, M., Henning, A., Striano, T., & Tomasello, M. (2004). Twelve-month-olds point to share attention and interest. *Developmental Science, 7*, 297–307.

Malcolm, N. (1991). Wittgenstein: The relation of language to instinctive behavior. In J. Hyman (Ed.), *Investigating psychology: Sciences of the mind after Wittgenstein* (pp. 27–47). London: Routledge.

McDonough, R. (1999). Bringing cognitive science back to life. *Idealistic Studies, 29*, 173–214.

Mead, G. H. (1934). Mind, self and society from the standpoint of a social behaviorist. Chicago: University of Chicago Press.

Mead, G. H. (1977). *George Herbert Mead on social psychology: Selected papers.* Chicago: The University of Chicago Press.

Meltzoff, A. N. (2002). Imitation as a mechanism of social cognition: Origins of empathy, theory of mind, and the representation of action. In U. Goswami (Ed.), *Blackwell Handbook of childhood cognitive development* (pp. 6–25). Oxford, U.K.: Blackwell.

Meltzoff, A. N., Gopnik, A., & Repacholi, B. M. (1999). Toddler's understanding of intentions, desires, and emotions; Explorations of the dark ages. In P. D. Zelazo, J. W. Astington, & D. R. Olson (Eds.), *Developing theories of intention: Social understanding and self-control* (pp. 17–41). Mahwah, NJ: Lawrence Erlbaum Associates.

Merleau-Ponty, M. (1962). *The phenomenology of perception.* New York: Humanities Press. (Original work published 1945)

Montgomery, D. E. (2002). Mental verbs and semantic development. *Journal of Cognition and Development, 3*, 357–384.

Montgomery, D. E. (2004). Challenging theory-theory accounts of social understanding: Where is the social constructivist advantage? *Behavioral and Brain Sciences, 27*, 118–119.

Moore, C. (1996). Theories of mind in infancy. *British Journal of Developmental Psychology, 14*, 19–40.

Moore, C. (1999). Intentional relations and triadic interaction. In P. D. Zelazo, J. W. Astington & D. R. Olson (Eds), *Developing theories of intention* (pp. 43–61). Mahwah, NJ: Erlbaum.

Moore, C., & Corkum, V. (1994). Social understanding at the end of the first year of life. *Developmental Review, 14*, 349–372.

Moore, C., & D'Entremont, B. (2001). Developmental changes in pointing as a function of attentional focus. *Journal of Cognition and Development, 2*, 109–129.

Morissette, P., Ricard, M., & Decaré, T. G. (1995). Joint visual attention and pointing in infancy: A longitudinal study of comprehension. *British Journal of Developmental Psychology, 13*, 163–175.

Müller, U., & Carpendale, J. I. M. (2000). The role of social interaction in Piaget's theory: Language for social cooperation and social cooperation for language. *New Ideas in Psychology, 18*, 139–156.

Müller, U., & Carpendale, J. I. M. (2004). From joint activity to joint attention: A relational approach to social development in infancy. In J. I. M. Carpendale, & U. Müller (Eds.), *Social interaction and the development of knowledge* (pp. 215–238). Mahwah, NJ: Lawrence Erlbaum Associates.

Overton, W. F. (1994). Contexts of meaning: The computational and the embodied mind. In W. F. Overton, & D. S. Palermo (Eds.), *The nature and ontogenesis of meaning* (pp. 1–18). Hillsdale, NJ: Lawrence Erlbaum Associates.

Overton, W. F. (2004). A relational and embodied perspective on resolving psychology's antinomies. In J. I. M. Carpendale, & U. Müller (Eds.) *Social interaction and the development of knowledge* (pp. 19–44). Mahwah, NJ: Lawrence Erlbaum Associates.

Perner, J. (1991). *Understanding the representational mind.* Cambridge, MA: The MIT Press.

Peterson, C. C., & Siegal, M. (2000). Insights into theory of mind from deafness and autism. *Mind & Language, 15*, 123–145.

Piaget, J. (1954). *The construction of reality in the child.* New York: Basic Books. (Original work published 1937)

Portmann, A. (1990). *A zoologist looks at humankind.* New York: Columbia University Press. (Original work published 1944)

Povinelli, D. J., & Eddy, T. J. (1996). What young chimpanzees know about seeing. *Monographs of the Society for Research in Child Development, 61*(Serial No. 247).

Povinelli, D. J., & Vonk, J. (2003). Chimpanzee minds: Suspiciously human? *Trends in Cognitive Sciences, 7*, 157–160.

Premack, D., & Woodruff, G. (1978). Does the chimpanzee have a theory of mind? *Behavioral and Brain Sciences, 4*, 515–526.

Racine, T. P. (2002). Computation, meaning and artificial intelligence: Some old problems, some new models. *Canadian Artificial Intelligence, 50*, 8–19.

Racine, T. P. (2004). Wittgenstein's internalistic logic and children's theories of mind. In J. I. M. Carpendale, & U. Müller (Eds.), *Social interaction and the development of knowledge* (pp. 257–276). Mahwah, NJ: Lawrence Erlbaum Associates.

Russell, B. (1921). *The analysis of mind.* London: Allen & Unwin.

Russell, J. (1996). *Agency: Its role in mental development.* Hove, UK: Erlbaum (UK) Taylor & Francis.

Savage-Rumbaugh, E. S., Shanker, S. G., & Talbot, J. T. (1998). *Apes, language, and the human mind.* New York: Oxford University Press.

Shatz, M., Wellman, H. M., & Silber, S. (1983). The acquisition of mental verbs: A systematic investigation of the first reference to mental state. *Cognition, 14*, 301–321.

Slaughter, V., & McConnell, D. (2003). Emergence of joint attention: Relationships between gaze following, social referencing, imitation and naming in infancy. *Journal of Genetic Psychology, 164*, 54–71.

Sinha, C. (1999). Grounding, mapping and acts of meaning. In T. Janssen, & G. Redeker (Eds.), *Cognitive linguistics: Foundations, scope and methodology* (pp. 223–255). New York: De Gruyter.

Tomasello, M. (1995). Joint attention as social cognition. In C. Moore, & P. Dunham (Eds.), *Joint attention: Its origins and role in development* (pp. 103–130). Hillsdale, NJ: Lawrence Erlbaum Associates.

Tomasello, M. (1999). *The cultural origins of human cognition.* Cambridge, MA: Harvard University Press.

Tomasello, M., Carpenter, M., Call, J., Behne, T., & Moll, H. (2005). Understanding and sharing intentions: The origins of cultural cognition. *Behavioral and Brain Sciences, 28*, 675–735.

Tomasello, M., Call, J., & Hare, B. (1998). Five primate species follow the visual gaze of conspecifics. *Animal Behavior, 55*, 1063–1069.

Tomasello, M., Hare, B., & Agnetta, B. (1999). Chimpanzees, Pan troglodytes, follow gaze direction geometrically. *Animal Behaviour, 58*, 769–777.

Tomasello, M., Call, J., & Hare, B. (2003a). Chimpanzees understand psychological states—the question is which ones and to what extent. *Trends in Cognitive Sciences, 7*, 153–156.

Tomasello, M., Call, J., & Hare, B. (2003b). Chimpanzees versus humans: It's not that simple. *Trends in Cognitive Sciences, 7*, 239–240.

Turnbull, W. (2003). *Language in action: Psychological models of conversation.* Hove, UK: Psychology Press.

Turnbull, W., & Carpendale, J. I. M. (1999). A social pragmatic model of talk: Implications for research on the development of children's social understanding. *Human Development, 42*, 328–355.

Turnbull, W., & Carpendale, J. I. M. (2001). Talk and social understanding. *Early Education and Development, 12*, 455–477.

Varela, F. J., Thompson, E., & Rosch, E. (1991). *The embodied mind: Cognitive science and human experience.* Cambridge, MA: MIT Press.

Williams, M. (1999). *Wittgenstein, mind and meaning: Toward a social conception of mind.* New York: Routledge.

Wittgenstein, L. (1958). *Philosophical investigations* (3rd ed.; G. E. M. Anscombe, Trans.). Englewood Cliffs, NJ: Prentice-Hall.

Wittgenstein, L. (1980). *Remarks on the philosophy of psychology* (Vol. 1; G. E. M. Anscombe, & G. H. Von Wright, Eds.; G. E. M. Anscombe, Trans.). Oxford, U.K.: Blackwell.

Wootton, A. J. (1997). *Interaction and the development of mind.* Cambridge, U.K.: Cambridge University Press.

8

EMBODIMENT AND CHILDREN'S UNDERSTANDING OF THE REAL AND REPRESENTED WORLD

Lynn S. Liben

The Pennsylvania State University

Joey the Disembodied Head adds some spirit to the 20K.

Figure. 8.1. The Doctor Fun cartoon, *Joey the Disembodied Head,* created by David Farley. The cartoon appeared on August 21, 1998. Reprinted with permission of the author.

DEFINING EMBODIMENT

Cartoons are good indices of the degree to which ideas are important beyond the rarified walls of the academy. Thus, *Joey the Disembodied Head*[1], shown in Fig. 8.1, provides a bit of folk evidence that the Cartesian position on the split between mind and body permeates our society. Of course, the cartoon does not accept, but rather pokes fun at, the absurdity of dualism. It thus sets the stage for the counter-position that forms the foundation for this chapter and the entire volume in which it appears: embodiment.

The concept of embodiment is a complex and far reaching one that is reviewed in depth in other contributions to this book (see especially, Overton, chapter 1, and Müller & Newman, chapter 12, this volume). For purposes of the current chapter, however, a relatively simple glossary entry for embodiment will suffice.

> The term is used to refer to the inseparability of a system's learning (and/or knowledge) and its physical being (and acting). The term embodiment is used both to convey both the particular processes used by a complex system to maintain its coherence and the manner in which it carries/expresses/lives its history. The term thus means different things for different complex forms. Individual humans, for example, are simultaneously biological and social beings who embody both the history of the species (biologically, in their bodily subsystems) and the cultural contexts of their existences (experientially, as participants in culture). Embodiment also points to the fact that complex systems often unfold from, and are enfolded in, other complex systems. (McMurtry, 2004)

Contemporary and Historical Interest in Embodiment

Recent scholarship in psychology has seen increased attention to embodiment, in part as a consequence of advances in neuroscience that have allowed empirical study of the relations among physical, emotional, and cognitive domains (e.g., see Damasio, 1994; Edelman, 1992), and in part as a consequence of increased attention to the body in the humanities. In a review of Roy Porter's *Flesh in the Age of Reason*, for example, Terry Eagleton (2004) offered this observation:

> If the body is such a fashionable topic at the moment, it is partly because it is nothing if not local and particular, which suits a postmodern age wary of universals and abstractions. Another reason is simply that the body is a more sexy topic than, say, the moral thought of Kant and is thus likely to sell more books in a

ferociously competitive market. Twenty or thirty years ago, you were unlikely to get your literary study published unless its title contained the word "dialectic"; nowadays, the obligatory word is "body." (p. 88)

Although one might take this quotation to suggest that embodiment is little more than a passing fad, this is far from the case, at least within developmental psychology. It is fitting to offer as evidence the writings of Piaget, given that the current volume emerged under the aegis of the Piaget Society. Piaget proposed that it was through sensorimotor action that individuals constructed knowledge; indeed, his entire project instantiates an embodiment theory. Unlike many theorists who both preceded and followed him, Piaget avoided split positions (see Overton, 2004, 2006). Thus, Piaget did not posit that bodily actions were separate from and causal of the mind, nor did he construe assimilation and accommodation as if they were sequential processes with one serving as an efficient cause of the other. Instead, Piaget's position was that these were mechanisms that function simultaneously and interdependently.

It is almost impossible to select a single quotation or two to document Piaget's (1936/1952) position because his entire oeuvre stands as evidence. Two brief passages chosen almost at random, however, can offer a flavor of the foundational intertwining of mind and body in his work:

The eye needs light images just as the whole body needs chemical nourishment, energy, etc. Among the aggregate of external realities assimilated by the organism there are some which are incorporated into the parts of the physicochemical mechanisms, while others simply serve as functional and general nourishment. In the first case, there is physiological assimilation, whereas the second may be called psychological assimilation. But the phenomenon is the same in both cases: the universe is embodied in the activity of the subject.

The existence of an organized totality which is preserved while assimilating the external world raises, in effect, the whole problem of life itself. But, as the higher cannot be reduced to the lower without adding something, biology will not succeed in clarifying the question of assimilation without taking into account its psychological aspect. At a certain level, life organization and mental organization only constitute, in effect, one and the same thing. (pp. 43, 46)

In the context of comments about the currency of the embodiment bandwagon, it is notable that these passages come from Piaget's *Origins of Intelligence*, originally published in French in 1936. The gist (if not the voice) of the Piagetian passages sounds remarkably like the following contemporary statement of embodiment by Mark Johnson (1999) in a book entitled *Perspectives on Embodiment:* "[A]ll of our cognitive mechanisms and structures are grounded in patterns of bodily experience and activities, such as our spatial and temporal orientations, the patterns of our bodily movements, and the ways we manipulate objects. Mental images [and] concepts are all tied . . . to these bodily structures of our sensorimotor activities" (p. 82).

Overview of the Chapter

Among the many implications of embodiment is the notion that our knowledge about the environment in which we live and move is part and parcel of the body with which we experience that environment. It is this implication that I have focused on in this chapter. In the second section of this chapter, I turn to identifying some of the ways in which the knowledge we construct from direct experience in the environment is embodied. While embodied experience in the real world supports the construction of some kinds of knowledge, it simultaneously constrains it. The human response to these constraints has been to develop tools that amplify our embodied knowledge of the environment. I define one category of tools that are the focus of this chapter: external spatial representations. I then argue that just as our experiences with the actual world are embodied, so, too, our experiences with the representational world are embodied. In the third section of the chapter, I draw on this notion to discuss our program of empirical work on the developmental understanding of external spatial representations. In the fourth section of the chapter, I discuss a general model of representational development and comment on the mechanisms that may facilitate developmental progress. I close the chapter with a brief comment about how we may conceptualize *Joey the Disembodied Head.*

EMBODIMENT IN EXPERIENCING THE
REAL AND REPRESENTED WORLD

Embodied Experience in the Real Environment

As previously explained, the foundational premise of this chapter is the notion that our bodies provide the context for us to have certain kinds of experiences as we move around in the world. There are many ways in which this is true. For example, our environmental experience is embodied in our muscular skeletal system. Our vestibular system keeps us erect. Unlike flies with sticky feet, we cannot fly or walk on walls.

Because of our upright stance, our human height, and our locomotor capacities and constraints, we see the landscape and horizon within some constrained range of angles and distances. The symmetries and asymmetries of our bodies affect our experience: the asymmetry of our body's longitudinal and sagittal axes means that it is very easy to discriminate above from below and in front from behind, whereas the symmetry of our transverse axis means that it is challenging to distinguish left from right. Our visual system is sensitive to only some energy levels. Thus, for example, a flower that to a bee appears to have a purple center looks to a human entirely white, because human eyes are insensitive to light in the ultraviolet range.

Others have made the argument—often in catchy ways—that bodies are important for the ways in which living beings experience and come to know the surrounding environment. Consider the following:

> Our rationality and animality are bound tightly together. If a caterpillar can be said to think at all, it cannot think about the world in the way we do. This is not only because it is unlikely to have read Simone de Beauvoir but also because its body, its sensory organization, presents it with a quite different environment about which to think. You do not reflect upon Nature in quite the way that Wordsworth does if your senses allow you to see only one square millimeter at any given time. (Eagleton, 2004, p. 88)

That caterpillars have access to only one square millimeter at a given time, however, is not simply what makes their environmental experience so different from that of humans. In fact, when humans rely on solely their own physical capacity for locomotion, they, too, have access to only small portions of the world when considered in the context of the region, country, continent, planet, or galaxy in which they live. True, the scale is on a different order of magnitude. On flat land, looking out in one direction, we can see, roughly, 16 square miles and—on a clear day, from a very high mountain—we can see thousands of square miles more. But if all we had to go on was what the eye could see, we, too, would have a limited "environment about which to think."

Amplifying Embodied Environmental Knowledge

The human response to these constraints has been to develop and use two major kinds of environmental amplifiers. First are what we might call *access amplifiers*, which are tools that in some way expand access to the physical environment itself. A telescope, for example, allows us to see more of the real environment than would otherwise be accessible to the human visual system. Similarly, cars, airplanes, and spaceships allow us to visit or at least see (real) environments that would be inaccessible if we were limited to the locomotor mechanisms provided by human biology alone.

Second are *representational amplifiers*. These are tools that serve to expand knowledge of the environment through some kind of symbolic mediator that stands for, but does not actually provide direct access to, the environment. Illustrative are maps and aerial photographs. It is important to note from the start that the term "representation" should *not* be interpreted in the sense of *re*-presentation (as in "to present again"), but rather should be interpreted in the sense of symbolic representation (see Liben & Downs, 1992). One reason for avoiding the *re*-presentation interpretation is simply that environmental representations such as photographs do not afford the same kinds of information nor the same kinds of actions that are afforded by the real, physical environment (see Gibson, 1966; 1971). It is only when the representation is a replica of an original that it could be said to afford similar actions (see Liben, 1999). A representation that is just like the original, however, offers no more than does the original itself. Lewis Carroll (1893) captured the absurdity of the notion of using replicas as representations in *Sylvie and Bruno Concluded*:

> What do you consider the largest map that would be really useful?
>
> About six inches to the mile.
>
> Only six inches! We very soon got to six yards to the mile. Then we tried a hundred yards to the mile. And then came the grandest idea of all! We actually made a map of the country on the scale of a mile to the mile!
>
> Have you used it much?
>
> It has never been spread out, yet, the farmers objected; they said it would cover the whole country and shut out the sunlight! So now we use the country itself as its own map, and I assure you it does nearly as well.

In the world of art, the absurdity of replication is captured succinctly by a quote attributed to Virginia Woolf: "Art is not a copy of the real world. One of the damn things is enough" (cited by Goodman, 1976, p. 3).

Thus, a second reason for avoiding the *re*-presentation interpretation is that such "representations" would serve no function. The intent of environmental representations is, like the intent of other kinds of representations, to offer new insights, not simply to duplicate those that might as easily be attained from the original referent. Environmental representations are thus of value as insofar as they offer creative "realizations" of the world in two senses of the word (Downs, 1985). First, they are realizations in the sense of making real or concrete. Maps and other kinds of place representations provide artifacts that can record information about the environment, compile it, store it, and allow manipulation of it in ways that would be impossible with the environment itself. Second, they are realizations in the sense of facilitating some discovery as in realizing something that had not been appreciated before, the "ah-ha!" sense of realization. Perhaps if caterpillars traveled on tractors, learned to use telescopes, and made use of maps, they, too, would be more reflective about the environments in which they live and crawl.

Representational amplifiers are the focus of the remainder of this chapter. Given the practical need to limit the scope of the chapter, I restrict the kinds of representations discussed along four dimensions. First, the representations I consider are *external*—that is, I consider here only representations that are open to inspection, either in interaction with others (e.g., as part of a communicative exchange) or by self (e.g., as a tool in support of one's own thinking). Second, I limit my discussion to representations with *spatial referents*. These are referents that themselves have some spatial extent; they must exist in real space. This includes everyday objects that one might find on a table or in a room (e.g., a stapler, a couch) or the physical environment that one might visit (e.g., New York City; the Rocky Mountains), but it excludes concepts that are not themselves inherently spatial (e.g., the Gross National Product).

Third, I discuss only representations that carry meaning through their own *spatial qualities*. These are representations in which at least some of the spatial information about the referent is carried by the spatial arrangement of the elements of the representation. Thus, for example, a room plan that depicts furniture with geometric shapes in sizes, shapes, and distributions that are analogous to the sizes, shapes, and distributions of the real furniture in the room would be included. A verbal description of the same room, however, would not. Finally, fourth, the representations I consider are *graphic*. These are representations composed of marks such as points, lines, shading, and colors on a two-dimensional surface. Thus, for example, an architectural blueprint would be included; an architectural model would not.

These criteria thus exclude a number of domains of inquiry, including research on (a) mental representation (e.g., cognitive maps), (b) the metaphorical or representational use of space for problems that are not themselves inherently spatial (e.g., spatial arrays that stand for premises in a nonspatial transitive reasoning task), (c) nonspatial symbol systems that are used to stand for spatial meaning (e.g., numerical or verbal representations of spatial information), or (d) three-dimensional models (e.g., models used in chemical or biological research). These domains are all equally important and fascinating in their own right (e.g., see Gattis, 2001; Levinson, 2003; Liben, 2006; National Research Council, 2005), but it would be impossible to discuss all within a single chapter.

EMBODIMENT AND INTERPRETING REPRESENTATIONS OF PLACE

The Role of Embodiment

The argument that I present in the remainder of the chapter is that embodiment is relevant not only for understanding how we build knowledge when moving around in the real environment, but also for how we use representations of the environment. In other words, embodied experiences in the real, physical environment inform the ways in which humans construct meaning from the symbolic, represented environment. This overarching thesis translates into the more specific prediction that environmental representations that are more similar to embodied environmental experience will be easier to understand than are environmental representations that are less similar to embodied environmental experience. Thus, representations that depict larger expanses of the world than those we encounter with normal human locomotion, or those that depict environments from viewing angles that we do not normally experience, may be difficult to interpret.

Illustrative is the image shown in Fig. 8.2.[2] If one were on the ground in this spot in Tunisia, looking straight ahead, it would be a simple matter to recognize that what appear to be dots in the image are individual trees, organized into neat rows in an olive-tree plantation. Furthermore, if one were standing in the actual environment, it would be easy to recognize that the trees were planted in hilly terrain. By instead exploring this environment via a representation that depicts it from a viewing distance and viewing angle that are not consistent with human embodied experience, it is difficult to interpret. A viewer might not recognize even the referential identity of the dots, and might have difficulty interpreting the physical referents of lines. (These are levees built to prevent soil erosion. Because they follow elevation levels, here they look like contour lines on a topographic map.)

Representational and Geometric Correspondences

Any environmental representation, including the one shown in Fig. 8.2, challenges viewers to understand two interconnected kinds of information. One concerns the identity of the referent (e.g., that there are trees or hills), and the other concerns spatial information about the referent. On the representation itself, the qualities of the graphic that provide clues to identity and spatial information are codetermined by qualities of the environment (e.g., that there are, in fact, trees in the photographed locale; that the trees are arranged in rows) and by the qualities of the representation (e.g., at what scale; with what colors; with what kind of geometric projection; from what direction). Any representation is a particular selection among a range of possibilities, both with respect to what content appears and how the content appears. It may be difficult to appreciate that *content* can differ across representations of the same environment for media often thought of as simple records of reality such as photography (e.g., see Bcilin, 1991; Sontag, 1977). Even with photography, however, depicted content varies with lighting, filters, film, and so on.

In cartography, these two components may be identified as *representational correspondences* and *geometric correspondences* (see Liben & Downs, 1989). Representational correspondences concern the links between categories of referents and their symbols (e.g., representing highway exits areas by white triangles; representing rivers by blue

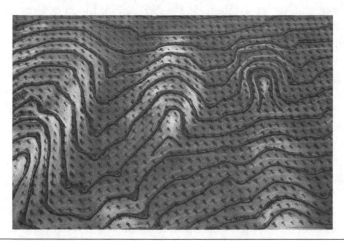

Figure. 8.2. A photograph from *Earth from Above,* © Yann Arthur-Bertrand, showing an overhead view of olive tree plantations in Tunisia. The original photograph is in color and is reproduced here by permission of the photographer. Additional information about the project is given in the Endnote.

lines). Geometric correspondences concern the links between the spatial characteristics of the referential environment and the spatial features of the map (e.g., how the land area of a continent that is part of the oblate spheroid of Earth is projected onto the two-dimensional surface of a piece of paper).

Although in theory the two may be distinguished, in reality the two are interrelated. First, identifying the referential identity of graphic marks in part depends on interpreting spatial information. In Fig. 8.2, for example, understanding that a given dot-like shape is an individual tree requires understanding that one is looking straight down from high above, and thus that even a big tree can look like a small, somewhat irregular dot rather than like a canonical tree with trunk, roots, and spreading branches. Second, the reverse is true as well—that is, identifying the spatial information in part depends on identifying the referent. Again, using Fig. 8.2 as the example, having identified that the dots are trees (with its entailed knowledge about tree size and shape), the user has access to information about viewing distance and viewing angle. Thus, the tasks of interpreting symbolic and spatial features are both distinct and interrelated processes.

From a psychological perspective, the challenge is for users to apply their symbolic and spatial concepts to understand a given representation. Because these symbolic and spatial concepts develop over childhood, it is especially interesting to examine children's developing understanding of environmental representations, and it is this interest that has been central to my research, much of it developed collaboratively (e.g., Downs & Liben, 1987, 1991, 1993; Liben & Downs, 1986, 1989, 1991, 2001). In the current chapter, I focus primarily on children's developing understanding of the spatial meaning contained in representations, although (as previously explained) this focus sometimes spills over into commenting on children's understanding of *what* is represented as well. Discussions more directly concerned with children's developing understanding of nonspatial symbolic meaning of place representations (e.g., understanding that on a road map, a red line stands for a road, but that the referent road itself is not colored red) are provided elsewhere (e.g., see Liben, 2001, 2006; Liben & Downs, 1989; 1994; Myers & Liben, 2005).

The Cartographic Eye

Having established a focus on the spatial domain, it is useful to structure the spatial component of representations in more detail. One way to conceptualize this component is with what has been called the *cartographic eye* (Downs, 1981). Before cataloguing its components, I offer two introductory comments about this conceptualization. First, the eye is labeled "cartographic" because the model was originally developed in relation to maps. It is suitable, however, for other kinds of graphic representations in which a systematic spatial correspondence exists between the referent space and the representation (e.g., photographs or representational paintings that use systematic geometries as in Renaissance art; see Hagen, 1986; Kubovy, 1986). To provide continuity with earlier writing, I use the word *cartographic* in this chapter, but the meaning should be interpreted more generally (e.g., as in "photographic eye"). Second, in the context of a chapter that eschews disembodiment, it is probably important to point out that one should think of the term *eye* here more as the sensing device of a machine, such as a camera, rather than as the organic eye of a sentient being. As should become clear from the section on empirical work and from the developmental model offered later, the human eye is unquestionably embodied.

Three dimensions of geometric correspondence are incorporated in the cartographic eye. The first, *viewing distance*, refers to how far away viewers are seeing the environment. For maps, viewing distance translates into scale, which we can simply express as a ratio contrasting the size of the representation to size of the referent. Thus, for example, if one uses a piece of 8½" × 11" paper to represent the city of Chicago, the ratio (or *representative fraction*) would be roughly 1:12,000. If the same paper were used to represent a classroom, the scale would be roughly 1:20. In cartography, a *small-scale* map means that the referent space looks small on the map; a *large-scale* map means the reverse. Thus, a small-scale map shows a large amount of land with little detail; a large-scale map shows a small amount of land with considerable detail. (These terms are often reversed in psychological literature on mapping.) In the case of photographs, viewing distance typically becomes a factor only when the photograph shows the referent at an unusually close distance (commonly referred to as a "close-up"). In painting, viewing distance is commonly captured implicitly by labeling its category (e.g., a landscape vs. a portrait).

The second dimension of the cartographic eye is *viewing angle*, which refers to the angle or the tilt at which the photographer has depicted the referent. In cartography, the most common viewing angle is 90°, or straight down, creating what is known as a "plan-view map" (also called "orthogonal," "nadir," or "vertical" views). This angle is measured as the deviation from 0° which is the eye-level, straight-ahead view. The 0° angle is, of course, the most natural, embodied experience of the environment, and the one most commonly used in representational art and snapshot photography. Angles falling in between these two extremes (e.g., 30° or 45°) are oblique views. In photography, oblique views commonly occur when pictures are taken from tall buildings or tall mountains. Cartographers often use oblique angles in tourist maps to provide information about the visual appearance of buildings, and in some cases, to provide information about the local topography (e.g., oblique maps are common in San Francisco, where tourists need to be apprised of steep roads).

The third dimension, *viewing azimuth*, refers to the direction from which the cartographer has depicted the space, which, by convention, is expressed as the deviation from north. In contemporary cartography, it is common to orient maps so that they are facing north (e.g., with north at the top of the paper). This is only a convention, however, and there are often reasons to do otherwise. For example, maps of lake recreation areas are commonly oriented so that the lake runs the width of the page, irrespective of the resulting azimuth. In addition, the north-facing convention is merely the modern one. In ancient and medieval eras, maps were conventionally oriented to face east—toward the Orient—thus explaining the origin of the term *orientation*. In photography, variations in azimuths occur routinely as the same object or environment is photographed from different directions (e.g., photographing the front vs. the side of a statue). In architecture, oblique renderings are often used to provide clients with a sense of how a proposed building will look in context. Any external spatial representation may be described in relation to these three dimensions.

Having identified some of the challenges of understanding, and having provided a structure for describing the spatial qualities of place representations, in the next section, I turn to empirical work on children's developing understanding of environmental representations.

EMPIRICAL ILLUSTRATIONS OF EMBODIED UNDERSTANDING OF SPATIAL-GRAPHIC REPRESENTATIONS

Consciousness and Perspective

Embodied experience is dynamic experience. Our eyes move, our heads move, and our bodies move. And as we move, we garner information of two kinds, simultaneously. One is about the world in which we move; the other is about ourselves, that is, about our own place in that world.

Consider this idea with respect to general theories of consciousness (Carlson, 1997):

> Subjectivity has the further consequence that all my conscious forms of intentionality that give me information about the world independent of myself are always from a special point of view. The world itself has no point of view, but my access to the world through my conscious states is always perspectival, always from my point of view. (Searle, 1992, p. 95)

> Whenever there is a conscious mind, there is a point of view. This is one of the most fundamental ideas we have about minds—or about consciousness. A conscious mind is an observer, who takes in a limited subset of all the information there is. . . . For most practical purposes, we can consider the point of view of a particular conscious subject to be just that: a point moving through space-time. (Dennett, 1991, pp. 101–102)

Both Searle and Dennett were using the notion of point of view in relation to consciousness in general; Gibson (1979) developed a similar argument with respect to visual perception.

> The optical information to specify the self, including the head, body, arms, and hands, accompanies the optical information to specify the environment. The two sources of information coexist. The one could not exist without the other. . . . Self-perception and environment perception go together. (p. 116)

Although these discussions were addressed to the ongoing stream of consciousness or perception, the same points are relevant for single, station-point, representational graphics as well. In other words, as implied by the earlier discussion of the cartographic eye, any static environmental representation provides information about a slice of the environment from a particular vantage point in a particular moment in time. The representation has some perspective or vantage point, just as a sentient viewer has a point of view. Thus, interpreting environmental representations requires understanding the view-specific nature of the image, and it is this understanding that is addressed in the research reviewed below.

UNDERSTANDING VANTAGE POINTS IN PHOTOGRAPHY

In this section, I review research concerning children's awareness or control of vantage point in the medium of photography. I describe findings from three kinds of tasks, including those in which participants were (a) shown pairs of photographs and asked to identify and explain vantage point differences between them, (b) given model photographs and asked to reproduce them, and (c) asked to create photographs that would depict a named referent in a specified manner.

Photographic Contrasts

To allow us to examine individuals' sensitivity to alternative vantage points, we prepared pairs of photographs that depicted the identical referent, but did so from different vantage points (Liben, 2003; Liben & Szechter, 2001). For each of the three dimensions identified in the cartographic eye (viewing distance, viewing angle, and viewing azimuth), we created five pairs of items. For example, a viewing distance pair depicted the base of a tree photographed from two distances; a viewing-angle pair showed a group of tulips photographed from the side or from directly overhead; and a viewing-azimuth pair showed a rooster on a painted tile photographed from two different sides of the tile. (The wood grain of the table on which the tile rested followed the same direction in both photographs, thus providing evidence that the camera had been moved to a different side of the table, rather than that the tile had been rotated by 90°.) In addition, we included filler pairs in which photographs were either entirely identical, or differed only because the referent itself had been changed in some way. For example, one referent-change item included a balloon that had been inflated to different sizes in the two photographs. Multiple clues indicated that it was balloon size, rather than viewing distance, that differed between the two photographs (e.g., the sizes of a nearby rubber duck and floor tiles were identical in the two photographs, as was the grain density of the wood wall). Illustrative photographs of all pair types may be found in Liben (2003, Figure 3).

For each pair of items, participants were first asked to decide whether or not the photographs were identical, and if not, to state what was different. Then they were asked to say whether they thought the difference was due to something that the photographer had done, or due to something that had changed "in this place" and in either case, to explain what had happened. These tasks were given to 3-, 5-, and 7-year-old children as well as to a sample of college students.

For the items in which the two photographs differed because of a change in viewing distance, three quarters of the 3-year-olds failed on every single item, and the remaining children answered only a single item correctly. By the age of five years, all levels of performance were represented (i.e., ranging from "none correct" to "all correct"), with over half the children correct on all or all but one item. By seven years, virtually all children were correct on all or all but one item, and by adulthood, with the exception of one person on one item, all participants correctly explained for all these pairs that the photographer had moved closer or further from the subject of the photograph.

Consistent with research on children's aesthetic development (e.g., Freeman, 1995; Parsons, 1987), young children's comments about differences between the photographs tended to focus on their referential *content* rather than on the way that they were created or the surface appearance of the photograph. Prototypical of a response to the distance item described above was a 5-year-old child who said, "Well, this one only has dandelions, and this one has dandelions and part of a tree."

Some young children were able to comment on some of the spatial qualities of the depictions, but again, the comments typically seemed to imply that they thought that differences in spatial appearance would be accounted for differences in the size of the referents rather than about differences in the image. For example, for a pair that showed a statue of a man photographed from two different distances, a one 3-year-old child explained that the difference was that, "This man is smaller and this man is bigger." Of course, with verbal explanations like these, there is always some ambiguity about what the child means. In this case, for example, it is possible that the child was commenting on depicted size rather than on actual size. Responses *from* older children and adults, however, were less ambiguous, as they tended to talk about the photographer's actions, providing clear statements that the photographer "got closer" or "moved further back." (It is interesting to note that even the adults seemingly failed to consider changes in the technology; for example, none suggested that perhaps the photographer had changed the lens on the camera to take the second photograph, or that perhaps the photographer had enlarged and cropped the photograph.)

Responses to the items designed to test understanding of viewing angle and viewing azimuth revealed similar developmental patterns, but with a slower progression. Among the 3-year-old children, none understood the change in viewing angle on even a single item. What was particularly striking in these data was the number of times young children did not appear to even see that there was anything spatially different about the two photographs. For example, when shown the tulips that had been photographed either from overhead or from the side, one 3-year-old child described the content, noting only differences of color: "I like tulips. My mom likes tulips. These ones are yellow"—pointing to the straight-ahead view—"and these ones are red"—pointing to the overhead view. Another 3-year-old said, "They're both the same." When the investigator responded, "Well, they're both of tulips, but is there anything different about the pictures?" the child responded, "Nope. This one"—points—"has the same stuff." Again, these responses are indicative of children focusing on the content of the photographs rather than on their appearance or the techniques used to create them.

By the age of five years, the modal response was still a score of zero, but by that age, almost half the children were able to answer correctly on one or two items. Although no 5-year-old child was correct on more than two items, even the quality of the 5-year-olds' errors suggested more advanced understanding. In other words, even when they were unable to show understanding of the photographer's viewing angle, they were at least able to notice differences between the two images. For the tulip pair, for example, one 5-year-old child attributed the difference to something the photographer did, albeit not related to viewing angle. Specifically, this child said that the photographs differed because the photographer "took this one when they were all curled up and those ones when they were all blooming." Another 5-year-old commented, "The tulips are up and the tulips are down . . . First, in the spring they were closed, and then in the summer they came out again." Still another commented: "This one is closed and this one is open." When the investigator probed by asking, "How did the photographer do that?" the child responded, "He took one sometime when they were closed and one sometime when they were open." Interestingly, then, although these children were able to recognize that any given image is open to change as a function of the photographer's action, they explained the change temporally rather than spatially.

Some 5-year-old children, however, were able to demonstrate excellent understanding of the effects of viewing angle. Illustrative was a child who offered this explanation: "Um, that one you're looking that way"—points straight ahead—"and that one you're looking down, this way"—bends over the picture. Another said, "Oh, I like these . . . He [the photographer] went sort of on the side of them and then like up above them to get the middle"—points hand down on top of the tulips and rises in chair—". . . because, um, like, this one is like straight across and this one's like you're looking down"—flexes hand to point all fingers down onto the tulips. Responses of this kind became increasingly common by seven years and almost universal by adulthood.

The patterns of performance on the pairs of photographs designed to tap children's understanding of viewing azimuth showed a similar developmental progression to that observed for viewing angle, except that in addition, even a few adults experienced difficulty. Thus, the youngest children often were not even able to see differences between the two images in the pair, and when they did notice differences, they more commonly believed that there had been a change "in the place" than a change in what the photographer had done. For example, with the item in which the rooster tile had been photographed from two different directions, a 3-year-old child said, "Hey, that's not the same rooster! There he's putting his head up and he's not the same!" Among both children and adults who erred, the common error was to say that the tile itself had been moved (a possibility that, as explained earlier, could be ruled out on the basis of the direction of the wood grain of the table).

Reproducing Photographic Models

A second approach used to explore understanding of the spatial, view-specific nature of photographs was one in which interviewers gave children (aged eight years) and adults (college students) a series of digital photographs as models. Investigators then asked the participants to reproduce them as precisely as possible using the same digital camera that had been used to create the initial photographs (Liben & Szechter, 2002). Again, of interest was participants' sensitivity to viewing distance, viewing angle, and viewing azimuth.

The photographer had taken all photographs in the same building and of relatively mundane subjects, but had designed the photographs so that they avoided canonical views. For example, a canonical photograph of a café called Otto's would be likely to place the "Otto's" sign at the center, and to use a viewing azimuth in which the sight line is orthogonal to the sign. In contrast, the model photograph of Otto's was taken from the side, with the sign off center. The rationale behind using noncanonical vantage points was to make it unlikely that a participant would create a good match to the model by chance, and to increase the probability that the participant would notice that there was a problem that they needed to solve.

By the time participants entered the building for the model task, they had already been given lessons about how to use the camera and had taken a number of photographs of their own choosing elsewhere on campus. Participants were given model photographs one at a time and were asked to take photographs that would look *exactly* the same. They were then asked to view their resulting photograph on the display screen to see how well they had done, and to try again to see if they could create an even more exact match.

Virtually all participants were successful in including the correct referents in their photographs. Thus, with only one exception (over all participants and over all four models), participants' photographs contained the same objects as did the model photographs (e.g., the correct flag, the mailbox, the table and plant). This finding is consistent with the observation made earlier with respect to the photographic pairs tasks that even by preschool, children are sensitive to *what* is in an image, even if they are not yet sensitive to *how* it is represented.

To quantify the degree to which participants were sensitive to the dimensions of the cartographic eye, we developed a scoring system that awarded points to each photograph on the basis of qualities that depended on the correct viewing distance, viewing angle, and viewing azimuth. In addition, we scored whether the correct camera orientation (vertical or horizontal) was used. Points from each of the four photographs were summed and performance was examined by trial. The data showed a large range of performance within both groups, but children performed worse than adults, and performance was higher on trial 2 than trial 1 (although the increase was significant only among the children). Taken as a whole, these data are consistent with the general conclusion from the photograph pair data described earlier that sensitivity to vantage point develops from childhood to adulthood. (Sample photographs and more detailed findings are found in Liben, 2003.)

Photographic Implementation of Verbal Descriptions

The third approach we used to study understanding of vantage point was a task in which interviewers asked participants to take photographs of a specified referent to achieve some specified appearance. Given that participants were using a camera that did not offer technical options (the camera's focal length lens was fixed, the user could not control exposure time or change the aperture setting), participants needed to control viewing distance, angle, or azimuth to implement the request.

Specifically, interviewers individually took children (eight years of age) and college students on a walk across campus. Before leaving for the walk, interviewers showed them how to use a digital camera, and told them that during the walk, they would be able to take some pictures of their own choosing, as well as specific photographs at the interviewer's request. As participants approached a large round pool containing a large, metal, water-fountain sculpture, the interviewer requested the first specific picture. Initially, participants were asked to take a photograph of the fountain, and were then helped to view the image on the camera's display. The interviewer then asked for a second image of the fountain. What the participant was asked to do depended on what the first image showed. If the first image showed all or most of the fountain, the interviewer asked, "What if you only wanted to see that spiral shaped part on top"—gesturing a sphere up in the air—"in your picture? What could you do to make that part take up most of the picture?" The interviewer then asked participants to try their solution. If, instead, only part of the fountain had been included in the first photograph, the interviewer asked what the participant might do so that the photograph would include the entire fountain, including the circular pool in which it rested. Again, the interviewer asked participants to implement their plan. Both of these verbal requests were intended to motivate participants to change viewing distance, viewing angle, or both.

To measure performance, we printed each photograph at a fixed size and then measured the circumference of the spherical part of the fountain (extrapolated beyond the picture frame, if necessary) as a proxy for viewing distance. With the exception of only two adults, all participants began by photographing the fountain from afar. Thus, first photographs almost always showed the full sphere, the stand on which it was mounted, and with only two exceptions, all or some of the larger pool in which the sculpture rests. The viewing distances used by children and adults were roughly comparable for their first photographs. Thus, the printed fountain sizes for children's and adults' first photographs were roughly equivalent.

Where children and adults differed was with respect to their ability to adjust vantage point to satisfy the experimenter's request for the second photograph. Only 65% of the children decreased the viewing distance sufficiently to create a measurably larger sphere in the print of the second photograph, sometimes with only a minimal change (e.g., less than a 10% increase in size). In contrast, all adults who were asked to increase the size of the sphere in the photograph did so successfully. Averaging across participants, for children, the second sphere was only 1.02 times larger than the first; for adults, the second sphere was 3.20 times larger.

The interviewer made a second request at the campus art museum, which displays two lion paw sculptures mounted on either side of the entrance. Here, the interviewer asked participants to take a photograph so that only one paw would show in the picture, a request that participants could meet by changing their viewing distance, angle, or azimuth. Adults were highly successful: All but two produced images with a single paw. Furthermore, even the two errors that occurred were simply technological errors insofar as both were cases in which the second paw appeared at the very edge of the print. This edge would not actually have been visible on the camera's display, which cuts off a small slice of what the photographer has actually recorded in the image.

Again, the pattern of children's performance was far more varied. Roughly one third of the children had photographs with two visible paws in the photograph, errors that were not attributable to the same technological explanation that held for adults. Among the children who succeeded, varied strategies were used. As anticipated, a common response was to change the viewing azimuth so that one of the paws was simply to the side of the camera's range, a strategy often used by adults as well. Some children, however, instead used noncanonical viewing angles (e.g., climbing to the top of one paw and photographing it from above) or noncanonical viewing distances (e.g., moving so close that a single paw filled the entire picture frame). One child simply "waited for people walking by to block one of the paws from view."

Summary of Photographic Vantage Points

The three types of tasks using photography converge on the general conclusion that there is a gradual developmental progression in coming to understand the view-specific nature of images. Very young preschool children focus on the referential content of representations almost exclusively. They have difficulty in even identifying the differences between photographs that have "the same stuff." They appear to be unaware of the ways in which referents and representations are linked. In the older-preschool and early-elementary years, children develop greater sensitivity to the way the same referent looks in a particular representation. They demonstrate greater skill in manipulating vantage points (e.g., in selecting a position for the camera) to achieve specified views. Parallel developmental progressions may be seen in other kinds of representational tasks discussed next.

UNDERSTANDING AND PRODUCING REPRESENTATIONS THAT DIVERGE FROM EMBODIED EXPERIENCE

In the research just described, all the images showed objects that are highly familiar, and depicted these objects in ways that are consonant with human embodied experience. In those studies, participants were required to identify some component of vantage point explicitly. In the first task, participants were asked to identify view-specific differences between pairs of photographs, and to explain the nature of the difference. In the second and third tasks, participants were required to bring vantage point under intentional control, either to create reproductions of model photographs or to create new photographs that would meet view-specific constraints about the way that specified referents were depicted.

The investigations described in the current section are also aimed at exploring developmental progressions in understanding vantage point. In these studies, however, the major challenges concern participants' ability to work with representations whose vantage points diverge from those of embodied experience in the environment. I discuss these studies in two sections. In the first, I review findings from tasks in which participants were asked to interpret or use environmental representations that were provided to them. In the second, I review findings from tasks in which participants were asked to draw their own representations.

Before turning to the research itself, I acknowledge that the boundaries are fuzzy both for divisions within this section, as well as for the division between this section and the previous one. For example, I include some data from children's drawings when making points about children's understanding of ready-made representations, and there is some use of ready-made representations in one of the drawing tasks. Further, one can easily argue that the act of "producing drawings" described below requires just as explicit attention to vantage point as does the act of "producing photographs" discussed above. Thus, one should view the section divisions as a rhetorical device whose purpose is to organize the presentation of diverse studies, rather than as a theoretical argument whose purpose is to argue for conceptual divisions among the various challenges and skills.

Interpreting and Using Environmental Representations

As explained in the introductory discussion of Fig. 8.2, an embodiment perspective leads to the expectation that it will be difficult to interpret environmental representations that depict vantage points that deviate from embodied experiences. Discussed below are relevant data from children's understanding of both aerial photographs and maps.

Understanding nadir and oblique aerial photographs. As part of our early research on children's developing understanding of representations of place (Liben & Downs, 1986, 1989; 1991), we interviewed preschool children (aged three to six years) about their understanding of a nadir (straight-down) aerial photograph of Chicago (approximately 1:20,000). In our interviews, we first solicited children's spontaneous interpretations, both of the meaning of the representation as a whole, and also of individual pieces of the representation, and then asked more specific questions about parts of the image.

Even the youngest children were very successful in interpreting the overall meaning of the image (what we called meaning at the *holistic* level) insofar as they were able to interpret it as a place. Illustrative were children who responded that it shows "a city" or "buildings and stuff." Children were, however, generally very inaccurate not only about the specific place, but even about the scope of the place, as in children who responded that it shows "states and stuff," or "the world," "the United States," or "Africa." These responses suggest that children have not yet come to understand viewing distance in that they misinterpret the scale of the representation taken as a whole.

Difficulty in understanding viewing distance and, thus, scale, was also evident in preschool children's interpretations of particular pieces of the image (what we called understanding at the "componential" level). Illustrative of scale errors were children who identified the boats in Lake Michigan as "fish," roads as "ropes," and the Chicago River as a "snake." We also observed componential errors that appeared to be motivated by children's failure to understand the overhead viewing angle of the aerial photograph. For example, children identified tennis courts as "doors" and a parking area that looked triangular from overhead as a "hill." Both of these erroneous interpretations make sense if one assumes that the child is interpreting the graphic patterns as they would be interpreted from embodied experience in the environment—that is, the lines of the tennis court could easily look like door panels viewed from straight ahead, and the triangular lines of the parking area could easily look like a hill seen from eye level.

A later study with preschool children and adults was conducted to investigate whether indeed it would be easier to interpret the meaning of components of aerial photographs if they were in viewing angles more compatible with embodied experience of the environment (Liben, Dunphy-Lelli, & Szechter, described in Liben, 2005). Children and adults were asked to identify components of aerial photographs that varied with respect to viewing distance (near vs. far) and viewing angle (nadir vs. oblique). Photographs that were both "near" and "oblique" were most similar to the experience one would have in looking at an environment from a hill, whereas those that were both "far" and "nadir" would be most dissimilar.

One illustrative item was a near nadir view on which a baseball field had been circled. Of the 33 adults asked to identify the referent, all were correct, with 31 answering either "baseball diamond" or "baseball field," and the remaining two answering "sport field." Preschool children, however, experienced far more difficulty, with only four of 40 children giving one of these correct responses. Many of children's errors were reasonable insofar as they named environmental features of the right general size and kind (e.g., responses such as "pool," "sand hole," "helicopter landing area," and "parking lot"). Approximately 20% of the preschoolers' responses, however, showed serious confusion (e.g., responses such as "eyeball," "mushroom," "New York City steam things," "parachute," "seashell," and "spiderweb"). Of particular relevance here was the interaction between age group and viewing angle; whereas adults performed equivalently on nadir and oblique photographs, children performed significantly better on oblique. These data suggest that it is a more extended process to learn to interpret representations with viewing angles that extend beyond embodied environmental experience.

Understanding and using maps. Investigators may ask parallel questions with respect to children's developing ability to understand maps depicting the environment from perspectives that differ from embodied experience. In one study, we directly compared preschool children's ability to understand and use plan versus oblique maps (Liben & Yekel, 1996). Children were given mapping tasks in their own familiar classroom. Before they arrived for the study, 12 novel objects (e.g., a teddy bear) were placed in the room. After some preliminary discussions about maps and after some general orientation to a map of the classroom (including aligning it with the space), investigators asked children to find and point to the novel objects. As children located each, they then asked children to place a colored sticker on a map of the room to show the object's location. Of particular relevance here was the between-subjects manipulation of order of map type. Half the children began by using a plan map for the sticker-location task and then an oblique perspective map, and half the children began with the oblique map and then used the plan map.

Children who received the plan map first tended to perform very badly, erring not only with respect to the precision of sticker placements, but also with respect to the quality of sticker placements—that is, children given the plan map first tended to place stickers on an entirely wrong category of symbol. For objects that were located on the floor, children commonly placed stickers on one of the representations for a piece of furniture. Consistent with this qualitative description of the data, analyses of the total number correct revealed a main effect of map type, with better performance on the oblique map than on the plan map, and an interaction with map order; children who received the oblique map first performed better on the plan map than did children who received the plan map first.

This study also provided another kind of data supporting the argument that children find it difficult to interpret plan view representations that offer perspectives at variance with their embodied experience. At the end of all the sticker-location items, investigators directly asked children whether there was any way that one could make the maps easier to understand. Over half of the children suggested that adding legs to the tables would help. It is easy to imagine that the embodied experience of a preschool child in the classroom offers far more opportunity to experience the legs of tables than to see their top surfaces.

Research on children's understanding of viewing azimuth was conducted in another study using maps of familiar classrooms (Liben & Downs, 1993). Each child in kindergarten, first-, second-, and combined fifth/sixth-grade classrooms received a map of their classroom. Maps were placed on children's desks so that the map was aligned with the room. After some general discussion about correspondence between the map and the room, an adult went to a sequence of six places within the room and pointed in a particular direction. Children were asked to place arrow stickers on their maps to show the adult's locations and pointing directions. After completing the six items, the map was collected and another copy of the map was distributed. This time, however, the maps were placed on children's desks so that they were turned 180°. With the maps in this unaligned condition, the adult asked children to complete the same arrow-placement task.

In the aligned condition, even the youngest children did fairly well, and children in the two oldest groups performed close to ceiling. The quality of errors also indicated reasonably good understanding—that is, in contrast to the high incidence of serious errors made by preschoolers on the plan map in the study by Liben and Yekel (1996) discussed above, first-grade children rarely placed arrows in referentially impossible locations (e.g., only rarely did children place arrows directly on furniture symbols rather than on the open area representing the floor). Furthermore, the large majority of the children placed their arrows in the right general area of the map and oriented their arrows in roughly the correct direction. Taken together, these data suggest that by first grade, most children have mastered the overhead (plan) viewing angle in general. At the same time, the dispersion of the arrows within the correct quadrant that may be seen on any particular arrow item (see Liben & Downs, 1993) shows that children of this age have not yet mastered the spatial correspondences linking the referent space and the representational space with precision.

The data from the unaligned condition showed a very different pattern. When children had to adjust for the mismatched azimuth, only rarely did they manage to place their arrows even close to the correct position or the correct orientation. Furthermore, there was evidence not only of quantitative inaccuracy, but also of symbolic confusion, with children placing arrows on symbols for tables or desks rather than on the floor area. Furthermore, even when arrows were placed on the symbolized floor, many were placed in the incorrect quadrant of the room, and many arrows deviated from the correct position by roughly 180°. What appears to be happening is that many of the children were having difficulty ignoring the position of their bodies in relation to the room when they responded to the task.

Producing Environmental Representations

Another way in which we have studied developmental understanding and flexibility in adjusting vantage points is by asking children to produce representations of various spaces. In one task, we simply asked children in kindergarten, first, second, fifth, and sixth grade to produce a map of their own classroom without specifying what vantage point they should use (Liben & Downs, 1994). When maps from one class at each grade were coded, we found increasing use of consistent overhead viewing angles (plan maps) with grade: 10%, 20%, 25%, and 100%, respectively. Children in the younger grades produced a variety of map types. Some were strictly elevation or straight-ahead views, as in drawing a single wall of their classroom. Others combined elevation and nadir viewing angles, as in maps that showed the tables in plan view, but showed the chairs in elevation. Overall, it appears that children gradually learn the convention of using an orthogonal viewing angles for maps, although as in art, it is likely that these age-linked differences may well vary from culture to culture (e.g., Hagen, 1986).

In another task, we asked first- and second-grade children to drawn a picture of what their school building would like to a bird flying directly overhead (Liben & Downs, 1994). Data from this task also showed that the incidence of elevation views was greater in younger children (32% in first grade vs. 8% in second grade) and that the incidence of plan views was greater in older children (27% in first grade vs. 44% in second grade).

In a third task, we distributed copies of an aerial photograph of Chicago to students in first- and second-grade classes. After some discussion about how an aerial photograph might be useful to someone trying to draw a map of a city, we asked each student to draw (without tracing) a map of Chicago based on information derived from the photograph (Liben & Downs, 1991). Interestingly, even with a vertical view, aerial photograph at their desk to use, approximately 20% of the first-grade children produced elevation drawings of a bit of a generic city (e.g., drawing the fronts of a few houses along a road).

In short, the data from a range of production tasks are consistent with those from the comprehension tasks described earlier in suggesting that it is initially difficult for children to understand viewing angles that fall outside their embodied experiences in interacting in the real environment. It is important to note, however, that although the preceding discussions have emphasized group comparisons across ages, with few exceptions, there is remarkable variability *within* age as well as the more predictable variability across age. In the next section of the chapter, I therefore turn briefly to some of the many factors that are involved in children's developing understanding of spatial graphic representations, and, more generally, to the way in which the child's developing understanding of representations is embedded within a broader context.

THE EMBEDDED MODEL OF UNDERSTANDING SPATIAL-GRAPHIC REPRESENTATIONS

My discussions thus far have emphasized one component of the meaning of the term embodiment given in the glossary definition cited at the beginning of this chapter: "the inseparability of a system's learning (and/or knowledge) and its physical being (and acting)." As discussed earlier, the position that knowledge is grounded in the body and in action is foundational for Piaget's (1952) constructive theory of development and for Gibson's (1979) ecological theory of perception. In prior sections of this chapter (and elsewhere; see Liben, 2005), I have posited that embodiment is also foundational for children's developing understanding of spatial-graphic representations of the environment.

The glossary entry for embodiment quoted earlier, however, contains a second component: "Embodiment also points to the fact that complex systems often unfold from, and are enfolded in, other complex systems." Here, the notion of the nonsplit nexus of mind and body becomes a metaphor for the nonsplit nexus of the individual (inter)acting and embedded in multilayered (intertwined) social and physical worlds. Again, the glossary subentry for embodiment on nestedness (McMurtry, 2004) makes the point concisely: "Individual human learners are one example of nested complex forms. They are, all-at-once, autonomous forms, complex collectives (e.g., they arise in the coactivity of bodily subsystems), and parts/subagents in a range of other emergent forms (including, for example, social collectives and culture)." A graphic instantiation of this nested aspect of embodiment proposed by Davis, Sumara, and Luce-Kapler (2000) shows an ever-expanding series of nested circles depicting, respectively, bodily subsystems (organs and cells); the person (the "body biologic"); the collective (social bodies or bodies of knowledge); the society or the body politic; the species; and finally, the biosphere or planetary body.

This general idea of nestedness is expressed in a wide range of disciplines. For example, in geography, it is contained in the concept of "expanding worlds" in which the individual is, simultaneously, located on a street, in a town, in a county, state, region, and country, as well as on a continent, on Earth, in a galaxy, and in a universe. In developmental psychology, it is represented in the concept of an "ecological" approach to development that recognizes that children develop in not only the microsystems of their own bodies, but also in the meso-, exo- and macro-level systems of family, neighborhood, religion, history, country and so on (Bronfenbrenner, 1977). At any moment, all these systems matter, even to the individual. They affect light, climate, seasons, gravity, roads; access to schools, books, movies, the Internet; physical safety, political constraints or freedoms, geometries of art, child care; the list is virtually endless. Simultaneously, the individual matters, perhaps nowhere more dramatically stated than in chaos theory where the beating of a wing in one location may affect weather on the other side of the globe (Lorenz, 1963).

Of course, neither a theorist nor an empirical researcher can possibly examine all levels and factors at once, and thus my own work is generally limited to focusing first, on the level of the individual child, and second, on the substantive topic of graphic representations. But even with these constraints, developmental pathways to competence are nested. In an earlier paper (Liben, 1999), I proposed the Embedded Model as one means of conceptualizing the major constructs and relations among them. Figure 8.3 shows the complete Embedded Model as originally conceptualized.

Of particular importance here are several points conveyed by this model. First, consistent with the point made in the earlier discussions of representational amplifiers and the cartographic eye, the inclusion of "representational strategies" highlights the argument that there is no singular, correct way to represent a referent. Instead, there are alternatives at every step of the way with respect to the representational medium, the content to be included, and the manner in which that content is depicted. The developmental challenges for the child involve (a) coming to realize that, indeed, there are choices to be made, (b) learning how to interpret meaning across different representational media, (c) understanding when some representational quality is a convention but only a convention (e.g., orienting maps with north at the top; using blue to represent water), and so on. As discussed at greater

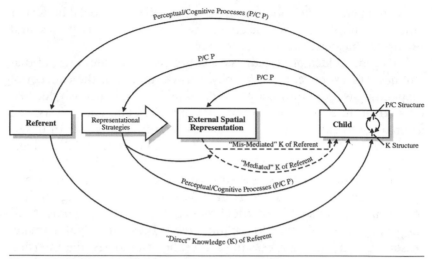

Figure. 8.3. The Embedded Model as described in Liben (1999).

length elsewhere (Liben, 1999), children may be expected to develop a better understanding of these strategies if they have the opportunity to create as well as use representations (see Callaghan & Rankin, 2002), if they are exposed to alternative representations of the identical referents, if their attention is directed to the representational surfaces via *ego-deictic* representations (those that explicitly point to themselves such as Escher's spatially impossible drawings), and if they are encouraged by adults to interpret the spatial meaning of graphic representations (e.g., see Szechter & Liben, 2004).

In Fig. 8.3, the arrows labeled "Perceptual/Cognitive Processes" flowing from the child are meant to convey that any given encounter with something in the environment—whether physical or representational—is driven by children's underlying cognitive processes, and these, themselves, are also embodied. This point is an instantiation of a constructivist account such as Piaget's, which posits that all knowledge is constructed, and that this constructed knowledge feeds back into the underlying cognitive structure of the embodied child (note the arrows feeding back to the child in Fig. 8.3). Although I have discussed the two sets of arrows here sequentially, the processes they depict are simultaneous and integrated, just as the nonsplit conceptualization of assimilation and accommodation described in the introductory section of this chapter.

Importantly, in order to derive appropriate (mediated) knowledge about the referent via external representations, children must have some appreciation for the links between the referent and representation, that is, some appreciation for representational strategies. Absent this understanding, children obtain what is referred to in the Embedded Model as "*mis-mediated* knowledge"—that is, distorted knowledge of the referent (e.g., interpreting tennis courts as doors on an aerial photograph). Only if one understands representational strategies is one in a position to derive "mediated knowledge" of the referent through representations.

CONCLUSION: REVISITING JOEY THE DISEMBODIED HEAD

In closing, I return to the cartoon with which I began. Perhaps it is reasonable to allow that Joey is right that "it is all in your head" as long as we are willing to concede that our heads are in our bodies (with, among other qualities, their muscular, vestibular, circulatory, respiratory, and visual systems, along with the histories that carried them to the day of the 20K race), and that our bodies are in the world (with, among other attributes, the surfaces that afford running, the gravity that keeps us on the road, the light that allows us to see obstacles, and whatever else has served as the aliment for our constructive processes). Both senses of embodiment—the individual mind-body nexus and the nested forms that span cell to stratosphere—shape the experiences and meaning we have from the physical world and from the graphic representations we encounter in it, even those as frivolous as Doctor Fun.

ACKNOWLEDGMENT

Portions of this work were supported by grants from the National Science Foundation (ESI 01-01758, RED-9554504, REC-0411686), although the opinions expressed are those of the author and not of the NSF.

ENDNOTES

1. Information about Doctor Fun may be found at http://sunsite.unc.edu/Dave/drfun.html.

2. The photograph by Yann Arthus-Bertrand reproduced in Fig. 8.2 is taken from *Earth from Above: An Aerial Portrait of Our Planet*. Below, respectively, are Arthus-Bertrand's verbatim descriptions of (a) the goals of his project and (b) the particular photograph in Fig. 8.2. I appreciate M.

Arthus-Bertrand's permission to reproduce the photograph and the accompanying text.

(a) Since 1990, Yann Arthus-Bertrand has flown over hundreds of countries. His aerial photographs, which cannot be dissociated from their captions, invite all of us to reflect upon the Earth's evolution and the future of its inhabitants. A report through words and images which makes us aware that, not only are we individually responsible for our planet, we must also decide what we bequeath to future generations, together. Over the past 50 years, humans have changed ecosystems more rapidly and extensively than in any comparable period of time in human history. Limits of our planet's ecosystem appear everywhere: fresh water, ocean water, forests, air, arable land, open spaces . . .

At this critical stage, the alternative offered by a sustainable development policy should help in bringing about the necessary changes in order to "meet the needs of the present without compromising the ability of future generations to meet their own needs." Inseparable from the accompanying text commentaries, *Earth from Above* images invite each one of us to reflect upon the planet's evolution and the future of its inhabitants. Each and every person can and must act and contribute to the future of the Earth and mankind, starting right now. Visit http://www.yannarthusbertrand.org; http://www.goodplanet.org

(b) NEWLY PLANTED OLIVE GROVES, ZAGHOUAN, TUNISIA (36°24′ N, 10°23′ E). These olive groves at the foot of the 4,250-foot-high (1,295 m) Jebel Zaghouan in northeastern Tunisia are planted in curved embankments to retain water and limit erosion, which viewed from above look like the lines on a relief map. A symbol of peace, the tree is native to the Mediterranean basin, where 90 percent of the planet's olive trees grow. An olive tree can live as long as 1,000 years, producing 11 to 65 pounds (5 to 30 kg) of olives yearly. In the past its oil was used in small clay lamps, but it has been replaced by petroleum. Today we consume both table olives and olive oil, which is renowned for its dietary and medicinal properties and also used in cosmetics. The lands of the Mediterranean are the greatest olive producers and also the greatest consumers. The Greeks consume 4.7 gallons (18 liters) of olive oil per person per year, and the Italians and the Spaniards 3.4 gallons (13 liters), compared to 0.4 gallons (1.6 liters) a year in France and 0.2 gallons (0.7 liters) in the United States.

REFERENCES

Beilin, H. (1991). Developmental aesthetics and the psychology of photography. In R. M. Downs, L. S. Liben, & D. S. Palermo (Eds.), *Visions of aesthetics, the environment, and development: The legacy of Joachim F. Wohlwill* (pp. 45–86). Hillsdale, NJ: Lawrence Erlbaum Associates.

Bronfenbrenner, U. (1977). Towards an experimental ecology of human development. *American Psychologist, 32*, 513–531.

Callaghan, T. C., & Rankin, M. P. (2002). Emergence of graphic symbol functioning and the question of domain specificity: A longitudinal training study. *Child Development, 73*, 359–376.

Carlson, R. A. (1997). *Experienced cognition*. Hillsdale, NJ: Lawrence Erlbaum Associates.

Carroll, L. (1893) *Sylvie and Bruno concluded*. London: Macmillan and Co.

Damasio, A. R. (1994). *Decartes' error: Emotion, reason, and the human brain*. New York: Putnam.

Davis, B., Sumara, D., & Luce-Kapler, R. (2000). *Engaging minds: Learning and teaching in a complex world*. Mahwah: Lawrence Erlbaum Associates.

Dennett, D. C. (1991). *Consciousness explained*. Boston: Little, Brown.

Downs, R. M. (1981). Maps and mappings as metaphors for spatial representation. In L. S. Liben, A. H. Patterson, & N. Newcombe (Eds.), *Spatial representation and behavior across the life span: Theory and application* (pp. 143–166). New York: Academic Press.

Downs, R. M. (1985). The representation of space: Its development in children and in cartography. In R. Cohen (Ed.), *The development of spatial cognition* (pp. 323–345). Hillsdale, NJ: Erlbaum Associates.

Downs, R. M., & Liben, L. S. (1987). Children's understanding of maps. In P. Ellen & C. Thinus-Blanc (Eds.), *Cognitive processes and spatial orientation in animal and man: Vol. l. Neurophysiology of spatial knowledge and developmental aspects* (pp. 202–219). Dordrecht, Holland: Martinius Nijhoff.

Downs, R. M., & Liben, L. S. (1991). The development of expertise in geography: A cognitive-developmental approach to geographic education. *Annals of the Association of American Geographers, 81*, 304–327.

Downs, R. M., & Liben, L. S. (1993). Mediating the environment: Communicating, appropriating, and developing graphic representations of place. In R. H. Wozniak & K. Fischer (Eds.), *Development in context: Acting and thinking in specific environments* (pp. 155–181). Hillsdale, NJ: Lawrence Erlbaum Associates.

Eagleton, T. (2004, March). I am, therefore I think: The plight of the body in modern thought. *Harper's Magazine, 308*, 87–91.

Edelman, G. M. (1992). *Bright air, brilliant fire: On the matter of mind*. New York: Basic Books.

Freeman, N. H. (1995). The emergence of a framework theory of pictorial reasoning. In C. Lange-Kuttner & G. V. Thomas (Eds.), *Drawing and looking: Theoretical approaches to pictorial representation in children* (pp. 135–146). New York: Harvester Wheatsheaf.

Gattis, M. (2001). *Spatial schemas and abstract thought*. Cambridge, MA: MIT Press.

Gibson, J. J. (1966). *The senses considered as perceptual systems.* Boston: Houghton Mifflin.

Gibson, J. J. (1971). The information available in pictures. *Leonardo, 4,* 27–35.

Gibson, J. J. (1979). *The ecological approach to visual perception.* Boston: Houghton Mifflin.

Goodman, N. (1976). *Languages of art.* Indianapolis: Hackett Publishing Co.

Hagen, M. A. (1986). *Varieties of realism: Geometries of representational art.* Cambridge: Cambridge University Press.

Johnson, M. L. (1999). Embodied reason. In G. Weiss & H. F. Haber (Eds.), *Perspectives on embodiment.* New York: Routledge.

Kubovy, M. (1986). *The psychology of perspective and Renaissance art.* Cambridge, UK: Cambridge University Press.

Levinson, S. C. (2003). *Space in language and cognition.* Cambridge: Cambridge University Press.

Liben, L. S. (1999). Developing an understanding of external spatial representations. In I. E. Sigel (Ed.), *Development of mental representation: Theories and applications* (pp. 297–321). Mahwah, NJ: Lawrence Erlbaum Associates.

Liben, L. S. (2001). Thinking through maps. In M. Gattis (Ed.), *Spatial schemas and abstract thought* (pp. 44–77). Cambridge, MA: MIT Press.

Liben, L. S. (2003). Beyond point and shoot: Children's developing understanding of photographs as spatial and expressive representations. In R. V. Kail (Ed.), *Advances in child development and behavior* (Vol. 31, pp. 1–42). San Diego: Academic Press.

Liben, L. S. (2005). The role of action in understanding and using environmental place representations. In. J. Rieser, J. Lockman, & C. Nelson (Eds.), *The Minnesota Symposium on Child Development* (pp. 323–361). Mahwah, NJ: Lawrence Erlbaum Associates.

Liben, L. S. (2006). Education for spatial thinking. In W. Damon & R. M. Lerner (Series Eds.), K. A. Renninger & I. E. Sigel (Vol. Eds.), *Handbook of child psychology: Vol. 4. Child psychology in practice* (6th ed., pp. 197–247). New York: Wiley.

Liben, L. S., & Downs, R. M. (1986). *Children's production and comprehension of maps: Increasing graphic literacy.* Final Report to National Institute of Education (#G-83-0025).

Liben, L. S., & Downs, R. M. (1989). Understanding maps as symbols: The development of map concepts in children. In H. W. Reese (Ed.), *Advances in child development and behavior* (Vol. 22, pp. 145–201). New York: Academic Press.

Liben, L. S., & Downs, R. M. (1991). The role of graphic representations in understanding the world. In R. M. Downs, L. S. Liben, & D. S. Palermo (Eds.), *Visions of aesthetics, the environment, and development: The legacy of Joachim Wohlwill* (pp. 139–180). Hillsdale, NJ: Lawrence Erlbaum Associates.

Liben, L. S., & Downs, R. M. (1992). Developing an understanding of graphic representations in children and adults: The case of GEO-graphics. *Cognitive Development, 7,* 331–349.

Liben, L. S., & Downs, R. M. (1993). Understanding person-space-map relations: Cartographic and developmental perspectives. *Developmental Psychology, 29,* 739–752.

Liben, L. S., & Downs, R. M. (1994). Fostering geographic literacy from early childhood: The contributions of interdisciplinary research. *Journal of Applied Developmental Psychology, 15,* 549–569.

Liben, L. S., & Downs, R. M. (2001). Geography for young children: Maps as tools for learning environments. In S. L. Golbeck (Ed.), *Psychological perspectives on early childhood education* (pp. 220–252). Mahwah, NJ: Lawrence Erlbaum Associates.

Liben, L. S., & Szechter, L. E. (2001, October). *Understanding the spatial qualities of photographs.* In L. S. Liben (Chair), Cognitive development: A photographic view. Symposium conducted at the biennial meeting of the Cognitive Development Society, Virginia Beach, VA.

Liben, L. S., & Szechter, L. S. (2002). A social science of the arts: An emerging organizational initiative and an illustrative investigation of photography. *Qualitative Sociology, 25,* 385–408.

Liben, L. S., & Yekel, C. A. (1996). Preschoolers' understanding of plan and oblique maps: The role of geometric and representational correspondence. *Child Development, 67,* 2780–2796.

Lorenz, E. N. (1963). Deterministic nonperiodic flow. *Journal of Atmospheric Physics, 357,* 130–141.

McMurtry, A. (2004). Complexity and education. Retrieved April 20, 2005, from http://www.complexityandeducation.ualberta.ca/Glossary/g_embodiment .htm

Myers, L. J., & Liben, L. S. (2005, April). *Can you find it? Children's understanding of symbol-creators' intentions in graphic representations.* Poster presented at the biennial meeting of the Society for Research in Child Development, Atlanta, GA.

National Research Council (2005). *Learning to think spatially: GIS as a support system in the K–12 curriculum.* Washington, DC: National Academy Press.

Overton, W. F. (2004). A relational and embodied perspective on resolving psychology's antinomies. In J. Carpendale & U. Müller (Eds.), *Social interaction and the development of knowledge* (pp. 19–44). Mahwah, NJ: Lawrence Erlbaum Associates.

Overton, W. F. (2006). Developmental psychology: Philosophy, concepts, methodology. In W. Damon & R. M. Lerner (Series Eds.) & R. M. Lerner (Vol. Ed.), *Handbook of child psychology: Vol. 1. Theoretical models of human development* (6th ed., pp. 18–88). New York: Wiley.

Parsons, M. J. (1987). *How we understand art: A cognitive developmental account of aesthetic experience.* Cambridge: Cambridge University Press.

Piaget, J. (1952). *The origins of intelligence in children* (Margaret Cook, Trans.). (Original work published 1936). New York: International Universitites Press.

Searle, J. R. (1992). *The rediscovery of the mind.* Cambridge, MA: MIT Press.

Sontag, S. (1977). *On photography.* New York: Anchor Books.

Szechter, L. E. & Liben, L. S. (2004). Parental guidance in preschoolers' understanding of spatial-graphic representations. *Child Development, 75,* 869–885.

9

LANGUAGE AND THE DEVELOPMENT OF CONSCIOUSNESS: DEGREES OF DISEMBODIMENT

Helena Hong Gao

Nanyang Technological University

Philip David Zelazo

University of Minnesota

> With the help of speech children, unlike apes, acquire the capacity to be both the subjects and objects of their own behavior. (Vygotsky, 1978, p. 26)

Child development is simultaneously a process of embodiment and a process of disembodiment. Embodiment occurs as the child grows physically and becomes enmeshed in an ever-expanding web of social and physical interactions with the environment. But at the same time, aspects of psychological development, including the development of language, allow the child to disengage from the flow of sensorimotor processing via increasingly complex forms of cognitive mediation. This cognitive mediation allows the child imaginatively to transcend time and space—to be disembodied.

The idea of development as disembodiment is inherent in a wide variety of theoretical accounts, from Baldwin to Piaget to Vygotsky to Bruner. It is also a central feature of the Levels of Consciousness model (Zelazo,

2004), according to which children are increasingly able to reflect on their own conscious experiences (e.g., from just seeing something, to knowing that they are seeing something, to knowing that they know this, etc.) and consequently able to formulate and use increasingly complex sets of rules for regulating their behaviors. Reflective processing is interposed between a stimulus and a response, and this permits children to "move away" from the stimulus and the response, creating "psychological distance"—it permits decontextualization, it permits abstraction, and it allows children to act on the basis of reason even when the recommendations of reason conflict with the exigencies of a situation (cf., Dewey, 1931/1985).

All of these accounts capture, in one way or another, what amounts to a fundamental observation: Infants, who are relatively stimulus-bound and context dependent, develop into articulate children who are able to reminisce about the past, plan for the future, and appreciate other people's points of view. This chapter explores the role of language in this age-related process of disembodiment. In what follows, we first describe several examples of children's behavior that we believe illustrate this process of disembodiment. We then note that disembodiment also occurs in the context of children's understanding and use of language. Finally, we point to a possible causal connection between language and children's developing capacity for disembodiment from sensorimotor processing.

EXAMPLES OF DISEMBODIMENT IN CHILDREN'S BEHAVIOR

Research on cognitive development provides numerous examples of age-related changes in children's abilities to disengage from a compelling construal of a situation. In children's pretend play, for example, children become more likely, over the course of the second year, to perform pretend actions (e.g., talking on the telephone) with pretense objects (e.g., a spoon) that bear little physical resemblance to the real objects, and they also become more likely to perform pretend actions without objects altogether (e.g., Ungerer, Zelazo, Kearsley, & O'Leary, 1981). Similar changes continue into the preschool years (Overton & Jackson, 1973; O'Reilly, 1995). As these changes occur, there are complementary changes in children's abilities to resist responding on the basis of the actions suggested by the real objects—putting the spoon into one's mouth, for example (Elder & Pederson, 1978; Pederson, Rook-Green, & Elder, 1981). Vygotsky (1978) described this type of development as a change in the relative influence of "object properties" versus "meaning." Initially, we might say that behavior is relatively stimulus-bound, or context-dependent. Eventually, however, representations that are less dependent on the external context and more internally determined come to control children's behaviors.

This general development pattern—from stimulus-dependent to cognitively controlled—is also well documented in the growing literature on children's executive function (for a review, see Zelazo & Müller, 2002). In the A-not-B task (Piaget, 1954; Marcovitch & Zelazo, 1999), for example, nine-month-old infants watched as researchers hid an object conspicuously at one of two or more locations, and then the infants retrieved it. When researchers then hid the object at a new location, nine-month-olds were likely to search for it at the first location, as if the context elicited a prepotent response. Older children evidently updated their representations of the object's location and used these representations to guide their searches, rather than responding in a perseverative, stimulus-bound fashion. As another example, consider the dimensional change card sort (DCCS; Frye, Zelazo, & Palfai, 1995; Zelazo, Müller, Frye, & Marcovitch, 2003). In this task, children are shown two target cards (e.g., a blue rabbit and a red car) and asked to sort a series of bivalent test cards (e.g., red rabbits and blue cars) according to one dimension (e.g., color). Then, after sorting several cards, children are told to stop playing the first game and switch to another (e.g., shape, "Put the rabbits here; put the boats there."). Regardless of which dimension researchers presented first, three-year-olds typically continued to sort by that dimension despite researchers telling them the new rules on every trial (e.g., Zelazo, Müller, Frye, et al., 2003). Rules that have become associated with the context seem to determine their behavior in a relatively bottom-up fashion by. By contrast, four-year-olds are sensitive to the experimenter's instructions, and they tend to respond flexibly despite the fact that the context pulls for perseveration.

LINGUISTIC DISEMBODIMENT

One can also observe examples of age-related disembodiment in children's linguistic development. With development, language use and understanding tied less are particular contexts and sensorimotor routines, as an entertaining program on Swedish national television some years ago illustrated. In the program, there were two groups of participants, preschool children and adults, who were supposed to play a version of the game "charades." That is, participants were asked to convey certain things, such as a vacuum cleaner, a computer mouse, a telephone, and so forth, by describing them but without naming them directly. Adults used language to accomplish this. Children, on the other hand, used hardly any words; instead, they used actions and sounds to mimic what they were supposed to describe. The fact that children at this age used linguistic input to recall sensorimotor experiences (actions and sounds in this case) is consistent with Bruner's (1973) notion of an "enactive mode." When in an enactive mode, children's understandings of linguistic input is closely tied to sensorimotor experience.

Gradually, however, linguistic meaning comes to dominate sensorimotor experience, as Vygotsky (1978) and Luria (1961) described. An example comes from a recent study of three- to five-year-olds' flexible understandings of the adjectives *big* and *little* (Gao et al., 2005, April). When shown a medium sized square together with a larger one, three-year-olds had little difficulty answering the question, "Which one of these two squares is a *big* one?" However, when researchers then paired the medium square with a smaller one, and they asked children the same question, only five-year-olds reliably indicated that the medium square was now the big one. This example shows an age-related increase in children's sensitivity to linguistic meaning when it conflicts with children's immediate experience, and it reveals that interpretation decouples, to some degree, from stimulus properties.

Another example of the same phenomenon comes from a study by Deák (2000), who examined three- to six-year-olds' uses of a series of different predicates. In this study, children heard a word for a standard object and generalized the word to one of four objects: one with the same body shape as the standard, one made of the same material, one with the same affixed part, and a nonmatching "foil." The predicate context implied the specific meaning of each word: either "This one *looks like a(n)* _____," "This one *is made of* _____," or "This one *has a(n)* _____." The results show that three-year-olds performed near ceiling in a control task that eliminated the need to use probabilistic inductive cues. However, three-year-olds showed limited use of predicates to infer word meanings, and they used predicates from previous trials to infer the meanings of later words. Four- to six-year-olds used predicate cues more consistently and made inferences that the most recent predicate cue implied. The data also reveal two developing abilities between three and six years of age. First, older children more consistently use predicate cues, including syntactic and semantic elements, to make specific, conventionally appropriate inferences about novel words. Second, flexibility across changing predicate cues increases between three and six years of age. Three-year-olds respond flexibly only when the task is variable *and* the cues to each problem are determinate. Most four-year-olds are flexible when *either* supportive factor is present.

In general, Deák (2000) found that three-year-olds typically used the first predicate appropriately to infer the meaning of the first novel word in a series, but then proceeded to use that same predicate to infer the meanings of subsequent words despite what the experimenter said. In contrast, older children used the most recent predicate cues. Deák suggested that researchers could understand age-related changes in the flexible use of predicate cues in part in terms of age-related increases in sensitivity to intertrial differences. That is, younger children fail to attend to the linguistic cues (e.g., the predicate cues) indicating that the inductive problem has changed; instead, the context strongly influenced their behaviors.

One can also see increasing sensitivity to linguistic information versus context in children's difficulties interpreting ambiguous adjectives. Preliminary research in our laboratory indicated that when shown medium-sized pictures of a rabbit and a bear, three-year-olds have no difficulty identifying the bear as "a big animal." However, when researchers show three-year-olds a big picture of a rabbit and a small picture of a bear and ask, "Which one of these two animals is a big animal?," children typically point to the rabbit. Slightly older children (four-year-olds) seem to sense the ambiguity in the questions; they typically hesitate and then reply in an inconsistent fashion. By five years of age, however, children often ask, "What do you mean? The animals here in the picture or real animals?," and they are more likely to point to the bear. Again, children's interpretations of language tied less are the characteristics of the perceptual context in which an utterance occurs, and children are increasingly likely to use verbal input to restrict their attention to the appropriate aspects of a situation (or referent)—in this case the normative context (Ebeling & Gelman, 1988, 1994).

Linguistic ambiguity can occur both at the lexical level (e.g., homonyms—*bear* and *bare, night* and *knight*) and at the sentence level (e.g., idiomatic expressions—"A cult is not a religion. A cult is *a different kettle of fish* entirely."). Recognizing and resolving ambiguity involves reflecting on language per se—it involves metalinguistic understanding. For example, in order to recognize and resolve the ambiguity in the spoken, "*At* night*, she practices at becoming the best* knight *in the land*," one first has to notice that *night* and *knight* sound identical [nait]. Further reflection yields an appreciation of the phonological ambiguity *in relation* to other aspects of semantic meaning. For example, it allows one to appreciate the dependency between the preposition *at* and the appropriate interpretation of [nait]. Metalinguistic understanding develops during the preschool years (and beyond). For example, Robinson, Goelman, and Olson (1983) found that even five-year-olds tended to confuse what experimenters meant with what experimenters said when they heard ambiguous verbal messages. In one study, the experimenter and child sat on opposite sides an opaque screen, and each had their own set of cards, which varied along two dimensions (e.g., large/small and red/blue flowers). They then played a game in which they took turns choosing a card from their set and describing the card in such a way that the other player could choose the identical card from his or her set. When acting as the speaker, the experimenter sometimes intentionally provided ambiguous descriptions. For example, the experimenter might tell the child, "Pick up the red flower," forcing the child to choose between the big red flower and the small red flower. The child generally chose one of the red flowers (e.g., the big red flower), and then the experimenter asked him or her to make a judgment about what was said. The child either heard a disambiguated version of the original utterance (e.g., "Did I say 'the big red flower'?"), a verbatim repetition of the original utterance (e.g., "Did I say 'the red flower'?"), or an incorrect version of the original utterance (e.g., "Did I say 'the blue flower'?"). Robinson et al. found that five-year-olds rejected the incorrect version 81% of the time and accepted the verbatim repetition 76% of the time. However, they incorrectly accepted the disambiguated version 60% of the time, suggesting that they did not understand that the two utterances expressed different intentions. Emphasizing the similarity to children's understandings of visual representations, Kamawar (1999) proposed that children "see through" linguistic expressions to the intended referent, failing to "see" expressions in and of themselves. Older children evidently come to distinguish between linguistic expressions and underlying intentions.

Examples such as this illustrate how children come to treat language as a thing in itself, abstracting it away from particular contexts. They also show how linguistic understanding is closely tied to understanding one's own and others' mental states (Pratt & Grieve, 1984; Rowe & Harste, 1986). Consider, for example, children's developing understandings of ironic and sarcastic expressions. Appreciating irony and sarcasm requires reflection on propositional content in relation to other things, such as paralanguage (e.g., intonation) or the context in which the utterance occurs. That is, it requires the co-ordination of two different perspectives on the same linguistic utterance. Consideration of two perspectives is made possible through metalinguistic awareness, at a level of consciousness that is one degree "higher" than each of the perspectives themselves, as shown in Fig. 9.1 using the type of tree structure used by Zelazo and Frye (1998) to illustrate children's hierarchical rule structures.

In this diagram, the same stimulus, in this case linguistic input in a particular context, can give rise to two different interpretations, a literal interpretation and a metaphorical interpretation. To understand the linguistic input, one needs to reflect on both the literal meaning and

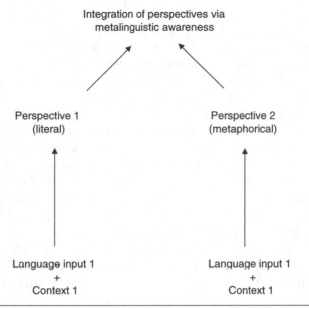

Figure 9.1. Perspective coordination required for metalinguistic awareness.

the metaphorical meaning, so that one can consider the meanings in relation to one another.

Notice that the problem is not simply one of accessing the metaphorical interpretation, which the paralanguage or context may favor, but rather of reflecting on this interpretation and considering it in contradistinction to the literal interpretation, which is consistent with the propositional content. Tomasello (2000) explained children's abilities to integrate all linguistic perspectives via metalinguistic awareness as "powerful skills of: (i) intention-reading and cultural learning, (ii) analogy making, and (iii) structure combining" (p. 235). The possibility that reflection, or disembodiment, is involved is perhaps clear from the fact that the same children who normally rely too heavily on context when it conflicts with linguistic meaning (e.g., Deák, 2000; Gao et al., 2005, April) rely too heavily on literal meaning when it comes to recognizing irony or sarcasm. That is, they appear to have difficulty resolving conflict. For example, when comparing children's interpretations of two types of irony (ironic criticisms and ironic compliments), Hancock, Dunham, and Purdy (2000) found five- to six-year-olds correctly recognized ironic utterances less than 50% of the time. Milosky and Ford (1997) found that the rate of recognition of sarcasm was rather low even in school age children: Six-year-olds recognized sarcasm 30% of the time, and nine-year-olds recognized it 50% of the time.

Children also rely too heavily on propositional content versus paralanguage and context when interpreting speakers' affect (e.g., Friend, 2000, 2003; Friend & Bryant, 2000; Solomon & Ali, 1972). For example, Lacks (1997) found that children as young as two to three years of age were unable to interpret affect when the literal or lexical content of utterances conflicted with both facial and vocal paralanguage. Morton and Trehub (2001) also found evidence that what one says influences children more than how one says it. For example, they found that six-year-olds had difficulty reporting that a speaker sounded sad when she uttered a positive proposition in a sad voice (e.g., "My mommy gave me a treat" in a sad voice.). In an initial experiment, four- and five-year-olds took longer to process conflicting than nonconflicting cues to emotion, but failed to report that there was anything odd about what was said. They also had a bias to judge the speaker's emotion on the basis of propositional content. By seven years of age, most children described the conflict sentences as odd. Subsequent experiments demonstrated that the younger children could respond on the basis of paralinguistic information when it was not in conflict with propositional content. For example, they could judge whether a speaker was happy or sad when she spoke a foreign language.

In another set of experiments, Morton, Trehub, and Zelazo (2003) looked more directly at the cognitive basis of younger children's difficulties with the conflict task. To do so, these authors used a rule-use paradigm, in which children heard conflicting sentences, and researchers first told them to judge on the basis of content and then told them to switch and judge on the basis of prosody. Results indicated that children who noticed the conflict and described it when asked, tended to switch successfully. This finding reveals an interesting link between children's reflections on the problem—their degree of disembodiment—and their abilities to resist interference from a salient aspect of the problem.

According to Mehrabian (1967; see also Mehrabian & Ferris, 1967; Mehrabian & Wiener, 1967), 55% of our communication consists of body language; we express 38% through tone of voice, and we communicate only 7% through words. That is, we actually decode or interpret a large proportion of verbal input with the help of nonlinguistic input, such as facial expressions, gestures, body language, and setting. However, it is unclear to what extent this is true for children at different ages, and it is unclear to what extent children, or even adults, are aware of the various influences on their interpretations. Indeed, it seems likely that sophisticated understanding of *relations* among influences on meaning is not something that comes naturally, even to native speaking adults—who might well have difficulty appreciating poetry, say, or the prose of a writer like Joyce (where both propositional content and various other aspects of language contribute to meaning). At the same time, however, intonation, rhythms, and rhymes more easily influence adult listeners, compared with children, and thus adult listeners tend to use them as interpretation tools when something challenges their comprehension abilities. We are reminded here of an anecdote that appeared in a French light magazine. A group of American tourists was having dinner together at a restaurant in Paris when they inferred that the waiter wanted to recite a French poem for the amusement of the party. His recitation was so full of changing intonation and sonorous rhymes, all accompanied by dramatic facial expressions, that all the guests, who could neither speak nor understand French, were deeply moved: they listened with rapt attention and, when he was done, they applauded and insisted on hearing which well-known poet wrote it. To their delight and discomfiture, the waiter explained in English that he had simply recited the evening's specials.

THE CAUSAL EFFECT OF LANGUAGE ON DISEMBODIMENT

Olson (1994) suggested that learning to read plays an instrumental role in helping children to become less dependent on paralinguistic context and better able to treat language as decontextualized—in the way that one can understand text even though it is normally abstracted away from the circumstances of its creation. He referred to this decontextualization of language as a change from understanding "language as utterance" to treating "language as text," and he described how understanding language as text can lead to an appreciation of the distinction between language and its meaning—how it fosters reflection on language per se.

As noted, the Levels of Consciousness model (Zelazo, 2004) provided an account of how reflection develops in childhood. According to this approach, there are age-related increases in the highest level of consciousness that children can muster in response to situational demands—there are increases in the extent to which children can be disembodied. These increases, brought about by the reprocessing of experienced information via neural circuits in prefrontal cortex, have important consequences for the quality of subjective experience, the potential for recall, the complexity of knowledge structures, and the possibility of action control. First, reprocessing adds depth to subjective experience because one can integrate more details into the experience before new environmental stimulation replaces the contents of consciousness. Second, each degree of reprocessing causes one to process information at a deeper, less superficial level, which increases the likelihood of retrieval (Craik & Tulving, 1975). Third, higher levels of consciousness allow for the formulation and use of more complex knowledge structures. The complexity of these knowledge structures determines the scope of one's cognitive control. In general, reprocessing moves consciousness further away from stimuli and responses, and this allows for the formulation of increasingly complex, and more decontextualized discursive reasoning.

According to this model, language can play a causal role in helping one to ascend to a higher level of consciousness—for children who are capable of mustering that particular level of consciousness. Previous research (e.g., using the DCCS and measures of children's theory of mind; Frye et al., 1995) suggested that four-year-olds are capable of considering two incompatible perspectives in contradistinction, even if they do not always do so. In a recent study, Jacques, Zelazo, Lourenco, and Sutherland (2006) presented four- and five-year-olds with the Flexible Item Selection Task (FIST). On each trial of this task, researchers showed children sets of three items designed so that one pair matches on one dimension, and a different pair matches on a different dimension (e.g., a small yellow teapot, a large yellow teapot, and a large yellow shoe; see Fig. 9.2).

Figure 9.2. Example stimuli used in the Flexible Item Selection Task (FIST). Note: These example stimuli all have the same color (e.g., yellow).

Children were first told to show the experimenter two things that go together in one way (e.g., on Selection 1), and then asked to show the experimenter two things that go together in a different way (e.g., Selection 2). To respond correctly, children must represent the pivot item (e.g., the large yellow teapot) first according to one dimension (e.g., size) and then according to another (e.g., shape). Four-year-olds generally perform well on Selection 1 but poorly on Selection 2, indicating that they have difficulty thinking about the pivot item in more than one way—they have difficulty disengaging from their initial construal of the item. However, when children were asked to label the basis of their initial selections (e.g., when they were asked, "Why do those two pictures go together?"), their performance on Selection 2 improved substantially. This was true whether children provided the label themselves or whether the experimenter generated it for them.

In terms of the Levels of Consciousness model, labeling the perspective adopted for Selection 1 caused children to step back from that perspective and reflect on it at a higher level of consciousness. According to this view, adopting a higher level of consciousness transformed children's initial perspective on the stimuli (e.g., seeing them in terms of size) from a subjective frame into an object of consideration, and it put psychological distance between the child and the perspective. From the vantage point of their higher level of consciousness, children were better able to adopt an alternative perspective on the stimuli (e.g., seeing them in terms of shape).

Fig. 9.3 abstractly illustrates this vantage point, as the highest point in the hierarchical tree structure. Like the tree structure in Fig. 9.1, this tree structure depicts two incompatible perspectives on a situation—a perspective (s1) that rules A and B define and a perspective (s2) that rules C and D define. The perspectives are incompatible because the same antecedent conditions (or aspects of the situation) lead to different consequents, and hence one is to treat them are differently, depending

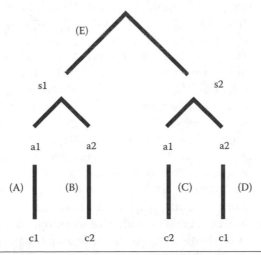

Figure 9.3. Hierarchical tree structure depicting formal relations among rules (adapted from Frye, Zelazo, & Palfai, 1995). Note. s1 and s2 = setting conditions; a1 and a2 = antecedent conditions; c1 and c2 = consequences. Reprinted with permission.

on the perspective. So, for example, rule A indicates that consequent 1 (c_1) should follow antecedent 1 (a_1) whereas rule C connects a_1 to c_2. In the FIST, four-year-olds typically adopt one perspective (e.g., s1) and have difficulty disengaging from it and considering it in contradistinction to the other. When the perspective is labeled, however, children are obliged to adopt the position at the top of this hierarchy—they are obliged to step back from the thing labeled and reflect on it—and from this position, the alternative perspective (e.g., s2) is easier to access. According to this model, language can promote reflection within developmental constraints on the highest level of consciousness that children are able to obtain. Reflection then permits the increasingly sophisticated selection and amplification of certain determinants of behavior when multiple determinants are present. Ultimately, linguistically influenced reflection allows our awareness to roam, unbounded, across time and space.

The adoption of a higher-order perspective allows for both greater influence of thought on language and greater influence of language on thought. On the one hand, it allows for more effective selection and manipulation of rules (e.g., it permits the control of language in the service of thought). On the other hand, it allows for top-down structuring of interpretive frames (as in the flexible interpretation of adjectives; Gao et al., 2005, April), permitting children to respond more appropriately to linguistic meaning despite misleading context—allowing language to influence thought. Notice that language and thought increasingly intertwine in a complex, reciprocal relation. Thus, language (e.g., labeling) influences thought (e.g., by promoting a temporary ascent to a higher level of consciousness) which in turn influences language, and so on. One can see this reciprocal relation in the growing richness of children's semantic understandings and increasing subtlety of their word usage. Consider, for instance, children's developing understandings of the semantics of the verb *hit*. Children first understand *hit* from its use to depict simple accidental actions (e.g., an utterance by a child at 2;4.0: *Table hit head;* Gao, 2001, p. 220). Usage is initially restricted to particular contexts. Eventually, however, reflection on this usage allows children to employ the word in flexible and creative ways (e.g., *I should hit her with a pencil and a stick* uttered metaphorically by the same child at 3;8.6; Gao, 2001, p. 219). As Tomasello (2000) explained, children's verb usage depends on imitative learning, with some understanding of functional roles. A process of analogy making then takes place to allow more flexible usage.

One can also understand the growing influence of language on thought in terms of linguistic relativity, the idea that language influences the way in which people experience the world. Sapir (1929/1958) stated this view as follows:

> Human beings do not live in the objective world alone, nor alone in the world of social activity as ordinarily understood, but are very much at the mercy of the particular language which has become the medium of expression for their society. . . The fact of the matter is that the "real world" is to a large extent unconsciously built on the language habits of the group. . . We see and hear and otherwise experience very largely as we do because the language habits of our community predispose certain choices of interpretation. (pp. 209–210)

More specifically, as Whorf (1956) stated, both grammatical categories and lexicons have a direct impact on the way in which people think. If a language explicitly codes for a certain distinction, making such a distinction might become relatively easy for speakers of that language (Gao, 1998). For instance, as children start to learn particular languages, their paths diverge. They learn to encode their experience using the grammatical and lexical options available in the language they learn as first language. But no language expresses every detail of the conceptual categories available, and thus children learn to pay attention to certain semantic properties in words and leave others aside. The selection is very much language determined. The task that confronts children is to map different linguistic forms and structures onto the conceptual domains of their experiences and express them. For instance, consider the domain of space. Spanish speaking children learn the same preposition, *en*, for three relations—containment, support, and attachment; English speaking children learn to map *in* onto containment and contrast it with *on*, which is mapped to both support and attachment. Dutch speaking children learn to use three prepositions: *in* for containment, *op* for support, and *aan* for attachment. So, one can assume that infants start with the same cognitive representations of spatial relations, but different language environments guide them to follow different paths as they learn how their own language maps onto these cognitive notions (Clark, 2004, p. 474).

Evidence that these cross-linguistic differences actually affect how children behave provides support for this hypothesis. Miller, Smith, Zhu, and Zhang (1995), for example, compared three- to five-year-old children from the United States and China (Beijing), asking children to count to the highest number they could. Although no differences were found for three-year-olds, four- and five-year-old Chinese children counted much higher than their American counterparts: 74% of the

Chinese children could count to 20, whereas only 48% of the American children managed as well. Once children could count to 20, however, differences between countries disappeared. Although there are many possible explanations for these results, such as differences in educational practices in schools (Stevenson & Stigler, 1992), differences in student and parental attitudes toward education (Chen & Uttal, 1988), and differences in parental practices (Huntsinger, Jose, Liaw, & Ching, 1997), Miller, Smith, et al. suggested that differences in counting were due to the difference in the number-naming systems between the two languages: the Chinese language starts its systematic naming of numbers following the first 10 digits; counting past the first 10 can be simply done by adding to 10 each of the first 10 digits. For example, 10 plus 1 is simply pronounced as "ten one," "ten two," and "ten three," and so forth. In contrast, English does not follow this type of consistent naming rule until the number 20. In the range 20–99, however, both languages follow a similar system that converges on roughly isomorphic rules (e.g., a decade unit; e.g., "six"; + "-ty" or "ten"+ a unit value, if any, in the range one to nine; see Miller, Major, Shu, & Zhang, 2000). The only morphological difference between Chinese and English names for numbers from 20–99 is that Chinese uses unit values for decade names (instead of modifying them as in English "twen-" or "thir-") and uses the unmodified name for 10 to designate decades, instead of the English "-ty"). This may explain why, once children were able to count more than 20, there were no differences between countries in counting up to 100. Other research, for example by Chen and Stevenson (1988) and Geary, Bow-Thomas, Fan, and Siegler (1993) showed that, starting at about age four years, Chinese children have longer digit spans than American children—a difference that persists into adulthood. This difference may reflect the fact that number words are shorter in Mandarin than in English, and so the rate at which one can pronounce them is higher.

From our perspective, linguistic relativity is something that *emerges* in development, not only as children learn language (of course) but also as the process of disembodiment unfolds. That is, linguistic relativity is part of the complex interaction between language and consciousness that emerges as children learn language and as consciousness develops through a series of levels of consciousness. The examples of disembodiment considered earlier are consistent with this suggestion: Sensitivity to the language habits of the group develops. As another example, try showing a three-year-old a toy train and telling him or her, "It's a special train; it can fly in the sky." Few three-year-olds will pick up the train and play with it as a plane. Instead, they will likely ignore the description (despite understanding it) and simply treat it as a train. This example shows the relative independence of language and thought early in development.

One might usefully explore the consequences of this developing sensitivity to linguistic relativity by looking at cultural differences in the development of understanding of abstract mental terms like *think*. For instance, one can normally answer questions such as, "What do you think of a peacock? Is it a big bird or a small bird?" in English in the following two ways: (a) "I think it is a big bird" and (b) "I don't think it is a big bird."

The English language, like most languages, allows one to express a certain fact as one's own thought in a subordinate clause, as in *a*. However, when one negates a certain fact as a result of one's thought, languages start to differ typologically. In English, one places the negation word *not* in the main clause with a sense of emphasizing that "that it is a big bird is not something that I thought." ("I don't think it is a big bird").

In Mandarin, possible responses differ: (c) Wo renwei ta bu shi yi zhi da niao. (I think it not be one classifier big bird. I don't think it is a big bird.); (d) Wo juede ta bu shi yi zhi da niao. (I feel it not be one classifier big bird. I don't feel that it is a big bird.); and (e) Wo xiang ta bu shi yi zhi da niao. (I think/guess/imagine/anticipate/gather/infer it not be one classifier big bird. I guess that it is not a big bird.).

From the corresponding equivalents, we can see that none of the sentences places the negation in the main clause as English does. In (c), the verb *renwei* in the main clause remains the equivalent of the English *think*, which gives an indication that what one expressed in the complement sentence is the result of careful thinking and reasoning. In (d), one changed the English *think* to the Mandarin for *feel*, which obviously indicates that one mainly bases the thought expressed here on one's personal perception of the reality; whether it is true or not is something minor. In (e), one Mandarin word *xiang* can be the equivalent of several English words, such as, *think, imagine, anticipate, gather, infer,* and *guess*. The senses are slightly different. When one interprets it as the English *think*, it is yet different from that of (c). *Xiang* in this context indicates a quick thought occurring to the mind without much reasoning—a wild guess. One may say the Mandarin terms reveal various elements of thinking that are implicit in the English verb *think*.

Researchers interested in children's developing theory of mind noted the presence of different mental verbs in English and Mandarin. These researchers noted, in particular, that Mandarin has a commonly used mental verb, *yiwei*, which indicates that one thought something. One can translate this term only into the English past tense of the verb *think*, which means that one is very likely to process it at a sentence level (sentential complement: *I thought that . . .*), with tense and aspect, but not as an independent lexicalized concept, as in Mandarin. Based on the differences between the languages, one might expect Chinese children to show better understanding of aspects of *think*, and in particular, false beliefs than children from English speaking countries. This does not appear to be the case, however—at least for false belief understanding (Liu, Wellman, Tardiff, & Sabbagh, 2004). Of course, the development of false belief understanding probably depends on many things, such as the number of siblings one has (mainland Chinese children have fewer, which in English speaking samples is associated with poorer theory of mind; e.g., Jenkins & Astington, 1996) and the way in which parents talk to children (e.g., Meins et al., 2002). Consistent perhaps with a general cultural difference in the degree of collectivism versus individualism (e.g., Markus & Kitayama, 1991), Cheung, Sabbagh, Seamans, and Callanan (2005) found that Cantonese speaking Chinese parents living in Toronto were less likely than American parents to talk to their children about their own and their children's epistemic mental states. They were also less likely to highlight the subjectivity of mental states. Differences in the way in which parents talk to their children may offset any effects of linguistic relativity.

Another possibility, however, is that young Chinese children cannot benefit from the presence of an explicit think falsely verb, *yiwei*, in their language until other developmental changes occur—development of the ability to adopt a level of consciousness that allows them to reflect on two incompatible perspectives and consider them in contradistinction. If so, then one might expect cultural differences in reasoning about false beliefs to emerge later in development, perhaps around five years of age and beyond. Naturally, testing this expectation may require the use of measures of false belief reasoning that are more difficult than the ones five-year-olds typically pass.

Incidentally, one can make a similar prediction of later emerging effects of linguistic relativity for other languages. Swedish, for instance, is a language similar to English, belonging to the Germanic branch of the Indo-European family of languages, but it offers more choices than English does to express aspects of thinking: (f) Jag tror inte, att det är någon stor fågel. (*tror*: same as the English *think* in *a*); (g) Jag tycker inte, att det är någon stor fågel. (*tycker*: indicating an imaging aspect); (h) Jag anser inte, att det är någon stor fågel. (*anser*: indicating a conclusive reasoning aspect); (i) Jag skulle inte tro, att det är någon stor fågel. (*skulle* inte *tro*: indicating that the result of reasoning can be claimed to be true); (j) Jag har svårt att föreställa mig, att det är någon stor fågel. (*har svårt att föreställa mig*: expressing one's feeling of diffi-culty in visualizing or depicting a scene as an answer); and (k) Såvitt jag förstår, är det inte någon stor fågel. (*såvitt jag förstår*: indicating one's own understanding, which might be different from others').

We know of no studies comparing theory of mind in Swedish and English speaking children, but we predict that Swedish children's understanding of the mental state under the general English term *think* would be very different from that of English children (as well as dif-ferent from that of Mandarin children). And again, differences in this understanding may emerge in the course of development, as language comes to interact with children's developing consciousness. Languages are not only tools that serve to express one's conscious thoughts, but, as Sapir (1929/1958) and Whorf (1956) argued, they are also epistemic frames that constrain one's thoughts. Thus, children's development in different linguistic environments is in part a process of refining their epistemic frames, as well as a process of internalizing cultural tools (Vygotsky, 1978).

CONCLUSION

Taken together, these suggestions lead to a model similar to one Vygotsky (1978) and Luria (1961) proposed. These authors proposed that thought and speech first develop independently only to become tightly inter-twined in the course of development. Initially, speech serves a com-municative purpose, but later it also acquires semantic, syntactic, and directive functions. What we are adding here is (a) the notion that lan-guage influences children's interpretations more (e.g., increasing lin-guistic relativity) as the relation between thought and language becomes increasingly reciprocal, and (b) the suggestion that the mechanism whereby this complex, reciprocal relation develops is one of disem-bodiment, through the development of levels of consciousness (Zelazo, 2004). Disembodiment, or psychological distancing as a result of an ascent through levels of consciousness, puts children in a position that allows them both to be more sensitive to various influences on their interpretations and to exert greater control over these interpretations.

ACKNOWLEDGMENTS

Grants to PDZ from the Natural Sciences and Engineering Research Council (NSERC) of Canada and the Canada Research Chairs Program supported preparation of this chapter. One should address correspondence to Dr. Helena Hong Gao, School of Humanities and Social Sciences, Nanyang Technological University, 12 Nanyang Drive, Singapore 639798; One may send electronic mail to helengao@ntu.edu.sg

REFERENCES

Bruner, J. (1973). Beyond the information given. New York: Norton.

Chen, C., & Stevenson, H. W. (1988). Cross-linguistic differences in digit span of preschool children. *Journal of Experimental Child Psychology, 46,* 150–158.

Chen, C., & Uttal, D. H. (1988). Cultural values, parents' beliefs, and children's achievement in the United States and China. *Human Development, 31,* 351–358.

Cheung, C., Sabbagh, M. A., Seamans, E. L., & Callanan, M. A. (2005). *Speaking minds: Mental state talk in Cantonese- and English-speaking parents' conversations with preschoolers.* Manuscript in preparation.

Clark, E. V. (2004) How language acquisition builds on cognitive development. *Trends in Cognitive Sciences, 8,* 472–478.

Craik, F. I. M., & Tulving, E. (1975). Depth of processing and the retention of words in episodic memory. *Journal of Experimental Psychology, 104,* 268–294.

Deák, G. O. (2000). The growth of flexible problem-solving: Preschool children use changing verbal cues to infer multiple word meanings. *Journal of Cognition and Development, 1,* 157–192.

Dewey, J. (1985). Context and thought. In J. A. Boydston & A. Sharpe (Eds.), *John Dewey: The later works, 1925–1953* (Vol. 6; pp. 3–21). Carbondale, IL: Southern Illinois University Press. (Original work published in 1931)

Ebeling, K., & Gelman, S. (1988). Coordination of size standards by young children. *Child Development, 59,* 888–896.

Ebeling, K., & Gelman, S. (1994). Children's use of context in interpreting "big" and "little." *Child Development, 65,* 1178–1192.

Elder, J. L., & Pederson, D. R. (1978). Preschool children's use of objects in symbolic play. *Child Development, 49,* 500–504.

Friend, M. (2000). Developmental changes in sensitivity to vocal paralanguage. *Developmental Science, 3,* 148–162.

Friend, M. (2003). What should I do? Behavior regulation by language and paralanguage in early childhood. *Journal of Cognition and Development, 4*(2), 161–183.

Friend, M., & Bryant, J. B. (2000). A developmental lexical bias in the interpretation of discrepant messages. *Merrill-Palmer Quarterly, 46,* 140–167.

Frye, D., Zelazo, P. D., & Palfai, T. (1995). Theory of mind and rule-based reasoning. *Cognitive Development, 10,* 483–527.

Gao, H., (1998, September). *Do languages have the same concepts? A comparison of some lexicalization patterns in Chinese, English, and Swedish.* Paper presented at Forskarseminariet i ASV, Lund, Sweden.

Gao, H. (2001). *The Physical foundation of the patterning of physical action verbs.* Lund, Sweden: Lund University Press.

Gao, H. H., Zelazo, P. D., & DeBarbara, K. (2005, April). *Beyond early linguistic competence: development of children's ability to interpret adjectives flexibly.* Poster session presented at 2005 Biennial Meeting of Society for Research in Child Development, Atlanta, Georgia.

Geary, D. C., Bow-Thomas, C. C., Fan, L., & Siegler, R. S. (1993). Even before formal instruction, Chinese children outperform American children in mental addition. *Cognitive Development, 8,* 517–529.

Hancock, J. T., Dunham, P. J., & Purdy, K. (2000). Children's comprehension of critical and complimentary forms of verbal irony. *Journal of Cognition and Development, 1,* 227–248.

Huntsinger, C. S., Jose, P. E., Liaw, F.-R., & Ching, W.-D. (1997). Cultural differences in early mathematics learning: a comparison of Euro-American, Chinese-American, and Taiwan-Chinese families. *International Journal of Behavioral Development, 21,* 371–388.

Jacques, S., Zelazo, P. D., Lourenco, S. F., & Sutherland, A. (2006). *Age-and language-related changes in preschoolers' performance on the Flexible Item Selection Task: The roles of labeling and abstraction in the development of cognitive flexibility.* Manuscript under review.

Jenkins, J. M., & Astington, J. W. (1996). Cognitive factors and family structure associated with theory of mind development in young children. *Developmental Psychology, 32,* 70–78.

Kamawar, D. (1999). *Children's understanding of the opaque and transparent uses of language.* Unpublished doctoral dissertation, University of Toronto, Canada.

Lacks, J. (1997). *The interplay of lexical, facial, and vocal affect during early language development.* Unpublished doctoral dissertation, Clark University, Worcester, MA.

Liu, D., Wellman, H. M., Tardif, T., & Sabbagh, M. A. (2004). *Development of Chinese and North American Children's Theory of Mind.* Poster session presented at the 28th International Congress of Psychology, Beijing, China.

Luria, A. R. (1961). *The role of speech in the regulation of normal and abnormal behavior.* New York: Liveright.

Marcovitch, S., & Zelazo, P. D. (1999). The A-not-B error: Results from a logistic meta-analysis. *Child Development, 70,* 1297–1313.

Markus, H., & Kitayama, S. (1991). Culture and the self: Implications for cognition, emotion, and motivation. *Psychological Review, 98,* 224–253.

Mehrabian, A. (1967). Orientation behaviors and nonverbal attitude communication. *Journal of Communication, 17,* 324–332.

Mehrabian, A., & Ferris, S. R. (1967). Inference of attitudes from nonverbal communication in two channels. *Journal of Consulting Psychology, 31,* 248–252.

Mehrabian, A., & Wiener, M. (1967). Decoding of inconsistent communications. *Journal of Personality and Social Psychology, 6,* 109–114.

Meins, E., Fernyhough, C., Wainwright, R., Das Gupta, M., Fradley, E., & Tuckey, M. (2002). Maternal mind-mindedness and attachment security as predictors of theory of mind understanding. *Child Development, 73,* 1715–1726.

Miller, K., Major, S. M., Shu, H., & Zhang, H. (2000). Ordinal knowledge: Number names and number concepts in Chinese and English. *Canadian Journal of Experimental Psychology, 54*(2), 129–140.

Miller, K. F., Smith, C. M., Zhu, J., & Zhang, H. (1995). Preschool origins of cross-national differences in mathematical competence: The role of number-naming systems *Psychological Science, 6,* 56–60.

Milosky, L. M., & Ford, J. A. (1997). The role of prosody in children's inferences of ironic intent. *Discourse Processes, 23,* 47–61.

Morton, J. B., & Trehub, S. E. (2001). Children's understanding of emotion in speech. *Child Development, 72,* 834–843.

Morton, J. B., Trehub, S. E., & Zelazo, P. D. (2003). Representational inflexibility in children's interpretation of emotion in speech. *Child Development, 74,* 1857–1868.

O'Reilly, A. W. (1995). Using representations: Comprehension and production of actions with imagined objects. *Child Development, 66,* 999–1010.

Olson, D. R. (1994). *The world on paper.* New York: Cambridge University Press.

Overton, W. F., & Jackson, J. P. (1973). The representation of imagined objects in action sequences: A developmental study. *Child Development, 44,* 309–314.

Pederson, D. R., Rook-Green, A., & Elder, J. L. (1981). The role of action in the development of pretend play in young children. *Developmental Psychology, 17,* 756–759.

Piaget, J. (1954). *Contruction of reality in the child.* New York: Basic Books.

Pratt, C., & Grieve, R. (1984). The development of metalinguistic awareness: An introduction. In W. Tunmer, C. Pratt, & M. Herriman (Eds.), *Metalinguistic awareness in children: Theory, research, and implications* (pp. 2–35). New York: Springer-Verlag.

Robinson, E. J., Goelman, H., & Olson, D. R. (1983). Children's understanding of the relation between expressions (what was said) and intentions (what was meant). *British Journal of Developmental Psychology, 1,* 75–86.

Rowe, D., & Harste, J. (1986). Metalinguistic awareness in writing and reading: The young child as curricular informant. In D. Yaden, & S. Templeton (Eds.), *Metalinguistic awareness and beginning literacy* (pp. 235–256). Portsmouth, NH: Heinemann.

Sapir, E. (1958). The status of linguistics as a science. In E. Sapir, & D. G. Mandelbaum (Eds.), *Culture, language and personality* (pp. 160–166). Berkeley, CA: University of California Press. (Original work published 1929)

Solomon, D., & Ali, F. A. (1972). Age trends in the perception of verbal reinforcers. *Developmental Psychology, 7,* 238–243.

Stevenson, H. W., & Stigler, J. W. (1992). *The learning gap: Wiry our schools are failing and what we can learn from Japanese and Chinese education.* New York: Summit.

Tomasello, M. (2000). Do young children have adult syntactic competence? *Cognition, 7,* 209–253.

Ungerer, J., Zelato, P., Kearsley, R., & O'Leary, K. (1981). Developmental change in the representation of objects in symbolic play from 18 to 34 months of age. *Child Development, 52,* 186–195.

Vygotsky, L. S. (1978). *Mind in society.* Cambridge, MA: MIT Press.

Whorf, B. L. (1956). *Language, thought and reality: Selected writings of Benjamin Lee Whorf.* Cambridge, MA: MIT Press.

Zelazo, P. D. (2004). The development of conscious control in childhood. *Trends in Cognitive Sciences, 8,* 12–17.

Zelazo, P. D., & Frye, D. (1998). II. Cognitive complexity and control: The development of executive function. *Current Directions in Psychological Science, 7,* 121–126.

Zelazo, P. D., & Müller, U. (2002). The balance beam in the balance: Reflections on rules, relational complexity, and developmental processes. *Journal of Experimental Child Psychology, 81,* 458–465.

Zelazo, P. D., Müller, U., Frye, D., & Marcovitch, S. (2003). The development of executive function in early childhood. *Monographs of the Society for Research in Child Development, 68*(3, Serial No. 274).

10

UNCOVERING THE BODY IN CONCEPTUAL DEVELOPMENT: A FEMINIST PERSPECTIVE

Ellin Kofsky Scholnick

University of Maryland

Patricia H. Miller

University of Georgia

"Embodiment is the claim that perception, thinking, feelings, desires—that is, *the way we behave, experience, and live the world*—is contextualized by our being *active agents* with this *particular kind of body* ([C.] Taylor, 1995)." (Overton, chapter 1, this volume)

Typically, we use the concept of embodiment to redress problematic, impoverished, or compartmentalized views of mental life by providing two solutions: (a) the biological and (b) the social. The biological solution heals the rift between mind and body by connecting mental contents and processing either to the brain or to "being an active agent with a particular body" that affords particular encounters with the world. The social solution enriches the study of mental life by situating the encounters with the world in a social, historical, and cultural context. The *particular kind of body* exists in a *particular kind of world* with a particular social structure. The mind is connected to specific social goals, tasks, and activities located in daily life. These seem easy solutions if embodiment simply integrates the spurious dichotomies of nature versus nurture or brain and behavior (Overton, 2003).

Why, then, has this proven to be the most difficult chapter we have ever written? The concept of embodiment hinges on the definition of each of the terms *mind, body,* and *lived world.* The Cartesian tradition presents insurmountable difficulties in finding bridges between the body, the mind, and the experiential context because its definitions of the terms *body, mind,* and *experiential context* impede finding their interconnections. Furthermore, the Cartesian framework uses diverse strategies to highlight the mind and hide or impoverish notions of the body or the lived world. We must, therefore, redefine each term in the triad and adopt new strategies in order to understand and investigate embodiment.

Consider this chapter an initial venture toward this redefinition. It begins with a discussion of how, why, and where developmental psychology's concept of the body is problematical, and then moves to the concept of the *lived* environment. In each section, we (a) identify the missing elements in traditional definitions, (b) analyze the techniques that some have used to delete the body and the lived world, and (c) use contemporary areas of cognitive research—such as concepts of biological essentialism, theory of mind, and gender constancy—as illustrations. The final section provides suggestions and strategies for an embodied view of conceptual development that might enable researchers to examine particular bodies in particular environments and to explore their interconnections. In doing so, we revisit—from an embodied perspective—the traditional research areas we have discussed.

BODY SNATCHING IN DEVELOPMENTAL PSYCHOLOGY

Those who attempt to use the framework of embodiment to provide a linkage between the mind and the body during the life span ultimately confront a mystery. The body is missing. The Cartesian framework does more than split mind from body. It buries or "snatches" the body (Duquin, 1994). How can one consider the mind and body as integrated if there is no body? Where is the body? Whose body is it? Who is the culprit who hid it, and how was the deed accomplished? The crime may even be the perfect one so beloved of mystery writers. Our culture, and our discipline, which reflects it, conceals the body so well that we do not even know that it is missing. Moreover, because our frameworks tend to eradicate the social locations in which bodies reside, there is no treasure map to indicate the body's hiding place. Consequently, the ways the discipline of developmental psychology conceptualizes the body and the social world impede our understanding of embodiment. We lack the conceptual language for studying it (e.g., Burman, 1994; Greene, 2003).

These are strong claims. What do we mean by the "body," and why do we claim it is missing? Biological determinism is not absent from developmental research. There is discussion of bodily disorders arising throughout the lifespan and their impact on behavior. Courses in human physiology are devoted to the body and the internal systems that contribute to our functioning, and when cognitive developmentalists track children's biological knowledge, they, too, focus on children's understanding of physiology and anatomy. There is more to the body, however, than its insides. The body we seek to uncover is the particular lived body, the body that others see, that which is the source of our emotions and agency, and serves as the basis for placing us into the social categories that contribute to our self-identity. This is the body that forms a bridge between the mind and the social world.

We have found it fruitful to draw on feminist scholarship to identify problems with accounts of the body in developmental psychology and to suggest possible solutions. Feminist sleuths can find the body because they critique the dualistic thinking that divorces and places in opposition the terms *male* versus *female*, as well as *mind* versus *body*, and produces stereotypes that align the masculine with the mental and the feminine with the corporeal (Labouvie-Vief, 1994; Lloyd, 1984; Spelman, 1982). Dualism obfuscates interconnections (Overton, 2003).

Feminist epistemology provides two insights that are especially useful in studying embodiment. The first highlights rather than hides the importance of the lived body for understanding psychological development. The mind develops in the context of a changing body. To be embodied is to grow and age. The body is a lived, material, physiological object that changes with age (Labouvie-Vief, 1994). These changes affect opportunities to explore the environment (Gibson, 1969) and they alter one's social status. Thus, bodily capacities and physical appearance influence cognitions regarding the environment, the self, and other people (Greene, 2003). The body provides a personal context for mental life and an object for thought. The next section of the chapter deals with the role of the lived body in cognitive development, and the ensuing sections present ideas about the nature of the lived environment.

The second insight, elaborated in a later section of the chapter, connects the body to the lived world by defining the historical and sociocultural context. It contextualizes the body itself. Living in an environment influences its shape and capacities. Feminists (e.g., Code, 2000) are particularly attentive to the hierarchical structure of society. They theorize that societies use bodily cues to categorize people by age, social class, gender, ethnicity, and so on, into particular social positions, which accord people differential access to the experiences that shape views of the world and of the self. In turn, these experiences shape the body in ways that perpetuate the extant social structure. Feminists approach the issue of embodiment by asking, "What does it mean to live with a particular kind of body in a world that is structured to categorize and position bodies?" Consequently, feminism provides some conceptual tools to uncover embodiment and unravel the mystery of how embodiment works.

Feminist theory also suggests the motive for the crime. Psychology as a discipline appears to have a deep ambivalence about the body and the environment. On the one hand, the current focus on neuroscience (e.g., Damasio, 1999; Edelman, 1992), the biologically based competencies emerging in early infancy (Wellman & Gelman, 1998), children's beliefs in folk biology (Gelman, 2003), and evolutionary models of cognition (Pinker, 2002) seem to emphasize the body. On the other hand, the preference for universal concepts masks bodies, especially specific individual bodies defined, positioned, and shaped by culture. Consequently, the attempts of feminists, critical psychologists, and philosophers (Burman, 1994; Foucault, 1977; Greene, 2003; Henriques, Hollway, Urwin, Venn & Walkerdine, 1998) to deconstruct developmental psychology and to call attention to lived bodies in a political environment disinter the embodied individual, but appear to leave psychology in ruins. Their focus on context-dependent cognitive development questions and draws attention away from the universals of traditional psychology. Thus, the concept of embodiment is problematic and revolutionary for psychology. Yet, without embodiment, psychology cannot understand the human condition.

Where is the Body?[1]

We illustrate the masking of the body by examining introductory child psychology textbooks and two areas of research. Open a textbook in developmental psychology. There is a prenatal body, growing in the womb in a fixed biological progression, potentially vulnerable to all sorts of diseases and disorders that the careful mother can prevent by adopting a healthy life style. Then there is the painstakingly charted sensory progression and motor control of an infant up to the point when the child can walk, pick up pellets, and articulate consonant blends. After about age three or so, the body disappears, except as the site of disorders like obesity, only to slowly reemerge as children enter their growth spurt at the onset of adolescence. At this point, the reproductive and sexual body enters the text and, for boys in particular, the athletic body. Active research areas in adolescence include the social effects of early or late puberty and, especially in girls, body image and eating disorders (Bordo, 1991; Brumberg, 1998; Piran, 2001). Because we define mature women's bodies as reproductive bodies, research focuses on reproduction in early adulthood and menopause, framed as "decline," during middle age (Brumberg, 1998). Cognitive psychologists continue to study the body's decline, and the impact of decline on psychological functioning during aging. Thus, attention to the body is selective after childhood. This departure of the body during much of development is ironic. In contrast to the research literature, popular books provide norms for changes in the body, skills, and behavior from birth to old age and offer advice about speeding the pace of acquisition of motor milestones, remediating developmental lags, and warding off the aging process (Hulbert, 2003). Parents use these norms to shape their children's toilet training, eating habits, and other forms of social etiquette. Adults encourage a child's progress by telling him he is a "big" boy. Consequently, children see age and size as the entry into more privileged roles in the social world. Bodily changes are associated with changes in the agency children *can* exert and the agency that their parents and society allows them to express.

We are bodies who change over time, and these changes are at the core of development. Indeed, psychologists have used the growth of the body as the basis for the organismic metaphor of development (Overton, 1984). The unrolling of motor capacities has been a seminal model for classic developmental theories (Brumberg, 1998; Greene, 2003), and it remains a central topic of investigation for its modern counterparts (Thelen, 2000b, Thelen & Smith, 1994, 1998). Yet we do not incorporate bodily growth thoroughly into our analysis of cognitive and social development, although surely a changing body is closely connected to a changing mind throughout development, not just in infancy (Thelen, 2000a). It is not only in adolescence that the child must construct a notion of selfhood in the face of changes in bodily appearance and motor capacity. Throughout childhood, certain dramatic bodily changes allow children to *do* more, not just think more competently, and engage in more frequent social interaction. The child encounters age-graded social expectations about appropriate behavior, experiences, and achievements, and age-graded means of regulating the self that physical growth cues (Greene, 2003). Children must be aware of and have attitudes, thoughts, feelings, and beliefs about their bodies. One would think that as children construct social schemas, such as gender and mind, heavily studied by developmentalists, they also would construct a body image schema (as attractive, powerful, gendered, etc.) and connect that schema to notions of gender and the mind. As they undergo growth spurts, they must face the challenge of reconstructing their images and of understanding the consequences of bodily changes. We know that children's construction of body concepts and body images emerges well before adolescence (Musher-Eizenman, Holub, Edwards-Leeper, Persson, & Goldstein, 2003), and may affect perceived social competence early in childhood. Yet we know little about the life course of personal body schemas and the impact of these schemas.

The potential for putting the body back into the mind exists. We know that the ability to locomote influences knowledge of the spatial environment and spatial competencies (e.g., Adolph, Eppler, & Gibson, 1993; Bertenthal, Campos, & Barnett, 1984). Surely, crawling, walking, and later biking provide increased social affordances, too (Gibson, 1969). It is interesting that although Piaget's (1974/1976) research on the emergence of the child's understanding of motor activities lays the groundwork for the research on the child's understanding of body image and understanding of the social interpretation of bodies, many have largely ignored this aspect of his work. In addition to *adapting* to their social world, children must *accommodate* to their changing body and its capacities. Some theoretical frameworks may provide the starting points for a developmental theory of embodiment. Bandura (1986; Bussey & Bandura, 1999) addressed the development and influence of physical self-efficacy, and Harter (1999) included the physical self as an aspect of the self-concept. Erik Erikson's (1963) theory pointed to the pervasive impact of the changing body on cognitive, emotional, and social interactions, as well as self-conceptions.

Strategies for Hiding the Body

Changes in the body are as dramatic as changes in cognition and language. Why do they receive so little attention and how are they divorced from the explanatory framework used to map mental development? The neglect of bodily change during middle childhood is an obvious instance of downplaying the body. Psychology also employs implicit strategies that de-emphasize or hide the lived body by *splitting* it, *reducing* it, *symbolizing* it, and *abstracting* it.

Splitting the body. The *splitting* strategy divides functioning into parts and privileges one part over another. Just as phrenologists divided the brain into diverse psychological functions, the splitting strategy divides individuals' lives into discrete, noninteractive modules, such as cognition, emotion, and motor activities, which psychologists then chop up and study. Dualisms are one example of *splitting*. Our culture splits the mind from body, privileges mind over body, and values autonomous minds that control the body. Ego governs id. Our models of development reflect this cultural belief system. Our descriptions of development emphasize self-regulation; we equate immaturity with lack of control. We expect infants and young children to gain *control* over their level of arousal, their bodies or body parts, and their emotions. Many pathologize lack of control as in aggression, hyperactivity, and obesity. Even in the cognitive realm, although Piaget (1936/1952) began his account of conceptual life with body and mind closely connected in the sensorimotor period, the body gradually drops out, and abstract thought eventually gains control over sensorimotor schemas. Thus, developmental accounts of cognition often progressively divorce cognitive and motor competence (Thelen, 2000a). Toward the end of his career, Piaget (1974/1976) returned to the link between actions (practical intelligence) and conceptualization in childhood and adolescence, but the primary focus remained the development of the capacity to plan and monitor behavior.

As an example of the negative effects of splitting, Lois Bloom (Bloom & Tinker, 2001) bemoaned the status of language acquisition research in which the emergence of a system of universal syntactic rules is separated from and privileged over semantics, a domain more susceptible to social input. In turn, the study of semantic development, as indexed in young children by the intellectual quest for the mapping of words onto their appropriate referents, is privileged over pragmatics, the emotional, corporeal quest for social communication and need satisfaction. When we divide language into three parts and separate it from acting and feeling, the whole speaker—and with her, her whole body—disappears. The modular approach discourages the investigator from examining the different ways that affective and verbal communication are coordinated when the child is struggling to produce the first words and first word combinations as compared to how emotion, movement, and speech are integrated when the child becomes a fluent speaker. Thelen (2000a) made a similar point about the way the study of cognitive development is divorced from the study of practical action. *Splitting* masks the way that mind and body are intertwined in an interacting system and hides the emergent properties that might arise from that interaction. When *splitting* subordinates one component under another, the process marginalizes the subordinate component, which receives less attention and fades from view. The body is often the subordinate component.

Reducing the body. The *reductionist* strategy complements *splitting*. Reductionists frame problems at the level of the finest grain, which is also supposed to be the most fundamental source of explanation. It is commonly thought that ultimate biological causation is at the level of the gene or the molecule. For example, one solution to the mind-body problem connects the neurological substrate to conceptual life. The body is reduced to cortical circuitry, and the frontal cortex is privileged, as seen in the focus on how executive functions *"control"* cognition. People tend to ignore the rest of the body, which represents the appearance we present to the world, and the social context for that body disappears from view.

Symbolizing the body: Figures of speech. The symbolic approach, derived primarily from rhetorical analyses (Lakoff & Johnson, 1980), links the metaphorical extension of basic schemas to conceptual development. Because one key schema is the body, it would seem as if this approach would be a promising framework for studying the growth of children's understanding of embodiment; however, idealized schemas may work against discovering the lived body. We use the "head" of state as a metaphorical term in which the head symbolizes the executive functions of the brain, not the physiognomy of a particular individual. Similarly, the "arm" of the law refers to the reach and power of an upper limb, not the body part of a particular individual. These figures of speech leave other parts of the individual and the particular vagaries of individual anatomical structures as ground. As we build "embodied" models of the mental life, it is important to examine what is included as figure and what we have left out or relegated to the background.

To illustrate how symbolic approaches relegate important aspects of embodiment to the background, we will briefly examine the highly influential work of Lakoff and Johnson (1980; Johnson, 1987; Johnson, chapter 2, this volume). Lakoff and Johnson proposed that our initial knowledge of the body is the basis for the concepts that populate our mind. Their books bear titles like "*The body in the mind*" and "*Philosophy in the flesh*." From the onset, the child is embodied. The baby's experiences of sensory and motor activities such as being fed, spitting up, or excreting are coalesced into a set of image schemas that serve as templates for organizing experiences in the visual-spatial world. For example, we think of the body as a container with particular entailments, such as "boundary," "in," and "out." The body may also be the starting point for understanding what is front and what is behind, or what is on top or below. Jean Mandler (1992) marshaled evidence that these image schemas may form the conceptual primitives children use to organize space and causality. Containment can also be used to understand mental states, which are thought of, metaphorically, as contained locations, allowing us to describe being "in the mood" or "out of it." Moreover, containment, depicted graphically as Euler circles, may configure our understanding of categories. Such containers presuppose that objects are either in a class or not, and we can think of inclusion relations, like nested dolls, as one set contained within a larger set. Thus, in the Johnson-Lakoff perspective, thought originates in embodied action. However, we have two concerns. First, as generic models of bodily activities become the basis for conceptual thought, it becomes harder to see the actual body. Second, the particular properties of the body, such as weight or containment, and the bodily activities that are chosen, such as seeing or paths of movement, are presented as universals, not socially constructed categories. Lakoff and Johnson (e.g., 1999) are well aware of the role of society in shaping what and how we categorize, but society does not seem to influence the basic image schemas. Our contention is that from the beginning, children's experience of containment varies. Some parents swaddle their children, and others allow their children to lie unrestrained and uncovered. In some cultures parents use clothing to constrain children's movement, for example, as in the process of binding the feet of Chinese women. Some children, usually girls, are contained within the home, while others, usually boys, are allowed to explore freely, to move "out of the box." Young children are allowed less freedom of movement than older children. Thus, containment of the body and movement leads to culturally specific concepts and attitudes toward the body.

Abstracting the body. Metaphor is but one form of *abstraction,* which is the prime tool that psychology uses to hide the body. Abstraction is the result of a process of finding similar elements across diverse phenomena while ignoring differences. It emphasizes commonalities at the expense of individual variations. What variations, however, are left out? Are those deletions systematic? We suspect the *lived body* is omitted even in examination of the child's biological knowledge. For example, recent work on children's naive biology (e.g., Medin & Atran, 1999) focuses on the understanding of generic functions such as digestion, and on the understanding of organs that occur in many species. The work on naïve biology does not explore the child's understanding of individual variations in bodies. Are valued cross-species commonalities over differences and their social interpretation, and are prized insides over outsides. Yet children have particular bodies, forged through a series of experiences that reflect their material conditions and the social evaluation of their stature, age, weight, skin color, gender, and physical attractiveness. They have bodies that change, and that change is the source of their embodiment.

Examples of Research that Hides the Body

Compartmentalization, reductionism, symbolization, and abstraction all obstruct our view of the body's role in conceptual development. These four implicit strategies encourage the study of the universal rational mind rather than the body. When the body *is* studied, it, too, is universalized and abstracted. Specific, concrete, changing bodies do not seem to be worthy of attention. To clarify and expand on the previous account, we turn to two active areas of research in cognitive developmental psychology: (a) biological essentialism and (b) gender constancy. These topics presumably could and should address the lived body, but in fact, they unknowingly work to hide it.

Biological essentialism. The study of biological essentialism illustrates how the body has disappeared from developmental psychology, even in the study of biological knowledge. Some have proposed that when children begin to construct an understanding of the biological world, they start with a default theory that hinges on biological essentialism (Gelman, 2003). Biological essentialism is the belief that each natural kind (be it herring, hippopotamus, or hawk) has a hidden, innate essence that defines what it is and how it functions. Essentialist beliefs, though seemingly based on biology, are not based on concrete knowledge of the body, but on a naive theory of idealized forms (Gelman & Hirschfield, 1999). In that theory, each creature's essence is inherent and immutable despite changes in its external appearance. In short, because the external body does not matter, essentialist theory creates a disembodied biology. This is evident from the techniques used to detect essentialist thinking.

One common method of investigating biological essentialism (Keil, 1989) involves imaginary surgery and cosmetic treatments that transform the appearance of an animal, for example, a raccoon into a skunk. This method has shown that even some young children are essentialists; they claim that this rearrangement of the animal's external appearance does not change what the animal truly is because the animal genetically remains itself and will give birth to its original kind. It is noteworthy that this procedure for the study of the representation of the body in the child's mind creates an abstraction that eliminates the situated external body from its inquiry and downplays physical change. In reality, the altered animal, depending on the type of surgery, may no longer have the adaptive capacities and behavioral repertoire it previously possessed. Being neither raccoon nor skunk, it might not attract a mate, nor even survive long enough to reproduce. Members of both the original and adopted species will quickly note the animal's changes in appearance and anomalies in behavior. Thus, developmental research favors paradigms that investigate the child's knowledge of the body by pitting essence against the material change in the body. An abstract (species-wide), universal essence wins out over a concrete, individual body. This method highlights certain biological functions and internal structures, but draws less attention to the external body, biological growth, and appearance and action in a social context. The body is eliminated in still another way. Essentialist concepts highlight differences between categories while ignoring variations within categories, variations that arise from bodily configurations, age, or social positions, for example, gender, race, and social class. A universal essence trumps a socially constructed set of essences.

Developmental studies of thinking about the body actually contain an additional layer of essentialism. The assumption that, universally, children are little essentialists also minimizes both the role of the child's embodied experiences with biological kinds and the role of the social environment in constructing the content of knowledge (see Ross, Medin, Coley, & Atran, 2003). The belief system of essentialism is based on inherent forms predetermining species characteristics. The claim that there is an essentialist child predisposed to construct such a theory minimizes two contexts for development, social experience and the rest of the child's conceptual life. The theory of biological essences is split off from other concepts the child is evolving.

Gender constancy. Research on gender constancy provides another illustration of the way that we ignore bodily change in the treatment of cognitive development by privileging abstract concepts. Gender constancy (Kohlberg, 1966) is the notion that one's gender assignment (identity) is permanent, presumably because innate sex differences determine it. Theories about gender constancy, as well as biological essentialism, originate in Platonic philosophy (Spelman, 1982). There is an ideal form for all natural objects. In the case of biological beings, it is their essence. Being idealized, that form resides in all humans, regardless of their social and cultural position and their age. We can extend what is true of biological beings to some aspects of their being, such as gender. Like biological essentialism, one facet of gender constancy is the belief that certain kinds of appearance do not affect gender assignment, such as the clothes one wears or the hairstyle one adopts. Males are males wherever they reside. Awareness of situational constancy complements by awareness of temporal constancy. Once a female, always a female. Although the child progresses from girlhood to womanhood, her gender identity remains unchanged.

Actually, neither type of consistency across time and situation is that simple. We "do gender" through our bodies (Butler, 1993). Therefore, the child who achieves gender constancy has to sort out carefully those aspects of biological sex that presumably are universal and invariant to each sex and those facets of the body that are the site of changing cultural inscriptions and definitions of gender. This is not an easy task because psychologists and biologists endlessly debate exactly which biological mechanisms are tied to sex differences (McGillicuddy-DeLisi & DeLisi, 2002). In the Victorian era, some alleged that the womb determined female behavior. Victorians were aghast if women exercised their intellectual abilities, because the general belief was that these activities weakened reproductive capacity (Brumberg, 1998). Current biological explanations focus on hormones and brain structure. However, the fact that behavior affects hormones and brain structure, as well as vice versa, makes these explanations problematic. By doing gender, humans influence the very biological phenomena proposed to define gender and account for its constancy.

Moreover, there are major changes during development in the very facets of the body that are at the core of biological definitions of gender. The body is not constant although the child's gender identity might be. A little girl does not look like a young woman. Females are fertile for less than half a modern woman's lifespan. The English language does not even use the same labels for a male (or a female) of different ages. No adult woman likes it when someone calls her a "girl," and men resent the appellation, "boy." It is true that a given person may be female or male for life, but the meaning of that designation is constantly undergoing revision based not merely on changing cultural and societal circumstances, but also based on a changing body. Even the sex of an infant cannot clearly be assigned in the approximately 1–2% of the population who are born intersexed (have some male and some female genitalia and reproductive organs). Assignment is based on cultural values as much as anatomical considerations (Fausto-Sterling, 2000). Additionally, it is well documented (Sinnott & Shiffrin, 2001) that gender is somewhat fluid and changing, rather than constant, throughout the lifespan. Greene (2003) made a very compelling point when she noted that so-called developmental theories are often adevelopmental because they highlight the static and abstract while ignoring the impact of a living, changing, aging body, a body that is at the core of gender. Transgendered adults and individuals with genital anomalies, such as hermaphrodites (Whelehan, 2001), also challenge the discrete categories of male and female.

Biological essentialism and gender constancy are fictional constructs. Reductionism and abstraction work in concert to hide the body. Essentialism ignores both variations in appearance among individuals and within individuals (Gelman & M. G. Taylor, 2000). Abstract, ideal essences trump outer manifestations of identity. Gender constancy assumes there is a dichotomy between males and females and that one's identity is biologically determined, although the content of that identity may be socially constructed. In addition, gender constancy ignores the age variations in the body that define what it is to be male or female by reducing the essence of gender to a permanent label. The label of "male" or "female" is privileged over the experiences and meaning of doing gender. The omission is particularly apparent when a concept like gender has a strong social component. Even if one were to emphasize biology, the body changes and those changes, in turn, alter gender and sexuality.

INVISIBLE CULTURAL CONSTRUCTIONS OF BODY

The concept of embodiment emphasizes both the body and its connection to the world. In the previous section, we focused on the body; however, it was difficult to separate the body from the body's situation in the lived world. The body is a both a material object and a social construct. The same strategies that hide and detach the mind from the body also disconnect the body from the social and material circumstances that influence the body and our interpretation of it. We devote this section to discussion of the way bodies are situated and how certain aspects of the positioning of bodies are hidden. We focus on the definition of the "lived world" and the nature of our connections to it. For feminists, living in the world involves assignment to roles that give individuals differential access to resources, status, power, and agency. These assignments affect social relations, belief systems, and the body. Although people may be unaware of the mechanisms societies employ or their impact, we *do* place bodies in social roles by virtue of their appearances, and their placement, in turn, affects their bodies. Feminists highlight two ways that societies work—(a) positioning and (b) inscription—to produce particular bodies that reflect and conform to the social structure or stratification of society. The term *position* has multiple meanings. Society places individuals in different social positions that provide them differential power and agency. One could argue that each social interaction involves putting the participants into positions according them relative power and agency. There are higher and lower status positions, as well as in-groups and out-groups. Positions in a social group also provide different perspectives. People who are on the margins are usually conscious of power differences; those in the center, however, may be unaware that some perspectives differ from their own (Code, 1995; Harding, 1991; Hekman, 1997). Consequently, psychologists who are often in positions of authority may not know that others do not share their worldviews, including beliefs about the body and the mind; hence, the impact of social stratification may be invisible to them. Yet another aspect of position is that positions are places with a spatial location, and different positions may occupy more space, allow more mobility and agency, and so forth. An obvious example is the concern of women and ethnic minorities that they will encounter a glass ceiling.

Second, as feminists (e.g., Butler, 1993; Greene, 2003) note, gender is *inscribed* on the child's body, not just inbuilt. Cultures work through inscription. Obviously, the material circumstances of one's life, such as income and occupation, shape the body. The body is also a discursive structure that people have represented differently across historical time and culture. The way society depicts the bodies of people of color, women, and peasants, for example, reflects the social structure and ethos of a society. Each culture defines, shapes, and presents images of each social category of body, and thus, these images become "natural" and "normal" (Code, 2000). This normalization makes the "cultural construction of the body" invisible. Cultural images of the child body, the boy body, the girl body, the youthful body, and the aging body not only define and construct the body, but also influence the sorts of experiences in which such bodies engage. Foucault (1977) drew attention to the ways that culture inscribes its structures on the body through developing norms for physical health and hygiene, and creating professions to monitor physical well being. Foucault's analysis applies to trends in developmental psychology. For example, there is significant debate about the first three years of life as a critical period in the growth and organization of the brain with profound effects on later learning (Bruer, 1999). Despite scientific uncertainty about the causes and consequences of infant brain development, the media and the toy industry have heightened parental interest in providing a stimulating environment for infants, and the government has become concerned about the impact of understimulation of infants in conditions of poverty (Bruer, 1999; Nadesan, 2002).

Foucault's analysis illuminates gender development, too. Socially constructed facets of gender influence the practices we engage in with children. For example, although boys are generally biologically more vulnerable as infants, American parents involve their infant boys in rough-and-tumble acrobatics, while they treat the sturdy girl as fragile and in need of vocal interaction. Parents start the little boy on the path to athletics by exposing him to athletic toys and activities at an early age, even though encouragement to sit still might buffer some of the learning difficulties in school more prevalent in boys. Boys are also encouraged to walk differently from girls, to take up more space when they sit, and to sit further apart.

Another way that society shapes the gendered and growing body is through clothing. Benson (1993) reported that children born in the summer and fall begin to crawl about three weeks later than do babies born in other seasons. She speculated that the summer babies reach the point when they might be exercising their lower limbs at a time when they are wearing layers of clothing that protect them against the cold, but impede their movements. Throughout the lifespan, traditional female attire often restricts movement. Gender constraints, as well as age strictures, exist on the kind of makeup, jewelry, and clothing that society considers acceptable for children—as opposed to adolescents and adults—to wear. It is generally acceptable for girls to wear makeup and jewelry, stressing their physical attractiveness; until recently, boys could not. The sexualization of young girls is beginning earlier and earlier, with midriff-baring tops and jeans (Brumberg, 1998). In contrast, society may censure a scantily clad 70-year-old woman as being inappropriate. The thesis of this chapter is that Cartesian dualism not only splits the mind from the body, but also divorces both from the lived world. It does so by ignoring not just the different kinds of bodies that people possess, but also the way living in different worlds shapes the mind and the body. In order to recover the body and place it within a lived context, the definition of the body must include appearance and agency, and the definition of the lived world must include the stratification of individuals on the basis of their bodies. The world that bodies inhabit is political, and those politics affect the body and the mind. A body is not a neutral vessel for the mind. Rather, it communicates role-related restrictions and values to girls and boys and to the young and old. The body inhabits the mind in that culturally sanctioned body images and personal body images may serve as guideposts for the growing child, who uses them as milestones on a culturally sanctioned imaginary life course. Because these "constructed" bodies appear to be "natural" and "normal," these cultural constructions of body are invisible—that is, not only is the body invisible in psychology, but the construction of bodies in any culture also is invisible (Henriques et al., 1998). We illustrate that invisibility through discussions of how typical contemporary

developmental texts and the experimental method itself decontextual-
ize and hide the "body politic" in general. We then examine how concepts like gender and our theory of mental life and social relations that
seem to have an embodied component have been decontextualized.

Decontextualized Children

Let us return to developmental textbooks. The photographs on their
covers depict diversity in gender, age, and ethnicity. Open the pages
and, with few exceptions (e.g., M. Cole & S. R. Cole, 2000), class, race,
and nationality are discussed in sidebars. Diversity in bodies is included
and addressed only in a superficial way; diversity is simply an "add-on"
to a universal, idealized, decontextualized body. Developmental psychology textbooks are scientific narratives relating the collective biog-
raphies of diverse children. These narratives, however, not only cloak
the bodies of children at certain points in development, they also hide
individual and social identities and their potent influences on mind
and body. Bodies have a social position. Who is the child whose story
the author has outlined? What is the setting and situation of the story?

Decontextualized Methods

The key strategy for erasing the social environment and decontextual-
izing the body has been the adoption of the experimental method that
dictates the control of extraneous variables in order to manipulate some
isolated process in the tiny moment of investigation (Bronfenbrenner,
1979). In stripping situations of meaning and people of their individu-
ality, we assign the particular body and its context to error variance and
they disappear from view. Behavior becomes easier to quantify, dissect,
and measure, but both the person and the setting vanish. The reduction and splitting of environmental influences to a set of manipulable
independent variables create the fiction that one can parse and control
the real environment in this way. In actuality, the environment has a
dynamically changing structure that influences individuals and positions them in ways that accord them different opportunities for agency
and different perspectives on the world. Moreover, individuals do not
shed their cultural locations upon entrance into an experiment, and the
experiment itself has a cultural location. British and Australian developmental psychologists (e.g., Burman, 1994; Walkerdine, 1997, 1998) have
been particularly vocal about the distortions and misinterpretations
that occur when the context for assessing development is abstract and
simplified. They contest privileging of abstract over contextual understanding, and they protest the unexamined assumptions about the way
children perceive and react to standardized assessment procedures. By

ignoring social positioning, we can neither understand its influence nor tap the children's awareness of their own social perspective. Thus, although embracing the experimental method has advanced developmental psychology, it also has introduced a bias that both reflects and reinforces the discipline's neglect of embodiment.

Decontextualized Thinking—Theory of Mind

Research on the child's *Theory of Mind* has explored the origin and nature of young children's understanding of the formation of beliefs and the relations among beliefs, emotions, and behavior. Researchers have honed in on a key milestone in understanding mental life: the ability to detect when people's beliefs are at variance from the reality they perceive due to lack of pertinent information (Flavell & Miller, 1998). Research has also explored young children's construction of a generic model explaining the psychology of human behavior. In that model, children assume that they can explain people's actions on the basis of their desires and their beliefs about the way those desires can be satisfied (Bartsch & Wellman, 1995; Wellman, 1990). A prominent explanation of the origins of these ideas is the "theory-theory." Gopnik and Meltzoff (1997), for example, claim that children acquire their understanding of representation and of the role of desires and beliefs through building a psychological theory, much as scientists build theories of diverse physical domains.

Feminists question these assumptions (e.g., Code, 2000; Nelson, Henseler, & Plesa, 2000) and highlight how the theory leads to (a) splitting the mind from the feeling body; (b) reducing understanding of daily social interactions to grand theories of mental representation; and (c) abstracting understanding of social interactions from the social context in which they occur. The standard Theory of Mind lacks corporeality, social location, and content. Of interest is universal, abstract knowledge about the nature of minds in general, for example, the knowledge that people can have false representations, and thus false beliefs, about the world, or that universally desiring, believing, and knowing cause certain behaviors. One can, of course, assume people are motivated without understanding what the motivations are. The skeletal theory does not provide insight into particular situations or people. Thus, the theory deals with disembodied, decontextualized, universal minds. Note that this account of theory of mind is not value neutral. It privileges abstract, theoretical, universal knowledge, as well as individualism, cognitive autonomy, and scientific reasoning. The theory considers similarities among human minds to be more important than their differences. Of less importance is cognition concerning a person's body, her emotional engagement with other people, her social position in communicative exchanges, her variable behaviors as she engages in social activities in various contexts, and the culture-specific content of her thinking and action. Usually, psychologists do not provide this information to children when asking them to inpret scenarios. Hence, psychologists may not include these as ingredients in a child's Theory of Mind. When asked to respond to disembodied stories, the child is likely to propose a disembodied explanatory theory.

The standard Theory of Mind (Gopnik & Meltzoff, 1997) takes a positivist view of knowledge that hides the social structure. Theory of Mind research is based on a view of an objective reality that the child takes in. It assumes that the most important representations are those that can be categorized as "true" or "false" by every observer (Fivush, 2000). Distortions arise when the child lacks information and, therefore, constructs a false belief. Usually the child lacks this information because he or she was not present at the right time to witness events. The false belief scenarios presented to children, however, are limited in content. Feminists argue that the creation of a false belief and the right to decide what is true or false are the products of social structures (e.g., Code, 2000), which give some people more authority to define the truth than others. Parents are prone to tell children what is in the child's mind, dictate what the child wants and ought to have, and insist on particular versions of past events (Fivush, 2000; Henriques et al., 1998). People at the center of the social structure assume their view of reality is accurate, while those on the margins may appreciate the relativity of perspectives. Restricting access to information reinforces social categories. In the Victorian era, people did not expect wives to read newspapers and in contemporary society, parents often prevent children from watching violent and sexually explicit television and films. We are just beginning to learn about young children's understanding of how inequities, power, and prejudice influence cognition and behavior (Killen, Lee-Kim, McGlothin, & Stangor, 2002).

Adults also know that some people are more motivated to voice false beliefs than are others. They know what to expect from a used-car salesman. The conveyers of information are not always to be trusted because their standpoints and self-interests distort the information that they perceive and convey. It is important to take into account the motivation of people who utter belief statements. It is not surprising that added information about the situation or the motivation of the believer affects children's understanding of false belief (Wellman, Cross, & Watson, 2001).

Our knowledge of people's mental life and people's interpretations of experience goes beyond situations where there is an objective reality (Chandler, 1988). The very same event can have different interpretations depending on the experiences and biases of the witnesses. The fluidity and ambiguity of events sometimes make it difficult to have a true belief or to categorize beliefs as false. The mind is not merely representational; it is interpretive. Research on mental life requires putting the social world that creates mental life into the child's beliefs about people's minds by tapping a wider range of social situations that influence people's interpretation of the thinking of other people.

Although many researchers continue to focus their research on the standard false belief task, a recent strand of developmental research has, in fact, placed explanations of the origin of understanding false belief in a social context. There is recognition that our concepts of mind reflect our culture's view of mental life and that we appreciate the way the mind works through discourse about it. This research makes the invisible context of living in a social context visible. Researchers have begun to explore the ways different family structures, discursive activities, and cultural conditions affect the timing of children's grasp of false beliefs (Carpendale & Lewis, 2004; Meins, Fernyhough, Wainwright, DasGupta, Fradley, & Tuckey, 2002; Vinden, 1999; Wellman et al., 2001). These data provide the grounds for a theory of mind constructed through living in a social environment (Carpendale & Lewis, 2004; Nelson et al., 2000).

In summary, three strategies work to mask the body and the workings of the body politic from discussions of the Theory of Mind. First, the Theory of Mind is an abstraction, a generic theory of the way minds universally work. Because theorists assume universality, their explanatory framework minimizes cultural input to the formation of the theory. The tasks presented to children do not require the child to consider the influence of the social system on the way events are registered and interpreted. Second, we often tend to reduce the Theory of Mind to a theory of the representational mind. In reality, understanding the origins of false beliefs, or even having a belief-desire theory of behavior, does not equip the child to interpret daily interactions. Understanding false beliefs is just a small portion of the psychological insight needed to become a good clinician (Chandler, 1988). Finally, the Theory of Mind epitomizes the splitting of mind and body. The Theory of Mind is fragmentary; the body is missing from the mind. Moreover, the mind is not always a rational mind. Emotions and self-interests influence beliefs and knowledge.

Gender Essentialism

Theory of Mind research is disembodied in that it abstracts mental life from its cultural location. Psychological research can diminish the influence of culture by oversimplifying its content. This oversimplification eliminates the social and power structure of society, and often reduces society to dyadic mother-child relations, or to a homogeneous group of persons or traditions that shapes the child. An example of this tactic is one of the research paradigms used to examine children's concepts of gender essentialism. Gender essentialism shares with gender constancy the belief that an individual's gender is inherent and that biological determinants play a predominant role in shaping gender roles (Gelman & M. G. Taylor, 2000). One paradigm for testing gender essentialism (M. G. Taylor, 1996) presents a scenario in which an infant of one sex joins others on an island populated only by people of the other sex. The interviewer then asks the participants in the experiment whether the growing child would manifest stereotyped behaviors usually associated with the gender of birth or the gender of the child's caretakers. Preschoolers usually take a nativist stance. They assume that little boys would still prefer to play with trucks rather than tea sets, wear army boots rather than hair ribbons, and aspire to be firefighters rather than ballet dancers. School-aged children gradually become more flexible in their stereotyping and accord more weight to environmental explanations for behavioral traits and activities.

An obvious target of feminist objections to this paradigm is the very notion of gender essentialism, which ignores within-group variation while exaggerating between-group differences. Our critique highlights how the nature-nurture contrast is constructed; it oversimplifies the social environment. The assumption is that on the fictional island, there is a new social structure, but it reproduces the same gender-divided roles (firefighters and ballet dancers), clothing (frilly dresses and army boots), and toys (trucks and tea sets) as before.[2] It is, of course, possible that if the island inhabitants were of just one gender, they would continue to display the behaviors associated with their gender, presumably because those behaviors are inherent in the sex. In that case, one might wonder how the little boy surrounded by females would even know about trucks, army boots, and firefighting. However, the island natives could instead adopt the behaviors associated with the other gender as their exclusive property. Again, a sharp gender division would exist, but not the "conventional" role assignment and the boy could simply learn the masculine role by socialization. Alternatively, the denizens of the society that the baby joined could have more than two categories of gender, as in some societies (Whelehan, 2001), or not even consider gender as a determinant of clothing, behavior, or occupational choice. Each of these possibilities might lead to different treatment of the infant, including differential exposure to the constituents of gender stereotyping. The mythological island seems to reproduce the current social structure and an inflexible nativist stance.

What about the child who joins the island? Would the society treat the child like the native island children are treated? Would the society treat the child as biologically different and therefore needing some special socialization? What would the treatment of this "other" and the position of the "other" be? Would every boy's growth under these social conditions be the same? Would there be a uniform reaction by each occupant of the island to this growing child, or is more than the child's gender the determinant of their behavior toward the child? The immediate consequence of a society in which gender is no longer a variation is that it changes the social structure and the meanings of the external attributes and activities that are associated with gender. The very term *nurture* used to describe environmental influence on gender development assumes that gender differentiation into two genders is an important goal of socialization in all cultures, when it is not (Whelehan, 2001). It ignores the way of the caretakers and children are positioned by a society with a set of beliefs and values. Moreover, this approach tends to ignore cultural differences in the methods of socialization for these roles. Mahalingam (2003) also pointed out that essentialist beliefs tend to perpetuate the status of people in power. It is advantageous for males to believe that gender is an immutable, innate, biological essence, whereas women, who have a lower status label, are more likely to affirm the powerful role of cultural and social factors and the potential for societal changes that might eradicate social status differences. Mahalingam has documented how the prevalence of essentialist beliefs decreases in lower caste individuals and those who adopt atypical gender roles.

Children may be little nativists because we implicitly present them with desert-island scenarios in our daily interactions with them. In these scenarios, gender, race, class, body type, and even development are isolated, individual difference variables. Children may eventually revise their scenarios to include beliefs about social structure. Those notions of the body and the social structure may change. Those changes, however, will not solely be the result of biological maturation, but of their attempt to incorporate and integrate the theories of gender, psychology, and social structure to which they are exposed.

In summary, reductionism, splitting, and abstraction hide the body, as well as veil or diminish contextual influences on the body. In our attempt to standardize the situations in which society assesses children and to universalize the participants in our assessment, we conceal the role of the culture. In our attempts to reduce the study of the child to behavior in the laboratory, the family, or homogeneous social groups, we ignore the larger features of the environment that work on the body and the body in the mind. We present children with simplified scenarios of false beliefs and homogeneous social structures because we assume that they cannot grasp complexity; however, we must take care regarding the components (e.g., the body) and interconnections (e.g., between body, mind, and social structure) that we omit. We can incorporate these components and interconnections into our experiments, and we can use observational methods to supplement our findings.

EMBODIED THEORY-RESEARCH ON EMBODIMENT

We began with the question, "Where is the body in cognitive developmental psychology?" The answer implies a close relationship between the mind, the body, and their location in a social world that positions bodies and influences ideas about them. Theories of embodiment have the potential of integrating the body in the mind, the mind in the body, and the body and mind in the social milieu. A theory of embodiment can examine how the social milieu is represented in the mind and body.

Developing such a theory presents challenges. We have argued that a tradition of reductionism and splitting works against holistic theories such as embodiment (Oyama, 1999) and that the quest for universal laws works against attempts to contextualize the body in its social and political context and to trace the implications of social inequalities and differences. Building a theory of embodiment first requires an understanding of growing bodies as a context for building concepts of the self and the physical and social world. What aspects of the body are relevant and why? Additionally, a theory of embodiment requires a theory of contexts. We have drawn on feminist theory and postmodernism to suggest that any context is political and that access to information and one's status as a knower relate to social status and power. One of the challenges of a theory of embodiment is the development of an acceptable theory of context, because such theories cross disciplinary borders into sociology or political science, and the choice of theory is inherently value laden. An additional ingredient of a theory of embodiment is an emphasis on connections. Bodies have a position. People may become aware of that position and its ramifications for their interpretation of the body, the self, and the social world. Not only does it matter whose body and what social context we study, but we also argue that close scrutiny of those connections between body and context will enrich our understanding.

We end this paper by suggesting a model of interconnected thinking as one framework for studying the embodied mind in cognitive development. We explore how we might examine what children understand about specific knowers positioned in a social system, and socially situated bodies.

Interconnected Thinking

Miller (2000) has proposed a feminist model of cognitive development, interconnected thinking, that stands as an example of an embodied epistemology. Thinking is interconnected in four ways that are themselves related (p. 46). The connections are variegated and the study of the implications of these variations provides a fruitful research agenda for an embodied psychology.

1. The objects of knowledge are not always isolated scraps of information. Many are interconnected with one another and with events in the external world. Much of knowledge is about relations among objects and events, rather than just the objects and events themselves. Interconnected thinking shifts attention from isolated concepts to connections, and to the system in which a single object, event, or phenomenon is a part. Examples include the understanding of (a) how another person's mind is connected to other minds through social relationships, (b) how exercise affects the physiology of the body, (c) how an ecological system operates, and (d) how social institutions affect healthy physical development and the acquisition of knowledge. From the perspective of interconnected thinking, researchers would explore how gender concepts are linked with a set of kinship relations, titles of address, age expectations, and so on. Another example is seeing the connections among politics, religion, economics, and geography at any moment in the history of a country.

2. The knower is connected to or located in a context that affords the knower evidence and epistemological authority. Interconnected knowing deconstructs the universal knower into specific socially constructed knowers and places the question, "Who is the knower?" at the forefront. Feminist scholarship focuses on the large social structures and discourses that shape the individual. Although a person constructs a self, that very construction is directed by social construals of male and female bodies, white bodies or those of color, thin or large bodies, and child and adult bodies. The knower has a body, and that body has a particular sex and color, socially constructed categories that create a gendered, raced, socially classed person. Thinking bodies occupy a particular position within a social matrix stratified according to gender, race, class, and age. That position has greater or lesser power and epistemic authority than other positions, depending on that person's gender, race, class, and age. This social position defines what experiences the person can have, how much authority the person's knowledge has in a particular setting, and what the person's subjectivity is like. It defines particular minds and thus the sorts of knowledge these minds construct.

A main tenet of feminist standpoint and women-of-color theories is that people at the margins of society—those with less power and authority because of their gender, race, and class—may have a richer understanding of people and social interaction than do people at the center (Collins, 1990). Because power resides in the center, those in the margins must understand not only their own experiences—which society has linked to being female, or "of color," or of low income—but also the dominant culture, which is mainly white, male, and middle class. In order to enter the dominant culture, they must understand it. People in the center typically see only their own views, because those views have constructed the mainstream culture. Their views about what sorts of knowledge are important appear to be natural, to be the reality, not just one of many possible realities. There is no such thing, however, as an "objective" view from nowhere; a view is always from somewhere. Thus, it matters *who* the knower is, what kind of body is undergoing cognitive development in culturally constructed situations. A Theory of Mind that focuses on the distinction between true and false belief, for example, oversimplifies human subjectivity and the social conditions that create it. Each social location entails a particular epistemological location.

All of this has implications for cognitive development. There is no such thing as a view from a genderless, raceless, classless developing body. Cognitive developmentalists have tended to study concepts believed to be universal and thus have ignored the specifics of the particular knower, other than his or her present cognitive structures. When culture is incorporated, developmentalists often investigate it as a moderator variable that speeds up or slows down development. Being of a *particular* gender, color, social class, and age, however, pushes children into *particular* social settings and discourages their access into other social settings. In addition, children themselves select particular settings as a result of their maturing gendered, raced, and classed bodies. Thus, these gendered, raced, and classed developing bodies have particular experiences that lead to particular concepts of both the self and the social and physical world.

If knowledge is always situated, then developmental psychologists must broaden their definition of "social cognition" beyond concepts such as friendship, conflict, and social rules. Interconnected thinking expands the social to issues of epistemic status and authority both as objects of thought and causes of cognition. What situations and statuses put particular people in the position to define truth? What do children know about epistemic authority and the conditions that produce it? From the perspective of interconnected knowledge, it is important to address questions such as, "Who can know?" and "Who has the right to define truth?"

3. *Knowers are connected to themselves.* Knowledge is connected to one's physical body, emotions, and needs. Interconnected thinking links mind and body. Knowing is connected to doing. The acquisition of concepts and strategies is linked to goal directed behavior and to the individual's feelings of self-efficacy (Bandura, 1986). There are no dichotomies between "knowledge that" and "knowledge how," and between "pure" knowledge and its uses in everyday life. Development charts not merely growth in abstraction, but also increasing competence in the transfer, application, and adaptation of knowledge. Knowers are also connected to themselves because they are often aware of and reflect on themselves—on their own bodies, thoughts, emotions, knowledge, and selfhood. Interconnected knowing provides a framework for studying how these connections arise and how social positions and social conditions mediate them.

4. *Interconnected knowing also posits an important source of knowledge and a particular way of arriving at knowledge.* The knower is connected to an epistemological community that constructs and interprets experience and gives it meaning. Interconnected knowing therefore contains elements of social constructionism (Vygotsky, 1978). It assumes, however, that societies are heterogeneous in terms of beliefs because the constituents of the society and its members are heterogeneous. Children are exposed to information from diverse sources and in diverse ways. Sometimes they are taught simple concepts and values, and sometimes they participate in activities that enable them to coconstruct interpretations of events. This latter process can occur because of the social relationships that have developed between the child and other people. Thus, social connections scaffold cognitive development. One research agenda for interconnected knowing examines how diverse

communities and diverse sources of information are transmitted, taken up, and interpreted by diverse children.

Recasting Research Agendas

Gender concepts. The four aspects of interconnected thinking recast the study of gender development and Theory of Mind. In exploring gender concepts, most research has focused on the child's acquisition of gender identity, gender constancy, and gender stereotypes. The perspective of interconnected thinking approaches gender concepts differently. As examples of the four aspects of interconnected knowing, a girl (a) develops an understanding of how gender is connected to a broader social system organized by age, race, social class, and ethnicity and (b) becomes aware of the epistemological privileges and authority that society accords each gender. She also (c) is taught to attend to and think about how a gender is a package of ideas, bodily states, and emotions (e.g., Adams, Kuebli, Boyle, & Fivush, 1995) and (d) becomes aware of the way her gender provides entry into certain epistemological communities, but not others. Consequently, researchers might explore how, and under what circumstances, the child recognizes that her gender may be a relevant variable in some situations but not others. What is her map of connected roadways for doing gender? When and how does she recognize that different cultures have different concepts of what it means to be a girl? How does she deal with the conflicting and diverse models of femininity presented by different sources such as schools and the media? How does she integrate her models of biological growth and of sexuality with her understanding of the nature of gender? How does her understanding of the social context affect her understanding of gender?

Theory of mind. Whereas current Theory of Mind research assumes an isolated observer representing the world, interconnected knowing starts with the claim that there is an interpersonal network of beliefs, desires, feelings, and intentions, as well as a social system of taking care of other bodies, especially those of children, the elderly, and the sick or disabled. This developing knowledge of a system of interacting minds and bodies, of a network of beliefs, desires, feelings, intentions, and physical behaviors *among people,* leads to a child's "theory-of-mind-and-body-in-society." A second claim is that because understanding minds is always from the perspective of the interpreter, the *relationship* between the knower and the person thought about makes a difference. Third, one's Theory of Mind is linked to other aspects of social and emotional life, and lastly, the content of a Theory of Mind and the proclivity to invoke it are rooted in the specifics of familial and social structure. Thus, feminist developmental theorists ask, "What do children of various ages understand about the relations among minds? When do children begin to think about a socially situated person with a body embedded in social relationships? How do children learn that people have mental representations of *each other's minds and bodies* that guide their interpersonal behavior?" We have suggested that identity politics is an essential ingredient of a theory of mind. The identity of the knower and the identity of the person the knower wishes to understand are important. The race, gender, social class, and nationality of the knower and known affect both the interpretation of behavior and the epistemic authority granted to the knower.

The body in the mind. An interconnected theory of knowing also looks at the body in the mind differently. The four aspects of interconnected knowing raise questions about how children (a) learn to categorize bodies on the basis of gender, age, ethnicity, etc.; (b) construct a body concept and social identity and learn the privileges and restrictions that this identity affords; (c) are taught to attend to and think about the connections between mental, emotional, and physical aspects of the body; and (d) become savvy about the ways cultures send messages about the body. This framework focuses on the study of the body as a social object. Within this framework, developmentalists could examine diverse children's developing understanding of themselves as growing beings and how the changing body brings with it potentials for negotiating and interacting with others, for entering new environments, for choosing some careers rather than others, and so forth. When do they discern that views of the body are relative? What is important about the body may differ among different social groups at different ages. How do diverse people feel embodied? How is embodiment interwoven with the self?

Researchers could also analyze (a) the culturally influenced processes by which children acquire their ways of displaying themselves and of moving through the world, (b) the child's awareness of the rules, and (c) the ways cultures assign strictures on display and movement. We know little about the development of children's knowledge that certain attributes of the body—such as a person's gender and race, and society's reactions to these attributes—affect that person's beliefs, desires, emotions, and intentions. In other words, we know more about young children's understanding about bodies in general than we do about their understanding of particular bodies and selves situated in a social system. Such research would rediscover the lived body in human development.

CONCLUSION

We began with a mystery, the hidden body in developmental psychology. We have argued that the body and its location were there all the time, but we designed our conceptualizations of each to mask them in order to produce a manageable and measurable psychological object. Although this simplification helped the field progress, developmental psychology is now established enough to consider a richer, more complex conceptualization of development and its study. Feminist epistemological theories provide the tools that reveal why and how the body was hidden. But what kind of body is it? Embodiment theory suggests a socially located body in the mind, a located mind in the body, and a material mind embedded in social positions. How do we define each of these terms , mind, body, and society, and the nature of the connections? The mystery is not ours alone; children also come to deal with these terms. What children know and how they know it reflect the circumstances of their embodiment. This is the true mystery of cognitive development. Acknowledging and studying the embodied and embedded mind would enrich our understanding of cognitive development by helping us identify the body and the lived world in both our own theories and in the conceptualizations children construct.

ENDNOTES

1. Our thanks to Jane Clark for illuminating discussions which helped us to elaborate our ideas. It was she who drew our attention to Duquin's (1994) analyses of "body snatching" in studies of sports.
2. Taylor did do one experiment with unfamiliar materials.

REFERENCES

Adams, S., Kuebli, J., Boyle, P., & Fivush, R. (1995). Gender differences in parent-child conversations about past emotions: A longitudinal investigation. *Sex Roles, 33*, 309–323.
Adolph, K. E., Eppler, M. A., & Gibson, E. J. (1993). Development of perception of affordances. In C. Rovee-Collier & L. P. Lipsitt (Eds.), *Advances in Infancy Research* (Vol. 8, pp. 51–98). Norwood, NJ: Ablex.
Bandura, A. (1986). *Social foundations of thought and action: A social cognitive theory.* Prentice-Hall.
Bartsch, K., & Wellman, H. M. (1995). *Children talk about the mind.* New York: Oxford University Press.
Benson, J. B. (1993). Season of birth and onset of locomotion: Theoretical and methodological implications. *Infant Behavior and Development, 16,* 69–81.

Bertenthal, B. I., Campos, J. J., & Barrett, K. C. (1984). Self-produced locomotion: An organizer of emotional, cognitive, and social development in infancy. In R. Emde & R. Harmon (Eds.), *Continuities and discontinuities in development* (pp. 175–210). New York: Plenum Press.

Bloom, L., & Tinker, E. (2001). *The intentionality model and language acquisition: Engagement, effort, and the essential tension in development* (Monographs of the Society for Research in Child Development, Serial No. 267, Vol. 66[4]). Boston: Blackwell Publishers.

Bordo, S. (1991). *Unbearable weight: Feminism, western culture, and the body.* Berkeley: University of California Press.

Bronfenbrenner, U. (1979). *The ecology of human development.* Cambridge, MA: Harvard University Press.

Bruer, J. T. (1999). *The myth of the first three years: A new understanding of early brain development and life long learning.* New York: Free Press.

Burman, E. (1994). *Deconstructing developmental psychology.* London: Routledge.

Butler, J. (1993). *Bodies that matter.* New York: Routledge.

Brumberg, J. J. (1998). *The body project: An intimate history of American girls.* New York: Vintage.

Bussey, K., & Bandura, A. (1999). Social cognitive theory of gender development and gender differentiation. *Psychological Review, 106,* 676–713.

Carey, S. (1999). Sources of conceptual change. In E. K. Scholnick, K. Nelson, S. A. Gelman, & P. H. Miller (Eds.), *Conceptual development: Piaget's legacy* (pp. 293–326). Mahwah, NJ: Erlbaum.

Carpendale, J. I. M., & Lewis, C. (2004). Constructing an understanding of mind: The development of children's social understanding within social interaction. *Behavioral and Brain Sciences, 27,* 79–151.

Chandler, M. (1988). Doubt and developing theories of mind. In J. W. Astington, P. L. Harris, & D. R. Olson (Eds.), *Developing theories of mind* (pp. 387–414). New York: Cambridge University Press.

Code, L. (1995). *Rhetorical spaces: Essays on gendered locations.* New York: Routledge.

Code, L. (2000). Naming, naturalizing, normalizing: "The child" as fact and artifact. In P. H. Miller & E. K. Scholnick (Eds.), *Toward a feminist developmental psychology* (pp. 215–237). New York: Routledge.

Cole, M., & Cole, S. R. (2001). *The development of children* (4th ed.). New York: W. H. Freeman.

Cole, M., Cole, S. R., & Lightfoot, C. (2004). *The development of children.* 4th edition, Freeman & Co.

Collins, P. H. (1990). *Black feminism.* Boston: Unwin Hyman.

Damasio, A. (1999). *The feeling of what happens: Body and emotion in the making of consciousness.* New York: Harcourt Brace.

Duquin, M. (1994). The body snatchers and Dr. Frankenstein revisited: Social construction and deconstruction of bodies and sport. *Journal of Sport and Social Issues, 18*(3), 268–281.

Edelman, G. M. (1992). *Bright air, brilliant fire: On the matter of the mind.* New York: Basic Books.

Erikson, E. H. (1963). *Childhood and society* (2nd ed.). New York: Norton.

Fausto-Sterling, A. (2000). *Sexing the body: Gender politics and the construction of sexuality.* New York: Basic.

Fivush, R. (2000). Accuracy, authority, and voice: Feminist perspectives on autobiographical memory. In P. H. Miller & E. K. Scholnick (Eds.), *Toward a feminist developmental psychology* (pp. 85–105). New York: Routledge.

Flavell, J. H., & Miller, P. H. (1998). Social cognition. In W. Damon (Series Ed.), D. Kuhn, & R. S. Siegler (Vol. Eds.), *Handbook of child psychology: Vol. 2. Cognition, perception, and language* (5th ed., pp. 851–898). New York: Wiley.

Foucault, M. (1977). *Discipline and punish.* London: Allen Lane.

Gelman, S. A. (2003). *The essential child: Origins of essentialism in everyday thought.* New York: Oxford University Press.

Gelman, S. A., & Hirschfield, L. A. (1999). How biological is essentialism? In D. Medin & S. Atran (Eds.), *Folk biology* (pp. 403–446). Cambridge, MA: MIT Press.

Gelman, S. A., & Taylor, M. G. (2000). Gender essentialism in cognitive development. In P. H. Miller & E. K. Scholnick (Eds.), *Toward a feminist developmental psychology* (pp. 169–190). New York: Routledge.

Gibson, E. J. (1969). *Principles of perceptual learning and development.* Appleton-Century Crofts.

Gopnik, A., & Meltzoff, A. (1997). *Words, thoughts, and theories.* Cambridge, MA: MIT Press.

Greene, S. (2003). *The psychological development of girls and women: Rethinking change in time.* London: Routledge.

Harding, S. (1991). *Whose science? Whose knowledge? Thinking from women's lives.* Ithaca, NY: Cornell University Press.

Harter, S. S. (1999). *The construction of the self: A developmental perspective.* New York: Guilford.

Hekman, S. (1997). Truth and method: Feminist standpoint theory revisited. *Signs, 22*(2), 341–365.

Henriques, J., Hollway, W., Urwin, C., Venn, C., & Walkerdine, V. (1998). *Changing the subject: Psychology, social regulation and subjectivity.* London: Routledge.

Hulbert, A. (2003). *Raising America: Experts, parents, and a century of advice about children.* New York: Knopf.

Johnson, M. (1987). *The body in the mind: The bodily basis of meaning, imagination and reason.* Chicago: University of Chicago Press.

Keil, F. C. (1989). *Concepts, kinds, and cognitive development.* Cambridge, MA: MIT Press.

Killen, M., Lee-Kim, J., McGlothin, H., & Stangor, C. (2002). *How children and adolescents evaluate gender and racial exclusion* (Monographs of the Society for Research in Child Development, Serial No. 271, Vol. 67[4]). Boston: Blackwell Publishers.

Kohlberg, L. (1996). A cognitive-developmental analysis of children's sex role concepts and attitudes. In E. E. Maccoby (Ed.), *The development of sex differences* (pp. 82–173). Stanford, CA: Stanford University Press.

Labouvie-Vief, G. (1994). *Psyche and Eros: Mind and gender in the life course.* Cambridge, England: Cambridge University Press.

Lakoff, G., & Johnson, M. (1980). *Metaphors we live by.* Chicago: University of Chicago Press.

Lakoff, G., & Johnson, M. (1999). *Philosophy in the flesh: The embodied mind and its challenge to Western thought.* New York: Basic Books.

Lloyd, G. (1984). *The man of reason: "Male" and "female" in Western philosophy.* London: Methuen.

Mahalingam, R. (2003). Essentialism, culture, and beliefs about gender among the Aravanis of Tamil Nadu, India. *Sex Roles, 49,* 489–496.

Medin, D. L., & Atran S. (Eds.). (1999). *Folkbiology.* Cambridge, MA: MIT Press.

Mandler, J. M. (1992). How to build a baby: II. Conceptual primitives. *Psychological Bulletin, 99,* 587–604.

McGillicuddy-DeLisi, A., & DeLisi, R. (Eds.). (2002). *Biology, society, and behavior: The development of sex differences in cognition.* Westport, CT: Ablex.

Meins, E., Fernyhough, C., Wainwright, R., DasGupta, M., Fradley, E., & Tuckey, M. (2002). Maternal mind-mindedness and attachment security as predictors of theory of mind understanding. *Child Development, 73,* 1715–1726.

Miller, P. H. (2000). The development of interconnected thinking. In P. H. Miller & E. K. Scholnick (Eds.), *Toward a feminist developmental psychology* (pp. 45–59). New York: Routledge.

Musher-Eizenman, D. R., Holub, S. C., Edwards-Leeper, L., Persson, A. V., & Goldstein, S. E. (2003). The narrow range of acceptable body types of preschoolers and their mothers. *Journal of Applied Developmental Psychology, 24,* 259–271.

Nadesan, M. H. (2002). Engineering the entrepreneurial infant: Brain science, infant development, toys, and governmentality. *Cultural Studies, 16,* 401–432.

Nelson, K., Henseler, S., & Plesa, D. (2000). Entering a community of minds: "Theory of Mind" from a feminist standpoint. In P. H. Miller & E. K. Scholnick (Eds.), *Toward a feminist developmental psychology* (pp. 61–84). New York: Routledge.

Overton, W. (1984). World views and their influence on psychological theory and research: Kuhn-Lakatos-Laudan. In H. W. Reese (Ed.), *Advances in child development and behavior* (Vol. 18, pp. 191–226). New York: Academic Press.

Overton, W. (2003) Embodied development: Ending the nativism-empiricism debate. In C. Garcia Coll, E. Bearer, & R. Lerner (Eds.), *Nature and nurture: The complex interplay of genetic and environmental influences on human behavior and development* (pp. 201–223). Mahwah, NJ: Lawrence Erlbaum Associates.

Oyama, S. (1999). Locating development: Locating developmental systems. In E. K. Scholnick, K. Nelson, S. A. Gelman, & P. H. Miller (Eds.), *Conceptual development: Piaget's legacy* (pp. 185–208). Mahwah, NJ: Erlbaum.

Piaget, J. (1952). *The origins of intelligence in children.* New York: International Universities Press. (Original work published 1936)

Piaget, J. (1976). *The grasp of consciousness: Action and concept in the young child.* Cambridge, MA: Harvard University Press. (Original work published 974)

Pinker, S. (2002). *The blank slate: The modern denial of human nature.* New York: Viking.

Piran, N. (2001). Eating disorders and disordered eating. In J. Worell (2001). *Encyclopedia of women and gender* (pp. 369–378). San Diego: Academic Press.

Ross, N., Medin, D., Coley, J. D., & Atran, S. (2003). Cultural and experiential differences in the development of folkbiological induction. *Cognitive Development, 181*, 25–47.

Sinnott, J. D., & Shiffrin, K. (2001). Gender and aging: Gender differences and gender roles. In J. E. Birren (Ed.), *Handbook of the psychology of aging* (5th ed., pp. 454–476). San Diego, CA: Academic Press.

Spelman, E. V. (1982). Woman as body: Ancient and contemporary views. *Feminist Studies, 8*, 109–131.

Taylor, C. (1995). *Philosophical arguments.* Cambridge, MA: Harvard University Press.

Taylor, M. G. (1996). The development of children's beliefs about social and biological aspects of gender differences. *Child Development, 67*, 1555–1571.

Thelen, E. (2000a). Grounded in the world: Developmental origins of the embodied mind. *Infancy, 1*, 3–28.

Thelen, E. (2000b). Motor development as foundation and future of developmental psychology. *International Journal of Behavioral Development, 24*, 385–397.

Thelen, E., & Smith, L. B. (1994). *A dynamic systems approach to the development of cognition and action.* Cambridge, MA: MIT Press.

Thelen, E., & Smith, L. B. (1998). Dynamic systems theory. In W. Damon (Series Ed.) & R. M. Lerner (Vol. Ed.), *Handbook of child psychology: Vol. 1. Theoretical models of human development* (5th ed., pp. 563–634). New York: Wiley.

Vinden, P. G. (1999). Children's understanding of mind and emotion: A multicultural study. *Cognition and Emotion, 13*, 19–48.

Vygotsky, L. S. (1978). *Mind in society: The development of higher psychological processes.* Cambridge, MA :Harvard University Press.

Walkerdine, V. (1997). *Daddy's girl: Young girls and popular culture.* Cambridge, MA: Harvard University Press.

Walkerdine, V. (1998). Developmental psychology and the child-centered pedagogy. In J. Henriques, W. Hollway, C. Urwin, C. Venn, & V. Walkerdine (Eds.). *Changing the subject: Psychology, social regulation, and subjectivity* (pp. –). London: Routledge.

Wellman, H. M. (1990). *The child's theory of the mind.* Cambridge, MA: MIT Press.

Wellman, H. M., Cross, D., & Watson, J. (2001). Meta-analysis of theory-of-mind development: The truth about false belief. *Child Development, 72,* 655–684.

Wellman, H. M., & Gelman, S. A. (1998). Knowledge acquisition in foundational domains. In W. Damon (Series Ed.), D. Kuhn, & R. S. Siegler (Vol. Eds.), *Handbook of child psychology: Vol. 2. Cognition, perception, and language* (5th ed., pp. 523–573). New York: Wiley.

Whelehan, P. (2001). Cross-cultural sexual practices. In J. Worell (Ed.), *Encyclopedia of women and gender* (pp. 291–302). San Diego: Academic Press.

11

COLORISM EMBODIED: SKIN TONE AND PSYCHOSOCIAL WELL-BEING IN ADOLESCENCE

Suzanne G. Fegley, Margaret B. Spencer,
Tyhesha N. Goss, Vinay Harpalani, and Nicole Charles
University of Pennsylvania, Graduate School of Education

Embodiment is a salient marker of the human experience. The physical constraints of our body and the ability of our mind to actively reflect on our body as we are interacting in the world shape our mental images of the world—our thoughts, feelings, and perceptions. In the absence of a physical body, there is no mind, and in the absence of a functioning mind, we are unable to perceive the world. Our abilities to self-reflect and make self-appraisals, including those based on our physical appearances, play an integral role in identity development and help define who we are as persons. Feelings of satisfaction and self-consciousness about our bodies influence the way we experience and perceive the world throughout the course of our lives, but especially during specific developmental periods such as adolescence. Moreover, these feelings take on especially important roles during specific developmental periods, including adolescence.

Although each of us experiences varying levels of bodily self-awareness depending upon the circumstances and current context (e.g., standing in front of a three-way mirror in the dressing room, being the only person of the opposite sex at a business meeting, being alone in a room with the door closed), adolescents are especially vulnerable to experiences of increased levels of bodily awareness due to their rapidly changing bodies and advancing cognitive capabilities. Being the only dark-skinned child in the sixth grade, the only overweight girl in gym class, or the shortest boy in the entire ninth grade exacerbates normative feelings of self-consciousness associated with entry into adolescence. Our bodies make us visible to others; other people view us and we perceive ourselves as *perceived*. This unavoidable social cognition contributes to the close monitoring of our bodies, as we as humans manage our appearance to create desired impressions.

Many factors influence body image and awareness of one's self as a physical being, but some, such as race and gender, have taken on a wider social and political significance. Race, for example, is unique in that the very definition of racial categories has often been dependent on a socially constructed, value-laden hierarchy of physical features—most notably skin color. Additionally, racial categories tie not only to physical features but also to various stereotypes related to intelligence and behavior. As social and cognitive skills develop, children gain increased awareness of societal messages regarding privileged phenotypic features (e.g., light skin, straight hair). Thus, society confronts many youth of color with a double quandary in regard to body image and appearance; society not only devalues their physical features as unattractive (or exotified), but they also link their appearances to negative cognitive and behavioral traits. For children who do not possess the socially valued traits (and, at times, even for those who do, but perceive that they do not), this can lead to decreased satisfaction with self. In order to promote positive coping responses in youth and to combat racism in the 21st century, it will be necessary to acknowledge the continued presence of societal biases (no matter how subtlety they are expressed) and understand how youth interpret and react to these biases.

In this chapter, we examine how minority status exacerbates the negotiation of body image and physical sense of self and creates challenges for youth of color. First, we present Spencer's (1995) theoretical framework, the Phenomenological Variant of Ecological Systems Theory (PVEST), to identify and interpret the risks, challenges, and coping strategies that youth employ in order to negotiate physical self-consciousness. We then present a social and historical overview of colorism (e.g., skin color bias) in the United States, followed by a review of literature on body image, skin color perceptions, and preferences, and the impact of skin color bias on psychological well-being, noting empirical findings, methodological challenges, and broader implications. Finally, we will present preliminary findings from our study of skin color perceptions and attitudes among our sample of racially diverse adolescents. The discussion covers the implications of our findings along with possibilities for future research.

PHENOMENOLOGICAL VARIANT OF ECOLOGICAL SYSTEMS THEORY (PVEST): AN IDENTITY-FOCUSED, CULTURAL-ECOLOGICAL PERSPECTIVE

As a synthesis of several frameworks, Spencer's (1995) PVEST combined a phenomenological perspective with Bronfenbrenner's (1979) ecological systems theory, linking context with perception. PVEST serves as a model to examine normative human development, framed through the interaction of identity processes and context. As such, it utilizes an Identity-Focused Cultural-Ecological (ICE) perspective, integrating issues of social, political, and cultural context with normative developmental processes. As a theory of human development, PVEST accounts generally for the differences in experience, perception, and dissonance, all of which are important to body image and physical sense of self. The PVEST model consists of five basic components that form a dynamic theoretical system, (a) net vulnerability, (b) net stress engagement, (c) reactive coping methods, (d) emergent identities, and (e) life-stage specific outcomes.

The first component, net vulnerability level, consists of the contexts and characteristics that pose potential challenges during specific developmental periods throughout the life course. Risk contributors are factors that may predispose individuals to adverse outcomes, depending on the context. Protective factors that serve as buffers against the experience of stress may offset risk, thus, defining the net vulnerability level for a given individual. For youth of color more generally, and for Black youth in particular, normative phenotypic features such as skin color are risk factors in a society that clearly and consistently devalues dark skin. Other risk factors may include socioeconomic conditions such as living in poverty, imposed expectations such as race and gender stereotypes, and larger historical processes such as racial segregation and discrimination. Self-appraisal is a key factor in identity formation, and perceptions of risks and resources are central to the process. Thus, the manner in which youth of color negotiate their own physical appearances and body images is contingent upon both macro- and micro-level characteristics of the social context and the availability of protective resources.

Net stress engagement, the second component of PVEST, refers to the actual experience of situations that challenge an individual's well-being. While net vulnerability represents the net balance between risk contributors and protective factors, net stress engagement represents the manifestation of risks as potential challenges; stressors are actualized risk factors. And, since social and structural supports can help youth negotiate the challenge of experienced stress, supports are actualized protective factors. Experiences of racism—both subtle and overt—and other related dissonance-producing situations are salient stressors for youth of color, exacerbating normative developmental issues encountered by all adolescents (e.g., puberty, identity exploration, peer relationships). With the onset of adolescence, body image and appearance become more salient, with physical features, such as skin color, serving as potential sources of dissonance for youth of color. Normative cognitive maturation makes awareness of dissonance acute and unavoidable, especially for those adolescents with no available support networks. Research suggests that, for youth of color, proactive racial socialization and positive ethnic identity are two protective factors that may serve as buffers against feelings of dissonance, directly impacting the level of stress they experience (e.g., Stevenson, H. C., 1994). Thus, within a given context, the net level of stress an individual experiences is the balance between his or her perception of risks and the availability of supports.

In response to the challenges that experiences of stress present, adolescents employ reactive coping methods to minimize or resolve dissonance-producing situations. Reactive coping responses include problem-solving strategies that can lead to adaptive or maladaptive solutions, depending on the context. It is important to remember that an adaptive solution in one context may be maladaptive in another context. For example, a Black adolescent boy walking through a predominantly Black neighborhood may adopt a certain body posture to avoid ridicule from his peers. However, the same body language may get him in trouble when walking through a predominantly White neighborhood because of residents' stereotypical beliefs about adolescent males based on the color of their skin. As youth employ different coping strategies, they are, at the same time, making self-appraisals, based in part on others' reactions to their behavior. Youth internalize those strategies that yield desired results for the ego (e.g., strategies that boost positive self-feelings or reduce feelings of anxiety and fear) and may replicate them in other situations. Over time, strategies that successfully protect the ego become stable coping responses, and, coupled, yield emergent identities. Emergent identities define how individuals view themselves within, and across, multiple contexts of their lives (e.g., family, school, and neighborhood). They provide stable ego processes experienced over time and place. The combination of racial and ethnic identity, sex role understanding, self, and other appraisals all help to define our identities, including our body images and physical self-appraisals.

Our identities lay the foundation for future perceptions, self-appraisals, and behaviors, leading to productive or adverse life-stage specific outcomes. Productive outcomes include good physical and mental health, academic competence, a sense of purpose, positive body image, and positive feelings about self, while adverse outcomes include poor physical and mental health, a lack of purpose, early parenthood, and self-destructive behaviors.

The PVEST framework represents dynamic, normative human processes that continue throughout the lifespan as individuals balance new risks against protective factors, encounter new stressors (potentially offset by supports), and establish novel and, ideally, more mature coping strategies. Throughout the process, individuals continue to refine and adjust their internal perceptions of themselves. Thus, identity is a process (as opposed to a static entity) that continues to evolve and develop throughout the lifespan. Spencer (1995) designed the PVEST model to elucidate salient challenges and developmental processes impacting identity formation during each successive stage of development, all occurring in a broader social context. The focus of this chapter is on one specific challenge, colorism, and the connections between body image, the perception of and attitudes toward skin color and positive feelings about self.

SOCIAL AND HISTORICAL ROOTS
OF COLORISM IN THE UNITED STATES

Colorism, or bias based on the lightness or darkness of a person's skin tone, is not a new phenomenon. In the early 17th century, when colonial plantation owners brought the first African slaves and White indentured servants to the American colonies, it was in the best interest of the planters to create a social hierarchy based on skin color. By elevating White servants to a higher rung on the social ladder than enslaved Blacks (who were relegated to the lowest rung), they were able to prevent dissatisfied slaves and servants from joining forces and starting an uprising against their landowners (Steinhorn & Diggs-Brown, 1999). In doing so, poor White servants suddenly found themselves with racial privileges, based solely on the color of their skin, that set them apart from the slaves and provided them with satisfaction in their newly acquired status over Blacks.

In their book, *The Color Complex*, Russell, Wilson, and Hall (1992) detailed the history of race mixing that contributed to the variation of skin color in America. Before slavery was abolished, it was not unusual for White slave masters to engage in coerced sexual relationships with enslaved Black women, resulting in light-skinned mulatto (one-half Black), quadroon (one-fourth Black), and octoroon (one-eighth Black) children that were sold for a large profit on the slave market (Izrael, 2001). Slaves with White fathers led more privileged existences than their "pure Black" counterparts (Frazier, 1957). White slave masters typically assigned tasks that required more training and intellectual ability to light-skinned slaves, while they left dark-skinned slaves to toil over the most physically demanding or menial work (Blackwell, 1985; Frazier, 1957). As a result, there was an assumption of privilege associated with light skin. The preferential treatment of light slaves caused the darker slaves to feel inferior and the lighter slaves to become further alienated from their families and communities. Nevertheless, this same treatment made the dream of freedom more attainable for light-skinned slaves. The close contact with Whites exposed them to improved basic needs (e.g., food, clothing, and shelter), opportunities to read and write, and exposure to White society (Franklin, 1980; Landry, 1987).

Lighter Blacks continued to experience skin color privilege even after the abolition of slavery. Opportunities for occupational training, education, and property acquisition were more accessible to light-skinned Blacks, in part, because racist ideology among Whites continued to dictate a preference for lighter skin, although Blacks themselves also helped to perpetuate this philosophy. Lighter skinned Blacks passed their phenotypic privileges on to their children by avoiding marriage with darker skinned Blacks and maintaining ties with the White community (Hunter, 2004). Further, they formed social clubs (e.g., the Bon Ton Society of Washington, DC and the Blue Vein Society of Nashville) in which the lightness of one's skin mainly determined membership. Even historically, Black universities discriminated against applicants based on the color of their skin. Universities granted lighter skinned Blacks (those with mixed blood) access to a liberal arts education while they denied darker skinned Blacks ("pure Blacks") the same privilege based on the implicit belief that they did not have the intellectual capacity to benefit from a more advanced education (Maddox, 1998). The belief that whiteness, and anything white-like, was good or superior, while darkness, and anything black, was evil or inferior drove these biased practices. Over time, the habit of associating white with good and black with evil was so automatic that it embedded itself deeply in the American psyche, helping to perpetuate the myth of White supremacy that continues to exist today.

Consider, for instance, the fact that skin color remains a frequent source of social and community acceptance or rejection even during the current climate of seemingly "color-blind" policies developed to eliminate skin color bias. Russell et al. (1992) claimed that the significance of one's skin color begins nearly at birth: "Many Black families can barely disguise their anxious concern about the color and features of a newborn" (p. 94). Families often pass on a range of attitudes about skin color to children (Boyd-Franklin, 1989). For example, in some Black families, light skin color is prized and regarded as special, while in other Black families, dark-skinned members are preferred and light-skinned members are viewed as a constant reminder of the considerable shame and guilt attached to slavery and miscegenation.

Skin tone continues to affect relationships throughout different developmental periods. During childhood and early adolescence, overt and covert within group color bias exists, particularly where peer relationships are concerned. Some of this literature has found evidence that some prefer children with lighter complexions as friends over those with darker complexions (e.g., Vaughn & Langlois, 1983).

Moreover, findings from more recent studies provide evidence that skin color continues to be a significant predictor of educational attainment and socioeconomic status among Blacks. Several studies have found that even after controlling for participants' gender, age, and parental socioeconomic status, lighter skinned Blacks completed more years of schooling than darker skinned Blacks (Hughes & Hartel, 1990; Keith & Herring, 1991). In addition, Keith and Herring (1991) reported that the personal income among lighter skinned participants in their study was 65% greater than that of Black participants with darker complexions. Unfortunately, the tendency to discriminate based on skin color is not unique to the continental United States. Studies have shown that colorism exists in a number of countries around the world including Puerto Rico (Hall, 1997), Japan (Wagatsuma, 1968), India (Beteille, 1968), and the Central and South American countries of Brazil, Portugal, and Mexico (Russell et al., 1992). In all of these societies, as in the United States, skin color serves to stratify individuals' educational, occupational, and economic opportunities, with fewer opportunities afforded to those with the darkest skin, even though our current government would have us believe otherwise.

SKIN TONE AS DEVELOPMENTAL CHALLENGE FOR ADOLESCENTS OF COLOR

Body Image: A Normative Adolescent Challenge Exacerbated by Color Bias

For all human beings, the body is a fundamental component of lived experience; our body is always with us, consciously and unconsciously affecting our thoughts, feelings, and behaviors. Self-understanding and knowledge about the physical world develop, in part, as a consequence of our physical motor capabilities. Our bodies provide the means for us to physically explore our environments and interact with others. Self-awareness—the understanding that we exist apart from objects and other people—develops through our social interactions. As Vallacher (1980) pointed out, we become aware of ourselves because other people are aware of us. Children's developing abilities to take the perspective of another allows them to develop a sense of who they are as persons. Over time, children begin to internalize the perspectives of others, especially significant others such as their parents, friends, and teachers (Vallacher, 1980).

Being persons with particular bodies influences how other people respond to us. In turn, our perceptions of others' reactions toward our physical appearances influence how we respond to them. Thus, the mental representation of our physical selves (e.g., our body images) develops, in part, from our perception of how others evaluate our appearances. Consequently, when we reflect on our physical appearance, we use criteria that we have inferred from others and internalized as ours, especially during earlier stages of development. As we get older, although we are aware of others' attitudes toward us, we do not necessarily accept them as valid, particularly if they widely contradict our internalized views of self.

Our body image may or may not be accurate, in terms of objective reality (Weinshenker, 2002). Nevertheless, it influences how we feel about our appearances, and how we respond to those feelings despite whether we base our mental pictures on fantasy or reality. The affective component of body image is the emotional response or level of satisfaction we experience when comparing perceptions of our actual to ideal body image (e.g., the perceived perfect body). Our perception of the physical traits that our family, friends, and larger society value influences our mental image of the ideal body. When the gap between our actual and ideal body image is too large, it can lead to the development of a negative body image, diminished self-satisfaction, and maladaptive coping behaviors (e.g., eating disorders, illegal use of steroids).

There is a wealth of research on body image among adolescents (especially among girls), primarily because the transition into adolescence precipitates an increased focus on the self—both the inner self and the outer self. It is difficult for young people to escape from being preoccupied with their physical appearance given the dramatic bodily changes puberty ushers in, especially when others are always pointing out those changes with comments such as, "Is that hair I see growing on your chin?" or "You don't look like a little girl anymore." Further, with the onset of formal operational thought, adolescents become more introspective and more likely to engage in thinking about what others are thinking about them. For the first time, they begin to really see and appraise themselves through the perceived eyes of others (a realization of what they believe they represent to others by virtue of their physical appearance).

According to Damon and Hart (1988), a normative shift occurs between the early and late stages of adolescent self-concept development. Adolescents' self-reflection shifts from a heightened awareness of the body to a recognition of more abstract psychological processes. During early adolescence, youth base self-evaluations predominantly on normative standards, social comparisons, and behaviors, evolving into personal beliefs and standards during late adolescence. Given that early adolescence is a period when youths' social environments are rapidly expanding and their bodies are quickly changing, the task of meeting new people and trying to make a good first impression becomes a more frequent occurrence, and for some, a common source of anxiety. Youth often base first impressions on physical appearance, prompting adolescents to focus even more on their looks and how they measure up in the eyes of others. As a result, young people are continuously modifying their body image in response to others' perceived reactions.

It has been well documented that girls typically report greater levels of body dissatisfaction than boys (e.g., Rosenblum & Lewis, 1999; Kenealy, Gleeson, Prude, & Shaw, 1991), with White girls consistently reporting higher levels of dissatisfaction than Black girls (see Franko & Striegel-Moore, 2002). For example, in a recent study of children between the ages of 8 and 17 years, Thompson, Rafiroiu, and Sargent (2003) found that girls, regardless of age, were more likely to report being overweight and more concerned about their weight than boys are. These findings were more pronounced for older White girls than for older Black girls, although researchers did not find these differences among younger girls. Similarly, Parker et al. (1995) noted that Black and White adolescent girls in their study differed in the criteria they use in forming their images of the ideal body. They found that White girls tended to use the "Barbie Doll" ideal as the criterion for the perfect body, while Black girls had more flexible notions of attractiveness, basing their ideal body image on the specific features of their appearance that they considered attractive. However, other research with more racially diverse samples found that diminished body image satisfaction is not limited to White adolescent girls. In a large health survey study of adolescents, Story, French, Resnick, and Blum (1995) found that among girls in their study,

Asians, Hispanics, and Whites reported lower levels of body image satisfaction than Black and Native Americans did.

Altabe (1998) suggested that the reason researchers consistently detect racial differences in body image is because most research assesses weight related body image rather than nonweight related body image. She designed her study of a racially diverse group of college students to help fill the gap in knowledge about racial and gender differences in nonweight related body image. In addition to completing more traditional measures of body image and perceived attractiveness, participants completed the Physical Appearance Discrepancy Questionnaire (PADQ; Altabe, 1996); this measure asked respondents to list the physical traits that best describe their actual physical appearancse, ideal body images, and perception of physical traits their cultures valued most. Findings concerning body image dissatisfaction and ratings of physical attractiveness among females in the study were consistent with other findings. Whites displayed the most weight related body dissatisfaction and Blacks rated themselves higher in physical attractiveness than Hispanics who, in turn, rated themselves higher than Asians and Whites. In addition to replicating earlier findings, examinations of the five most frequently listed ideal body image traits revealed some interesting patterns—males and females in all racial groups listed height as an ideal trait; Asian and White males and all of the females listed being thinner; Black and White females and all of the males listed being more toned; Black, Hispanic, and Asian females listed having long or longer hair; and all of the groups listed having a different shade of skin color (either darker or lighter) as an ideal trait. Asians valued light skin the most, followed by Blacks. Conversely, all of the groups except Black females and Asian males included having a darker shade of skin color on their list of the top five ideal traits. However, when examining cultural values of attractiveness, a similar proportion of Asians and Blacks listed light or lighter skin as a culturally valued trait (23.5% and 21.2% respectively), with a smaller proportion of Hispanics and Whites listing light or lighter skin as a trait their cultures valued (10.5% and 8%, respectively). Findings from this study highlight the importance of examining physical traits other than body weight when examining racial differences in body image. Further, as indicated by participants' lists of culturally valued traits, college students from different racial groups were easily able to pinpoint physical traits they perceived as those that their cultural group valued. When does this awareness develop, and how does it affect our individual life outcomes? The following section addresses these questions by briefly reviewing research on children's skin color awareness and attitudes toward skin color.

RESEARCH ON SKIN COLOR
PERCEPTION AND ATTITUDES

Many of the early research findings on the perception of, and attitudes toward, skin color came from studies designed to assess young children's awareness of race and racial identity. For example, K. B. Clark and M. P. Clark (1939; 1940) studied racial identity and self-esteem among Black children and reported that children as young as three years old had knowledge about, and attitudes toward, skin color. Additionally, the children correctly self-identified as Black (e.g., African American), although K. B. Clark and M. P. Clark claimed that they were able to do so only because they based their self-selections on skin color (a concrete physical trait) rather than race (an abstract concept that is too advanced, cognitively, for children to understand). These studies led to perhaps the most well known study of skin color attitudes among Black children, the Clark Doll Study (Clark, K. B., & Clark, M. P., 1947). In this study, researchers presented children with a brown doll and a pinkish-white doll and asked them to make a series of forced-choice selections concerning things such as which doll they would like to play with, which doll is the good doll, or which doll has a nice color. In almost every situation, the majority of children selected the pinkish-white doll over the brown doll, findings that the Clarks believed were an indication of Black children's self-hatred and pro-White attitudes.

The results from this now legendary doll study helped determine the Supreme Court's 1954 landmark decision to strike down "separate but equal schooling" in *Brown v. Board of Education of Topeka, Kansas*. The court assumed that, by the early 1960s, schools would racially integrate and Blacks would simply assimilate into the mainstream culture (Steinhorn & Diggs-Brown, 1999). Theoretically, future studies of children's skin color attitudes should reflect the changing times. Ideally, Black children would no longer prefer light skin tones to darker skin tones, and White children would no longer automatically judge individuals by the color of their skin. Mandated racial integration of public schools would put the United States on the fast track to a "color-blind" society, one whose conscience dictates equal treatment for all. The problem, as Steinhorn and Diggs-Brown (1999) pointed out, is that ". . . integration is about people, not laws. It is about the way we *perceive* each other, about the way we act toward each other, about whether there will ever be room in our hearts, homes, classrooms, and communities to welcome each other as neighbors and friends" (p. 5). Unfortunately, it is difficult to change people's perceptions. As we will demonstrate, there is still a long road to travel in the quest for equality.

Subsequent research on children's skin color preferences and racial identifications generally supported the K. B. Clark and M. P. Clark's (1947) findings. Despite different types of props and stimuli (e.g., puppets, dolls, line drawings of children and animals, photographs of children and adults, etc.), researchers continued to find that both White and Black children evaluated light-skinned people more positively than dark-skinned people, and that all groups of children routinely displayed pro-White/anti-Black biases, although these biases were more pronounced among White children (e.g., Anderson & Cromwell, 1977; Landreth & Johnson, 1953; Moreland, 1963; Spencer & Horowitz, 1973; Spencer, 1984; Williams, Boswell, & Best, 1975). Moreover, preferences for light-skinned figures or the color white were found among children from both southern and northern regions of the United States (e.g., Asher & Allen, V. L., 1969; Greenwald & Oppenheim, 1968; Radke, Sutherland, & Rosenberg, 1950; Stevenson, H. W., & Stewart, 1958), suggesting that the tentacles of skin color bias extended beyond regions that overtly displayed racial bias and bigotry to regions that were seemingly more open-minded and less tolerant of blatant racism. It would appear that children are equally skilled in identifying overt and covert expressions of colorism.

Unfortunately, findings from skin color studies conducted within the past 20 years suggest that not much has changed. Studies among racially diverse groups of children, adolescents, and adults indicate that society has made little progress in changing pro-White/anti-Black biases (e.g., Averhart & Bigler, 1997; Bond & Cash, 1992; Cramer & Anderson, 2003; Porter, 1991). This is true despite technological improvements in stimuli that allow for more realistic, digitally altered images and the relatively recent use of neutral stimuli, such as color wheels and color bars, that eliminate bias based on physical appearance, in addition to allowing for a wider range of skin color selections. For example, in Averhart and Bigler's (1997) study of perceived skin color and racial attitudes among a sample of younger Black elementary school students, researchers presented children with five ceramic tiles, ranging in color from light tan to dark brown, and asked them to select the tile with the color that was most like their own skin color. The researchers then examined the association between children's skin color selections and their racial attitudes. Investigators read racially stereotypical and counterstereotypical stories about light- and dark-skinned Black characters to the children and later tested them for their memory of story details. They found that children who selected the lighter tiles as being most like their own skin color were more likely to remember racially stereotyped stories (those in which darker skinned characters were described with negative qualities and lighter skinned characters were described with positive qualities) than children who selected the darker tiles. Interestingly, experimenter ratings of children's actual skin colors did not relate to skin color attitudes and memory. Averhart and Bigler suggested that this was an indication that children's racial attitudes may alter their perceptions (or self-reports) of their own skin colors. If children perceive that dark skin is associated with negative traits, and if these traits do not fit into how they see themselves, they may change their perceptions of their own skin colors as a way of reducing dissonance.

The Developmental Significance of Race and Skin Color

During middle childhood and early adolescence, children's awareness of minority status differs substantially from earlier periods (Spencer, 1984). Very young children often conceive their race and gender as alterable, something that may change when they get older (Semaj, 1985; Allen, Spencer, & Brookins, 1985; Vaughan, 1987). Similar to preschool boys who sometimes aspire to be a Mommy when they grow up, young Black children may aspire to be White (Tatum, 1997). Pulido-Tobiassen and Gonzalez-Mena (1999) illustrated young children's logic concerning racial constancy in the following questions two preschoolers asked, "If I don't speak Spanish, can I still be a Mexican?" and "I want to have eyes like Miyoko's. If I learn Japanese, will my eyes change?" (p. 3).

In contrast to young children, older children have the ability to interpret differences in physical appearance based on the social meaning attached to them. For youth of color, an increased sensitivity to how members of the majority culture appraise their own minority groups compounds anxiety stemming from heightened bodily self-awareness (Comer, 1975; Fordham & Ogbu, 1986; Muga, 1984). With the inception of more advanced social perspective-taking abilities, young people become more vulnerable to messages transmitted through racially stereotyped media images, derogative labels, and sayings used to convey attitudes about dark skin tones (Brown, Ward, Lightbourn, & Jackson, 1999). One such catchphrase is, "If you're white you're alright, if you're yellow you're mellow, if you're brown stick around, if you're black get back." Regardless of the lightness or darkness of one's skin, perceptions of stereotypes based on skin color serve as a risk factor for all minority adolescents. Moreover, the awareness of negative societal appraisals can influence not only their social and emotional development, but also the choices they make in life and the tactics they choose to achieve them (Spencer & Dornbusch, 1990). Thus, for youth of color, and particularly for Black Americans, the task of integrating the frequently devalued physical characteristics of their race exacerbates the normative task of negotiating body image (e.g., facial characteristics, hair texture, and skin color) into their physical self-schemas (Fullilove & Reynolds, 1984).

If dark skin is such a liability, how is that some of these youth are thriving despite the dire odds? In the past, researchers have attempted to answer this question using a circuitous route. Instead of studying youth who were succeeding and attempting to uncover what makes these young people resilient, researchers concentrated their efforts on extreme groups of youth who were not successful (e.g., juvenile offenders, drug users, school dropouts, unwed parents, gang members) and tried to rehabilitate them or uncover traits or conditions (e.g., risk factors) that appeared to be related to their maladaptive behaviors. The problem with this approach is twofold. First, it pathologizes individuals and perpetuates the notion that youth of color are an inherent liability rather than an asset. Second, even if all of the risk factors (and combinations of risk factors) could be identified, they cannot all be eliminated (e.g., race, gender). It would be more beneficial and cost effective to ask what one could do to prevent detrimental outcomes and to identify supports or buffers that one could put in place to support their optimal developments.

Research suggests that one source of support is the racial socialization of children by parents and other adults. Minority parents can, and often do, socialize their children to understand the importance and implication of race and skin color. Peters (1985) claimed that racial socialization is necessary for "raising physically and emotionally healthy children who are Black in a society where Black has negative connotations" (p. 161). Concurring with this sentiment, Spencer, Dupree, and Hartman (1997) suggested that the childrearing efforts of minority parents demand, of necessity, the imparting of clear and explicit explanations to their children concerning the meaning and significance of their children's skin colors and races. Research has found that racial socialization practices can help children learn to cope more adaptively with experiences of racism and discrimination (Stevenson, H. C., 1994).

It is important to note that skin color can serve as both a risk and a protective factor. For lighter skinned minority youth, the privilege associated with light skin might initially serve as a protective factor because others (especially peers, teachers, and other adult figures) tend to judge adolescents with a lighter skin color more positively, thus hindering the perception and internalization of mainstream cultures' negative racial stereotypes. This same privilege, however, may also be a risk factor because, as is the case for more affluent White youth, privilege may preclude the development of adaptive coping skills. Thus, when faced with adversity for the first time, these youth may be shocked to learn that they are not immune from being a target of racial discrimination and bigotry. In the absence of previously developed coping skills, these experiences might cause young people to employ maladaptive coping skills that may temporarily reduce their psychological distress, but, in the long run, serve to undermine their ultimate life outcomes (e.g., quitting college, limiting opportunities due to fear of rejection).

Viewed against the backdrop of the history of colorism in the United States, we have tried to illustrate the impact that bodily self-awareness and color bias can have on multiple domains of life, including psychological development. For youth of color, experiences related to skin color bias are stress encounters that they must negotiate in conjunction with normative developmental challenges such as rapidly changing bodies and developing a positive body image. Ultimately, the ways in which youth cope with these challenges (e.g., reactive coping responses) can lead to either adaptive or maladaptive solutions that, over time, may become a stable part of adolescents' identities. We know that our perceptions of self and other peoples' attitudes toward us influence our behaviors (e.g., Spencer, 1995). It is less clear how the mental images that adolescents construct of their physical appearances (including skin color) and their perceptions about what physical traits society values (or devalues) most affect adolescents' identities and psychological well-being.

The following exploratory study is an initial attempt to untangle the processes that might be important in understanding the role of the embodied self in psychosocial development. It would be imprudent to test a model of skin color perceptions and attitudes before understanding the links between various constructs and processes. Thus, as a beginning point, we selected a limited set of variables to represent the five components of PVEST including perceived skin color and preferences as the *risk* component, ideal body image stereotypes as the perceived *challenge*, ethnic identity as a *protective* factor, worrying about neighborhood-related risks as a *reactive coping* response, and positive self-attitudes as an emergent *identity*. It is expected that adolescents who express dissonance about the color of their skin (e.g., those who indicate that they prefer a skin color other than the color they select as being most like their own) will report engaging in less ethnic identity exploration, will be less satisfied with their body images, and will have less positive attitudes about self and more anxiety related to neighborhood characteristics than adolescents who do not experience dissonance concerning their skin color (e.g., those whose perceived skin color is consonant with their preferred skin color). We will conduct post hoc exploratory analyses to examine within group differences.

An Exploratory Study of Skin Color Perceptions and Attitudes

Study Sample. The sample for the present study is comprised of a subsample (Cohort 1) of adolescents who were part of a longitudinal randomized field trial looking at the effect of monetary stipends on the academic achievement of low resource urban youth. Two groups of low-income[1] adolescents, high-academic performers (A/B students), and marginal-academic performers (C/D students) attending public high school in a large northeastern city of the United States were recruited from grades 9, 10, and 11 and were randomly assigned to "control" and "treatment" groups. Researchers drew the data for this study from baseline data collected in 1999 and 2000; 779 participants completed their baseline assessment; 65% were high-achieving students; 69% were females; 15% were Asian/Asian American, 56% were Black/African American, 11% were Hispanic/Latino, 7% were White/European American, and 11% indicated their race/ethnicity as "Other."

Procedures. A team of trained research assistants administered annual surveys to participants. Survey administrations took place either in large group settings at geographically central locations or in smaller group settings at students' schools and at our research center. We offered participants $25 incentives to complete their annual surveys and informed them that tokens for public transportation would be available for students who took public transportation to and from the survey site.

Demographic Variables. Researchers took demographic information from respondents' answers to questions on their baseline survey including age, race, ethnicity, family household structure, and maternal employment. Respondents' mean age was 15.36 years (SD = 1.18); 35% lived in two-parent households, 53% lived in single-parent households (2% father only), and 12% lived with their grandparents or other relatives and adults. Among students who reported living with their mother (including two-parent and single-parent households), 64% of the mothers were employed, with 71% of the employed mothers working full time.

The Measurement of Skin Color. Adolescents *perceptions* of, and *attitudes* toward, skin color were assessed using the *Skin Color Opinions and Perceptions Evaluation* (SCOPE), a 17-item questionnaire comprised of questions related to participants' perceptions of their own skin colors, the skin colors they would *most* like and *least* like to have and questions assessing their perceptions of the skin colors that "referent others," such as teachers, peers, and other adults, value most. Adolescents indicated their skin color choices using the *Visual Inventory for Skin Tone Assessment* (VISTA)—a commercially produced, glossy-finished, 15-inch color bar developed specifically for this project. The VISTA is comprised of 10 colors arrayed across the bar from lightest to darkest. Researchers selected colors on the VISTA from a wide range of human skin-tone colors that they presented to a pilot group of students who they then asked to select the color that was most like their own shade of skin color. Based on information gathered during the pilot period, researchers ultimately reduced the selection of colors to 10.

Psychosocial Measures

Body image satisfaction.[2] We assessed body image satisfaction using the seven-item appearance evaluation subscale of Cash's *Multidimensional Body Self-Relations Questionnaire* (as cited in Thompson, Heinberg, Altabe, & Tanleff, 1999); a measure that assesses overall satisfaction with one's appearance (e.g., feelings of attractiveness and unattractiveness). Students rated, on a scale of one to four, the extent to which they agreed or disagreed with statements such as, "I am physically unattractive" and "Most people would consider me good looking." The alpha reliability for this measure was .88 and the mean was 48.01 (SD = 10.08).

Ethnic identity. We assessed ethnic identity using Phinney's *Multigroup Ethnic Identity Measure* (Phinney, 1992), a 23-item scale designed to explore the structure of ethnic identity in adolescents and young adults from diverse ethno-cultural groups. We used only the 16 items included in the *revised MEIM* (see Roberts et al., 1999) to construct the scaled scores used in these analyses. Participants rated, on a scale of one to four, the extent to which they agreed or disagreed with statements such as, "I have spent time trying to find out more about my own ethnic group, such as its history, traditions, and customs" and "I have a clear sense of my ethnic background and what it means for me." The alpha reliability for this measure was .83 and the mean was 48.71 (SD = 10.01).

Worry about neighborhood-related risks. We assessed the extent to which adolescents' worry about risks in their neighborhood using an eight-item version of the *Fear of Calamity Scale* (Riechard & McGarrity, 1994). Students rated, on a scale of one to five, how much they worried about various risks in their neighborhood, such as getting stabbed or getting beat up. The alpha reliability for this measure was .91 and the mean was 46.55 (SD = 15.57).

Positive attitudes about self. Positive attitudes about self were assessed using the *Hare/Funder/Block Ego-Esteem/Resilience Scale* (Hare, 1977;

Shoemaker, 1980; Block, 1985; Hare & Castenell, 1985), a self-report inventory comprised of 23 items drawn from the Hare Self-Esteem Scale (items are expressions of individuals' perception of others' positive views of self) and the Funder/Block ego-resiliency Q-sort measure (items are self-assertions of attitudes and behaviors). Respondents rated, on a scale of one to four, the extent to which they agreed or disagreed with statements such as, "I am generous with my friends" or "Most of the people I meet are likeable." The alpha reliability for this measure was .85 and the mean was 48.95 (SD = 9.99).

Gender, achievement and racial group differences in scores on psychosocial measures. We used the analysis of variance and t-test statistical methods to examine mean group differences on measures of body image satisfaction, positive attitudes about self, ethnic identity, and fear of calamity. Scores on measures of body image satisfaction, positive attitudes about self, and ethnic identity did not differ significantly between males and females. However, the mean fear of calamity score for females ($M = 47.46, SD = 15.31$) was significantly higher than the mean score for males ($M = 44.47, SD = 15.96$), $t(775) = -2.47, p = .014$), indicating that adolescent girls reported worrying more about risks in their neighborhood than did the boys.

High- and marginal-achieving adolescents' mean group scores differed for all psychosocial measures except fear of calamity. The mean body image satisfaction score for the marginally performing group of adolescents ($M = 49.08, SD = 10.13$) was significantly higher than that for the high performing group ($M = 47.44, SD = 10.02$), $t(759) = 2.14, p = .033$). Conversely, the high performing group was significantly more likely than the marginally performing group to score higher on measures of positive attitudes about self ($M = 50.15$ and $46.77, SD = 9.88$ and 9.85, respectively), $t(775) = -4.56, p < .0001$), and ethnic identity ($Ms = 50.06$ and $46.24, SDs = 9.56$ and 10.35, respectively), t(773) = -5.17, p < .0001$).

Racial mean group scores differed on measures of body image satisfaction ($F(4, 756) = 33.03, p < .0001$), positive attitudes about self, $F(4, 772) = 10.98, p < .0001$, and fear of calamity, $F(4, 772) = 2.51, p = .04$. Exploratory post hoc analyses using Tukey's Standardized Range test (alpha = .001) revealed that the mean body image satisfaction scores and positive attitudes about self scores for the Asian group were significantly lower than the average mean scores for all other racial groups ($Ms = 50.63, 49.12, 47.44, 44.68$ and 39.78 for body image satisfaction and $50.11, 48.51, 50.34, 49.74,$ and 43.56 for positive attitudes about self for Black, Other, Hispanic, White, and Asian groups, respectively). Further, post hoc analyses revealed that the White mean group score on the measure of fear of calamity was significantly lower (at the .005 alpha level) than the mean scores for all other racial groups (Ms = 48.52, 47.31, 45.9, 45.2 and 41.21 for Hispanic, Black, Asian, Other, and White groups, respectively).

Skin Color Analyses. Analyses using variables from the SCOPE questionnaire omitted 23 participants due to incomplete or inconsistent data (e.g., participants who selected the same answer for most preferred and least preferred skin color were omitted from the analyses). These participants did not differ significantly from participants in the analysis group by gender, race/ethnicity, or academic achievement.

Perceived skin color. The variable *perceived skin color* is a categorical variable created from adolescents' responses to the following item on the SCOPE, "Choose the color that you think best represents the color of your facial skin." We constructed the variable by collapsing the 10 skin tone selections into three categories: (a) light, which includes participants who selected one of the four lightest skin tones, (b) medium, which includes participants who selected one of two medium skin tones, and (c) dark, which includes participants who selected one of the four darkest skin tones.

We conducted chi-square analyses to examine gender, achievement, and racial group differences in adolescents' perceived skin color group (see Table 11.1). We used analysis of variance to examine mean perceived skin color group differences on measures of body image satisfaction, positive attitudes about self, ethnic identity, and fear of calamity. We conducted post hoc analyses using Tukey's Standardized Range test (alpha = .001) to examine pair-wise comparisons on scores for measures where the omnibus F test reached the .05 level of significance.

As indicated in Table 11.1, there were no significant differences in adolescents' scores on measures of ethnic identity and fear of calamity as a function of their perceived skin color. And, although the omnibus F test for perceived skin color group differences in scores on positive attitudes about the self reached the .05 level of significance, the post hoc analyses showed only a slight tendency (alpha = .05) for the group of participants who self selected one of the four lightest skin tones to score lower in positive attitudes about the self than those in groups who selected medium and dark skin tones. However, there was a robust difference between perceived skin color group mean scores on the measure of body image satisfaction, with the light skin tone group mean score being significantly lower than the mean scores of the medium and dark perceived skin color groups.

Table 11.1 Perceived Skin Color Distribution by Demographic (%) and Psychosocial Mean Group Scores

Demographic Group	Perceived Skin Color (Self Rating)		
	Light Tones	Medium Tones	Dark Tones
Gender	($n = 206$)	($n = 324$)	($n = 225$)
% Male ($n = 230$)	25.65	36.52	37.83
% Female ($n = 525$)	28.00	45.71	26.29
Achievement			
% High Achievers ($n = 491$)	33.20	41.55	25.25
% Marginal Achievers ($n = 264$)	16.29	45.45	38.26
Race/Ethnicity			
% Asian/Asian Am. ($n = 112$)	58.93	35.71	5.36
% Black/African Am. ($n = 424$)	8.25	46.70	45.05
% Hispanic/Latino ($n = 79$)	41.77	51.90	6.33
% White/Euro. Am. ($n = 57$)	91.23	8.77	-
% 'Other' ($n = 83$)	24.1	48.19	27.71
Psychosocial Measures			
Body Image Satisfaction $F(2, 737) = 18.89, p < .0001$	$M = 44.4$	$M = 49.29$	$M = 49.55$
General Positive Attitude $F(2, 752) = 3.47, p = .031$	$M = 47.44$	$M = 49.7$	$M = 49.35$
Ethnic Identity Development	$M = 48.39$	$M = 49.03$	$M = 48.84$
Fear of Calamity	$M = 45.12$	$M = 47.63$	$M = 46.03$

Perceptions of actual and ideal skin color. We constructed the variable *skin color preference* using two items from the SCOPE, "Choose the color that you think best represents the color of your facial skin" (e.g., actual skin color) and "Choose the facial skin color that you would prefer to have" (e.g., ideal skin color). We classified adolescents who selected the same color for their actual an ideal skin colors as *consonant* for skin color preference, and we classified those who selected two different skin tones for their actual and ideal skin color as *dissonant* for skin color preference.

Gender, academic, racial and perceived skin color group differences in scores on psychosocial measures. We conducted chi-square analyses to examine gender, achievement, racial, and perceived skin color group differences in adolescents' skin color preference. As depicted in Table 11.2, there were no gender differences in skin color preference. Adolescent boys were no more likely than girls were to be *consonant* in

Table 11.2 Demographic and Perceived Skin Color Differences (%) in Skin Color Consonance and Dissonance

Demographic Group	Consonant	Dissonant
Gender	($n = 384$)	($n = 365$)
% Male ($n = 226$)	51.33	48.67
% Female ($n = 523$)	51.24	48.76
Achievement: $\chi^2 = 5.52, p = .02$.		
% High Achievers ($n = 485$)	54.43	45.57
% Marginal Achievers ($n = 264$)	45.45	54.55
Race: $\chi^2 = 9.95, p = .04$		
% Asian/Asian Am. ($n = 110$)	39.09	60.91
% Black/African Am. ($n = 421$)	54.87	45.13
% Hispanic/Latino ($n = 79$)	53.16	46.84
% White/Euro. Am. ($n = 56$)	53.57	46.43
% 'Other' ($n = 83$)	45.78	54.22
Perceived Skin Color: $\chi^2 = 11.1, p = .004$		
% Light Tones ($n = 206$)	50.97	49.03
% Medium Tones ($n = 319$)	57.37	42.63
% Dark Tones ($n = 224$)	42.86	57.14

their actual and ideal perceived skin colors, and adolescent girls were no more likely than boys were to be *dissonant* in their actual and ideal perceived skin colors. However, there was a slight tendency for high-achieving adolescents to be in the *consonant* skin preference group and for the adolescents who were not doing as well academically to be in the *dissonant* group. Further, in terms of racial group differences, Asian students, in comparison to their peers in other racial groups, were more likely to be *dissonant* in their skin color preference.

Finally, when examining whether skin color preference differed as a function of adolescents' perceptions of their actual skin color, adolescents in the light skin color group were just as likely to be in the *dissonant* skin preference group as they were to be in the *consonant* group. However, adolescents in the medium skin color group were more likely than their peers in the light and dark skin color groups to be *consonant* in skin color preference, while adolescents in the dark skin color group were more likely than their peers in the light and medium skin color groups to be *dissonant* in their skin color preference.

T-tests were conducted to examine whether group scores on body image satisfaction, positive attitudes about the self, ethnic identity, and fear of calamity differed by skin color preference (see Table 11.3). Over-

Table 11.3 Mean Scores on Psychosocial Measures by Skin Color Consonance and Dissonance

Psychosocial Measures	Consonant ($n = 384$)	Dissonant ($n = 365$)
Body Image Satisfaction $t (731) = -6.00, p < .0001$	50.2 ($SD = 9.83$)	45.87 ($SD = 9.67$)
General Positive Attitude $t (745) = -4.81, p < .0001$	50.7 ($SD = 9.7$)	47.21 ($SD = 9.94$)
Ethnic Identity Development $t (723) = -3.48, p = .0005$	50.04 ($SD = 9.35$)	47.5 ($SD = 10.5$)
Fear of Calamity $t (742) = 2.69, p = .007$	45.04 ($SD = 16.5$)	48.08 ($SD = 14.4$)

all, adolescents who reported preferring a skin color other than the color they selected as best reflecting their own skin color (e.g., the *dissonant* group) reported being less satisfied with their physical appearance, less positive views about self, and experiencing more fear of calamity than their peers who selected the same color for their actual and ideal skin color (e.g., the *consonant* group). In addition, the mean ethnic identity score for the dissonant group was significantly lower than that for the consonant group. These findings suggest that the affective component of adolescents' actual and ideal skin color perceptions is related to their self-reports of body image satisfaction, positive attitudes about self, and the extent to which they have begun to explore their ethnic identity. However, are these findings more salient among different groups of youth?

In light of the fact that scores on various psychosocial measures differed as a function of race and perceived skin color, we conducted a second series of *t*-tests within these groups to see if the same pattern of skin color preference findings would be detected for different groups of youth. We first examined differences within racial groups. We found the same pattern of findings among our samples' Black youth; the dissonant group's mean scores were lower for body image satisfaction, positive attitudes about self, and ethnic identity, and higher for fear of calamity than those for the consonant group. And, although the mean scores for the consonant and dissonant groups within the Hispanic and "Other" groups of youth followed the same overall pattern, the only significant mean score differences between youth in the consonant and dissonant groups were in positive attitudes about self and body image satisfaction (although a trend only in the "Other" group). Among youth in the White group, there were no significant differences between the dissonant and consonant group mean scores on ethnic identity, fear of calamity, and positive attitudes about self, although the mean body image satisfaction score for the consonant group was significantly higher than that for the dissonant group. Interestingly, among our sample of Asian youth, scores on body image satisfaction, positive attitudes about self, and ethnic identity development did not differ by virtue of skin color consonance or dissonance, although there was a trend for adolescents in the dissonant group to express higher levels of fear of calamity than their peers in the consonant skin preference group. Given that our sample of Asian youth scored significantly lower overall on body image satisfaction and positive attitudes about the self than participants from all other racial groups, it is difficult to conclude whether these findings are a result of a ceiling effect or whether skin color preference makes no significant contribution to Asian participants' scores on body image satisfaction and positive feelings toward self.

When examining differences between consonant and dissonant groups of youth within preferred skin color groups, we detected the same general pattern of findings. Overall, the dissonant group within the light, medium, and dark skin tone groups had significantly lower mean body image satisfaction scores than their counterparts in the consonant group. However, the pattern of findings for positive attitudes about self, ethnic identity, and fear of calamity deviated slightly from the overall pattern depending upon perceived skin color. When examining differences between groups of consonant and dissonant youth, there were no significant differences in positive attitudes about self among adolescents in the light skin tone group, within the medium skin tone group there were no significant differences in ethnic identity development, and within the dark skin tone group, there were no significant differences in fear of calamity.

DISCUSSION OF EMPIRICAL FINDINGS

Consistent with early speculations, specifically about African Americans (Franklin, 1968; Kardiner & Ovesey, 1951; Pettigrew, 1964), there continues to be long term interest in the role that skin color serves in individuals' social experiences and psychological well-being. In fact, for the virtual 50-year interim period between early touted, and often incendiary, assumptions concerning color/racial group membership as a "mark of oppression" (see Kardiner & Ovesey, 1951), interest in the topic has not abated. However, exploratory and empirical efforts to disentangle the relationships between race, color, context, and psychological development remain sparse. Specific measurement challenges along with the need for studies that directly link skin color with psychological *processes* (e.g., as opposed to a priori assumptions of psychopathology for minority groups) were suggested over 30 years ago (e.g., see Spencer & Horowitz 1973; Spencer 1977, 1983). Unfortunately, evidence supporting the assumed relationship continues to be elusive while pathology linked speculations remain evident across disciplinary lines.

Researches have cited a variety of reasons for the lack of advancement in colorism research; one of the most frequently noted is the lack of good measurement tools. However, as demonstrated in Kardiner and Ovesey's (1950) widely cited volume, *Mark of Oppression*, another important conceptual shortcoming of the literature has been the assumption of a *linear* (and *pathological*) relationship between skin color/ racial group membership and psychological well-being. The intent of this chapter was to introduce a systems perspective for understanding the complex processes underlying the impact of individuals' skin color perceptions and attitudes on psychological development and to open discussion of possible intervening, context-linked, mediating factors that might suggest strategies for exploring and testing more complex sets of relationships.

This chapter provides a first step toward understanding the role of adolescents' self-perceptions of skin color for psychological processes. The reported research introduced an alternative theoretical framework that views human development from a systems perspective that includes an individual's contextually linked phenomenology or perceptions. As a systems perspective, PVEST affords a conceptual strategy that is different from the traditional linear models frequently employed when considering issues of colorism. As mentioned, analyses of data from our multiethnic sample utilized measures generally associated with *risk* factors (e.g., race and skin color), their transformation into specific perceived *challenges* (e.g., the degree of consonance between perceptions of actual and ideal body image), *protective* factors (e.g., ethnic identity as proxy for racial socialization), *reactive coping* methods (e.g., degree of neighborhood-related worry and fear), and emergent *identities* (e.g., self-concept).

The most salient overarching trend in this study is that adolescents' skin color consonance or dissonance, rather than perceived skin tone itself, was most relevant to their psychosocial outcomes. We illustrated the utility of a contextually sensitive, identity-focused perspective, such as PVEST, here. Contrary to the assumption that dark skin leads to maladaptive coping and poor psychosocial outcomes, the findings indicate that one can attain consonance—relative satisfaction with one's skin color—regardless of skin tone, in spite of the fact that a large bias toward light skin remains in American society. Individuals with darker skin tone must cope with these biases, but they can learn to do so in adaptive ways, given adequate social and cultural capital. This highlights the importance of proactive racial and cultural socialization—a necessity to prevent societal biases from adversely impacting the development of children of color.

The lack of significant differences in ethnic identity and fear of calamity scores for adolescents who differed in self-perceived skin color (e.g., those in the light, medium, and dark self-rated skin color groups) stands in contradiction to previous assumptions. As noted, one might presume, based on cultural socialization theorizing, that parental cultural socialization of ethnic identity would serve as a protective factor. However, ethnic identity scores did not vary as a function of distance from the "societal norm" relative to skin color. Also somewhat surprising were the significantly lower scores on body image satisfaction *and* positive attitudes about self among adolescents in the lightest skin tone group relative to their peers in the two darker skin color groups. One explanation may be that young people having lighter skin tone self-ratings are also sensitive to externally based expectations for stereotypic body image attitudes; thus, a consequence of feeling less satisfied with your physical appearance may be an emergent identity that is less positive overall, than those who feel more satisfied with their appearance. However, does this pattern suggest that these youth, in fact, are more psychologically vulnerable and require particular types of support?

The findings also raise other questions. Higher achieving youth were more likely to report skin color consonance, and marginal performers more often reported skin color dissonance. Does this indicate that one links marginal performance, as an outcome, to such youths' "misuse" of psychic energy? That is, are youth focusing their limited psychological resources on concerns about skin color perception and skin color-based biases (e.g., feelings of dissonance) that instead one might ideally better use for academic pursuits? The fact that the analyses examining differences in scores on psychosocial variables by both skin color consonance and dissonance and skin tone ratings were similar to patterns obtained *within* racial groups suggests interesting speculations. Are the color stereotypes concerning "Whiteness" psychologically powerful enough on their own to have such an effect for the several racial groups or do adolescents associate "power and privilege" with a specific shade of skin color that one desires to the point of generating dissonance? The sets of analysis presented in this chapter cannot answer these questions. However, they suggest far more complex interactions between skin tone values and psychosocial well-being than previously explored.

Finally, the study initiates the process of placing skin color, as a salient physical attribute, within the realm of body image and physical appearance concerns of adolescents. For people of color, one should examine colorism, skin color attitudes, and perceptions in conjunction with the numerous other social biases governing appearance, such as those related to body weight and dimensions, eye and hair color, and so forth. Moreover, one should factor the additional sociopolitical significance of color—the legacy of Jim Crow and other manifestations of White supremacy—into this analysis.

CONCLUSION

As America enters the 21st century, we are in the post-Civil-Rights era—a time where formal legal distinctions based on race and color are moot. However, we should not be naïve enough to assume that color-blind law translates to a color-blind society, nor should we hold to the simplistic, pathological formulations regarding skin color that were espoused in the past. We hope that this chapter will help researchers move beyond past errors to understand the changing, albeit continuing, significance of race and skin color in shaping children's lives.

ENDNOTES

1. Adolescents who were eligible for the study provided verifiable proof that their family's total household income met the financial criteria guidelines for the Federal Free Lunch Program (130% of the poverty line).

2. For each psychosocial scale or subscale, researchers computed students' raw scale scores as the unit-weighted sum of salient items and then transformed to area T conversion scores, a method of standardizing scores that does not assume linearity.

REFERENCES

Allen, W. R., Spencer, M. B., & Brookins, G. K. (1985). Synthesis: Black children keep on growing. In M. B. Spencer, G. K. Brookins, & W. R. Allen (Eds.), *Beginnings: The social and affective development of Black children* (pp. 301–314). Hillsdale, NJ: Lawrence Erlbaum Associates.

Altabe, M. (1996). Issues in the assessment and treatment of body image disturbance in culturally diverse populations. In J. K. Thompson (Ed.), *Eating disorders, obesity, and body image: A practical guide to assessment and treatment* (129–147). Washington, DC: American Psychological Association Books.

Altabe, M. (1998). Ethnicity and body image: Quantitative and qualitative analysis. *International Journal of Eating Disorders, 2*, 153–159.

Anderson, C., & Cromwell, R. L. (1977). "Black is beautiful" and the color preferences of Afro-American youth. *Journal of Negro Education, 46*, 76–88.

Asher, S. R., & Allen, V. L. (1969). Racial preference and social comparison processes. *Journal of Social Issues, 25*(1), 157–166.

Averhart, C. J., & Bigler, R. S. (1997). Shades of meaning: Skin tone, racial attitudes, and constructive memory in African American children. *Journal of Experimental Child Psychology, 67*, 363–388.

Beteille, H. (1968). Race and descent as social categories in India. In J. H. Franklin (Ed.), *Color and race* (166–185). Boston: Beacon Press.

Blackwell, J. E. (1985). *The Black community: Diversity and unity.* New York: Dodd, Mead.

Block, J. (1985). *Some relationships regarding the self emanating from the Block and Block longitudinal study.* Paper presented at the SSRC conference, Center for Advanced Study in the Behavioral Sciences, Stanford, CA.

Bond, S., & Cash, T. F. (1992). Black beauty: Skin color and body images among African American college women. *Journal of Applied Social Psychology, 22*, 874–888.

Boyd-Franklin, N. (1989). *Black families in therapy.* New York: Guilford.

Bronfenbrenner, U. (1979). *The ecology of human development: Experiments by nature and design.* Cambridge, MA: Harvard University Press.

Brown, K. T., Ward, G. K., Lightbourn, T., & Jackson, J. S. (1999). Skin tone and racial identity among African Americans: A theoretical and research framework. In. R. L. Jones (Ed.), *Advances in African American psychology* (pp. 191–215). Hampton, VA: Cobb & Henry Press.

Clark, K. B., & Clark, M. P. (1939). The development of consciousness of self and the emergence of racial identity in Negro preschool children. *Journal of Social Psychology, 10*, 591–599.

Clark, K. B., & Clark, M. P. (1940). Skin color as a factor in racial identification of Negro preschool children. *Journal of Social Psychology, 2*, 159–169.

Clark, K. B., & Clark, M. P. (1947). Racial identification and preferences in Negro children. In T. M. Bewcomb, & E. L. Hartley (Eds.), *Readings in social psychology* (pp. 169–178). New York: Holt.

Comer, J. P. (1975). Black child care: How to bring up a healthy Black child in America: A guide to emotional and psychological development. New York: Schuster.

Cramer, P., & Anderson, G. (2003). Ethnic/racial attitudes and self-identification of Black Jamaican and White New England children. *Journal of Cross-Cultural Psychology, 34*, 395–416.

Damon, W., & Hart, D. (1988). *Self understanding in childhood and adolescence.* New York: Cambridge University Press.

Fordham, S., & Ogbu, J. U. (1986). Black students' school success: Coping with the "burden of 'acting White.'" *The Urban Review, 18*(3), 176–206.

Franklin, J. H. (Ed.). (1968). *Color and race.* Boston, MA: Beacon Press.

Franklin, J. H. (1980). *From slavery to freedom* (5th ed.). New York: Knopf.

Franko, D. L., & Striegel-Moore, R. H. (2002). The role of body dissatisfaction as a risk factor for depression in adolescent girls: are the differences Black and White? *Journal of Psychosomatic Research, 53,* 975–983.

Frazier, E. F. (1957). *The Black bourgeoisie.* New York: Free Press.

Fullilove, M. T., & Reynolds, T. (1984). Skin color in the development of identity: A biopsychosocial model. *Journal of the National Medical Association, 76,* 587–591.

Greenwald, H. J., & Oppenheim, D. B. (1968). Reported magnitude of self-misidentification among Negro children-artifacts? *Journal of Personality and Social Psychology, 8,* 49–52.

Hall, R. E. (1997). *The psychogenesis of color based racism: implications of projection for dark-skinned Puertorriqueños* (JRSI Research Report No. 21). East Lansing, MI: The Julian Samora Research Institute, Michigan State University.

Hare, B. R. (1977). Racial and socioeconomic variation in preadolescent area-specific and general self-esteem. *International Journal of Intercultural Relations, 3,* 31–51.

Hare, B. R., & Castenell, L. A., Jr. (1985). No place to run, no place to hide: Comparative status and future prospects of black boys. In M. B. Spencer, G. K Brookins, & W. R. Allen (Eds.), *Beginnings: The social and affective development of Black children* (pp. 201–214). Hillsdale, NJ: Lawrence Erlbaum Associates.

Hughes, M., & Hartel, B. R. (1990). The significance of color remains: A study of life chances, mate selection, and ethnic consciousness among Black Americans. *Social Forces, 68,* 1105–1120.

Hunter, M. (2004). Light, bright, and almost white: The advantages and disadvantages of light skin. In C. Herring, V. M. Keith, & H. D. Horton (Eds.), Skin deep: How race and complexion matter in the "color-blind" era (pp. 22–44). Chicago: University of Illinois Press.

Izrael, J. (2001). Skin games: Color and skin tone in the black community. *Africana: Gateway to the Black world.* Retrieved December 15, 2003, from http://www.africana.com/articles/daily/index_20010108.asp

Kardiner, A., & Ovesey, L. (1951). *The mark of oppression.* Cleveland, OH: World Publishing.

Keith, V., & Herring, C. (1991). Skin tone and stratification in the Black community. *American Journal of Sociology, 97,* 760–778.

Kenealy, P., Gleeson, K., Prude, N., & Shaw, W. (1991). The importance of the individual in the "causal" relationship between attractiveness and self-esteem. *Journal of Community and Applied Psychology, 11,* 45–46.

Landreth, C., & Johnson, B. C. (1953). Young children's responses to a picture and inset test designed to reveal reactions to persons of different skin color. *Child Development, 24,* 63–80.

Landry, B. (1987). *The new middle class.* Berkeley, CA: University of California Press.

Maddox, K. B. (1998). *Cognitive representation of light- vs. dark-skinned blacks: Structure, content, and use of the African American stereotype.* Unpublished doctoral dissertation, University of California, Santa Barbara, CA.

Moreland, J. K. (1963). Racial self-identification: A study of nursery school children. *American Catholic Sociological Review, 24,* 231–242.

Muga, D. (1984). Academic sub-cultural theory and the problematic of ethnicity: A tentative critique. *Journal of Ethnic Studies, 12,* 1–52.

Parker, S., Nichter, M., Nichter, M., Vuckovic, N., Sims, C., & Ritenbaugh, C. (1995). Body image and weight concerns among African American and White adolescent females: Differences that make a difference. *Human Organization, 54,* 103–113.

Peters, M. F. (1985). Racial socialization of young Black children. In H. P. McAdoo, & J. L. McAdoo (Eds.), *Black children: Social, education and parental environments* (pp. 159–173). Newbury Park, CA: Sage.

Pettigrew, T. F. (1964). *A profile of the Negro American.* Princeton, NJ: D. Van Nostrand Company, Inc.

Phinney, J. S. (1992). The multigroup ethnic identity measure: A new scale for use with adolescents and young adults from diverse groups. *Journal of Adolescent Research, 7,* 156–176.

Porter, C. P. (1991). Social reasons for skin tone preferences of Black school-age children. *American Journal of Orthopsychiatry, 61,* 149–154.

Pulido-Tobiassen, D., & Gonzalez-Mena, J. (1999). *A place to begin: Working with parents on issues of diversity.* Oakland, CA: California Tomorrow.

Radke, M., Sutherland, J., & Rosenberg, P. (1950). Racial attitudes of children. *Sociometry, 13,* 154-171.

Riechard, D. E., & McGarrity, J. (1994). Early adolescents' perceptions of relative risk from 10 societal and environmental hazards. *Journal of Environmental Education, 26,* 16–23.

Roberts, R., Phinney, J., Masse, L., Chen, Y., Roberts, C., & Romera, A. (1999). The structure of ethnic identity in young adolescents from diverse ethnocultural groups. *Journal of Early Adolescence, 19,* 301–322.

Rosenblum, G. D., & Lewis, M. (1999). The relations among body image, physical attractiveness, and body mass in adolescence. *Child Development, 70,* 50–64.

Russell, K., Wilson, M., & Hall, R. (1992). *The color complex: The politics of skin color among African Americans.* New York: Anchor Books.

Semaj, L. T. (1985). Afrikanity, cognition, and extended self-identity. In M. B. Spencer, G. K. Brookins, & W. R. Allen (Eds.), *Beginnings: The social and affective development of Black children* (pp. 173–183). Hillsdale, NJ: Lawrence Erlbaum Associates.

Shoemaker, A. L. (1980). Construct validity of area specific self-esteem: The Hare Self-Esteem Scale. *Educational and Psychological Measurement, 40,* 495–501.

Spencer, M. B. (1977, July). The social-cognitive and personality development of the Black preschool child: An exploratory study of developmental process. *Dissertation Abstracts International, 38*(1), 970.

Spencer, M. B. (1983). Children's cultural values and parental child rearing strategies. *Developmental Review, 3*, 351–370.

Spencer, M. B. (1984). Black children's race awareness, racial attitudes and self-concept: A reinterpretation. *Journal of Child Psychology and Psychiatry, 25*, 443–441.

Spencer, M. B. (1995). Old issues and new theorizing about African-American youth: A phenomenological variant of ecological systems theory. In R. L. Taylor (Ed.), *Black youth: Perspectives on their status in the United States* (pp. 37–70). Westport, CT: Praeger.

Spencer, M. B., & Dornbusch, S. (1990). Challenges in studying minority youth. In S. Feldman, & G. Elliot (Eds.), *At the threshold: The developing adolescent* (pp. 123–146). Cambridge, MA: Harvard University Press.

Spencer, M. B., Dupree, D., & Hartmann, T. (1997). A phenomenological variant of ecological systems theory (PVEST): A self-organization perspective in context. *Development and Psychopathology, 9*, 817–833.

Spencer, M. B., & Horowitz, F. D. (1973). Effects of systematic social and token reinforcement on the modification of racial and color concept attitudes in Black and in White pre-school children. *Developmental Psychology, 9*, 246–254.

Steinhorn, L., & Diggs-Brown, B. (1999). *By the color of our skin: The illusion of integration and the reality of race.* New York: Dutton.

Stevenson, H. C. (1994). Racial socialization in African American families: The art of balancing intolerance and survival. *The Family Journal: Counseling and Therapy for Couples and Families, 2*, 190–198.

Stevenson, H. W., & Stewart, E. C. (1958). A developmental study of race awareness in young children. *Child Development, 29*, 399–410.

Story M., French S. A., Resnick M. D., & Blum R. W. (1995). Ethnic/racial and socioeconomic differences in dieting behaviors and body image perceptions in adolescents. *International Journal of Eating Disorders, 18*, 173–179.

Tatum, B. (1997). *Why are all the Black kids sitting together in the cafeteria?* New York: Harper-Collins.

Thompson, J. K., Heinberg, L. J., Altabe, M., & Tanleff, S. D. (1999). Exacting beauty: Theory, assessment, and treatment of body image disturbance. Washington, DC: American Psychological Association.

Thompson, S. H., Rafiroiu, A. C., & Sargent, R. G. (2003). Examining gender, racial, and age differences in weight concern among third, fifth, eighth, and eleventh graders. *Eating Behaviors, 3*, 307–323.

Vallacher, R. R. (1980). An introduction to self theory. In D. M. Wegner, & R. R. Vallacher (Eds.), *The self in social psychology* (pp. 3–30). New York: Oxford University Press.

Vaughan, G. M. (1987). A social-psychological model of ethnic identity development. In J. S. Phinney, & M. J. Rotheram (Eds.), *Children's ethnic socialization: Pluralism and development* (pp. 73–91). Newbury Park, CA: Sage Publications.

Vaughn, B. E., & Langlois, J. H. (1983). Physical attractiveness as a correlate of peer status and social competence in preschool children. *Developmental Psychology, 19,* 561–567.

Wagatsuma, A. (1968). The social perception of skin color in Japan. In J. H. Franklin (Ed.), *Color and race* (129–165). Boston: Beacon Press.

Weinshenker, N. (2002). Adolescents and body image: What's typical and what's not. *Child Study Center, 6,* 1–4.

Williams, J. E., Boswell, D. A., & Best, D. L. (1975). Evaluative responses of preschool children to the color White and Black. *Child Development, 46,* 501–508.

12

THE BODY IN ACTION: PERSPECTIVES ON EMBODIMENT AND DEVELOPMENT

Ulrich Müller

University of Victoria

Judith L. Newman

Penn State Abington

Until recently, the body has been almost completely ignored in theories and empirical research in psychology in general, and in developmental psychology in particular. This neglect is partly due to Descartes' split between mind and body, which has held sway over philosophy and psychology for centuries. Lately, increasing dissatisfaction with Descartes' dualism has been expressed in different scientific disciplines, including biology and neuroscience (Damasio, 1994; Gallese & Lakoff, 2005), philosophy (Gallagher, 2005; Taylor, 1995), anthropology (Sheets-Johnstone, 1990), and psychology (Barsalou, Simmons, Barbey, & Wilson, 2003; Hobson, 2002; L. B. Smith, 2005). Common to this movement is the conviction that Descartes' dualist conception does not adequately capture the relation between body and mind. Hence, several alternative conceptions of the relation between body and mind have been developed that share the idea that the body plays an important role in human emotional, social, and cognitive life.

This volume brings together efforts from different theoretical perspectives to properly situate the role of the body in psychological functioning, and to link the body to the development of consciousness and meaning. One thread that runs through several chapters is the view that embodiment itself provides the very foundation for psychological functioning and experience. Embodiment is considered as the foundation of cognition in general (Thelen; Vonèche), as well as source of conceptual meaning (Johnson; Miller & Scholnick), social understanding (Racine & Carpendale), emotions (Colombetti & Thompson), spatial cognition (Liben), and religious experience (Csordas). These chapters reflect the effort to put the mind (i.e., psychological experience) back into the body. A second thread that runs through a number of chapters (Fegley, Spencer, Goss, Harpalani, & Charles; Miller & Scholnick; Vonèche) is the idea that the mind forms particular images about and conceptualizes the body. These chapters reflect the effort to put the body into the mind. Finally, in one chapter, Gao and Zelazo proposed that development is a process of both embodiment and disembodiment. The idea of development as disembodiment appears, at first, to be at odds with the efforts of the other chapters; however, as we will argue, disembodiment is indeed an essential characteristic of how we sometimes experience our relation to the body.

Our goals in this final chapter are twofold. First, we place the contributions to the current volume within the historical context of the mind-body dualism. To this end, we discuss Descartes' distinction between two qualitatively different substances, *res extensa* and *res cogitans*, which has had a tremendous influence on both psychology and philosophy (see Jonas, 1966; Rozemond, 1998; Straus, 1932/1963, pp. 3–25). After a brief review of some of Descartes' key ideas, we contrast Descartes' dualistic approach to body and mind with a radically different approach that has been developed mainly in the tradition of phenomenological psychology (e.g., Buytendijk, 1974; Merleau-Ponty, 1942/1963, 1960/1964; Plessner, 1928, 1941/1970; Scheler, 1913/1954, 1916/1973), a tradition to which we also count Piaget's (1937/1954a, 1936/1963) writings on sensorimotor development. Within this tradition, some conceive mind and body as intrinsically related: The mind is incarnated, and the body is ensouled. We next provide three examples that demonstrate that the Cartesian legacy is still alive in contemporary developmental theorizing. These examples are drawn from the areas of sensorimotor functioning, the development of causality, and early social development. We show how, by adhering to the Cartesian dualism, these approaches run into problems and briefly sketch an alternative and, as we think, more fruitful perspective that reconceptualizes development in these areas from an embodiment perspective.

The second goal of this chapter is to clarify different aspects of the multifaceted concept of embodiment. Specifically, we address three larger issues that the concept of embodiment raises. The first issue concerns the relation between felt or lived embodiment and (neuro-) physiological embodiment, an issue that surfaces in a number of chapters (Johnson; Colombetti & Thompson; Thelen; Vonèche). The second issue concerns the relation between body and context. A number of chapters (Fegley et al.; Miller & Scholnick; Liben; Racine & Carpendale; Thelen) promote a broad notion of embodiment by suggesting that the embodied person is embedded in a larger social-cultural context. The final aspect of embodiment pertains to the notion of disembodiment (Gao & Zelazo). We propose that there is a "truth to dualism" (Merleau-Ponty, 1942/1963, p. 209) in the sense that humans not only are embodied but can also distance themselves from, take a position vis-à-vis, and form images about their body (Fegley et al.). We suggest that, in the course of ontogenesis, the development of elementary perspective-taking abilities lead to the body becoming an object of consciousness, and we examine some processes that contribute to this more complex level of (still embodied) consciousness.

DESCARTES: DISEMBODIED MINDS AND MACHINE-LIKE BODIES

As is well known, Descartes distinguished between two substances, *res extensa* and *res cogitans* (P. Smith & Jones, 1986; Rozemond, 1998). Descartes conceived of *res extensa* as having physical characteristics such as being extended (e.g., taking up a certain amount of space) but as lacking mental characteristics such as consciousness. *Res cogitans*, by contrast, has mental characteristics such as consciousness but lacks physical properties. In the sixth meditation, Descartes (1641/1960a) set up this sharp contrast:

> And although perhaps, or rather certainly, as I will soon show, I have a body with which I am closely united, nevertheless, since, on the one hand I have a clear and distinct idea of myself, in so far as I am only a thinking and not an extended being; and since on the other hand I have a distinct idea of body, in so far as it is only an extended being which does not think, it is certain that this "I" is entirely distinct from my body and that it can exist without it. (p. 132)

Descartes' position on the relation between body and mind, however, is not entirely consistent (Alanen, 2003; Leder, 1990; Rozemond, 1998).

At times, he appears to acknowledge that we are closely connected with our bodies. In the end, however, he argued that the nature of the mind is such that it has an existence that is completely independent of the body:

> I then examined closely what I was, and saw that I could imagine that I had no body, and that there was no world nor any place that I occupied, but that I could not imagine for a moment that I did not exist. On the contrary, from the very fact that I doubted the truth of other things . . . it followed evidently that I existed. On the other hand, if I had ceased to think while my body and the world and all the rest of what I had ever imagined remained true, I would have had no reason to believe that I existed during that time; therefore I concluded that I was a substance whose whole essence or nature was only to think, and which, to exist, has no need of space nor of any material thing or body. Thus, what I am is entirely distinct from the body and is easier to know than the latter, and that even if the body were not, the soul would not cease to be all that it now is. (Descartes, 1637/1960b, p. 25)

For Descartes, then, the human body belonged to the world of material things—*res extensa*—and is, like other physical bodies, extended in space and time and driven by mechanical forces. Like other physical bodies, the human body belongs to the domain of what is measurable and can be approached with the methods of mathematical physics (see Straus, 1932/1963, pp. 189–191; Welton, 1999). Accordingly, Descartes (1662/1972) systematically reduces various types of human experience (e.g., the will, moods, and passions) to the mechanical interactions between fluids and parts of the body. For Descartes, then, the human body is nothing but a machine, a view that is evident in the following two remarks:

> Death comes to pass by reason of the soul, but only because some one of the principal parts of the body decays: and we may judge that the body of a living man differs from that of a dead man just as does a watch or other automaton (i.e., a machine that moves of itself), when it is wound up and contains in itself the corporeal principle for its actions, from the same watch or other machine when it is broken and when the principle of its movement ceases to act. (Descartes, 1649/1911, p. 333)

> A clock, composed of wheels and counterweights, is no less exactly obeying all the laws of nature when it is badly made and does not mark the time correctly than when it completely fulfills the

intentions of the maker; so also the human body may be considered a machine, so built and composed of bones, nerves, muscles, veins, blood, and skin that even if there were no mind in it, it would not cease to move in all the ways that it does at present when it is not moved "under the direction of the will, nor consequently with the aid of the mind." (Descartes, 1641/1960a, p. 138)

Because body and mind are qualitatively different substances, Descartes ran into problems when he had to specify the interaction between body and mind. As an *ad hoc* solution, he placed the interaction in the pineal gland, which, of course, did not resolve the conceptual problem of how it is possible for two qualitatively different substances to interact with each other.

Descartes' view of human nature, the mind, and the relation between mind and body has dominated philosophy and psychology for centuries. Although rationalism and empiricism represent two different ways of dealing with the dualism set up by Descartes, they both consider the body a physical object in the world. In the rationalist framework, judgment and reflective thought are invoked to explain how bodily movements and experiences attain meaning. In the empiricist tradition, the body is treated as a device that follows the mechanistic laws of association. Neither rationalism nor empiricism move beyond the dichotomy between body and mind and, *nolens volens*, subscribe to Descartes' view that the human body is a machine.

THE LIVED BODY

In contrast to the rationalist and empiricist frameworks, some developed a fundamentally different view of the body within the tradition of phenomenological philosophy. Within this tradition, Max Scheler (1916/1973) introduced the distinction between a "lived body" and a "thing-body":

> If, in thinking, we suppressed the functions of all the external senses by which we perceive the external world, then all possible perception of our own "thing-body" would be abolished, along with the perception of all other different bodies. . . . But the phenomenon of our "lived body" would by no means be annihilated in this case. For—no matter how closely one may focus on this point—in the case of our lived body we have, in addition to its possible external consciousness, an internal consciousness that we lack in regard to inanimate bodies. (p. 399)

The terms *lived body* and *thing body* derive from the German words *Leib* and *Körper,* respectively. In German, the term *Leib* is employed when one is referring to living bodies, while the term *Körper* is used to refer to inanimate bodies or physical things (e.g., the body of a rock). The Cartesian paradigm annihilates the essential difference between lived body and physical body (i.e., between Leib and Körper) because, within the Cartesian paradigm, the lived body is subsumed to the class of physical things. This difference is reinstated with the introduction of the concept of the lived body.

Within the phenomenological tradition, it is probably Maurice Merleau-Ponty who worked out the notion of the lived body in most detail (see Good, 1998; Taylor, 1986; Waldenfels, 1980). Following Scheler (1916/1973), Merleau-Ponty (1945/1962) elaborated on the distinction between the lived body and physical things. He illustrated the difference between the lived body and physical things in terms of their permanence and spatiality. The permanence of the lived body is different from the permanence of things: Whereas physical objects can disappear from our field of vision such that their presence always entails their possible absence, our body cannot disappear completely. Our body is always with us and participates in all our activities. The spatiality of the body also differs from the spatiality of living things. Physical things are located next to each other in a coordinate system that assigns each position its fixed place. By contrast, body parts envelop each other, and we know the position of the limbs without having to think about it:

> If my arm is resting on the table I should never think of saying that it is beside the ash-tray in the way the ash-tray is beside the telephone. The outline of my body is a frontier which ordinary spatial relations do not cross. This is because its parts are interrelated in a particular way: they are not spread out side by side, but enveloped in each other.... Similarly, my whole body for me is not an assemblage of organs juxtaposed in space. I am in undivided possession of it and I know where my limbs are. (Merleau-Ponty, 1945/1962, p. 98)

Merleau-Ponty emphasized that the lived body is not just a causal condition of experience. Rather, "the body is the vehicle of being in the world" (Merleau-Ponty, 1945/1962, p. 82). As a vehicle, the lived body mediates and creates our relation with the world through its sensorimotor powers. These sensorimotor powers comprise bodily needs and capabilities that together define an actional field and polarize the world by providing orientation and separating figure and background (Leder, 1990). For example, the perceptual field has vertical orientations such as top and bottom which are derived from the direction of our action and from how we interact with objects in a gravitational field (Taylor, 1986). Similarly, the meaning of objects is dependent upon our motility and action capabilities to engage them, and we assign functional values and practical significance to objects based on our sensorimotor powers. For example, the lived body evaluates objects according to whether they are graspable or not, within reach or not, threatening or inviting, obstacles or aids (Merleau-Ponty, 1945/1962, pp. 439–440).

The lived body thus casts a web of intentionality over the environment (Merleau-Ponty, 1945/1962, pp. 105–106; see Taylor, 1986). Merleau-Ponty (1945/1962) termed this type of intentionality "operative intentionality" (p. xviii). Operative intentionality is that intentionality by means of which the lived body projects its goals onto the world. Operative intentionality casts an intentional arc:

> [It] projects round about us our past, our future, our human setting, our physical and moral situation, or rather which results in our being situated in all these respects. It is this intentional arc which brings about the unity of the sense, of intelligence, of sensibility and motility. (Merleau-Ponty, 1945/1962, p. 136)

At the primordial level of being-to-the-world, intentionality is lived and not an act of consciousness. The concept of operative intentionality points to a primordial, unreflective, pretheoretical, and preobjective being-in-the-world that gives meaning and valence to situations, and that provides the ground of any explicit and voluntary act of intentionality (Kelly, 2003; Merleau-Ponty, 1945/1962). For example, in reaching for an object, there is contained the following:

> [A] reference to the object, not as an object represented, but as that highly specific thing towards which we project ourselves, near which we are, in anticipation, and which we haunt. Consciousness is being-towards-the-thing through the intermediary of the body. A movement is learned when the body has understood it, that is, when it has incorporated it into its "world," and to move one's body is to aim at things through it; it is to allow oneself to respond to their call, which is made independently of any representation. (Merleau-Ponty, 1945/1962, pp. 138–139)

Operative intentionality does not involve symbolic representations. To illustrate, our motor actions are guided by the following:

> A motor power, a "motor project," . . . a "motor intentionality". . . . [E]very movement has a background . . . [T]he background is

not a representation associated with or linked externally with the movement itself, but is immanent in the movement inspiring and sustaining it every moment. To plunge into action is, from the subject's point of view, an original way of relating himself to the object. (Merleau-Ponty, 1945/1962, pp. 110–111)

Reflective and theoretical attitudes toward the world are founded on and derived from this primordial bodily being in the world. We must have been engaged with and immersed in the world before we can contemplate and theorize about the world from a neutral, distanced perspective. To elucidate this foundation of our knowledge, we must return to the following:

[T]hat world which precedes knowledge, of which knowledge always speaks, and in relation to which every scientific schematization is an abstract and derivative sign-language, as is geography in relation to the countryside in which we have learnt beforehand what a forest, a prairie or a river is. (Merleau-Ponty, 1945/1962, p. ix)

To summarize, according to Merleau-Ponty's (1945/1962) theory, the lived body is bound up with, directed toward, and acting within the physical world. It is a being in relation to that which is other: other people and other things in the environment. Moreover, the lived body helps to constitute this world-as-experienced. We cannot understand the meaning and form of objects without reference to the bodily powers through which we engage them—our senses, motility, and desires. The lived body is not just one thing in the world but a way in which the world comes to be.

As Merleau-Ponty (1945/1962) pointed out, the primordial unity of experienced objects is not accomplished through interpretation, hypothesis testing, or the conscious categorization of experience, but through a preconscious power of bodily synthesis (p. 232). The primordial level provides an example of the following:

[A] non-positing consciousness, that is, of consciousness not in possession of fully determinate objects, that of a logic lived though which cannot account for itself, and that of an immanent meaning which is not clear to itself and becomes fully aware of itself only through experiencing certain natural signs. (Merleau-Ponty, 1945/1962, p. 49)

By distinguishing a nonreflective and a reflective way of being in the world, Merleau-Ponty introduced a genetic perspective (see Taylor, 1986). Self-consciousness and theoretical, neutral, and reflective knowing develop out of and are anchored in a primordial form of life.

Because the body is a vehicle of being in the world, it has "from-to" structure (Polanyi, 1966): We attend from the body to objects in the world. As a consequence, the body itself is not perceived: "Insofar as I perceive through an organ, it necessarily recedes from the perceptual field it discloses" (Leder, 1990, p. 14). Similarly, our actions are directed toward the goal, and our sensorimotor capabilities are used to attain this goal. "My body as a sensorimotor means . . . recedes before this experiential primacy of ends" (Leder, 1990, p. 19). Furthermore, once skills are incorporated into the bodily repertoire and once they have become habitualized and automatized, they disappear from conscious awareness: For example, in learning how to swim, "the thematization of rules, of my own embodiment, falls away once I truly know how to swim" (Leder, 1990, p. 31). The fact that our body is a vehicle of being in the world and as such has a from-to structure may be one reason why the body is absent in contemporary psychological theories (Scholnick & Miller, this volume).

Let us turn to Piaget's (1936/1963) description of the initial stage of psychological functioning, the sensorimotor stage, which is strikingly similar to Merleau-Ponty's (1945/1962) concept of the primordial level of being-in-the-world. During the sensorimotor stage, infants engage with the world through perception-action cycles. Infants employ action schemes like sucking, pushing, hitting, and grasping to explore and manipulate the world. These schemes are directed toward the world and give meaning to the things with which they interact. Thus, during the sensorimotor stage, objects have a practical meaning; they are things at hand, utensils for practical use or manipulation (Overton, 1994). Meaning is originally embedded in and bound up with practical, embodied activities, and practical, unreflective interactions with objects and other people constitute a necessary condition for the emergence of a theoretical attitude: "Sensory-motor intelligence aims at success and not at truth; it finds its satisfaction in the achievement of the practical aim pursued, and not in recognition (classification) or explanation. It is an intelligence only lived and not thought" (Piaget, 1936/1963, p. 238).

For Piaget (1936/1963), the emergence of a theoretical attitude requires the differentiation and coordination of action schemes and the construction of symbols and signs (i.e., differentiated signifiers; see Müller, Sokol, & Overton, 1998; Vonèche, this volume). With the differentiation and coordination of action schemes, things acquire more complex meanings and become gradually detached from the immediate situation; however, even more abstract and reflective knowledge remains founded on and is ultimately derived from embodied interactions with the world (Piaget, 1974/1976).

DESCARTES' LEGACY: THREE EXAMPLES
FROM DEVELOPMENTAL PSYCHOLOGY

Even though Cartesian dualism is generally disdained and considered a flawed view belonging to an era long since gone, closer examination shows that the Cartesian split between body and mind is still influencing contemporary developmental theories. Here, we use three examples to illustrate the way in which dualist assumptions shape developmental theories and arguments. These issues are (a) the interpretation of sensorimotor functioning, (b) the explanation of the origin of causality, and (c) the explanation of the origin of social understanding. Because Cartesian dualism ultimately leads to an impasse, we will draw on the concept of the lived body to indicate a potential way out.

Sensorimotor Functioning

Instead of conceptualizing the infant as being involved with the physical and social environment through embodied practical interactions, more recent developmental approaches argue that sensorimotor functioning is not a rich enough basis for cognitive and social development (Mandler, 1992). As a consequence, developmental mechanisms that are not based on embodied sensorimotor interactions with the world are proposed. Interestingly, ideas that have been expressed within the rationalist and empiricist tradition can be discerned as lurking behind these proposals. The rationalist tradition is manifest in the claim that the infant is a little theoretician (*theory theory*; Gopnik & Meltzoff, 1997; Gopnik, Meltzoff, & Kuhl, 1999). The empiricist tradition is manifest in the failure to understand that sensorimotor functioning constitutes a meaningful relation to the world (Mandler, 1992).

According to theory theory (Gopnik & Meltzoff, 1997; Gopnik et al., 1999), the infant is a little scientist who holds and tests theories that "involve abstract theoretical entities, with coherent causal relations among them" (Gopnik & Meltzoff, 1997, p. 41). This position implies that all kinds of knowledge—"even apparently 'ordinary' kinds of knowledge, like our knowledge that this is a jar and that is a table" (Gopnik & Meltzoff, 1997, p. 44)—are considered to be theoretical knowledge, based on "the application of everyday theories" (Gopnik & Meltzoff, 1997, p. 44). In addition, infants are said to behave like scientists in that they make predictions, produce interpretations, and give abstract, coherent, and causal explanations (Gopnik & Meltzoff, 1997, pp. 36–38).

Although a contemplative, "theoretical" attitude is certainly important in more advanced levels of cognitive functioning, it is implausible that it characterizes the initial stage of development. Wittgenstein

(1958) forcefully made this point in the context of his discussion of rule following (see Racine & Carpendale, this volume). Wittgenstein argued that the relation between a rule and its application cannot be grounded in the mediation by a third term such as an internal representation. Representational theories of rule following commit the psychologism fallacy by assuming that a rule must be interpreted by an internal mental representation or theory, which then determines whether an application accords with the rule. The introduction of the concepts of internal representation, theory, and interpretation, however, merely shifts the problem of the relation between rule and application to another level because any internal representation can be interpreted in different ways. In other words, representational theories of rule following ignore the fact that the interpretation itself must be used (Wittgenstein, 1958, §139–§140). The view that the application of a rule is mediated by an interpretation, therefore, cannot explain the transition from the interpretation of a rule to its application. Rather, this view leads to an infinite regression of interpretations: "Any interpretation still hangs in the air along with what it interprets, and cannot give it any support. Interpretations by themselves do not determine meaning" (Wittgenstein, 1958, §198).

Following the logic of Wittgenstein's argument, then, the infant cannot start out as a "scientist in the crib," pondering different theories and testing hypotheses; rather, the starting point must be an unreflected practice: "In the beginning was the deed" (1969, §402).

The empiricist tradition is evident in Jean Mandler's (1998a) interpretation of sensorimotor functioning. Mandler argued that sensorimotor functioning is procedural knowledge and is inaccessible to consciousness. Because conceptual (declarative) knowledge cannot be derived from something that cannot be brought to consciousness, she suggested that a special process, perceptual analysis, is necessary. Perceptual analysis recodes the incoming perceptual information into abstract, nonperceptual image schemas, which are simplified and condensed redescriptions of spatial structure. These image schemas then serve as the basis for conceptual thought.

Mandler's (1998a) interpretation of sensorimotor functioning as inaccessible to consciousness is rooted in the empiricist tradition. Mandler conceived of sensorimotor functioning as the mechanistic strengthening of stimulus-response associations. Consequently, Mandler (1998b) fails to understand the concept of action meaning:

> What does it mean that an infant is conscious that a ball is pushable but has no representation of pushing? How can you be conscious of pushable without any representation of pushing. . . .

What exactly is action meaning? A feeling in the muscles? If we put an EMG to the baby's arm would we see increased activity when the baby looks at the ball? (pp. 118–119)

In the embodiment tradition, however, sensorimotor functioning is characterized by operative intentionality. Piaget (1965/1971a), for one, explicitly rejected the idea that the acquisition of sensorimotor knowledge occurs through associative strengthening:

Even before language begins, the young infant reacts to objects not by a mechanical set of stimulus-response associations but by an integrative assimilation to schemes of action, which impress a direction on his activities and include the satisfaction of a need or an interest." (p. 131; see also Piaget, 1936/1963, pp. 122–143; Müller & Overton, 1998)

Within Piaget's (1965/1971a) theory, the concept of assimilation is synonymous with the concept of intentionality, although, on the sensorimotor level, intentionality is a lived, operative intentionality rather than a reflective intentionality. Because Mandler (1998a) fails to ground knowledge in the infant's embodied interactions with the world, her own image-schema theory, as has been shown elsewhere (Müller & Overton, 1998), runs into the problem of grounding meaning.

Causality

The influence of the Cartesian framework is also noticeable in recent approaches to the development of causality because these approaches ignore the contribution of the lived body to the emergence of causality. Take, for example, the modular approach to the development of causality that has been advanced by Alan Leslie (1982, 1984; Leslie & Keeble, 1987). On the basis of habituation experiments, which show that 6-months old infants distinguish between visual displays in which movement patterns of objects either suggest causality or not, Leslie postulates an innate visual module that accounts for the understanding of causality in infants (Leslie & Keeble, 1987; see Müller & Overton, 1998, for an alternative interpretation of these findings). Although Leslie leaves open what the crucial information is that accounts for the causal perception, he suggests that continuity plays an important role (Leslie & Keeble, 1987).

Continuity, however, is a spatiotemporal quality of events and does not explain the specific difference between spatiotemporal qualities and causality. Furthermore, as Hans Jonas (1966) has shown, if we try to derive causality from perception without considering our body through which we are part of the world, our knowledge of the world is reduced to the following:

> [S]sequences of contents external and indifferent to one another, regarding which there could not even arise the suspicion of an inner connection, of any relation other than spatio-temporal ones, nor the least justification for postulating it. Causality here becomes a fiction—on a psychological basis left groundless itself. (pp. 20–21)

Crucial features of causal relations are that we consider them as productive and forceful, and these features cannot be accounted for by passive information-processing devices and modules. An alternative account grounds the generative force of causality in our experience of bodily action and agency (Baldwin, 1995; Jonas, 1966). Specifically, according to this alternative account, causality originates in our experience of effort that we must use to overcome the resistance of "the worldly matter in . . . [our] acting and to resist the impact of worldly matters" (Jonas, 1966, p. 22) upon ourselves. Jonas explained the following:

> This happens through and with my body, with its extensive outwardness and its intensive inwardness at once . . . [Causality] is rooted in just the point of actual live "transcendence" of the self, the point where inwardness actively transcends itself into the outward and continues itself into it with actions. The point is the intensive-extensive body in which the self exists, at once, for itself (intensive) and in the midst of the world (extensive). (Jonas, 1966, p. 23)

Similar to Jonas (1966), Piaget (1937/1954a) derived causality from an intensive (internal) and extensive (external) pole. The internal pole is the dynamic feeling of efficacy that expresses the consciousness of the infant's activity. The external pole initially consists in whatever the infant perceives when acting. At the beginning of development, these two poles are not differentiated, and elementary causality lacks both physical spatiality and the feeling of self-acting as internal cause (Piaget, 1937/1954a, p. 220). The perceived qualities are not yet detached from the action itself, and, as a consequence, infants experience complex aggregates in which tactile, visual, gustatory, and auditory sensations are intermingled with sensations of desire, effort, and expectations. It is only through the resistance of things to our bodily actions that these two poles of causality become differentiated, and that, as a consequence, causality becomes objectified and spatialized.

The Origin of the Notion of the Other

Contemporary approaches to the development of social understanding likewise operate with assumptions that are rooted in the Cartesian mind-body dualism. For Descartes (1641/1960a), a fundamental epistemological problem was how we can possibly know of other minds. If behavior simply consists in the mechanical movements of the body, how do we know that another living being is not an automaton? Descartes addressed this question in the Second Meditation:

> So I may by chance look out of a window and notice some men passing in the street, at the sight of whom I do not fail to say that I see men. . . . And nevertheless: what do I see from this window except hats and cloaks which could cover automata? But I judge that they are men, and thus I comprehend, solely by the faculty of judgement which resides in my mind, that which I believed I saw with my eyes. (p. 89)

Because the body is considered a physical thing, in the Cartesian framework, the inner is something hidden behind the outer and must be inferred from perceptible behavior by analogy. As a consequence, the mind, feelings, and the very notion of the other have frequently been derived from reasoning by analogy. Dilthey (1989) formulated the analogical argument in terms of the following syllogism:

> Major Premise: A specific bodily process B has as its correlate or antecedent a specific psychic process A. (Whenever B appears, it has A as its antecedent.)

> Minor Premise: A bodily process b contained in my present perception is similar to the bodily process B.

> Conclusion: The affinity between b and B allows us to posit a psychic state a, similar to A, as the antecedent or correlate of b. (pp. 388–389)

The analogical argument is also employed in contemporary theories of the development of social understanding. We will use the theory by Meltzoff and colleagues as an illustrative example (Gopnik & Meltzoff, 1994, 1997; Meltzoff, Gopnik, & Repacholi, 1999). According to Meltzoff et al. (1999), "Our sensory experience of other people tells us about their movements in space but does not tell us directly about their mental states" (p. 17). As a consequence, we must arrive at the notion of other minds by analogical reasoning from our own ego:

We envision a three-step developmental sequence: (a) When I perform that bodily act I have such and such a phenomenal experience, (b) I recognize that others perform the same type of bodily acts as me, (c) the other is sharing my behavioral state; ergo, perhaps the other is having the same phenomenal experience. (Meltzoff et al., 1999, p. 35)

The analogical argument has been criticized for a variety of reasons (see Müller & Runions, 2003; Müller & Carpendale, 2004). Scheler (1913/1954) criticized the assumption underlying the analogical argument that we cannot directly perceive the emotion of others. He argued that the body is a field of expressions and that we can directly perceive emotional expression:

It is *in* the blush that we perceive shame, *in* the laughter joy. To say that "our only initial datum is the body" is completely erroneous. This is true only for the doctor or the scientist, i.e. for man in so far as he abstracts *artificially* from the expressive phenomena. (p. 10)

The idea that emotions are directly perceived has been further worked out by Gestalt psychologists (Koffka, 1928; Köhler, 1947; Werner, 1948) and philosophers (Cassirer, 1929/1957; Merleau-Ponty, 1960/1964; Wittgenstein, 1958).

Furthermore, Scheler (1913/1954) and Lipps (1907) showed that analogical inference can, for logical reasons, not lead to the notion of other, let alone the notion of other minds. Rather, the analogical inference can only lead to the conclusion that "I double my experience in consciousness" (Lipps, 1907, p. 708). In other words, the correct conclusion to the major and minor premises in the analogical argument is, "There is another of my psychic states again." The conclusion that the bodily processes given in my perception are accompanied by a psychic state of an *alter* ego is not warranted. The notion of alter ego is illicitly introduced into the conclusion, and the illicit introduction is due to the equivocal use of the word *ego*. In the analogical argument, the word *ego* indiscriminately refers to both my ego and the alter ego, thereby annihilating the fundamental difference between ego and alter ego. Based on the logical analysis of the structure of the analogical argument, Scheler (1913/1954) concluded that the analogical argument would be logically correct only if it implied the following:

[T]hat on occurrence of expressive movements similar to those I perform myself, *it is my own self that is present here as well—and not some other and alien self.* If the conclusion refers to an alien self distinct from my own, it is a false conclusion, . . . the analogical argument can never, in any case, imply the existence of other selves, except in so far as they are like myself; hence it can never establish the existence of other conscious individuals. (pp. 240–241)

Following Scheler's (1913/1954) lines of argument, Meltzoff et al.'s (1999) theory of the development of social understanding fails—as do other theories based on similar assumptions—because the theory cannot explain the origin of alter ego and other minds. This failure is symptomatic of the assumption that we only perceive physical movements in space and not a lived body.

According to an alternative account, inner and outer, bodily and mental aspects of behavior, and ego and alter ego are not initially differentiated, and the mind is not yet understood as "being closed in on itself and inaccessible to anyone but me" (Merleau-Ponty, 1960/1964, p. 116). Because the other is not yet a separate, independent person, the infant does not have to infer the emotions from behavioral indicators; rather, the behavioral expression discloses its meaning first in immediate bodily interactions (Hobson, 1994, 2002), and later (e.g., from 6 months on; Adamson & Bakeman, 1991) in interactions centered around objects.

Likewise, by changing the perspective from an infant who discovers other minds by generalizing her own mentality to an infant who learns about self, other, and minds through bodily interactions it becomes easier to explain social development:

> If I am a consciousness turned toward things, I can meet in things the actions of another and find in them meaning, because they are themes of possible activity for my own body. . . . At first, the child imitates not persons but conducts. The problem of knowing how conduct can be transferred from another to me is infinitely less difficult to solve than the problem of knowing how I can represent to myself a psyche that is radically foreign to me. (Merleau-Ponty, 1960/1964, p. 117)

MIND AND BODY

An important question that comes up in a number of chapters (Colombetti & Thompson; Johnson; Thelen; Vonéche) concerns the relation between mind and body. As we have previously indicated, the question cannot be answered from the Cartesian perspective. Currently popular is the interpretation of embodiment in terms of brain mechanisms. For example, Gallese and Lakoff (2005) have made a case for conceptual knowledge being embodied and originating in the sensorimotor system, which, in turn, is interpreted in terms of neurophysiological functioning (sensorimotor brain mechanisms). The question arises of whether one can reduce embodied sensorimotor functioning to neurophysiological functioning.

In this context, Piaget's (1950) discussion of the mind-body problem is relevant (see Vonèche, this volume). Piaget acknowledged that every conduct has a physiological aspect and that physiological mechanisms are a causal condition for conduct (p. 139). The fact that physiological mechanisms are a causal condition for every conduct, however, does not imply that conduct is reducible to physiological explanation. There are limits to physiological explanation, and these are set by consciousness of logical-mathematical necessity and the awareness of moral obligation:

> [The] truth of $2 + 2 = 4$ is not the "cause" of the truth of $4 - 2 = 2$ in the same way that a cannon causes the movement of two billiard balls, or a stimulus is one of the causes of a reaction: the truth . . . of $2 + 2 = 4$ "implies" that of $4 - 2 = 2$, which is quite a different matter. In the same way the value attributed to an aim or moral obligation is not the "cause" of the value of the means or of an action connected with the obligation; one of the values implies the other in a way similar to logical implication, and one can call this implication between values. (Piaget, 1963/1968, pp. 187–188)

Thus, Piaget (1963/1968) concluded that material or physical causality and logical mathematical implications are irreducible to each other. All states of consciousness are related by implication. "Enlarging the meaning of the word "implication" we therefore find a relation by implication to be the basic relationship between two states of consciousness, whereas physiologic connections are characterized by causal relationships" (Piaget, 1954b, p. 143). Implications can already be found at the level of sensorimotor functioning. Sensorimotor functioning can be explained by neurophysiological mechanisms, but a neurophysiological approach to sensorimotor functioning does not explain the intrinsic connection between actions, which alone, from the perspective of the infant, confers a meaning on the object. For example, when an infant grasps an object in order to shake it, the sensorimotor scheme of shaking implies the scheme of grasping and the assimilation of the object to these schemes constitutes an inclusion (Piaget, 1950).

If reduction of consciousness to physiology is excluded, what then is the nature of the link between the conscious judgment and the physiological connections underlying them? Conceived as a working hypothesis that permits physiologists and psychologists to collaborate, Piaget (1950) proposed to adopt the principle of psycho-physiological parallelism (pp. 170–181). The principle of psycho-physiological parallelism

states that every psychological phenomenon has a physiological concomitant and that there is no causal connection between psychological and physiological phenomena. Accordingly, we have two series;
phenomena in one series cannot be explained by phenomena in the
other series. Thus, neither can states of consciousness be introduced
as causes into the system of physiological inquiries, nor can a state of
consciousness be explained through physiological processes. Rather,
the structures of nervous processes and consciousness are isomorphic
to each other, which amounts to an isomorphism between a system of
implication and a causal system; however, psycho-physiological parallelism encounters the problem of explaining why consciousness has
a distinct function and is not just an epiphenomenon. Piaget's (1963/
1968) answer to this problem is that consciousness has a function that
arises from the construction of increasingly complex conduct. This
function of consciousness must be studied genetically—that is, ontogenetically and phylogenetically (Piaget, 1950, pp. 158–170; 1967/1971b).

Ontogenetically, necessity is the result of a long, protracted development. At the beginning of ontogenesis, there is neither logical nor
moral necessity. Rather, initially, conduct simultaneously encompasses
physiologically conditioned movements of the body and the states of
consciousness within one undifferentiated reality. With development,
the causal aspect of conduct loses and the implicative aspect gains in
importance (Piaget, 1950).

Implication, however, has also a deeper, organic root. This follows
from the fact that assimilatory schemes are an extension of biological organization. Every biological organization presupposes at every level self-
organization; life is essentially self-organization (Piaget, 1967/1971b;
see also Bruun & Langlais, 2003). Cognitive functions are the result
of and reflect the processes of organic self-regulation, and they continue the exchange processes with the world on a new, functional level.
Piaget argued that cognitive processes are the outcome of a continuous
evolution and that cognitive self-regulation uses the general systems of
organic autoregulation which can be found on all genetic, morphogenetic, physiological, and nervous stages, and adapts them to new circumstances. In a way, consciousness not only represents an incomplete
translation of the organic series but also adds value and understanding
to the causal mechanism. Many functional and structural analogies
between cognitive functions and organic life support this view, and
Piaget examined many forms of life that are intermediaries between
organic and cognitive activity. In the end, consciousness is bound to
general functioning of an organization that, through its activity, maintains and transforms itself.

To summarize Piaget's (1963/1968) view, the inner or subjective aspect of conduct—that is, consciousness—cannot be reduced to causal explanation as used in physiology (p. 185). Rather, conscious states are governed by implications between meanings that at higher levels of ontogenetic development evolve into necessary relations between meanings in the cognitive realm and into hierarchical relations between values in the affective realm. Ultimately, the polarity between psychology and physiology is superseded by a genetic account that derives cognitive functions and meanings from the self-organization of life. The genetic account secures the unity of implications of consciousness and organic causes. The bridging concept is assimilation that by partaking in material self-organization incorporates an explanatory point of view without excluding the subjective point of understanding introduced by functional assimilation.

As Vonèche (this volume) points out, however, Piaget's solution to the mind-body problem is insufficient. Particularly, one wonders whether Piaget's strict separation between, on the one hand, consciousness and implication (i.e., intentionality, personal processes), and, on the other hand, physiology and causality (subpersonal processes; see Bruun & Langlais, 2003) is tenable. For example, in cutting ourselves with a knife, the knife is not just an intended object but is experienced in its real effectiveness. Intended reality and effective reality are thus one and the same: What is phenomenally given is effective reality and what is effective reality is the phenomenally given:

> The injury we suffered is intentional experience and a real occurrence at once. In the course of our embodied interactions with the world, something happens to us; we experience our body in its vulnerability. The attempt to take the phenomenon of suffering and to separate sense and physical reality of the object, lived body and physical body of the subject, and to assign one to the sphere of original experience and the other to a derived natural sphere destroys the phenomenon to be understood. (Waldenfels, 1980, p. 107)

Piaget's identification of mechanistic causality with organic processes is similarly problematic. For example, von Schelling (1797/1988) argued that biological self-organization excludes the notion of mechanistic cause and effect relations:

> For as soon as we enter the realm of *organic nature,* all mechanical linkage of cause and effect ceases for us. Every organic product exists *for itself*; its being is dependent on no other being. But

now the cause is never the *same as* the effect; only between quite *different* things is a relation between cause and effect possible. The organic, however, produces *itself*, arises *out of itself*; every single plant is the product only of *its own kind*, and so every single organism endlessly produces and reproduces *its own species*. Hence no organization progresses *forward*, but is forever turning back always into *itself*. Accordingly, an organization as such is neither *cause* nor *effect* of anything outside it, and so is nothing that intrudes into the nexus of mechanism. (p. 30)

In a way, Piaget's psycho-physical parallelism appears to construe a new dualism: that between lived body and physical thing. To be a lived body, however, also means to be a physical body with:

[B]ones and tendons, nerves and sinews, all of which can be scientifically characterized. These are not two different bodies. *Korper* [sic!] is itself an aspect of *Leib*, one manner in which the lived body shows itself.... [O]nce relativized within a broader phenomenological reading, scientific references need not be reductionistic; they can open up a rich experiential domain. For science itself arises out of lived experience. (Leder, 1990, p. 6)

Because the lived body is also a physical thing, intentionality and causality intertwine in our experience. Specifically, the level of primordial, embodied consciousness is the joint that connects intentionality/implication and causality. This level is neither completely personal or transparent to the human agent nor reducible to subpersonal, neurophysiological processes (Bruun & Langlais, 2003). Rather, functioning at this level is psychophysically neutral or impersonal (Merleau-Ponty, 1945/1962; Plessner & Buytendijk, 1925/1983). We are always already open to the world, perceiving the world that remains there even if we close our eyes. We are always already directed to the world, with desires, feelings, and a spontaneity that outstrips and escapes our conscious and voluntary decisions (Csordas, this volume). Our body represents the prefigured direction of life, lives its own life at the border of our personal life: "There is, therefore, another subject beneath me, for whom a world exists before I am here, and who marks out my place in it. This captive or natural spirit is my body ... the system of anonymous functions" (Merleau-Ponty, 1945/1962, p. 254). The lived body, then, constitutes the impersonal background of my conscious and intentional activity, thereby uniting the subpersonal and the personal.

THE SITUATED BODY

A number of contributors to the volume conceptualize embodiment as being contextualized (Liben; Racine & Carpendale; Scholnick & Miller). For example, Racine and Carpendale (this volume) argue that embodiment is situated in particular social activities and participates in a form of life. Here, we will offer a few other arguments for why it is plausible to suggest that embodiment is intrinsically context bound.

The context relatedness of embodiment follows from two features of embodiment. First, embodiment highlights the material basis of the human being. Materially, each organism is an open system that is part of the world and depends on its environment for survival. Second, the concept of a primordial level of embodied consciousness implies that first and foremost, the human being is rooted in the midst of the world. Furthermore, the lived body is intrinsically directed toward the world, giving meaning and relevance to particular aspects of the world. Because we are part of the world and the world is part of us, embodied actions are constitutionally (and not just contingently) dependent on the environment (Bruun & Langlais, 2003). Human beings are not just contained in the environment as one independent object in another independent object (e.g., sand in a bucket). Rather, they intrinsically relate to the environment, which is why descriptions of human beings and their actions must include descriptions of part of the environment (Taylor, 1986).

The human environment is not a ready-made environment; rather, the human environment is a socially and culturally constructed environment that undergoes historical change. The unique sociality of human beings follows from the peculiar birth state of human infants compared to other mammals (Portmann, 1944/1990). Compared to nonhuman primates and other mammals, human infants are born one year too early because, to attain the degree of development characteristic of other primates at birth, human pregnancy would have to last for about 21 months. This "early" birth gives human infants an extra-uterine year—a period of dependency that does not take place in the constrained environment of the womb where species-specific behavior appropriate for a genetically assigned environment matures. Rather, already during the formative period of rapid growth, infants interact with the physical and social environment. In contrast to other species,

[Human development] corresponds to the situation of a creature open to the world. . . . Our mental structures do not mature through self-differentiation to become finished behavior patterns, capable of only the slightest subtleties, as we know maturation to occur in other animals" (Portmann, 1944/1990, p. 94).

The upshot of Portmann's (1944/1990) position is that our sociocultural history and biology are not two separate strata, one added on to the other. Rather, the particular human biological constitution already embodies the dialectic between openness to the world and mediation through culture (Plessner, 1928). The extrauterine year provides a period of social gestation during which the human infant lives through the other (Vygotsky, 1998), experiences an intercorporeity with the other (Merleau-Ponty, 1945/1962), and develops more complex forms of interaction with the world through exchanges with others. The close social interaction between infant and caregiver signals the onset of cultural mediation.

Ultimately, the peculiar human condition also provides the reason for why our abilities to build implements, tools, and artifacts (that are often merely projections of our body organs, see Kapp, 1877) transform our agency, interactions, experience of embodiment, and relation to the world. These tools can then themselves acquire a constitutive function for human action (Bruun & Langlais, 2003).

THE AMBIGUITY OF THE BODY

Although our psychological life is grounded in the lived body, there is, as Merleau-Ponty (1942/1963) stated, a "truth to dualism" (p. 209; see Gao & Zelazo, this volume). Although consciousness cannot be conceived except as embodied (e.g., I am my body), in another sense, there are times when we can identify consciousness as distinct from although still related to the body (e.g., I have a body). For example, we distinguish between mind and physical body when we are ill or our body poses an obstacle to our projects. Also, in timidity and embarrassment, we do not experience the body as a spontaneous expression of our intentions but as a barrier or mask separating ourselves from the world.

In many ways, the relation of human beings to their bodies is fundamentally different from that of other animals, a point well captured by Plessner (1928). According to Plessner, animals are centered beings: they act out of an embodied center and relate objects to this lived center. Because animals act out of a center, they take a stance vis-à-vis the world and confront a field determined by their position or perspective. Plessner called this form of consciousness characteristic of animals "frontality." Animals' centric form of life implies that they cannot distance themselves from and position themselves in relation to this lived center. Rather, the lived center is the sole point of reference, the dynamic center onto which body and environment converge.

As a consequence, the experience of animals is absorbed in the immediate here and now (see Vonèche, this volume). Although their living center of activity constitutes a self, they are not reflexively aware of this self (Grene, 1974).

In contrast to animals, human beings have what Plessner (1928) called an "eccentric position" (pp. 288–346). This term implies that humans have a more complex, ambiguous relation to their body. It also suggests that for them, the body has a double role: A "human being always and conjointly is a living body (head, trunk, extremities, with all that these contain) . . . and has this living body as this physical thing" (Plessner, 1941/1970, p. 35). The lived body is experienced from within and constitutes the absolute focal point of reference of all things in the environment. By contrast, to understand the body as a physical thing, the absolute focal point of reference must be left behind and the lived body (including consciousness) must be localized relative to and on the same plane as other things (Plessner, 1970, 1983). Crucial to the understanding of the body as a physical thing is the ability to objectify the body from the outside. This ability is closely related to the ability to take an instrumental attitude toward one's body: Whereas animals live the instrumentality of their body but are not aware of having an instrumental relation to their body, human beings are aware of this instrumental relation, and their body becomes the instrument on which they play (Plessner, 1983, p. 319).

By distinguishing between the lived body and the body as a physical thing, human beings not only have an inner life as distinct from their physical existence; they, in addition, "stand over and against both of these, holding them apart from one another and yet together" (Grene, 1974, p. 341). As a consequence, a human being can experience him- or herself the center of his or her inner life, as being enclosed by the lived body into which he or she is stuck as if in a case (Plessner, 1983, pp. 178, 321).

The body as lived body and as a physical thing are intertwined, and human beings live this dual relationship:

> I go walking with my consciousness, my body is its bearer, on whose momentary position the selective content and perspective of my consciousness depend; and I go walking in my consciousness, and my body with its changes of position appears as the content of its sphere. (Plessner, 1941/1970, p. 36)

From a developmental perspective, it would be interesting to study the development of an eccentric position in children. When do children start to objectify their bodies? What are the processes that lead to this objectification?

Socially coordinated imitative games are one process that contributes to self-objectification. Empirical studies have shown that infants' interactions with other persons become increasingly complex in the course of the second year of life. For example, around 18 months, peer play can be maintained for longer periods, becomes more organized around consistent, meaningfully related themes, and develops into imitative games that exhibit increasingly coordinated role relations between the players, such as chaser and being chased, or coordinated object exchanges (Brownell & Brown, 1992; Eckerman, 1993; Eckerman & Stein, 1982; Eckerman, Davis, & Didow, 1989; Ross, 1982).

As Sinclair (1987) pointed out, imitative games have a double character: there is somebody who imitates and somebody else who lets him- or herself be imitated. In other words, imitative games have a recipient-design structure, in which agent and recipient are intrinsically related (Auwärter & Kirsch, 1984). By coordinating and then internalizing the agent and recipient roles, the infant learns to take the attitude of the other toward his or her own behavior. This recipient-design structure thus captures the process of taking an external perspective on the self.

By learning to take the attitude of the other toward herself in imitative games, the infant learns to objectify herself, which, in turn, leads to the emergence of the concept of self and of explicit self-consciousness and body images and concepts. Self-recognition in the mirror is a good indicator for the infant's rudimentary ability to take an external perspective on the self (see Case, 1991; Lewis, 1992; Merleau-Ponty, 1964; Müller & Runions, 2003). In order to recognize herself in the mirror, the infant must relate her own embodied, active center to the external, visually displayed body in the mirror. In other words, the infant's active, psychic point of view is broken and "reflected" by an external perspective. As a consequence, the infant is able to understand herself simultaneously as agent and as recipient. The ability to adopt an external social perspective onto the self is not only important in early childhood. For example, as Fegley and colleagues (this volume) have shown, it is an important factor affecting body image and self-esteem in late childhood and adolescence.

Language builds on social imitation and leads to a further distancing from and conceptualization of the body. Language is necessary for logical necessity (2 + 2 must be 4) and higher forms of moral self-regulation, in which we act according to what we think is right and can forgo our bodily desires and feelings (Plessner, 1983; Waldenfels, 1980). Language thus promotes disembodiment (Gao & Zelazo, this volume), but remains grounded in our bodily interactions with the world (Merleau-Ponty, 1962).

CONCLUSION

Despite the fact that we all happily avow that we are anti-Cartesians now and are prone to view Cartesian dualism as a kind of infantile disease of philosophy which we all have outgrown, that dualistic picture, in subtle and insidious ways, still dominates contemporary thought (Bennett & Hacker, 2003; Overton, 1998). We have illustrated how the Cartesian framework still influences thinking in contemporary developmental psychology. This influence is evident in the tendencies either to ignore the role of the lived body in the constitution of the world or to conceive of the body as a physical thing.

Within the phenomenological tradition, by contrast, the lived body is an intertwining (Merleau-Ponty, 1968, pp. 130–155), both perceiver and perceived, intentional and material. This intertwining is torn apart within the Cartesian framework. The concept of the lived body leads to a reconceptualization of the human position. It helps us ground meaning and acknowledges the divergence of perspectives and languages through which the person can be approached. It bridges the biological, psychological, and cultural by realizing the inherent context-embeddedness and ambiguity of the human position.

The notion of the lived body thus overcomes the dualism inherent in empiricism and rationalism. The body is not just a physical object—being an embodied agent is constitutive for our relations to the world. In contrast to rationalism, the mind is not a "ghost in the machine" (Ryle, 1949). Rather, the mind is incarnated.

> It is because it is a pre-objective view that being-in-the-world can be distinguished from every third person process, from every modality of the *res extensa*, as from every *cogitatio*, from every first person form of knowledge—and that it can effect the union of the "psychic" and the "physiological." (Merleau-Ponty, 1962, p. 80)

The lived body provides the intermediary that allows a synthesis between pure thought and physical body. This synthesis is foreclosed for empiricism as well rationalism.

REFERENCES

Adamson, L. B., & Bakeman, R. (1991). The development of shared attention during infancy. *Annals of Child Development, 8*, 1–41.
Alanen, L. (2003). *Descartes's concept of mind.* Cambridge, MA: Harvard University Press.

Auwärter, M., & Kirsch, E. (1984). Zur Ontogenese der sozialen Interaktion: Eine strukturtheoretische Analyse [On the ontogenesis of interaction: A structure theoretical analysis]. In W. Edelstein, & J. Habermas (Eds.), *Soziale Interaktion und soziales Verstehen* (pp. 167–219). Frankfurt am Main, Germany: Suhrkamp.

Baldwin, T. (1995). Objectivity, causality, and agency. In J. L. Bermudez, A. Marcel, & N. Eilan (Eds.), *The body and the self* (pp. 107–125). Cambridge, MA: MIT Press.

Barsalou, L. W., Simmons, W. K., Barbey, A. K., & Wilson, C. D. (2003). Grounding conceptual knowledge in modality-specific systems. *Trends in Cognitive Sciences, 7,* 84–91.

Bennett, M. R., & Hacker, P. M. S. (2003). *Philosophical foundations of neuroscience.* Oxford: Blackwell.

Brownell, C. A., & Brown, E. (1992). Peers and play in infants and toddlers. In V. B. Van Hasselt & M. Hersen (Eds.), *Handbook of social development: A lifespan perspective* (pp. 183–200). New York: Plenum Press.

Bruun, H., & Langlais, R. (2003). On the embodied nature of action. *Acta Sociologica, 46,* 31–49.

Buytendijk, F. J. J. (1974). *Prologomena to an anthropological physiology.* Pittsburgh, PA: Duquesne University Press.

Case, R. (1991). Stages in the development of the young child's first sense of self. *Developmental Review, 11,* 210–230.

Cassirer, E. (1957). *The philosophy of symbolic forms, Vol. 3: The phenomenology of knowledge.* New Haven: Yale University Press. (Original work published 1929)

Damasio, A. (1994). *Descartes' error: Emotion, reason, and the human brain.* New York: Grosset/Putnam.

Descartes, R. (1911). *The philosophical works of Descartes* (Vol. 1). Cambridge, U.K.: Cambridge University Press. (Original work published 1649)

Descartes, R. (1960a). The meditations concerning first philosophy. In R. Descartes (Ed.), *Discourse on method and meditations* (pp. 67–141). Indianapolis, IN: Bobbs-Merrill Educational Publishing. (Original work published 1641)

Descartes, R. (1960b). Discourse on method. In R. Descartes (Ed.), *Discourse on method and meditations* (pp. 3–57). Indianapolis, IL: Bobbs-Merrill Educational Publishing. (Original work published 1637)

Descartes, R. (1972). *Treatise on man.* Cambridge, MA: Harvard University Press. (Original work published 1662)

Dilthey, W. (1989). *Selected works, Vol. 1: Introduction to the human sciences.* Princeton, NJ: Princeton University Press.

Eckerman, C. O. (1993). Imitation and toddlers? Achievement of co-ordinated actions with others. In J. Nadel, & L. Camaioni (Eds.), *New perspectives in early communicative development* (pp. 116–138). New York: Routledge.

Eckerman, C. O., Davis, C. C., & Didow, S. M. (1989). Toddlers' emerging ways of achieving social coordinations with a peer. *Child Development, 60,* 440–453.

Eckerman, C. O., & Stein, M. R. (1982). The toddler's emerging interactive skills. In K. H. Rubin, & H. S. Ross (Eds.), *Peer relationships and social skills in childhood* (pp. 41–71). New York: Springer.

Gallagher, S. (2005). *How the body shapes the mind.* Oxford, U.K.: Clarendon Press.

Gallese, V., & Lakoff, G. F. (2005). The brain's concepts: The role of the sensory-motor system in conceptual knowledge. *Cognitive Neuropsychology, 22,* 455–479.

Good, P. (1998). *Maurice Merleau-Ponty: Eine Einführung* [Merleau-Ponty: An Introduction]. Düsseldorf, Germany: Parerga.

Gopnik, A., & Meltzoff, A. N. (1994). Minds, bodies, and persons: Young children's understanding of the self and others as reflected in imitation and 'theory of mind' research. In S. Parker, M. Boccia, & R. Mitchell (Eds.), *Self-awareness in animals and humans: Developmental perspectives* (pp. 166–186). New York: Cambridge University Press.

Gopnik, A., & Meltzoff, A. N. (1997). *Words, thoughts, and theories.* Cambridge, MA: MIT Press.

Gopnik, A., Meltzoff, A. N., & Kuhl, P. K. (1999). *The scientist in the crib.* New York: William Morrow and Company.

Grene, M. (1974). *The understanding of nature.* Dordrecht: D. Reidel Publishing Company.

Hobson, R. P. (1994). Perceiving attitudes, conceiving minds. In C. Lewis, & P. Mitchell (Eds.), *Children's early understanding of mind: Origins and development* (pp. 71–93). Hove, U.K.: Lawrence Erlbaum Associates.

Hobson, R. P. (2002). *The cradle of thought.* London: Macmillan

Jonas, H. (1966). *The phenomenon of life: Toward a philosophical biology.* New York: Harper & Row Publishers.

Kapp, E. (1877). *Grundlinien einer Philosophie der Technik* [Basic Principles of a Philosophy of Technic]. Braunschweig, Germany: Georg Westermann Verlag.

Kelly, S. D. (2003). Merleau-Ponty on the body. In M. Proudfoot (Ed.), *The philosophy of body* (pp. 62–76). Oxford, U.K.: Blackwell.

Köhler, W. (1947). *Gestalt psychology.* New York: Liveright Publishing Corporation.

Koffka, K. (1928). *The growth of the mind.* New York: Harcourt, Brace and Company.

Leder, D. (1990). *The absent body.* Chicago: The University of Chicago Press.

Leslie, A. M. (1982). The perception of causality in infants. *Perception, 11,* 173–186.

Leslie, A. M. (1984). Spatiotemporal continuity and the perception of causality in infants. *Perception, 13,* 287–305.

Leslie, A. M., & Keeble, S. (1987). Do six-month-old infants perceive causality? *Cognition, 25,* 265–288.

Lewis, M. (1992). *Shame: The exposed self.* New York: Free Press.

Lipps, T. (1907). Das Wissen von fremden Ichen [The knowledge of alter egos]. *Psychologische Untersuchungen, 1,* 694–722.

Mandler, J. M. (1992). How to build a baby: II. Conceptual primitives. *Psychological Review, 99,* 587–604.

Mandler, J. M. (1998a). Representation. In W. Damon, D. Kuhn, & R. Siegler (Eds.), *Handbook of child psychology: Vol. 2: Cognition, perception and language* (5th ed., pp. 255–308). New York: Wiley.

Mandler, J. M. (1998b). Babies think before they speak. *Human Development, 41,* 116–126.

Meltzoff, A. N., Gopnik, A., & Repacholi, B. M. (1999). Toddlers' understanding of intentions, desires, and emotions: Explorations of the dark ages. In P. D. Zelazo, J. W. Astington, & D. R. Olson (Eds.), *Developing theories of intention* (pp. 17–41). Mahwah, NJ: Lawrence Erlbaum Associates.

Merleau-Ponty, M. (1962). *The phenomenology of perception.* New York: Humanities Press. (Original work published 1945)

Merleau-Ponty, M. (1963). *The structure of behavior.* Boston: Beacon Press. (Original work published 1942)

Merleau-Ponty, M. (1964). *The child's relations with others.* In M. Merleau-Ponty (Ed.), *The primacy of perception* (pp. 96–155). Evanston, IL: Northwestern Press. (Original work published 1960)

Merleau-Ponty, M. (1968). *The visible and the invisible.* Evanston, IL: Northwestern University Press.

Müller, U., & Carpendale, J. I. M. (2004). The development of social understanding in infancy (pp. 215–238). In J. I. M. Carpendale, & U. Müller (Eds.), *Social interaction and the development of knowledge.* Mahwah, NJ: Lawrence Erlbaum Associates.

Müller, U., & Overton, W. F. (1998). How to grow a baby: A re-evaluation of image schema and Piagetian action approaches to representation. *Human Development, 41,* 71–111.

Müller, U., & Runions, K. (2003). The origins of understanding self and other: James Mark Baldwin's theory. *Developmental Review, 23,* 29–54.

Müller, U., Sokol, B., & Overton, W. F. (1998). Reframing a constructivst model of the developmental of mental representations: The role of higher-order operations. *Developmental Review, 18,* 155–201.

Overton, W. F. (1994). Contexts of meaning: The computational and the embodied mind. In W. F. Overton & D. S. Palermo (Eds.), *The nature and ontogenesis of meaning* (pp. 1–18). Hillsdale, NJ: Lawrence Erlbaum Associates.

Overton, W. F. (1998). Developmental psychology: Philosophy, concepts, and methodology. In W. Damon, & R. M. Lerner (Eds.), *Handbook of child psychology: Vol. 1, Theoretical models of human development* (5th ed., pp. 107–188). New York: Wiley.

Piaget, J. (1950). *Introduction à l'épistemologie génétique, Vol. 3: La pensée biologique, la pensée psychologique et la pensée sociologique* [Introduction to genetic epistemology, Vol. 3: Biological, psychological, and sociological thought]. Paris: Press Universitaires de France.

Piaget, J. (1954a). *The construction of reality in the child.* New York: Basic Books. (Original work published 1937)

Piaget, J. (1954b). The problem of consciousness in child psychology: Developmental changes of awareness. In H. A. Abramson (Ed.), *Conference on problems of consciousness* (Vol. 4, pp. 136–177). New York: Joisah Macy Foundation.

Piaget, J. (1962). *Play, dreams, and imitation.* New York: Norton. (Original work published 1945)

Piaget, J. (1963). *The origins of intelligence.* New York: Norton. (Original work published 1936)

Piaget, J. (1968). Explanation in psychology and psychophysiological parallelism. In P. Fraisse, & J. Piaget (Eds.), *Experimental psychology: its scope and method, Vol. 1* (pp. 153–191). London: Routledge & Kegan Paul. (Original work published 1963)

Piaget, J. (1971a). *Insights and illusions of philosophy* (translated by Wolfe Mays). London: Routledge & Kegan Paul. (Original work published 1965)

Piaget, J. (1971b). *Biology and knowledge.* Chicago: The University of Chicago Press. (Original work published 1967)

Piaget, J. (1976). *The grasp of consciousness.* Cambridge, MA: Harvard University Press. (Original work published 1974)

Plessner, H. (1928). *Die Stufen des Organischen und der Mensch* [The levels of the organic and the human being]. Berlin, Germany: Göschen.

Plessner, H. (1970). *Laughing and crying: A study of the limits of human behavior.* Evanston, IL: Northwestern University Press. (Original work published 1941)

Plessner, H. (1983). *Gesammelte Schriften, VIII: Conditio Humana* [Collected writings, Vol. 8: The human condition]. Frankfurt, Germany: Suhrkamp.

Plessner, H., & Buytendijk, F. J. J. (1983). Die Deutung des mimischen Ausdrucks: Ein Beitrag zur Lehre vom Bewusstsein des anderen Ichs [The interpretation of mimic expression: A contribution to the idea of the consciousness of alter egos]. In H. Plessner, *Gesammelte Werke* (Vol. VII, pp. 69–129). Frankfurt am Main, Germany: Suhrkamp. (Original work published 1925)

Polanyi, M. (1966). *The tacit dimension.* Garden City, NJ: Doubleday & Company.

Portmann, A. (1990). *A zoologist looks at humankind.* New York: Columbia University Press. (Original work published 1944)

Ross, H. S. (1982). Establishment of social games among toddlers. *Developmental Psychology, 18,* 509–518.

Ryle, G. (1949). *The concept of mind.* Harmondsworth, U.K.: Penguin Books.

Rozemond, M. (1998). *Descartes's dualism.* Cambridge, MA: Harvard University Press.

Scheler, M. (1954). *The nature of sympathy*. Hamden, CT: Archon Books. (Original work published 1913)

Scheler, M. (1973). *Formalism in ethics and non-formal ethics of values*. Evanston, IL: Northwestern University Press. (Original work published 1916)

Sheets-Johnstone, M. (1990). *The roots of thinking*. Philadelphia: Temple University Press.

Sinclair, H. (1987). Symbolic systems and interpersonal relations in infancy. In J. Montangero, A. Tryphon, & S. Dionnet (Eds.), *Symbolism and knowledge* (pp. 129–141). Geneva, Switzerland: Jean Piaget Archives Fondation, Cahier No. 8.

Smith, L. B. (2005). Cognition as a dynamic system: Principles from embodiment. *Developmental Review, 25*, 278–298.

Smith, P., & Jones, O. R. (1986). *The philosophy of mind: An introduction*. Cambridge, U.K.: Cambridge University Press.

Straus, E. (1963). *The primary world of senses*. London: Glencoe. (Original work published 1932)

Taylor, C. (1986). Leibliches Handeln [Embodied action]. In A. Metraux, & B. Waldenfels (Eds.), *Leibhaftige Vernunft: Spuren von Merleau-Pontys Denken* (pp. 194–217). München, Germany: Wilhelm Fink Verlag.

Taylor, C. (1995). *Philosophical arguments*. Cambridge, MA: Harvard University Press.

von Schelling, F. W. J. (1988). *Ideas for a philosophy of nature*. New York: Cambridge University Press. (Original work published 1797)

Vygotsky, L. S. (1998). Infancy. In R. W. Rieber (Ed.), *The collected works of L. S. Vygotsky, Vol. 5: Child psychology* (pp. 207–241). New York: Plenum Press.

Waldenfels, B. (1980). *Der Spielraum des Verhaltens* [The scope of behavior]. Frankfurt am Main, Germany: Suhrkamp.

Welton, D. (1999). Introduction: Foundations of a theory of the body. In D. Welton (Ed.), *The body: Classic and contemporary readings* (pp. 1–8). Oxford, U.K.: Blackwell Publishers.

Werner, H. (1948). *Comparative psychology of mental development*. New York: International Universities Press.

Wittgenstein, L. (1958). *Philosophical investigations*. New York: Macmillan.

Wittgenstein, L. (1969). *On certainty*. Oxford, U.K.: Blackwell.

AUTHOR INDEX

S

Sabbagh, M. A., 240, *242, 243*
Sampson, E. E., 5, *17*
Sanders, J. T., 5, *17*
Santostefano, S., 12, *17*
Sapir, E., 237, 241, *245*
Sargent, R. G., 289, *310*
Saussure, F. de, 96, *98*
Savage-Rumbaugh, E. S., 161, 162, 180, *189*
Saxe, G. B., 13, *18*
Schachter, S., 51, 61, 64, *67*
Scheier, C., 12, *18*, 46, 54, *67*, 117, 119, *129*
Scheler, M., 314, 317, 318, 327, 328, *342*
Scherer, K. R., 52, 53, 54, *67*
Schoner, G., 12, *18*
Schöner, G., 46, 54, *67*, 117, 119, *129*
Schwartz, A. B., 109*t, 126, 127*
Scott, S. H., 109*t, 128*
Seamans, E. L., 240, *242*
Searle, J., 2, 3, *18*
Searle, J. R., 203, *224*
Semaj, L. T., 293, *309*
Sergio, L. E., 109*t, 128*
Shadmehr, R., 123, *128*
Shanker, S. G., 161, 162, 180, *189*
Shanon, B., 7, *18*
Sharrock, W., 161, *186*
Shatz, M., 160, *190*
Shaw, W., 289, *308*
Sheets-Johnstone, M., 12, *18*, 313, *342*
Shen, L., 109*t, 128*
Shepard, R., 24, *43*
Shiffrin, K., 258, *278*
Shoemaker, A. L., 298, *309*
Shu, H., 238, *244*
Shulman, G. L., 39, *42*
Shweder, R. A., 101, *128*
Siegal, M., 182, *189*
Siegler, R. S., 238, *243*
Silber, S., 160, *190*
Simmons, W. K., 313, *338*
Sims, C., 289, *309*
Sinclair, H., 336, *342*
Singer, J. E., 51, 61, 64, *67*
Sinha, C., 161, 175, *190*
Sinnott, J. D., 258, *278*
Skinner, B. F., 50, *67*
Slaughter, V., 172, *190*

Smart, N., 155, *158*
Smith, C. A., 64, *67*
Smith, C. M., 237, *244*
Smith, L., 12, *18*
Smith, L. B., 46, 54, *67*, 101, 107*f*, 117, 119, 120, 122, *126, 128, 129*, 251, *278*, 313, *342*
Smith, P., 315, *342*
Smyrnis, N., 109*t, 126*
Snyder, L. H., 109*t, 125*
Sokol, B., 321, *340*
Solomon, D., 232, *245*
Solomon, R. C., 49, 50, 51, 52, 64, 65, *67*
Sontag, S., 199, *224*
Spelke, E. S., 100, *128*
Spelman, E. V., 249, 257, *278*
Spencer, M. B., 282, 283, 285, 292, 293, 294, 295, 304, *306, 310*
Spinoza, B., 48, *67*
Sporns, O, 101, *125*
Stangor, C., 264, *276*
Stein, M. R., 336, *339*
Steinhorn, L., 285, 291, *310*
Stevenson, H. C., 284, 294, *310*
Stevenson, H. W., 238, *242, 245*, 292, *310*
Stewart, E. C., 292, *310*
Stigler, J. W., 238, *245*
Story M., 289, *310*
Straus, E., 314, 316, *342*
Striano, T., 172, *188*
Striegel-Moore, R. H., 289, *308*
Sumara, D., 216, *221*
Suomi, S. J., 10, *18*
Sutherland, A., 234, *243*
Sutherland, J., 292, *309*
Szechter, L. E., 204, 212, 218, *223, 224*
Szechter, L. S., 207, *223*

T

Taira, M., 109*t, 126*
Talbot, J. T., 161, 162, 180, *189*
Talmy, L., 101, *128*
Tanleff, S. D., 297, *310*
Tardiff, T., 240, *243*
Tatum, B., 293, *310*
Taussig, M., 152, *158*

SUBJECT INDEX